The Condition of American Liberal Education/

The Condition of American Liberal Education/
Pragmatism and a Changing Tradition

An essay by
BRUCE A. KIMBALL *with commentaries
and responses*

ROBERT ORRILL, *executive editor*

College Entrance Examination Board, New York

The College Board is a national nonprofit association that champions educational excellence for all students through the ongoing collaboration of more than 2,900 member schools, colleges, universities, education systems, and associations. The Board promotes—by means of responsive forums, research, programs, and policy development—universal access to high standards of learning, equity of opportunity, and sufficient financial support so that every student is prepared for success in college and work.

In all of its publishing activities, the College Board endeavors to present the works of authors who are well qualified to write with authority on the subject at hand and to present accurate and timely information. However, the opinions, interpretations, and conclusions of the authors are their own and do not necessarily represent those of the College Board; nothing contained herein should be assumed to represent the official position of the College Board.

Copies of this book can be ordered from College Board Publications, Box 886, New York, New York 10101-0886. The price is $18 (paper) $28 (hardcover).

Library of Congress Catalog Number: 95-074744
International Standard Book Number 0-87447-524-4 (hardcover) 0-87447-522-8 (paper)

Printed in the United States of America.

Table of Contents

Editor's Preface

This book had its beginnings in a day-long invitational seminar convened by the College Board on November 10, 1994. The purpose of the seminar was to bring together a group of college faculty and academic administrators to discuss the current condition and future prospects of liberal education in the United States. This subject, of course, has been much written about in recent years, but, for whatever reason, those voices that reflect the most gloomy or desperate points of view have received the most general attention. I have referred to this phenomenon in the introduction as a literature of lamentation, most notably reflected by the late Allan Bloom's national best-seller *The Closing of the American Mind*. Our sense was that Bloom and like-minded colleagues represent a minority voice in the academy, and therefore we sought in this seminar to take a broader perspective on the health of liberal education. This was not to ignore much that is clearly problematic about liberal education, but it was to assume that a constructive, forward-looking stance toward the issues is still possible.

To provide a point of departure for the day's discussion, we invited Bruce Kimball to prepare a paper that addressed the contemporary condition of liberal education. Moreover, we asked him to focus especially on liberal education in its twentieth century American setting. Professor Kimball was an obvious choice for this role in that he is the author of our most comprehensive and coherent history of the idea of liberal education, an account entitled *Orators and Philosophers: A History of the Idea of Liberal Education*. In the event, he produced an extended essay entitled "Toward Pragmatic Liberal Education" which is itself a significant extension, and something of a revision (or "reconstruction"), of his earlier work. In this essay, he makes the somewhat startling proposal that a consensus is emerging in reform efforts related to liberal education and that this coming together of points of view owes much to the current resurgence of American pragmatic thought—hence for the first time in history we are on the verge of having a distinctively American version of liberal education.

Much of the seminar was given over to a discussion of the several lines of argument opened by Bruce Kimball's essay. Not surprisingly, there was much debate about the "consensus" hypothesis and considerable time needed to clarify whether the essay was intended to express a normative point of view ("what should be") or a descriptive one ("what seems to be happening"). Professor Kimball said it was the latter. Nonetheless, the discussion also took on a life of its own, and its many interwoven strands are now reflected in the commentaries that make up the second part of this book. Indeed, readers will find bits and pieces of the days interactions still remaining in the texture of these writings. Overall, however, participants were invited in their written responses to take up any aspect of Bruce Kimball's argument or the day's conversation that seemed to them of special importance. The result, we think, is a uniquely rounded contemplation of the challenges that currently confront all concerned with the fate of liberal education.

The College Board is pleased to make this valuable set of essays and commentaries available to a wider audience. We believe that they will be useful in addressing current educational needs and help illuminate our way for some time to come. A very special thanks goes to Madelyn Roesch for her deft and careful editorial attention to this book. Thanks also to Dorothy Downie and Geoffrey Kirshner. As much as anyone, these three colleagues made possible the appearance of this book. A further word of appreciation to Hannah Selby for copy editing and to Lianna Kelly for her research support. Finally, I am pleased to take this opportunity to acknowledge Donald Stewart and Janice Weinman for their welcome support and especially for all they do to make the College Board a forum for the discussion of educational ideas.

Robert Orrill
Office of Academic Affairs
The College Board

An End to Mourning: Liberal Education in Contemporary America

ROBERT ORRILL

"The picture we form of history becomes a factor in our volition."

Karl Jaspers

While readying this book for publication, I began to read with renewed interest the recently updated edition of Clark Kerr's *The Uses of the University*.[1] On this reading, what most struck me is the sense of loss that occasionally emanates from this seminal, if controversial, account of the expansion of American higher education. Kerr's predominate theme, of course, is that of growth. In this regard, however, the price of growth from an overall perspective is what Kerr perceives to be the near demise of liberal education in our time. This is not, I hasten to add, an impression of the current status of liberal education shared by most of the essays and commentaries collected in *The Condition of American Liberal Education*. Nevertheless, it is not an uncommon perception. It is one shared, in fact, by some of liberal education's most publicly visible advocates—individuals who, in other respects, agree with Kerr about almost nothing else. Moreover, it is a perspective that has attracted a large readership and much media attention in recent years.[2] At the outset, therefore, it may be useful to place the viewpoints expressed by the contributors to this book in the context of the more mournful appraisals of liberal education presented by Kerr and others.

As indicated, *The Uses of the University* is about the transfiguration of American higher education. First published in 1963, this now augmented series of lectures is best known as an attempt to focus attention on how the American university had undergone a radical transformation in the decades following WW II. The primary agent of this change was a "federal initiative" that opened unprecedented access for universities to an abundant, ever-increasing flow of government dollars. In a Cold War environment, these dollars were provided largely to support scientific and technical research. According to Kerr, the modern research university in the United States responded with little hesitation to this "external" stimulus, and, in so doing, had without prior design become "a new

---

[1] Clark Kerr, *The Uses of the University* (Cambridge, Mass.: Harvard University Press, 1995).

[2] Most notably, of course, through the attention given Allan Bloom's *The Closing of the American Mind* (New York: Simon & Schuster, 1987).

type of institution in the world." As a result, the characteristic that now most defines this expansive institution is precisely its lack of definition and sense of self-direction, at least in terms of any "single animating principle." Unlike its historical predecessors, Kerr proposed, this emerging "multiversity" has "no single vision of its nature and purpose." Rather, it is an administratively mediated "mechanism" that manages to support "several competing visions of true purpose," each of which is related to a "different layer of history" and a "different web of forces." Prominent among these competing purposes, of course, is the idea of providing undergraduate students with a liberal education.

The story that Kerr tells of research universities, then, is in part one in which rival claims of purpose compete for preeminence in the growing enterprise of American higher education. As he saw it in the early 1960s, the attempt of the modern university to accommodate this clash of "ideals" did not impede its expansion; but, in becoming "so many things to so many different people," a situation was created in which the university "must, of necessity, be partially at war with itself." This was the source, he thought, of much of the "malaise" in university communities circa 1960, though it is fair to add that Kerr also believed this internal distress was (and is) an unavoidable consequence of institutional "progress." In addition, Kerr fully acknowledged that there were winners and losers among the contending constituencies. The flow of federal (and later corporate) dollars from outside the university overwhelmingly favored the "research" ideal, with a corresponding expansion of graduate schools, centers, and institutes devoted to the production of specialized knowledge. What most suffered, in turn, was attention to undergraduate teaching and learning except as a means of student induction into the specialized disciplines. Revisiting these observations in the mid-1990s, Kerr reminds those who criticized him for delivering this message that his intent was to advocate at least a partial restoration of the balance among university purposes: not least that "liberal knowledge would be (as well as should be) more central in the education of undergraduates." This was integral to Kerr's "vision" for the future of the American university and much of the import of his call for the academy "once again, to become more of a community of people and of interacting intellectuals across fields of knowledge."

In the event, however, the future did not unfold as Kerr had hoped. On the contrary, his current reckoning in the mid-1990s is that "liberal knowledge" in the university is "in retreat" more than ever. Liberal education in the 30 years since his original publication, he writes, has been "greatly mourned, but not even slightly revived." Kerr, of course, takes the precaution of saying that he speaks only of the situation in research universities, not about "the totality of higher education." Nonetheless, he also notes that since 1963 the number of research institutions with "multiversity" ambitions has increased from "about 20, with Harvard and Berkeley as leaders among them" to perhaps 125 all told in the early 1990s. These currently enroll approximately 20 percent of all college students. Moreover, their prestige influences other institutions to strive for a "comprehensive" status, even as those that determinedly remain liberal arts colleges enroll a smaller proportion of students entering higher education. One can reasonably say, I believe, that Kerr thinks the "multiversity," and the trends that it incorporates, casts a broad shadow across most of U.S. higher education.

Nonetheless, Kerr's caution about extending his analysis beyond the sector of the research university reminds us that any appraisal of the current condition of liberal education must include a recognition of how difficult it is to generalize about postsecondary education in this country. As Francis Oakley observes in this volume and elsewhere, there is nothing like a "system" of higher education in the United States. Rather, we have a vast, sprawling, markedly variegated and extremely decentralized non-system—or, some would argue, anti-system. Stanley Katz and many other contributors to this book extend this observation by questioning whether the sheer complexity of higher education makes anything other than "local knowledge" of specific institutions possible or perhaps desirable. I will return to this point later, but it is worth mentioning here that the absence of an explicit system does not necessarily mean that the overall educational enterprise is exempt from the effects of common "organizing" or "determinative" forces. In his contribution, for example, Richard Freeland argues that it is competition among institutions for "prestige and resources" in such decentralized conditions that most drives change throughout the whole of higher education. Further, Freeland observes that for most of the post-WW II period "the terms of inter-institutional competition in higher education have been determined by the model and values of the research university." Since Freeland believes that the effects of the research model have been even more harmful to the quality of undergraduate education than Kerr concedes, he argues that a forceful resurgence of liberal learning depends on the creation of "new paradigms of excellence that [will] enable colleges and universities to compete with each other on the basis of the quality of teaching and learning that they foster rather than the scholarly output of their faculties."

Thirty years after his original publication, however, Kerr is increasingly pessimistic that any such new paradigm is likely to succeed in accommodating both the research interests of graduate schools and the idea of a revitalized liberal education for undergraduates. Contrary to his hopes in 1963, he has come more and more to believe that these are two distinctive and diverging "visions" and that they probably "are not inherently fully compatible." The research ideal points institutions in the direction of "larger size and more specialization" while liberal learning implies "smaller size and more commonality of interests." Largely resigned to the defeat of his hopes, Kerr retains only the wish that ways might yet be found to make the two visions "more compatible rather than less," although he accepts that "this may be only unguarded utopianism."

Now extended over more than three decades, Kerr's account of the major determinative trends shaping higher education remains one of the more forthright and plainspoken—if also controversial and contested—analyses available to us. Unfortunately, for those especially concerned about the future of liberal education, the relevant part of Kerr's message has a dispiriting ring. Simply put, the story he tells (somewhat unwillingly) is of an endangered tradition in decline and all but swamped by forces "external" to university communities. If this were not enough, it is also the story of a tradition most fully realized some time in the past history of Western Europe. In this regard, the narrative includes the implication that this tradition was never made fully American in its passage across the Atlantic, leaving it forever vulnerable in this country to the charge that it is appropriate only for a time and place that, if not lost to us altogether, shares little in common with indigenous conditions and needs. Indeed, almost the sole image that Kerr evokes of liberal education is that "never so well expressed" as by Cardinal Newman's lectures on "The Idea of a University" (1852), or so completely embodied as in the cloistered colleges of nineteenth-century Oxbridge. With respect to the United States, the closest approximation to the ideal that Kerr can summon is "the Swarthmore of the early 1930s." This, he acknowledges, is an impression saturated by much sentiment and sense of loss.

By and large, of course, Kerr adopts a pragmatic stance in carrying forward his analysis. It is the inescapable "imperative" of adapting to political and pecuniary forces at play in the environment that dominate in his account of the place and prospects of higher education in today's world. Nostalgia enters only when he considers the possibilities of a continuing, albeit subordinate, role for liberal education in the larger mix of educational purposes. In an appraisal of the current condition of American liberal education, it is also worth taking note that this tendency to associate liberal education with a bygone time and a European setting is even more prevalent among the most severe critics of the trends that Kerr identifies. For these ardent advocates of liberal education, among whom the late Allan Bloom is probably the most prominent, even Newman and nineteenth-century Oxbridge are distant echoes of the real thing. They find the true and essential home of liberal education, insofar as it ever took earthly form, in often eloquent evocations of Plato's Athens. Everything thereafter in liberal education has been an ever-fainter facsimile of that enchanted time and place. As Bloom puts it, if we are to recover this tradition, our passionate intent must be, not to join with the present, but to experience "that magic Athenian moment reproduced."[3]

In these introductory remarks, the only point I wish to underscore is that neither Kerr nor Bloom sees liberal education as well-equipped to address the here and now. The difference between them is that Bloom sees this as a latent strength whereas Kerr finds it a near lethal weakness. For the latter, not to adapt to current trends and contingencies clearly puts the survival of this tradition in jeopardy, while, for the former, doing so—given the utilitarian and "illiberal" nature of these trends— would be to kill the redemptive power of the ideal. In saying as much, let me quickly acknowledge that I cannot in this introduction do full justice to Bloom's point of view. Probably owing more to Matthew Arnold than to Plato, it reflects a latter-day invocation of a reform tradition that entered the American setting of higher education in the late nineteenth century largely as a critique of prevailing commercial and egalitarian tendencies in the society at large.[4] Often referred to as "liberal culture," this reform program sought to replace conformity to prevailing norms with more "permanent" standards exemplified in the "best that had been thought and said" in past literatures—or, as Bloom later paraphrased Arnold, it directed utmost attention to "the rare, the refined and the superior." In the last century and now, most in the academy have thought that the estrangement from American society entailed in this position involves a futile alienation. In seeking to separate itself from this or any other present moment, Santayana later wrote, liberal culture "liberated the studious mind from obligatory or national discipline, and as far as possible from all bonds of time, place, utility, and co-operation." However, in rejecting the "local," the "partisan," and all thought that emerged from the soil of "dire necessity," it necessarily offered in return

---

[3] Allan Bloom, *The Closing of the American Mind* (New York: Simon & Schuster, Inc., 1987). In another exercise in complaint, Russell Jacoby characterizes liberal education as having "vanished" from today's world altogether, except perhaps for a few tantalizing hints about its Greek epiphany left to us by Leo Strauss. See Russell Jacoby, *Dogmatic Wisdom: How the Culture Wars Divert Education and Distract America* (New York: Doubleday, 1994).

[4] Laurence Veysey, *The Emergence of the American University* (Chicago: University of Chicago Press, 1965).

only "a wealth of vicarious experience" and the dubious and shallow "joy of living every life but one's own."[5] At least for me, this measured judgment remains a telling one.[6]

Is there no perspective, then, on American liberal education to set against one that consigns this tradition to a receding and perhaps irrecoverable past? Or that sees it as other than foreign to, and alienated from, contemporary American life and culture? Or that, in consequence, assigns it an ever-diminishing role in our educational enterprise? These were some of the questions inevitably set in motion when we asked a number of faculty and academic administrators to join in a discussion of the current status of liberal education in the United States. This book is the result of that conversation. What readers will discover, I think, is that overall there is little inclination among the contributors to join in producing the kind of literature of lamentation and complaint that some might have anticipated. This is not to say that the essays and commentaries are uniformly upbeat. On the contrary, many reflect a deep concern about the current condition and future prospects of liberal education. Taken together, however, these writings seem to me to take a reconstructive stance toward the tradition and none is indifferent to the issue of its current applicability to the nation's educational needs. In this sense, they build upon and extend a small but growing body of literature that has much enriched our understanding of the liberal arts tradition and its contemporary uses. In this regard one thinks of such recent books as Charles Anderson's *Prescribing the Life of the Mind* (1993) and W. B. Carnochan's *The Battleground of the Curriculum: Liberal Education and American Experience* (1993). Both authors, it is perhaps

---

[5] George Santayana, "Liberalism and Culture," in Norman Henfrey, *Selected Critical Writings of George Santayana*: Volume 2 (London: Cambridge University Press, 1968).

[6] Santayana, of course, wrote most eloquently of the need for an "indigenous" American philosophy in "The Genteel Tradition in American Philosophy." When it came to John Dewey's attempt to produce such a philosophy, however, he was a good deal less than satisfied. Santayana asserted that Dewey's thought "was calculated to justify all the assumptions of American society" and, as such, reduced "metaphysics" to an equation with the American social experience. With the cultural achievement of Athens and Rome in mind, Santayana wrote that casting philosophy in this way was "what Sparta and Carthage would have done if they had produced philosophers." For his part, Dewey thought that Santayana overdid the "urbane and ironical" and tended to adopt "the attitude of 'le bon Dieu' surveying the over-excited and vain struggles of mankind." See Santayana's "Dewey's Naturalistic Metaphysics," in Sidney Morgenbesser, *Dewey and His Critics* (Lancaster: Lancaster Press, 1977). Also see Dewey's review of "The Genteel Tradition at Bay," in Jo Ann Boydston, *The Later Works, 1925-1953 John Dewey: Volume 6: 1931-1932 Essays, Reviews, and Miscellany* (Carbondale and Edwardsville: Southern Illinois University Press, 1985).

worth noting, are long-time faculty members of major research universities. From a different sector, we also have Francis Oakley's immensely informative *Community of Learning: The American College and the Liberal Arts Tradition* (1992). Drawing on both past and present experience, Oakley is especially concerned to delineate "the very particular strengths of that quintessentially *American* contribution to the vitality of higher education—the free-standing, undergraduate liberal arts college."[7]

These studies are engaged rather than elegiac in tone, and all reject fixed, unchanging conceptions of the liberal arts tradition. Oakley, in particular, deplores the absence in most current critiques of higher education of "any historically informed sense of the range, looseness, variability and flexibility of the liberal arts tradition itself across the course of its large history, or of the tensions which have wracked it for centuries and may well account for much of its enduring vitality and strength." An important corrective, Oakley points out, is to be found in the superb scholarship conducted by Bruce Kimball and first published in his *Orators and Philosophers: A History of the Idea of Liberal Education* (1986).[8] In this book, Kimball very effectively examines the voluminous textual materials reflective of the idea of liberal education and brings conceptual coherence to the tensions that have characterized its history from antiquity to the late twentieth century. Assisted by the breadth and depth of perspective that Kimball provides, Oakley observes, one must be impressed by the long-lasting evolutionary vitality of the liberal arts tradition.

Longevity and a rich heritage are, of course, no guarantees against eventual extinction. If the historical record often reflects permanence and continuity, it also shows that even once-robust ideas disappear or continue on only in fossilized form. We must continue to ask, therefore, if the tradition of liberal education still has the power and evolutionary capacity to animate the overall educational enterprise. To address this question, there seemed no better way to begin than by inviting Bruce Kimball to extend the analysis begun in *Orators and Philosophers* to the present moment. It also seemed pertinent to ask him to focus especially on this tradition in the context of its twentieth-century American setting. In *Orators and Philosophers*, he had emphasized the defining importance of Western European sources in the making of the tradition

---

[7] Francis Oakley, *Community of Learning: The American College and The Liberal Arts Tradition* (New York: Oxford University Press, 1992).

[8] The College Board has recently issued an expanded edition of this study. See Bruce A. Kimball, *Orators and Philosophers: A History of the Idea of Liberal Education* (New York: College Entrance Examination Board, 1995).

and so at the end of the book was inclined to accept the opinion that "there is no such thing as the American theory of liberal education." Nonetheless, we included in our invitation the specific request that he revisit this question. In a time seemingly committed to an "international" outlook, this query may seem to pose a somewhat unfashionable issue; but we thought it not inconsequential. As briefly indicated, the issue of whether education springs from "indigenous" or imported sources runs very deep in our national experience.

The first part of this book presents an extended essay in which Bruce Kimball addresses these questions. Its title, "Toward Pragmatic Liberal Education," suggests that he has come out in a somewhat surprising place. Closely examining recent reform proposals, he makes a carefully wrought argument that a new and distinctly American version of liberal education *is* emerging in the closing years of the twentieth century. This reform "consensus" can best be grasped, he believes, if we understand how its core elements or themes—of which he identifies seven—fit with and are "deeply rooted in the resurgent intellectual tradition of pragmatism." As he sees it, this turn of events involves a long-delayed convergence of two lines of development that have until recently remained largely separate—that of liberal education and American pragmatic thought. With transformative results, Kimball sees the latter as now having a "widespread and significant influence on liberal education." Indeed, he proposes that pragmatic thought is the animating impetus in a reconstruction of the meaning and purpose of the liberal arts tradition. In a summative statement, Kimball observes that it can now be said "that pragmatism is pouring over and through the academic dikes that long kept it outside the liberal arts and that a broad consensus is therefore emerging around a view of liberal education that may be termed 'pragmatic'!"

The second part of the book consists of commentaries on Bruce Kimball's essay. These reflect the views of a large number of faculty and academic administrators, though no claim is made that the participants "represent" or reflect the whole of U.S. higher education. Contributions were invited based on individual interest in the issues addressed, not on institutional affiliation or geographic location. Most of the commentaries are direct responses to Kimball's argument; a few use the essay to open new lines of thought. Taken together, they constitute an unusually rich basis for appraising the current condition of American liberal education. Do they fully agree, though, with Kimball's description of a new consensus in the making? Few, if any, are entirely persuaded. Many, however, do agree, at least to some extent or with qualifications that they specify. There are some exceptions, but almost none find the case that

Kimball makes to be without a substantial basis in fact or lacking in descriptive power. Moreover, as David Steiner indicates, it does not necessarily detract from Kimball's essay that one can think of examples that do not fit the argument. Kimball's claim, he correctly says, "is for evidence of a pragmatic pattern in higher education, not proof that it constitutes a universal condition." Importantly, the contributors mostly agree that a new pattern is in the making. In this regard, none sees liberal education as in a static, unchanging condition—though several, with Eva Brann, see its future in problematic terms. Louis Menand, I think, is representative of the conversation generally when he accepts Kimball's argument up to the point of acknowledging "that the consensus philosophy of liberal education is undergoing an alteration."

Will, then, the academy itself shape and direct this remaking? Not surprisingly, this question plays in and out of many of the commentaries and is prominent in several. Clark Kerr's analysis of the course of development in higher education over the last three decades provides ample evidence that external forces, rather than internal design, can often direct the course of events and make an immense difference in determining outcomes. As we know, this brute fact has often led some in the academy to advocate what, in criticizing the views of Robert Hutchins, John Dewey called the "policy of aloofness."[9] From this perspective, the great threat to academic ideals is too much contact with the American public. Dewey, of course, never left any doubt about where he stood on this issue of the need for constructive (or "reconstructive") interaction between higher education and the society at large. As he told a conference on curriculum held at Rollins College in 1931, "educational confusion" is the only result possible when higher education fails to connect what it seeks to teach with "the dominant interests and activities of the great body of the American people."[10]

One intent of Dewey's pronouncement was to press those in the academy to declare their own inclinations. In this regard, Stanley Katz probably speaks for the majority of the contributors to this book in agreeing "that liberal education cannot prosper as a backward-looking set of principles, but must constantly adapt itself to social change." Still, he quickly adds, "the question remains—are university faculty and administrators up to the challenge?" On this point, the writings in this book do not speak with a single voice. Menand suggests that faculty in particular may be caught in a difficult bind. Their changing intellectual interests, he suggests, can be understood as just now in especially sharp conflict

[9] John Dewey, "Rationality in Education," in Boydston, *The Later Works*.
[10] John Dewey, *The Way Out of Educational Confusion* (Cambridge: Harvard University Press, 1931).

with their professional responsibilities. The former tend toward interdisciplinarity and ease of interaction across branches of knowledge, but
the latter are dependent upon traditional scholastic structural arrangements that divide faculty along familiar departmental lines. In this connection, for example, consider the matter of academic standards.
Because they are almost all trained in the traditional disciplinary structures of a very small number of graduate institutions, faculty serve as the
agents for providing equitable standards of excellence across our heterogeneous "system" of higher education. As Menand puts it, "this common background insures that standards for professors, and thus for
curricula and scholarship, are universal, so that a student at a state
school and a student at an Ivy League school will be taught by professors
whose training is virtually identical." Performing this function, however, is dependent upon a principle of "academic freedom" and privilege
of professional self-regulation rooted in structural arrangements that
date from a century-old scheme for the organization of knowledge. It is
precisely this structure, he points out, that the new pragmatic impetus
in the academy regards as intellectually retrograde and would seek to
dissolve or radically reconfigure.[11]

These are fundamentally important considerations, but, if they can be
resolved, there may be help in moving forward that is generated from an
unexpected quarter. What I have in mind relates to the changes that
Menand suggests may be taking place in the upper reaches of the
"mulitversity" itself. It appears, for example, that graduate programs of
study have begun to suffer from the same problem that has long plagued
both K–12 and undergraduate education. Or, to put it another way, graduate education may now have more in common than ever before with
long-standing K–12 and undergraduate concerns. That is, knowledge
now grows and changes at such a rapid rate that attempts to organize it
into fixed and stable "subject-matter" categories are routinely thwarted.
As Julie Klein and others indicate, even research universities cannot now
proliferate structured specializations fast enough to keep up with the pace
at which knowledge is transformed—often through a process in which disciplinary boundaries are crossed, erased, or redrawn. John Dewey foresaw
this situation long ago. Even at the time he wrote, the existing "body of
knowledge" had long since grown much too large and various to be "transmitted" to students at the school and college levels. The attempt

---

[11] Menand believes that this impetus owes more to the brand of pragmatism advanced by
Richard Rorty than that of John Dewey. For the debate about the divergence of Rorty
from Dewey see Herman Saatkamp, *Rorty & Pragmatism: The Philosopher Responds
to His Critics* (Nashville: Vanderbilt University Press, 1995).

to do so by adding "subject" on top of "subject" had resulted in curricular and pedagogic gridlock. In such a situation, therefore, the only alternative was to focus the education of students on the activity of acquiring and using knowledge—on nurturing intelligence, that is, rather than storing information in memory. Education, in this conception, should be primarily about the learning process itself, with the question of its content determined by present need rather than inherited tradition. Richard Hofstadter accurately described the goal of this educational alternative as the creation of "the capacity for still further education."[12] Hofstadter, of course, thought this a damning criticism, but do we really have any better definition of our educational aims?

The help that I mentioned depends, in part, on how the resurgence of pragmatism that Kimball describes works its way through graduate education. On this score, Dewey himself may provide little direct assistance. He saw change in education, and society generally, as occurring from the "bottom up." Hence, his life-long attention to the reform of the public school system. Menand, however, suggests that internally-directed change in higher education might more likely be "top down," with its source in the graduate school experience of teaching faculty. As Clifford Gertz once pointed out, it is through the graduate experience that faculty acquire their "way of being" in the world.[13] If this is so, and if the graduate research realm is now much more attuned to how disciplines connect and cross in formulating resolutions for problems, might this not begin to have a significant impact on the undergraduate curriculum?[14] Could it not, in fact, have the effect of orienting undergraduate teaching and learning more toward the integrative and connective aims that have always been central in the idea of liberal education? This, of course, is a conjecture, not a forecast. If there is anything to it, however, it is possible that we are experiencing a remaking of liberal education in part because its long-time "bête noire," the research ideal, is also undergoing a kind of intellectual transformation unnoticed by Clark Kerr.

[12]Richard Hofstadter, *Anti-Intellectualism in American Life* (New York: Vintage Books, 1962).

[13] Clifford Gertz, *Local Knowledge: Further Essays in Interpretive Anthropology* (New York: Basic Books, 1983).

[14] For example, see a recent report in which the president of Harvard, Neil Rudenstine, cites a "genuine shift in outlook" within his university toward "a greater integration of knowledge, rather than increasing subdivision and separateness." In this connection, he describes a trend toward programmatic mergers and notes with interest "that the plan for the Faculty of Arts and Sciences does not propose the creation of any new departments–something that would have been nearly impossible to imagine in 1955 or 1965." *The President's Report, Harvard University 1991–93.*

But, as a pragmatist would say, nothing is ever settled. Eva Brann is doubtless close-to-the-mark in pointing out that Bruce Kimball has alerted us to the emergence of a "definable intellectual atmosphere" which, for good or ill, is likely to have significant implications for the remaking of liberal education. The outcome itself, however, is less certain. Perhaps better than anyone, Alan Ryan catches the spirit of these writings when he concludes "that the competition for the soul of the liberal educator is still on."

Introduction

I recant. No, I reconstruct. After devoting more than a decade to reading, thinking, and writing about the history of the liberal arts, I had come to understand liberal education in terms of two long-standing intellectual traditions, and thereby to agree with Thomas Green that there is no such thing as the American theory of liberal education.[1] Developments within higher education and American culture in these closing years of the twentieth century indicate, however, that a new tradition of liberal education is emerging, one that stems from the host of intellectual and social forces contributing to the seemingly intractable confrontations that have been called our "culture wars." This American tradition of liberal education, however new, is deeply rooted in the resurgent intellectual tradition of pragmatism.

How could it have been otherwise? How could liberal education in the United States have remained insulated from the efflorescence of pragmatism during the twentieth century? After all, John Dewey is well known for identifying philosophy and education, while fellow pragmatist William James virtually equated philosophy and liberal education.[2] What sensible alternative is there for interpreting the history of liberal education? How and why did pragmatism resurge and influence liberal education in the closing decades of the twentieth century?

This essay attempts to address these questions by first reviewing an interpretation of the history of liberal education that identifies two

[1] Thomas F. Green, "Liberalism and Liberal Education: The Good Life and the Making of the Good Man," *Seminar Reports, Program of General Education in the Humanities, Columbia University* 5 (Fall 1976): 27.
[2] John Dewey, *Democracy and Education: An Introduction to the Philosophy of Education* (New York: Free Press, 1966), 383; William James, *Some Problems of Philosophy: A Beginning of an Introduction to Philosophy* [incomplete in 1910], ed. by Frederick H. Burkhardt et al., in *The Works of William James*, ed. F. H. Burkhardt (Cambridge, Mass.: Harvard University Press, 1975-), 9-10.

prominent traditions: one emphasizing "reason," the other emphasizing "speech." This interpretation relies on a pragmatic historical method that tries to solve the historiographical problem of entwining descriptive and normative purposes in examining the issue. The rise of pragmatism is then briefly considered, and a set of six points is proposed to serve as a general framework for understanding the movement during the opening decades of the twentieth century. The challenge and the intent here is to offer a reasoned and general characterization of this elusive movement in light of the pragmatists' writings and the discordant, often contentious, scholarly literature on the topic.

The ensuing analysis of the course of pragmatism in twentieth-century America suggests that the development of the movement is perceived in different ways by different groups of scholars, notably, by philosophers and historians. Hence, the way in which pragmatism is interpreted depends on the context and community within which it is discussed. This understanding aids in explaining the shifting course of pragmatism over the twentieth century. The "turn" to pragmatism in recent thought and the rise of neo-pragmatism are then considered, followed by an examination of the relationship between pragmatism and twentieth-century liberal education. Notwithstanding some good reasons to expect that pragmatism would have significantly influenced liberal education, a pattern of disjunction between these two movements appears to have prevailed throughout most of the twentieth century, with three exceptions: a period of convergence during the 1920s and 1930s, the continuing efforts of certain Progressive Education Colleges, and a persistent thread of interest in general education.

Turning to the current situation, this essay concludes by proposing that the long-standing disjunction is nearing an end. Pragmatism and liberal education seem to be converging, for pragmatism is now exerting an influence on liberal education in a number of ways. The more direct and explicit influence can be seen in the multiple and varied invocations of pragmatism, pragmatists, and progressivism by commentators on liberal education. But this impact is accompanied by intellectual and cultural influences that are subtle and indirect. Recent developments in liberal education, while appearing to be disparate responses to particular demographic, economic, or disciplinary changes, are actually related to one another through deep intellectual and cultural roots. Though perhaps individually prompted by such changes, these recent developments exhibit a collective pattern that is shaped by the historical and cultural context in which they occur. Hence, the proposed influence of pragmatism lies in providing a deeply-rooted rationalization, or intellectual justification, for recent changes and reforms in liberal education. To be sure, the rationalization may not conventionally be called "pragmatic" or even identified as a coherent philosophy or viewpoint. Nevertheless, I suggest that pragmatism provides an intellectual framework within which recent developments in liberal education "make sense during the current era."

Accordingly, it may be said that an interpretation of liberal education that is at once new and traditional appears to be gaining significant support in U.S. higher education, even becoming a matter of consensus, notwithstanding the cacophony of recent debate. And this interpretation may be termed "pragmatic." Whether this convergence of pragmatism and liberal education is a good thing is for others to decide. This essay explores what the convergence means and why it is happening now.

BRUCE KIMBALL

The Condition of American Liberal Education/

Part 1/

*Toward Pragmatic
Liberal Education*

Acknowledgments

I am indebted to Kathleen Mahoney and Darlene Abel for their research assistance in preparing this essay, and to my colleague, Philosophy Professor Randall Curren, for helpful criticism of pragmatism and of this essay.

1/

Orators and Philosophers

A cogent argument can be made for interpreting the history of what has been called "liberal arts" or "liberal education" in terms of two basic traditions.[1] To be sure, any historical generalization involves exceptions and qualifications and may be disaggregated or deconstructed. But to make some general sense out of the long and confusing debate over liberal education, it is helpful to contrast a tradition that has privileged "reason"—including its various denotations of a rationale, a faculty of thinking, and an act of thinking—with a tradition that has privileged "speech" with all its meanings—the pronouncing of words, the faculty of talking, and a formal act of communication. These are the two semantic branches of the Greek term *logos*, which was thought to define the nature of civilization and of a civilized human being, as illustrated in a noted passage by Isocrates (436–338 B.C.).[2]

[1] The following account draws on Bruce A. Kimball, *Orators and Philosophers: A History of the Idea of Liberal Education*, expanded ed., (New York: College Entrance Examination Board, 1995).

[2] "For in our other faculties we (human beings) do not excell the animals. Many of them are fleeter or stronger or otherwise better than we. But because we were endowed with the power of persuading one another and explaining [ourselves], we were not only released from beastial ways of living, but came together and founded states and established laws and invented arts. It was *logos* which enabled us to perfect almost everything we have achieved in the way of civilization. For it was this which laid down the standards of right and wrong, nobility and baseness, without which we should not be able to live together. It is through [*logos*] that we convict bad men and praise good ones. By its aid we educate the foolish and test the wise.... With the help of *logos* we dispute over doubtful matters and investigate the unknown. If we sum up the character of this power, we shall find that no significant thing is done anywhere without the power of *logos*, that *logos* is the leader of all actions and thoughts and that those who make most use of it are the wisest of all humanity," Isocrates, *Antidosis* 253-7, translation adapted by the author from Werner Jaeger, *Paideia: The Ideals of Greek Culture*, trans. Gilbert Highet, 2d ed. (Oxford, England: Basil Blackwell, 1939-1944), 3:89-90.

On one branch were orators and rhetors, who emphasized the newly invented arts of grammar and rhetoric and the skills of composing, delivering, and analyzing a speech. These skills were paramount in a democratic city-state or a republic where persuasion determined the outcome of every question arising in the political and judicial assemblies. On the other branch were those who regarded rhetoric as an imprecise and practical tool that constituted but a shadow of the true essence of *logos*. These others, including Plato (427–347 B.C.) and Aristotle (384–322 B.C.), searched for a precise, rational method of pursuing knowledge, and regarded the new arts of mathematics and syllogistic logic as conveying the essential nature of *logos*.

The debate between advocates of mathematics and logic, on one side, and grammar and rhetoric, on the other, passed to the Romans, who introduced the terms *ratio* and *oratio*. This terminology reflected both the connection and the tension between reason and speech that were expressed by Cicero (106–43 B.C.) in his major treatise on education: "As rivers flow out of the Apennines, the course of learning, from a single mountain ridge of wisdom, diverged, so that philosophers...flowed into the Greek Adriatic Sea of many ports, and orators cascaded on our craggy, barbarous Tuscan shore."[3] The Romans, being builders, lawyers, and administrators of an emerging empire, felt most sympathetic toward a theory of education emphasizing public expression, political and legal discourse, and general and ethical training in the literary tradition that described the noble virtues and orderly society of the past.

Consequently, the foundation of the Roman *artes liberales* lay in "grammar," which included the study of literature as well as language and was emphasized throughout the course of education. Meanwhile, a modicum of attention was occasionally given to arithmetic, geometry, and astronomy, which were regarded as bodies of facts, useful for speeches, but not as formal or theoretical disciplines in the way that Plato and Aristotle had understood them. Music was sometimes studied as practical training for the ear and voice and as an aid to appreciating poetry, but not as one of the formal and theoretical sciences. Logic, or dialectic, was offered as a means of providing the skeletal arguments for public speeches, while rhetoric became the crowning art, which taught the methods of constructing a persuasive discourse on any topic, be it political, religious, military, aesthetic, or legal. This Roman preference for rhetorical, public, practical, prescriptive, and literary education over the precision and clarity of logic and mathematics is exactly what, cen-

---

[3] Cicero, *De Oratore* (Cambridge, Mass.: Harvard University Press, 1942), 3:69. Author's translation.

turies earlier, Plato, Aristotle, and many of their students had found objectionable in the orators' interpretation of the liberal arts.

The literary and rhetorical Roman liberal arts eventually deteriorated toward sophistry, but were gradually adopted and reinvigorated by Christian scholars and educators. They initially observed, as did Paul (died circa 64), that classical learning was refracted into both "oratory and philosophy."[4] Faced with the choice between speech and reason, however, Christians such as Jerome (347–420) and Augustine (354–430) embraced the pagan liberal arts that were concerned with interpreting and expounding the meaning of normative texts. They made the study of grammar and rhetoric preeminent in the *artes liberales*, regarded logic as an adjunct to rhetoric, and studied music primarily in its sonorous and practical dimensions. They treated mathematical and scientific disciplines as bodies of facts providing technical information useful for exegesis. Specialization and advanced study were not encouraged by the Christians and were even criticized as leading to self-indulgence—the same criticism that the orators Cicero and Isocrates had expressed about Plato's vision of a philosophical education extending into adulthood and about Aristotle's idea of education for leisure.

As invasions and turmoil brought an end to the period now called antiquity, the Christian philosopher Boethius (475–525) tried to recover the Platonic and Aristotelian view of the liberal arts, which emphasized the study of mathematics and logic to train the mind in critical analysis and speculative thought. Boethius died at a relatively young age, however, and his influence was not as great as that of three other writers who adopted the practical, literary, and rhetorical model of liberal education: Martianus Capella, Cassiodorus, and Isidore of Seville. In the fifth and sixth centuries, they each wrote handbooks codifying liberal education into a program of seven liberal arts: grammar, logic, rhetoric, arithmetic, geometry, music, and astronomy. The three handbooks served as textbooks for the Christian medieval schools throughout western Europe.

In the twelfth and thirteenth centuries, the rhetorical model of liberal education was challenged when the newly recovered texts of Aristotle and of Islamic philosophers and mathematicians prompted a revival of critical and speculative thought on the part of the Scholastics at the newly arising medieval universities. The challenge was expressed by John of Salisbury (1110–1180) in the observation that "*logos* means both 'word' and 'reason.'"[5] The outcome was that the theoretical and ration-

---

[4] Paul, 1 Corinthians 2:1-4. (Jerusalem Bible)

[5] John of Salisbury, *The Metalogicon of John of Salisbury, A Twelfth-Century Defense of the Verbal and Logical Arts of the Trivium*, trans. Daniel D. McGarry (Berkeley, Calif.: University of California Press, 1955), bk. 1, ch. 10.

alistic orientation of these university Scholastics, or professors, such as Thomas Aquinas (1225–1274), transformed the meaning and content of the liberal arts. Logic emerged supreme as a refined analytic tool, and mathematics and music increasingly addressed abstract number rather than sonorous or practical matters. Rhetoric almost dropped from sight, while grammar was transmuted into linguistic analysis and stripped of its association with literature and texts. Overall, the liberal arts became narrow and relatively cursory *scientiae speculativae* intended to prepare students for advanced and specialized study in the graduate faculties of the universities.

During the fourteenth and fifteenth centuries, the provocative logical disputations that represented the core of the Scholastic liberal arts deteriorated into sophistry. At the same time, the Ciceronian conception of liberal education, along with the works of Cicero, were being rediscovered by the Humanists of the Renaissance. The Humanist movement began outside of the universities and gradually infiltrated those institutions during the fifteenth and sixteenth centuries through the efforts of individuals such as Desiderius Erasmus (1466–1536), who affirmed in his *Plan of Study* that "All knowledge falls into one of two divisions: the knowledge of 'truths' and the knowledge of 'words.'"[6]

Inclining toward the latter, the Humanist model of rhetorical and literary learning was amplified with Christian ethics and with notions of courtesy derived from the medieval tradition of knighthood. These three normative traditions—the Humanist model of learning, the social etiquette of courtesy, and Christian ethics—coalesced to yield the ideal of Christian gentility, which became the archetype of a liberally educated person in sixteenth- and seventeenth-century England. Treatises addressing liberal education during this period proclaimed the orator, the statesman, or what Sir Thomas Elyot called the "governor," as the model for a student engaged in liberal education. At the same time, the fundamental tension between reason and speech was recalled, for example, by Bathsua Pell Makin (1608–1675) in the first English-language treatise arguing on behalf of higher education for women: "There was a Contest between twenty Grecian and twenty Roman Ladies, which were most excellent in learning. The Romane Dames were the best Oratours; But the Grecian Ladies the best Philosophers."[7]

<hr>

[6] Desiderius Erasmus, *De Ratione Studii* [ca. 1511], translated in *Desiderius Erasmus Concerning the Aim and Method of Education*, by William H. Woodward (Cambridge: Cambridge University Press, 1904), 162.
[7] Bathsua Pell Makin, "An Essay to Revive the Antient Education of Gentlewomen," in *First Feminists, British Women Writers, 1578-1799*, ed. Moira Ferguson (Bloomington, Ind.: Indiana University Press, 1985), 132.

The model of Christian gentility was readily endorsed by the founders of Harvard College in 1636, as well as in the eight other colleges subsequently founded in the American colonies. The bulk of the curriculum leading to the degree of bachelor of arts was devoted to rhetoric and grammar, and to reading, memorizing, and interpreting literary and theological texts that defined the virtues of a citizen in God's commonwealth. Meanwhile, leaders of the seventeenth-century Scientific Revolution and eighteenth-century Enlightenment endeavored to resurrect the philosophical tradition with its commitment to mathematical laws and Socratic rationality. The ideas of scientists and *philosophes* began to inform discussion of liberal education in the late eighteenth and early nineteenth centuries, as can be seen in the writings of the Unitarian chemist Joseph Priestley and in the essays that won a contest sponsored in 1795 by the American Philosophical Society, which called for descriptions of "the best system of liberal education and literary instruction, adapted to the genius of the government of the United States."[8]

Conflict inevitably developed between the rhetorical and philosophical models of liberal education, just as it had in the medieval universities and in Athens in the fifth and fourth centuries B.C. During the 1880s, the literary critic and essayist Matthew Arnold and the Darwinian scientist Thomas Henry Huxley toured the United States lecturing on diametrically opposed conceptions of liberal education. Contemporaneously, James McCosh, Presbyterian minister and president of Princeton, and Charles Eliot, chemist and president of Harvard, were engaged in the same debate. Each of these confrontations repeated the centuries-old debate as to which pole of *logos*—reason or speech—should predominate in culture and in the liberal arts. Even as Arnold and McCosh spoke, however, it seemed that Huxley, Eliot, and their allies had carried the day in the United States. A new generation of Scholastics established a flock of universities devoted to advanced and specialized research: Cornell in 1868, Johns Hopkins in 1876, Clark in 1889, Stanford in 1891, and Chicago in 1892. The devotion of the new university professors to the scientific method and to specialized research transformed liberal education once again into preparation for graduate study and the pursuit of knowledge.

Defenders of the rhetorical, practical, and textual liberal arts were not easily brushed aside, however, particularly at the small, special-interest colleges that emerged to serve religious denominations, women, or

---

[8] Frederick Rudolph, ed., *Essays on Education in the Early Republic* (Cambridge, Mass.: Harvard University Press, 1965), xv; *see also* 167-224, 273-372.

African Americans. A vigorous debate ensued in the late nineteenth and early twentieth centuries that eventually became as acrimonious as those of the thirteenth century and the fourth century B.C. Sectarian colleges and universities, particularly Roman Catholic institutions, clung to the Humanist program of studies with its emphasis on literary and rhetorical training that could be traced back through Ignatius Loyola to Cicero and Isocrates. That program was amplified by the teaching of divinity and Scholastic theology in order to mold the Christian citizen. At the same time, many of the universities, encouraged by the scientific emphasis on value-free research, abandoned the idea of training the virtuous citizen. Commensurately, they introduced the undergraduate major, a specialized preparation for the pursuit of truth that was modeled on graduate study and grounded in precise, rational method.

The philosophical, rationalist model of liberal education, enshrined in the American research university, became increasingly dominant as the twentieth century unfolded, although the historical challenge of the oratorical tradition has recently been renewed. This, at least, was the argument put forward in my own attempt to relate this interpretation of a twofold tradition of liberal education to the spirited discussion about undergraduate education in the 1980s. In a lecture sponsored by the Fund for the Improvement of Post-Secondary Education (FIPSE),[9] I attempted to show that, notwithstanding some disagreement, the discussion in the early and mid-1980s suggested a general consensus that undergraduate education should place more emphasis on:

- The study of language and the tradition of the culture;
- The values of students;
- Citizenship and community;
- The coherence and unity of general education; and
- Teaching.

The general consensus on these ideas, I proposed, constituted a reaffirmation of the oratorical tradition of liberal education in response to the century-old dominance of the philosophical tradition. This shift toward an oratorical concept of liberal education, I further suggested, reflected a sea change in the meaning of knowledge and value that was widespread in U.S. culture and that resembled closely the historical changes that precipitated shifts toward the oratorical tradition in earlier periods. For confirmation of these proposals, I pointed to the "linguistic turn" in virtually all areas of scholarship in the humanities and social sciences,

[9] *See* Bruce A. Kimball, "The Historical and Cultural Dimensions of the Recent Reports on Undergraduate Education," *American Journal of Education* 96 (1988).

which was, in certain respects, analogous to the shift toward an oratorical view of liberal education.

In concluding this narrative sketch, it should be noted that advocates of the philosophical and oratorical traditions tend not to fully appreciate one another's positions. Proponents of the rational and precise philosophical tradition often criticize the rhetorical tradition for relying on a crude understanding of knowledge and, therefore, of liberal education. Conversely, advocates of the oratorical tradition claim that overemphasis on rational method artificially narrows the scope and meaning of knowledge because language is the primary conduit of knowledge and, therefore, lies at the heart of liberal education. Proponents of each tradition hold a diminished view of the other because each makes different assumptions about the nature of reason, language, knowledge, and value.

Poised now to address the topic of pragmatism, its relation to liberal education, and the reconstruction of the above argument concerning recent discussion of liberal education, it is necessary, and fitting, to address first the problem of method.

2/

A Pragmatic Historical Method

Efforts to understand liberal education and its history have often foundered on the problem of relating normative and descriptive purposes, that is, relating value and fact. What tends to happen is that a view about the nature of education is developed and then "liberal education" is defined in terms of that view, thus implicitly or explicitly draping the favored position with the mantle of distinguished tradition (or the targeted position with a despised tradition). Philosopher Jane Roland Martin discussed this problem, while seeking to replace what she considers to be the dominant view of liberal education, derived from Paul H. Hirst, with "a new paradigm of liberal education" drawn from feminist thinking. Martin wrote:

> "[L]iberal education" is an honorific title. Suppose [Hirst] had used the label "intellectual education" instead. Would his theory have been taken as seriously as it has been by philosophers of education? Would it have come to dominate thinking in the field so that to all intents and purposes it has become a theory of the whole of education deemed valuable? Surely not.... [W]e should recognize that his theory has taken on a life of its own at least in part because Hirst has traded on the label "liberal education." The... theory has become the received theory not just of intellectual education but of that education deemed valuable, at least in part because Hirst has presented it as a theory of liberal education and liberal education is thought to exhaust that education which is valuable.[1]

[1] Jane Roland Martin, "Needed: A New Paradigm for Liberal Education," in *Changing the Educational Landscape: Philosophy, Women, and Curriculum* (New York: Routledge, 1994), 174. *See* Paul H. Hirst, "Liberal Education and the Nature of Knowledge," in *Philosophical Analysis and Education*, ed. Reginald D. Archambault (London: Routledge and Kegan Paul, 1965).

Though insightfully identifying the problematic connection between definition and evaluation, Martin's analysis overlooks an important distinction between two different causal relationships. Thinkers may label their theories "liberal education" *because* they implicitly or explicitly desire to trade on the honor accruing to the term. However, theories probably do not become accepted *because* they adopt the term "liberal education" (though they may become noticed because they are so called). "Progressive liberal education" is a case in point.[2] Furthermore, Martin does not address the question of whether "liberal education" has meant something more than "valuable education." Is it possible to identify characteristics historically associated with what has been called "liberal education" in addition to its being considered valuable?

A similar attempt to circumvent the "trad[ing] on the label 'liberal education,'" of which Martin accuses Hirst, may be found in the stimulating historical analysis of liberal education in the United States by W. B. Carnochan. Carnochan disavowed the identification of "a transhistorical value" or "the abstract ideal" of liberal education, apparently wishing to avoid an essentialist definition. Instead, he looked for the "purpose" of liberal education. It is hard to see, however, how identifying "criteria of purposefulness" escapes an essentialist definition. In fact, this approach appears to beg the question, because it is difficult to talk about the purposes of something, say *hashi-oki*, without knowing what *hashi-oki* is. This objection may be rebutted by Carnochan's explanation that discussion of liberal education should focus on "the specific purpose of whatever it is, educationally, that we are trying to do."[3] This effectively defines liberal education as whatever educators are "trying to do," a definition that is (pragmatically) close to Martin's, that liberal education is about what is "valuable." In both cases, the historical investigation is subtly transformed into a philosophical discussion of purpose or value. This approach sidesteps the historical account of liberal education, as is demonstrated by the fact that what some educators tried to do or considered valuable was called "liberal education" while what others tried or considered was not. Hence, value or purpose cannot have been the sole, or even necessary, criterion underlying the definition of "liberal education" in the past.

These examples from highly sophisticated scholarship demonstrate a major stumbling block in the way of understanding the history, and pres-

[2] *See* Sidney Hook, "Thirteen Arrows Against Progressive Liberal Education," *The Humanist* 4 (Spring 1944).

[3] W. B. Carnochan, *The Battleground of the Curriculum: Liberal Education and American Experience* (Stanford, Calif.: Stanford University Press, 1993), 6, 115, 23, 119, 115.

ent situation, of liberal education: entwining normative and descriptive purposes in assessing the nature of the tradition and its significance today. In response to this problem in the historiography of liberal education—as well as in the historiography of professions—I have adopted what I now understand to be a pragmatic approach to assessing historical meaning. Those familiar with pragmatism will immediately recognize that this approach to meaning makes perfect sense in assessing a topic freighted with multiple and complicated relationships between fact and value. But it was only in preparing to write this essay that I came to understand my approach to studying the history of liberal education and of professions as pragmatic. The reader, I trust, will excuse this personal aside, inasmuch as the point is to demonstrate that one scholar who wrote a history of liberal education in 1986 realized in 1994 that he was clearly employing a pragmatic approach to that history in order to navigate through the Strait of Messina where commentators on liberal education, or professions, have foundered between the Scylla and Charybdis of fact and value.

What is this pragmatic method? First, it proposes that there is no necessary, universal, or essential meaning of liberal education or liberal arts, "not a sort of Hegelian cloud, building over the *scholae*." Second, this approach maintains that, in the absence of essences or universals, the meaning of liberal education or liberal arts is determined by how the terms are used; thus, "the fundamental method will be to follow the words 'liberal education' or 'liberal arts' through history." Third, the approach attempts to infer, in line with Charles Sanders Peirce, the logical consequences that attend the use of the term. The meaning thus becomes the abstracted propositions that are associated with its use and that are rationally consequent on and inferable from those propositions. What thereby results is "a general frame of reference...[that] constitutes a logically coherent whole...systematizing the ideas generally associated with the words 'liberal education' and 'liberal arts.'" In sum, this pragmatic approach intends to arrive at (1) a nominalist or anti-essentialist, but nevertheless (2) empirical and (3) rationally systematic appraisal of (4) how the terms "liberal arts" or "liberal education" have been *used* by the community of interpreters, and of (5) how that use has changed over time.[4]

Responses to this approach have varied. Terry Gourvish has derogated it as "an exercise in intellectual history, with a strong emphasis on

[4] Bruce A. Kimball, *Orators and Philosophers: A History of the Idea of Liberal Education*, expanded ed., (New York: College Entrance Examination Board, 1995), 37, 2-3, 36-37, 52. *See also* Kimball, *The "True Professional Ideal" in America: A History* (Oxford, England: Basil Blackwell, 1992), ch. 1.

semantics," while Christopher Lasch has suggested that the approach "yields such an abundance of insights and now seems such an obvious strategy that it is hard to understand why this kind of analysis has been neglected."[5] Whatever the judgment, it must be acknowledged that there is a good deal of indeterminacy, speculation, and judgment attending both the evidence and the inferences concerning the tradition of what has historically been called "liberal education" or "liberal arts." With regard to etymology, we need only examine the admirable essays of Lambert de Rijk on *enkuklios paideia* or Pio Rajna on the *quadrivium* and, with regard to teaching practice, the recent books concerning Renaissance Humanists, tutors, and grammar masters by Anthony Grafton and Lisa Jardine and by Paul Gehl.[6] Nevertheless, a survey of the historical discussion explicitly addressing liberal education or liberal arts does evince certain patterns, which account for much of what has often been regarded in twentieth-century discussion as confusion in the historical debate.

Finally, it is worth considering the application of this pragmatic concept of meaning to "pragmatism" itself. The leading commentators on the pragmatist philosophers have tended to discount the use of the term "pragmatism" for the sake of the concepts that it supposedly mediates. "[A]fter all, what's in a name?" asked Philip Wiener when discussing the denotations of "pragmatism," "Practicalism," and "pragmaticism." John Smith observed that the problems of William James's "'slipshod' and 'elliptical'" language "belong essentially to the rhetoric rather than the logic of the situation."[7] A prominent exception is provided by William Van Orman Quine, who stated, "I suspect that the term 'pragmatism' is one we could do without. It draws a pragmatic blank.... It is

---

[5] Terry Gourvish, "The Professionals," *History Today* (May 1994): 58; Christopher Lasch, personal correspondence with the author (20 July 1990).

[6] Lambert de Rijk, "*Enkuklios Paideia*: A Study of Its Original Meaning," *Vivarium* 3 (1965); Pio Rajna, "Le denominazioni *Trivium* e *Quadrivium*," *Studi Medievali* 1 (1928); Anthony Grafton and Lisa Jardine, *From Humanism to the Humanities: Education and the Liberal Arts in Fifteenth- and Sixteenth-Century Europe* (Cambridge, Mass.: Harvard University Press, 1986); Paul F. Gehl, *A Moral Art: Grammar, Society, and Culture in Trecento Florence* (Ithaca, N.Y.: Cornell University Press, 1993).

[7] Philip P. Wiener, *Evolution and the Founders of Pragmatism* (Philadelphia: University of Pennsylvania Press, 1972), 25; John E. Smith, *Purpose and Thought: The Meaning of Pragmatism* (Chicago: University of Chicago Press, 1978), 69-70. It is interesting that Peirce, James, and Dewey are all regarded as having problems in expressing themselves. William Van Orman Quine, "Pragmatists' Place in Empiricism," in *Pragmatism: Its Sources and Prospects*, ed. Robert J. Mulvaney and Philip M. Zeltner (Columbia, S.C.: University of South Carolina Press, 1981), 29; Smith, *Purpose and Thought*, 7-8; Oliver Wendell Holmes, Jr., in *Holmes-Pollock Letters: The Correspondence of Mr. Justice Holmes and Sir Frederick Pollock, 1874-1932*, ed. Mark DeWolfe Howe, (Cambridge, Mass.: Harvard University Press, 1941), 2:272, 287.

not clear in what ways the philosophers who have been called pragmatists are nearer in outlook to one another than to philosophers who are
not so called." Paradoxically, Quine thus employs a pragmatic method
to show that the term "pragmatism" mediates no concepts, although
the paradox may be partly explained by the fact that Quine was attempting here to dissociate himself from pragmatism.[8] What this exception
and paradox demonstrate is that the pragmatic historical method and
concept of meaning lead to a consideration of the complex relationship
between scholars' wishes, or purposes, and their conceptions. And this
consideration weighs prominently in the following examination of how
pragmatism and liberal education are now converging.

[8] Quine, "Pragmatists' Place in Empiricism," 23. Meanwhile, Quine explicitly approved
of the pragmatic approach to meaning while endorsing John Horne Tooke's observation
of 1796 that if the term "word" were substituted every place where Locke wrote the
term "idea," the *Essay Concerning Human Understanding* would be improved. In the
same vein, Quine observed that "Dewey long preceded Wittgenstein in insisting that
there is no more to meaning than is to be found in the social use of linguistic forms"
("Pragmatists' Place in Empiricism," 36-37). Thus, Ludwig Wittgenstein said, "if we had
to name anything which is the life of the sign, we should have to say it was its *use*"
(*Preliminary Studies for "Philosophical Investigations Generally Known as 'The Blue
and Brown Books'"* [Oxford, England: Basil Blackwell, 1958], 4). Cf. John Dewey,
Experience and Nature [1925], 2d ed. (La Salle, Ill.: Open Court, 1929), ch. 6; H. S.
Thayer, *Meaning and Action: A Critical History of Pragmatism* [1968], 2d ed. (Indianapolis, Ind.: Hackett, 1981), 311-13.

3/

Pragmatism

Notwithstanding claims that pragmatism extends back to the British empiricists,[1] Francis Bacon,[2] or the sophist Protagoras,[3] the philosophical movement of this name stems most directly and notably from Charles S. Peirce (1839–1914), William James (1842–1910), and John Dewey (1859–1952), as well as from George Herbert Mead (1862–1931) and Clarence Irving Lewis (1883–1964). Even the lineage among this group is somewhat uncertain because "the founders of pragmatism were neither very clear nor consistent in the accounts they gave concerning the historical origins of their doctrine."[4] Nevertheless, it may be said that the "doctrine" was discussed among a small group of intellectuals meeting informally in Cambridge, Massachusetts, during the 1870s, and was first formulated in writing by Peirce and published in two articles in *Popular Science Monthly* after the group stopped meeting.[5] Two decades later, these papers were praised by another member of the group, William James, in a lecture at the University of California in which "pragmatism" was first publicly called by that name.[6] Academics at the

[1] William James, *Pragmatism: A New Name for Some Old Ways of Thinking* [1907] (New York: Longmans, Green, 1925), 46-48.
[2] John Dewey, *Reconstruction in Philosophy* (New York: Henry Holt, 1920), 38, 93.
[3] A. J. Ayer, *The Origins of Pragmatism* (San Francisco: Freeman, Cooper, 1968), 3.
[4] H. S. Thayer, *Meaning and Action: A Critical History of Pragmatism* 2d ed. [1968], (Indianapolis, Ind.: Hackett, 1981), 5. *See also* John E. Smith, *Purpose and Thought: The Meaning of Pragmatism* (Chicago: University of Chicago Press, 1978), 9.
[5] *See* Charles S. Peirce, "The Fixation of Belief," *Popular Science Monthly* 12 (1877), in *Collected Papers of Charles Sanders Peirce*, 5:358-87, ed. Charles Hartshorne and Paul Weiss (vols. 1-6), with A. Burks (vols. 7-8) (Cambridge, Mass.: Harvard University Press, 1931-58); Peirce, "How To Make Our Ideas Clear," *Popular Science Monthly* 12 (1878), in *Collected Papers* 5:388-410.
[6] William James, "Philosophical Conceptions and Practical Results," [1898], published in *University of California Chronicle*, reprinted in *Collected Essays and Reviews*, ed, Ralph Barton Perry (New York: Longmans, Green, 1920).

University of Chicago, especially Dewey and Mead, were meanwhile being influenced by James, although Dewey left Chicago contemporaneously with the publication of what he later recalled as his first mature writings in *Studies in Logical Theory* (1903), which he edited and James praised.[7] By 1910 these "pragmatists," who scarcely formed a movement or school, were moving in distinctive directions. In 1905, Peirce coined the term "pragmaticism" to distinguish his doctrine from that of James and, as he said, from the parodies of pragmatism already appearing in "literary journals."[8] In 1909, James expounded a doctrine of "radical empiricism," which he called "a sequel to 'Pragmatism,'" and Dewey soon was writing under the flag of "instrumentalism" or "experimentalism."[9]

Consequently, it is hazardous to generalize about the views of these thinkers, who were briefly and scarcely associated, whose views are elusive, and who disagreed with each other and apparently misunderstood each other.[10] One must heed David Hollinger's astute warning against identifying tenets whereby "the tradition of Peirce, James, and Dewey is flattened into a style of thought." Even so, "pragmatism" came to refer to the doctrine or viewpoint of these individuals, and Hollinger himself proceeded to offer "my account of the combination of [three] elements peculiar to the pragmatists," as have many others with all the customary apologies.[11] In attributing the following six points to pragmatism, I

[7] *See* Bruce Kuklick, *Churchmen and Philosophers: From Jonathan Edwards to John Dewey* (New Haven, Conn.: Yale University Press, 1985), 240; Andrew Feffer, *The Chicago Pragmatists and American Progressivism* (Ithaca, N.Y.: Cornell University Press, 1993), 4ff., passim; William James, *Collected Essays and Reviews*, ed. Ralph Barton Perry (New York: Longmans, Green, 1920), 445-47.

[8] Charles S. Peirce, "What Pragmatism Is," *Monist* 15 (1905), in *Collected Papers* 5:414.

[9] William James, *The Meaning of Truth: A Sequel to 'Pragmatism'* (New York: Longmans, Green, 1909), Pref. John Dewey, "The Development of American Pragmatism," published originally in French in 1922, English translation reprinted in *Philosophy and Civilization* (New York: Minton, Balch, 1931), 13: "The purpose of this article is to define the principal theories of the philosophical movements known under the names of Pragmatism, Instrumentalism, or Experimentalism."

[10] Murray Murphey observed, "even today there is little agreement as to the nature of [Peirce's] philosophy" (*The Development of Peirce's Philosophy* [1961] [Indianapolis, Ind.: Hackett, 1993], 1). David W. Marcell went so far as to say, "pragmatism is so varied and protean a mode of philosophy that lumping Peirce, James, Dewey, and Mead into a 'school' may justifiably raise eyebrows" (*Progress and Pragmatism: James, Dewey, Beard, and the American Idea of Progress* [Westport, Conn.: Greenwood, 1974], x).

[11] David A. Hollinger, "The Problem of Pragmatism in American History," *Journal of American History* 67 (1980):91, 93, 93-99. Cf. the general accounts offered in Thayer,

wish to underscore my reliance on the commentary offered by "the rather more orthodox interpretation"[12] and "the finest analysis we have of the main figures and themes of the movement"[13] by H. S. Thayer, as well as on the careful analyses of John Smith, Israel Scheffler and certain other philosophers.

The first point of pragmatism is an emphasis on the "fallibilism" of meaning and belief, in contrast to the certainty of truth. This emphasis was expressed by Peirce in his two seminal essays of 1877 and 1878 through the general formulation that belief and meaning are ever revisable and improvable. This formulation relied on Peirce's insight that what he called the "fallibilism" of belief or meaning is compatible with a "realist" view of abstractions and truths.[14] James, "much more of a nominalist than Peirce," as Dewey noted, emphasized the particular and behavioral consequences of thought, rather than the generality of logical rules, which attracted Peirce.[15] As a result, James raised the prospect that any particular conception of truth we might have is fallible. In this way, James elaborated Peirce's insight about the fallible nature of belief and meaning into a theory of truth.[16] This undermining of the certainty of truth was a leitmotif of the pragmatist era, as James Kloppenberg has shown, and Dewey became perhaps the chief excavator, by attacking "the theory of knowledge, and especially the belief that it is the

Meaning and Action, 4, 348, 348-414, 431; John J. Stuhr, ed., *Classical American Philosophy: Essential Readings and Interpretive Essays* (New York: Oxford University Press, 1987), 5-11; Philip P. Wiener, *Evolution and the Founders of Pragmatism* [1949] (Philadelphia: University of Pennsylvania Press, 1972), 190-91; James T. Kloppenberg, *Uncertain Victory: Social Democracy and Progressivism in European and American Thought, 1870-1920* (New York: Oxford University Press, 1986), 3-4, 79-94, 113-15; Israel Scheffler, *Four Pragmatists: A Critical Introduction to Peirce, James, Mead, and Dewey* (New York: Humanities, 1974), 1-2, 8; Ernest Gellner, "Pragmatism and the Importance of Being Earnest," in *Pragmatism: Its Sources and Prospects*, ed. Robert J. Mulvaney and Philip M. Zeltner (Columbia, S.C.: University of South Carolina Press, 1981), 60; Richard Rorty, *Consequences of Pragmatism (Essays 1972-1980)* (Minneapolis: University of Minnesota Press, 1982), 162ff.; (but *see* Richard Rorty, "Comments on Sleeper and Edel," *Transactions of the Charles S. Peirce Society* 21 (1985): 39ff.).

[12] Garry Brodsky, "Rorty's Interpretation of Pragmatism," *Transactions of the Charles S. Peirce Society* 18 (1982): 322.

[13] Mulvaney and Zeltner, eds., *Pragmatism*, viii.

[14] Peirce, *Collected Papers*, 1:8-14, 171; "The Fixation of Belief," 5:384.

[15] Dewey, "The Development of American Pragmatism," 18-19. *See also* James, *The Meaning of Truth*, 209-10; Murphey, *The Development of Peirce's Philosophy*, 2-3; Thayer, *Meaning and Action*, 140-41; Smith, *Purpose and Thought*, 24.

[16] Smith, *Purpose and Thought*, 32-35, 43-44.

inescapable starting point of all philosophical thought.... In place of this ['epistemological'] approach, Dewey proposed a *methodological* solution to the problem of knowing."[17] The link between the attack on certainty and an emphasis on method was made most notably by Dewey in *The Quest for Certainty*.[18]

This emphasis on method leads to a second point of pragmatism: a belief in a universal and experimental method of inquiry obtaining in science and all reflective thought. This emphasis originated in Peirce's often-quoted "Pragmatic Maxim" proposing a "practical" way to clarify meaning, and in his view that "the method of science" is comparatively the best method "to satisfy our doubts."[19] In 1907, James wrote that pragmatism "does not stand for any special results. It is a method only," although in the next breath he adumbrated that methodological emphasis, "Such then would be the scope of pragmatism—first a method; second, a genetic theory of what is meant by truth." A method to disclose "the meaning of truth," James held, would require that truth claims be tested; that such testing involve at some point the consideration of empirical consequences—"What difference would it practically make to anyone if this notion rather than that notion were true?"—and, finally, that all tested and empirically validated conclusions remain tentative and subject to further revision.[20]

In line with James's ideas, Dewey drew on what he understood to be scientific method to propose a pattern of "reflective experience," which he also called a "method of knowing" and the "experimental method." This pattern was elaborated in a number of works over the period between the first edition of *How We Think* (1910) and *Logic: The Theory of Inquiry* (1938), while its direct implications for education were

[17] Smith, *Purpose and Thought*, 10. *See also* Kloppenberg, *Uncertain Victory*, 64-94.
[18] *See* John Dewey, *The Quest for Certainty: A Study of the Relation of Knowledge and Action* (New York: Minton, Balch, 1929), chs. 2, 9.
[19] Peirce, "The Fixation of Belief," 5:384. The "maxim" was set forth in "How to Make Our Ideas Clear," 5:402: "Consider what effects, that might conceivably have practical bearings, we conceive the object of our conception to have. Then, our conception of these effects is the whole of our conception of the object." The meaning of "practical bearings" or "practical consequences" has been much debated. Reformulating the original pragmatic maxim in 1905, Peirce restated "practical bearings" in terms of experimental results ("What Pragmatism Is," 5:411-13). Dewey tried to clarify the meaning in "What Pragmatism Means by Practical" [*a review of William James, Pragmatism*], *Journal of Philosophy* 5 (1908), reprinted in John Dewey, *Essays in Experimental Logic* (Chicago: University of Chicago Press, 1910; New York: Dover, 1954). *See also* John Dewey, "The Pragmatism of Peirce," *Journal of Philosophy* 13 (1916).
[20] James, *Pragmatism*, 50, 64-65, 45, 46-47. *See also* James, *Essays in Radical Empiricism* (New York: Longmans, Green, 1912), 42; Smith, *Purpose and Thought*, 45; Thayer, *Meaning and Action*, 160.

expressed in *Democracy and Education* (1916). Dewey's method of reflecting, knowing, inquiring, and experimenting involved identifying a problem arising out of an experienced situation, surveying the relevant evidence, inferring a hypothesis to explain or solve the problem, conducting a test of the hypothesis, and inferring the results of the test both with respect to the hypothesis and with respect to new problems.[21]

The belief of the pragmatists, particularly Dewey, "that they now understood the real nature of the scientific method—the key to understanding the social universe"[22] has been widely discussed and often criticized from a number of perspectives. One such criticism that bears mention here is that pragmatists did not understand how science and scientists work, a contention often accompanied by invocations of Thomas Kuhn's *The Structure of Scientific Revolutions*. This criticism tends to overlook the point made by both Douglas Sloan and John Smith that Dewey consciously diverged from the scientists of his day in, for example, stressing "the interconnectedness of all experience" and "the essential connection between thought and action."[23] Dewey was not mimicking scientists. Moreover, this criticism is somewhat beside the point, inasmuch as pragmatism "takes science as suggestive of more general concepts of critical thought, in terms of which the continuities among all modes may be revealed, and in light of which all may be refined and advanced."[24] The point was that science was only one instance, however exemplary, of "a common 'pattern'" of human

[21] John Dewey, *Democracy and Education: An Introduction to the Philosophy of Education* [1916] (New York: Free Press, 1966), 150, 163, 173, 338. *See also* Dewey, "The Pattern of Inquiry," in *Logic: The Theory of Inquiry* (New York: Henry Holt, 1938), 101-19; Sandra B. Rosenthal, "John Dewey: Scientific Method and Lived Immediacy," *Transactions of the Charles S. Peirce Society* 17 (1981); Rosenthal, "Pragmatism and Scientific Method: A Revisit," *Southwest Philosophy Review* 1 (1984). Noting that "Dewey's conception of inquiry is heavily indebted to the theory of Peirce," Thayer maintained that "what Dewey calls 'the pattern of inquiry'. . . exhibits four stages—or five, if we count as a first stage the antecedent troubled and indeterminate situation within and from which inquiry is generated"—(i) recognition of a problem within a situation; (ii) formulation of hypotheses, "suggestions," or potential solutions to the problem; (iii) "reasoning" to determine the relevancy of the solution to the problem; and (iv) experiment or testing of the solution to determine if it performs the function (*Meaning and Action*, 171, 191-92).

[22] Edward A. Purcell, Jr., *The Crisis of Democratic Theory: Scientific Naturalism and the Problem of Value* (Lexington, Ky.: University of Kentucky Press, 1973), 29.

[23] Douglas Sloan, "The Teaching of Ethics in the American Undergraduate Curriculum, 1876-1976, "*Teachers College Record* 82 (1980): 224ff.; Smith, *Purpose and Thought*, 58.

[24] Israel Scheffler, *Four Pragmatists: A Critical Introduction to Peirce, James, Mead, and Dewey* (New York: Humanities, 1974), 2.

thought extending from common sense to the most sophisticated inquiry.[25]

This putative commonality, however, becomes a target of criticism for others who contend that "the natural and physical sciences have the closest connections to political and economic structures" and that "scientific studies reflect cultural values."[26] The charge that pragmatists failed to recognize the influences of culture and gender on scientific findings and method is another way of stating a long-standing criticism made by philosophers ranging from Sidney Hook to Smith and Thayer. The latter criticism is that the pragmatists, especially Dewey, failed to see that method is not "neutral" and that specifying a universal method of inquiry implies certain presuppositions about "the generic traits of existence which make that method a fruitful one in revealing them."[27]

This second criticism is acute, but may be rebutted by two points, which are also relevant to the first criticism. On the one hand, Dewey was not offering a formalistic recipe, but a fallible understanding of method as it had appeared to work in past inquiry. Thus, the criticism that Dewey's view needs to be reconstructed in light of Kuhnian and constructivist views is compatible both with Dewey's approach and, in fact, with the method he proposed.[28] On the other hand, what is lost in dismissing the commonality and universality of Deweyan method is a deep-seated egalitarianism. As Dewey wrote in the preface to *How We Think*: "This scientific attitude of mind might, conceivably, be quite irrelevant to teaching children and youth. But this book also represents the conviction that such is not the case; that the native and unspoiled attitude of childhood, marked by ardent curiosity, fertile imagination, and love of experimental inquiry is near, very near, to the attitude of the scientific mind."[29] Thus, Dewey's "unified conception of thinking...reveals the continuity between the humblest bit of learning

---

[25] Smith, *Purpose and Thought*, 97. *See also* Sandra B. Rosenthal, *Speculative Pragmatism* (Amherst, Mass.: University of Massachusetts Press, 1986), ch. 1.

[26] Margaret L. Anderson, "Changing the Curriculum in Higher Education," *Signs: A Journal of Women in Culture and Society* 12 (1987): 240-42. *See also* Evelyn Fox Keller, *Reflections on Gender and Science* (New Haven, Conn.: Yale University Press, 1985); Sandra Harding, *The Science Question in Feminism* (Ithaca, N.Y.: Cornell University Press, 1986).

[27] Sidney Hook, Ph.D. dissertation, published as *The Metaphysics of Pragmatism* (Chicago: Open Court, 1927), 6. *See also* Smith, *Purpose and Thought*, 44-45; Thayer, Meaning and Action, 454.

[28] *See* Smith, *Purpose and Thought*, 101-3; Thayer, *Meaning and Action*, 192-93; Cornel West, *The American Evasion of Philosophy: A Genealogy of Pragmatism* (Madison, Wis.: University of Wisconsin Press, 1989), 98.

[29] John Dewey, *How We Think*, "Preface to the First Edition," [1910], V. *See also* Dewey, *Democracy and Education*, chs. 11, 12, 13.

by a child exploring its room and the most refined piece of theorizing by an experimental scientist investigating the natural world."[30] In contrast to Peirce or Quine, Dewey did not concede to a group of experts an esoteric method whose results were then to be reported to the general community. Such "a hierarchical and monopolistic conception" was precluded by the commonality and universality of method that is criticized by some, ironically, who abhor such a conception.[31]

This rebuttal leads directly to a third point of pragmatism: that belief, meaning, and truth depend on the context and the intersubjective judgment of the community in which they are formed. James provided the classic example of this perspectivity and subjectivity in posing the question: Does a person circling a tree also circle a squirrel moving around the tree, on the side opposite from the person?[32] But James gave less attention to the intersubjective and communitarian basis of belief than did Peirce,[33] who maintained that belief expresses the fallible and working consensus of a community of inquirers. Peirce reconciled this view with his realism through "a cheerful hope" that the beliefs of the community of individual inquirers, bound by the discipline of experimental method, will converge toward a working consensus that approaches truth as if it were a mathematical limit. Thus, truth is "the opinion which is fated to be ultimately agreed to by all who investigate," which is "that concordance of an abstract statement with the ideal limit towards which endless investigation would tend to bring scientific belief." In Peirce's view, the historical record of "three centuries" of practicing scientific method "encourages us to hope that we are approaching nearer and nearer to an opinion which is not destined to be broken down."[34]

[30] Scheffler, *Four Pragmatists*, 2.

[31] Scheffler, *Four Pragmatists*, 87. West astutely observed, "Quine…unlike Dewey, invokes the *authority* of physics as that which tells us the way the world is, subject to revision. Dewey accepts the authority of physics (or of common sense or of any other authority) only insofar as that authority works effectively" (*The American Evasion of Philosophy*, 188). *See also* Daniel J. Wilson, *Science, Community, and the Transformation of American Philosophy, 1860-1930* (Chicago: University of Chicago Press, 1990), 21-22, 34-35, 126-27, 132-33, 138-41, 188-92; William Van Orman Quine, "Pragmatists' Place in Empiricism," in *Pragmatism: Its Sources and Prospects*, ed. Robert J. Mulvaney and Philip M. Zeltner (Columbia, S.C.: University of South Carolina Press, 1981), 33-34.

[32] James, *Pragmatism*, 43-44.

[33] Commensurately, James's doctrine gave greater emphasis to individualism than did those of other pragmatists. Cf. Wiener, *Evolution and the Founders of Pragmatism*, 125; Thayer, *Meaning and Action*, 151; Kloppenberg, *Uncertain Victory*, 97.

[34] Peirce, *Collected Papers* 5:407, 565, 384 n. 1.

C. I. Lewis subsequently qualified Peirce's view by proposing that different communities of scientific investigators might arrive at "alternative conceptual systems, giving rise to alternative descriptions of experience, which are equally objective and equally valid."[35] But, among the pragmatists, Dewey most notably challenged Peirce's realism and "ideal limit" by arguing for the perpetually reconstructive nature of science and inquiry and speaking in terms of "warranted assertibility" or "warranted assertions." For Dewey, the warrant of belief stems not from the proximity of belief to the true or the real, as Peirce suggested, but purely from the consensus of the community, whose members employ the experimental method.[36] It is worth noting here that this idea of warranted assertibility led Dewey to associate science and democracy. Indeed, the two are analogous in Deweyan pragmatism, inasmuch as both experimental method and democratic decision making are said to rely on the warrant of a consensus among rational minds attending to evidence and testing the results.[37]

A fourth point of pragmatism is an understanding of experience as the dynamic interaction of organism and environment, which results in a close interrelationship between thought and action. This theme receives less support in Peirce, who was, nevertheless, both "an empiricist" and "a logician," as Dewey observed.[38] The dynamic quality of experience was forcefully expressed by James in his seminal psychological doctrine that consciousness is not a set of "states" but a "wonderful stream."[39] His emphasis on particular and behavioral experience led to his doctrine of "radical empiricism," which will "neither admit into its constructions any element that is not directly experienced, nor exclude from them any element that is directly experienced."[40] This conception was extended by Dewey, who held that thought and action cannot be understood apart from their close interrelationship in "experience," which he viewed as the dynamic interaction of organism and environment. Here the biological tincture of Dewey's thought was most pronounced, although the hard edge of the "struggle for existence" was softened:

[35] Clarence I. Lewis, *Mind and the World Order: Outline of a Theory of Knowledge* (New York: Charles Scribner's Sons, 1929), 271.

[36] *See* Dewey, *Logic: The Theory of Inquiry*, 8-9; Dewey, "Propositions, Warranted Assertibility, and Truth," in *Problems of Men* [1941] (New York: Philosophical Library, 1946), 331-35.

[37] *See* Dewey, *Democracy and Education*, 229, 344-45.

[38] Dewey, "The Development of American Pragmatism," 13-14.

[39] William James, *The Principles of Psychology* (New York: Henry Holt, 1890), 1:243.

[40] James, *Essays in Radical Empiricism*, 42.

The nature of experience can be understood only by noting that it includes an active and a passive element particularly combined. On the active hand, experience is *trying*—a meaning which is made explicit in the connected term experiment. On the passive, it is *undergoing*. When we experience something we act on it, we do something to the thing and then it does something to us in return. Such is the peculiar combination.[41]

In the end, Dewey arrived at a fuller, more dynamic and complex conception of what it means to "have an experience," which represents another distinction between his understanding of experimental method and that of others of his day.

This conception of experience and that of the universal method of inquiry lead to a fifth point of pragmatism: that purpose is intrinsic to thought and inquiry. In explaining his choice between the Kantian terms *pragmatisch* and *praktisch*, Peirce observed, "the most striking feature of the new theory was its recognition of an inseparable connection between rational cognition and rational purpose; and that consideration...determined the preference for the name *pragmatism*."[42] The "inseparable connection" lies in the proposition that all inquiry begins with genuine doubt, "The irritation of doubt causes a struggle to attain a state of belief. I shall term this struggle *Inquiry*....With the doubt, therefore, the struggle begins, with the cessation of doubt it ends. Hence, the sole object of inquiry is the settlement of opinion."[43] James concurred in holding that "a *conception*...is a *teleological instrument*," while Mead, writing on "A Pragmatic Theory of Truth," likewise observed that "truth is then synonymous with the solution of the problem."[44]

Mead's terminology and his close association with Dewey are significant because "problem," rather than "doubt," was the word that Dewey preferred. The underlying point—that all intelligent inquiry is guided by purpose—remained unchanged, however. "The realness of error, ambiguity, doubt and guess poses a problem....The right, the true and good...is that which carries out satisfactorily the specific purpose for

[41] Dewey, *Democracy and Education*, 139. *See also* Dewey, *Democracy and Education*, ch. 11. Note, too, that Dewey said, "Experience. . .has depth. It also has breadth and to an infinitely elastic extent. It stretches. That stretch constitutes inference" (*Experience and Nature* [1925], 2d ed. [La Salle, Ill.: Open Court, 1929]), 4.

[42] Peirce, "What Pragmatism Is," 5:412.

[43] Peirce, "The Fixation of Belief," 5:374, 375. *See also* John E. Smith, "Purpose in American Philosophy," in *Themes in American Philosophy* (New York: Harper & Row, 1971); Thayer, *Meaning and Action*, 83-86, 138-40.

[44] William James, *Collected Essays and Reviews*, ed. Ralph Barton Perry (New York: Longmans, Green, 1920), 86; George Herbert Mead, *Selected Writings*, ed. Andrew J. Reck (New York: Bobbs-Merrill, 1964), 328.

the sake of which knowing occurs," Dewey wrote in "The Practical Character of Reality."[45] And in *The Quest for Certainty*, he said, "intelligence is a quality of some acts, those which are directed."[46] This central emphasis on purpose led Dewey to employ the term "instrumentalism," along with "experimentalism," for his version of pragmatism.

From the instrumental conception of thinking as solving problems or resolving doubts follows a sixth point of pragmatism: the evaluative and normative character of all inquiry. Thinking cannot be separated from choosing or preferring; knowledge cannot be separated from evaluation; fact cannot be separated from value. "The shift in content and direction that James brought upon Peirce's original formulation of pragmatism" was a shift from logical toward particular and behavioral consequences of thought, which entailed "fundamentally a shift from the analysis of meanings of ideas to an analysis of their value or moral uses."[47] The tension of reconciling the scientific view with moral questions is evident throughout *The Principles of Psychology* because, on the one hand, James attempted to adhere strictly to scientific procedure, while, on the other, his teleological view of the mind as "*a fighter for ends*" led him inexorably to questions of purpose and value.[48]

In Dewey's view, "the problem of restoring integration and cooperation between man's beliefs about the world in which he lives and his beliefs about the values and purposes that should direct his conduct is the deepest problem of modern life."[49] Indeed, as Ernest Nagel and others have observed, the relation of science and human values was "at the focus of Dewey's attention during his long philosophical career."[50] Dewey's effort in this regard is often analyzed in terms of "naturalism,"

[45] Dewey, "The Practical Character of Reality," in *Philosophy and Civilization*, 47.

[46] Dewey, *The Quest for Certainty*, 245.

[47] Thayer, *Meaning and Action*, 134. *See also* Thayer, *Meaning and Action*, 147-48; Smith, *Purpose and Thought*, 33-35.

[48] James, *The Principles of Psychology*, 1:141.

[49] Dewey, *The Quest for Certainty*, 255.

[50] Ernest Nagel, "Dewey's Theory of Natural Science," in *John Dewey: Philosopher of Science and Freedom, A Symposium*, ed. Sidney Hook (Westport, Conn.: Greenwood, 1950), 234. Dewey's concern has led, even today, to serious misreadings, asserting that he "held firmly. . .that value judgments could be drawn from scientific data" or "that the scientific method could turn all moral issues into questions of experiential fact" (John Patrick Diggins, *The Promise of Pragmatism: Modernism and the Crisis of Knowledge and Authority* [Chicago: University of Chicago Press, 1992], 46, 246). According to Wilson, however, "Dewey did not seek to reduce morals, ethics, or other considerations of value to the physical sciences. Rather, he argued that the scientific method of inquiry was appropriate to 'matters of conduct' as well as to 'physical matters'" (*Science, Community, and the Transformation of American Philosophy*, 128-29).

and, along with the views of other pragmatists, compared to those of Darwin.[51] A more helpful approach to understanding the pragmatists' viewpoint, however, may lie in examining the kinds of statements they made, rather than their views of nature. By this approach, "pragmatism might almost be defined as the contention that all judgments of truth are judgments of value; that verification is a value-determination; and the criterion of truth is realization of some kind of value," according to C. I. Lewis.[52] In other words, "to be pragmatic is to adhere to the view that all questions are to be answered pragmatically, that there is only one kind of assertion."[53]

Hence, the "doctrine I called Pragmatism," stated Peirce, is "that the meaning and essence of every conception lies in the application of it."[54] Dewey concurred, while extending this idea of meaning to value, "Thus we are led to our main proposition. *Judgments about values are judgments about the conditions and the results of experienced objects; judgments about that which should regulate the formation of our desires, affections and enjoyments.*"[55] Many were not convinced by Dewey's attempt to reconcile science and value. Nevertheless, pragmatism became "the most ambitious and important effort in our time to accomplish the...critical synthesizing of knowledge and the methods of science with the moral heritage and aspirations that shape human conduct."[56]

---

[51] *See* Purcell, *The Crisis of Democratic Theory*, 10, 42-43, passim; Smith, *Purpose and Thought*, 144, passim; Kuklick, *Churchmen and Philosophers*, 247; Quine, "Pragmatists' Place in Empiricism," 28.

[52] Clarence I. Lewis, *Collected Papers*, ed. John D. Goheen and John L. Mothershead, Jr. (Stanford, Calif.: Stanford University Press, 1970), 280. It is significant to note that "naturalism" has been understood to refer to theories that treat moral judgments as being equivalent to nonmoral, factual statements. *See* R. M. Hare, *The Language of Morals* (Oxford, England: Clarendon, 1952), ch. 5. Important statements by Dewey in this regard are found in *The Quest for Certainty*, ch. 10; Dewey, *Theory of the Moral Life*, Part II in Dewey and James H. Tufts, *Ethics* [1932], rev. ed. (New York: Holt, Rinehart, and Winston, 1960), ch. 5; Dewey, "Logical Conditions of a Scientific Treatment of Morality," in *The Middle Works, 1899-1924*, vol. 3, *1903-1906* (Carbondale, Ill.: Southern Illinois University Press, 1903).

[53] Mark Okrent, *Heidegger's Pragmatism: Understanding, Being, and the Critique of Metaphysics* (Ithaca, N.Y.: Cornell University Press, 1988), 10.

[54] Charles S. Peirce, "[Review of] Clark University, 1889-1899: Decennial Celebration, Worcester, Mass.: Clark University, 1899," in *Science* n.s. 11 (20 April 1900): 621.

[55] Dewey, *The Quest for Certainty*, 265.

[56] Thayer, *Meaning and Action*, xviii. On the response to Dewey's attempt, *see* Purcell, *The Crisis of Democratic Theory*, 42-43; Wilson, *Science, Community, and the Transformation of American Philosophy*, 128-29.

4/

The Course of Pragmatism

The six points of pragmatism sketched in the previous chapter—

1. that belief and meaning, even truth itself, are fallible and revisable;

2. that an experimental method of inquiry obtains in all science and reflective thought;

3. that belief, meaning, and truth depend on the context and the inter-subjective judgment of the community in which they are formed;

4. that experience is the dynamic interaction of organism and environment, resulting in a close interrelationship between thought and action;

5. that the purpose of resolving doubts or solving problems is intrinsic to all thought and inquiry; and

6. that all inquiry and thought are evaluative, and judgments about fact are no different from judgments about value

—constitute an interpretation of the views generally held by those who began to embrace the term "pragmatism" early in the twentieth century. The question of whether this kind of thinking is particularly characteristic of or derived from the culture of the United States has attracted a good deal of attention in the past, although the tendency in recent scholarship is to regard that question as unanswerable, insignificant, or misleading.

Without attempting to address directly the "Americanness" of pragmatism, we may observe that discussion of this issue appears to be linked in complex ways to scholars' definitions and evaluations of pragmatism. Reviewing the discussion concerning the place of pragmatism in American history, Hollinger, an eminent intellectual historian, incisively observed that the argument that pragmatism is emblematic of America stemmed from the effort to legitimate and popularize this philosophical approach over the first half of the twentieth century. He also states, "some nonhistorians may continue to believe that pragmatism is a distinctive contribution of America to modern civilization and somehow emblematic of America, but few scholarly energies are devoted to the exploration or even assertion of this belief."[1] In this fashion, Hollinger tends to discount the scholarship of nonhistorians, particularly philosophers, and his conclusions are based primarily on historians' writings about the Americanness of pragmatism.

Discussion among philosophers yields a different picture. Although some philosophers who write sympathetically on pragmatism, such as Smith, have associated pragmatism with American culture,[2] Thayer appraised the general tenor of the discussion thus, "Pragmatism has *sometimes* been praised and *often* condemned as a typically American philosophy."[3] Whereas the historian Hollinger sees the association between the United States and pragmatism as correlated primarily with praise of pragmatism (and suspects it for this reason), the philosopher Thayer sees the association as correlated primarily with condemnation of pragmatism (and suspects it for this reason).[4] Discussion of its "Americanness," therefore, alerts us to the fact that the way in which pragmatism is interpreted depends on the context and community within which it is discussed. In this fashion, discussion of pragmatism appears to validate certain views of pragmatism.[5] Be that as it may, the contrast between discussions of pragmatism among communities of

[1] David A. Hollinger, "The Problem of Pragmatism in American History," *Journal of American History* 67 (1980): 88, 106-7.

[2] John E. Smith, *Purpose and Thought: The Meaning of Pragmatism* (Chicago: University of Chicago Press, 1978), 50. In *America's Philosophical Vision* (Chicago: University of Chicago Press, 1992), Smith retreated from this position, though with some ambivalence, cf. 1-2, 193-95.

[3] H. S. Thayer, *Meaning and Action: A Critical History of Pragmatism*, 2d ed. [1968] (Indianapolis, Ind.: Hackett, 1981), 432 (emphasis added).

[4] In a word, the attack to which Thayer responded is that pragmatism expresses the commercialism and crass utility that characterize American culture. Thayer conceded that commercialism and crass utility characterize a segment of American culture, but denied that they constitute any part of the meaning of pragmatism (*Meaning and Action*, 5-6, 88, 432-34, 439).

[5] This point generally goes unnoticed in discussions on the pragmatic evaluation of pragmatism. *See* William James, "The Pragmatist Account of Truth and Its Misunderstanders," in *The Meaning of Truth: A Sequel to "Pragmatism"* (New York: Longmans, Green, 1909), 180-216; William Van Orman Quine, "Pragmatists' Place in Empiricism," in *Pragmatism: Its Sources and Prospects*, ed. Robert J. Mulvaney and

historians and among those of philosophers deserves some attention before considering the course of pragmatism over the twentieth century.

In general, historians and philosophers have tended to talk past, or away from, each other, when discussing pragmatism. One of the few scholars to observe this tendency is Hollinger. Despite this important insight, he appears to discount the philosophers' discussion and to regard analysis of the ideas of Peirce, James, and Dewey as "increasingly the business of philosophers addressing other philosophers...increasingly isolated—even when carried out by historians—from the study of the rest of American history." Thus, Hollinger discounted "the confining of pragmatism to its philosophic contributions," which means that "this theory is projected as an ideal type," that is, having the aim "to recover the completed structure of Dewey's philosophy," a project that Hollinger attributed to Thayer and Smith, whom the philosophical community regards as the most judicious commentators. Hand in hand with discounting the philosophical commentators on Dewey is the derogation of his work. Its "vague," "question-begging," and "mushy" character over the first 40 years of the twentieth century is said to be tightened up retrospectively by the ideal-seeking philosophical commentators who "focus on [Dewey's] most rigorous climactic work."[6]

To all this it may be responded that while it is helpful to distinguish, say, among early, middle, and late Plato or between the kingly Christ of *Matthew* and the pastoral Christ of *Luke*, it seems gratuitous to dismiss commentators' efforts to offer a comprehensive interpretation of the thinking of Plato, Christ, or any other figure, particularly one such as Dewey, who, after the turn of the century, was generally elaborating a consistent view. In addition, and notwithstanding Dewey's notoriously murky prose, it seems excessive to discount as "40 years of mushy work" the four decades that saw the publication of *Art as Experience* (1934), *The Quest for Certainty* (1929), *Human Nature and Conduct* (1922), and *Democracy and Education* (1916), wherein Scheffler, albeit a philosopher, finds that "the combination of shrewd description, brilliant criticism, plain common sense, and practical wisdom permeating his discussions...is characteristic of Dewey's best writing."[7]

Philip M. Zeltner (Columbia, S.C.: University of South Carolina Press, 1981), 23; Mark Okrent, *Heidegger's Pragmatism: Understanding, Being, and the Critique of Metaphysics* (Ithaca, N.Y.: Cornell University Press, 1988), 291-92; Daniel J. Wilson, *Science, Community, and the Transformation of American Philosophy, 1860-1930* (Chicago: University of Chicago Press, 1990), 193; Smith, *America's Philosophical Vision*, 70-75;

[6] Hollinger, "The Problem of Pragmatism in American History," 89-91, 98, 98n.

[7] Israel Scheffler, *Four Pragmatists: A Critical Introduction to Peirce, James, Mead, and Dewey* (New York: Humanities, 1974), 236.

Nevertheless, the tendencies to discount, or neglect, the leading philosophical commentators on pragmatism, to emphasize the importance of historical scholarship, to devalue Dewey's thinking in particular, and, often, to attribute to Dewey the popularly conceived ills of "progressive education," are evident in the recent work of other eminent historians writing on pragmatism. These tendencies appear, for example, in the recent book by John Diggins, who underscored the criticisms of early British commentators who did not read the pragmatists carefully, while according relatively less attention to Smith and Thayer. Proposing that in Dewey's view "there would be no essential need for historical knowledge or belief," Diggins maintained that "humankind can be understood only historically, and knowledge itself is conditioned and mediated by its historical context." Indeed, "philosophy left behind the world of knowledge and moral tension to enter the world of power unprepared for the ironies and dilemmas of politics."[8] Similar views were put forth in a significant essay by historian Laurence Veysey, which will be discussed later. Such views depart from the positive evaluations offered in the past and illustrated in the comment of historian Henry Steele Commager that pragmatism is "almost the official philosophy of America."[9] Consequently, in the words of Andrew Feffer, historians' "changing interpretations of Dewey generally paralleled changing assessments of the progressive reform movement to which historians linked Deweyan pragmatism."[10]

On the other hand, the historians' criticism of philosophical discussion is not off the mark. Though providing acute analysis of what may on the surface appear to be vague or mushy thinking, the philosophical commentary sometimes neglects the context surrounding an issue. One type of such neglect can be seen in studies of the meaning of a philosopher's work that do not take into account the personal situation of the philosopher. For example, "in the 1950s...the Harvard Philosophy Department refused to give scholars access to what it considered Peirce's biographical papers."[11] Not only was this dualistic distinction

[8] John Patrick Diggins, *The Promise of Pragmatism: Modernism and the Crisis of Knowledge and Authority* (Chicago: University of Chicago Press, 1992), 206, 439, 46. Cf. Scheffler, *Four Pragmatists*: From Dewey's view that doctrines, theories, and procedures "are to be judged by their fruits rather than their origins...it emphatically does not follow...that the...past is to be rejected in a wholesale manner" (244).

[9] Henry Steele Commager, *The American Mind: An Interpretation of American Thought and Character Since the 1880s* (New Haven, Conn.: Yale University Press, 1950), 97-98.

[10] Andrew Feffer, *The Chicago Pragmatists and American Progressivism* (Ithaca, N.Y.: Cornell University Press, 1993), 7. Cf. Morton G. White, *Pragmatism and the American Mind* (New York: Oxford University Press, 1973), 190ff.

[11] Murray G. Murphey, *The Development of Peirce's Philosophy* [1961] (Indianapolis, Ind.: Hackett, 1993), vi.

between "biographical" and "philosophical" papers suspect in general, but it was also a paradoxical position to assume in regard to a philosopher espousing pragmatism, especially one whose professional and personal life was so checkered and quirky. That this policy obtained in the 1950s is telling both philosophically and historically, because that period marked the full eclipse of pragmatism by analytic philosophy.

Here arises a second type of philosophical neglect of context. Disagreements between philosophical commentators or between schools, such as between analysts and pragmatists or between British empiricists and pragmatists, are often interpreted in the philosophical literature as stemming entirely from conceptual differences or from misreadings and misunderstandings of various sorts. Rarely are personal, professional, or national interests given weight or even mentioned as factors in philosophers' evaluations of each other's work, although such interests are manifest in the debate over pragmatism, as is noted in the historical writings by Cornel West and Daniel Wilson.[12] Finally, the philosophical analysis of pragmatism, however acute, seems to ignore context in stepping around the emotive and nonrational issues that crop up. Peirce's reflections on "Evolutionary Love," which "will probably shock my scientific brethren," and his analogues between "the Law of Love and the Law of Reason" and between devotion to "logical method" and love of a "bride, whom he has chosen from all the world" are passed over in philosophical commentary.[13] By the same token, some philosophical analyses of Peirce's famous "Pragmatic Maxim" make no reference to his annotation that the maxim "is only an application of the sole principle of logic which was recommended by Jesus; 'Ye may know them by their fruits,' and it is very intimately allied with the ideas of the gospel."[14]

In sum, the suggestion is that the leading philosophical commentators on pragmatism are more careful and acute analysts of the thinking of the pragmatists, but the recent historians of pragmatism are more

[12] *See* Cornel West, *The American Evasion of Philosophy: A Genealogy of Pragmatism* (Madison, Wis.: University of Wisconsin Press, 1989), 183; Wilson, *Science, Community, and the Transformation of American Philosophy*, ch. 8.

[13] Charles S. Peirce, "Evolutionary Love," in *Collected Papers of Charles Sanders Peirce*, ed. Charles Hartshorne and Paul Weiss (Cambridge, Mass.: Harvard University Press, 1931-58), 6:295; Peirce, "[Review of] Clark University, 1889-1899: Decennial Celebration (Worcester, Mass.: Clark University, 1899," in *Science* n.s. 11 (20 April 1900): 621; Peirce, "The Fixation of Belief," in *Collected Papers*, 5:387.

[14] Charles S. Peirce, "How to Make Our Ideas Clear," in *Collected Papers*, 5:401-2, 402 n. 2. Cf. Thayer, *Meaning and Action*, 79ff.; Smith, *Purpose and Thought*, 18ff.

closely practicing what pragmatism prescribes. It may not be too much
to say that if we want to learn about pragmatism, read the philosophers;
but if we want to see how to do it, study the historians. These differences
are not without practical import for how the story of pragmatism in the
twentieth century is told.

Every student of the movement agrees that the course of pragmatism
has run through an initial flourishing, a lull or retrenchment, and finally a
resurgence. But two differences of interpretation stand out, and these have
been given little attention. One is the dating of the respective periods; the
other is the reasons given for such changes over time. These differences are
related to each other and to the differences between the historical and
philosophical communities of interpreters proposed above.

During the initial flourishing of pragmatism, it became the most significant American philosophical movement in the late nineteenth and
early twentieth centuries, which are variously called the "classical"
period or "the Golden Age" of American philosophy.[15] The rankings vary
as to who, among the leading pragmatists, was the "philosophers'
philosopher," but it is generally agreed that pragmatism was "the major
contribution of America to the world of philosophy."[16] Dewey's stature
in this regard is worth recalling. He has been the target of such frequent
and sharp criticism, even to the point of dismissing "Dewey's reputation
as a puzzling form of intellectual aberration, sociologically intelligible
but philosophically mysterious,"[17] that it is difficult sometimes to
understand why "when Dewey died in 1952, he was widely regarded as
the preeminent philosopher in the United States and the twentieth
century's foremost American intellectual,"[18] and why he is still considered by many today "the most important twentieth-century American
thinker."[19] The stature of a philosopher is, of course, ultimately dependent on the evaluation of the quality of the philosophy. But purely in

[15] Max H. Fisch, gen. ed., *Classic American Philosophers: Peirce, James, Royce,
Santayana, Dewey, Whitehead* (New York: Appleton-Century-Crofts, 1951), Pref.;
Bruce Kuklick, *Churchmen and Philosophers: From Jonathan Edwards to John Dewey*
(New Haven, Conn.: Yale University Press, 1985), 196; John J. Stuhr, ed., *Classical
American Philosophy: Essential Readings and Interpretive Essays* (New York: Oxford
University Press, 1987), 4-5.

[16] Thayer, *Meaning and Action*, 3, 432. Cf. Sidney Hook, ed., *John Dewey: Philosopher of
Science and Freedom: A Symposium* (New York: Dial, 1950), v; Garry Brodsky, "Rorty's
Interpretation of Pragmatism," *Transactions of the Charles S. Peirce Society* 18 (1982),
311; Murry G. Murphey, *The Development of Peirce's Philosophy*, vi.

[17] John Passmore, "Philosophical Scholarship in the United States, 1930-1960," in Roderick
M. Chisolm et al., *Philosophy* (Englewood Cliffs, N.J.: Prentice-Hall, 1964), 123.

[18] Kuklick, *Churchmen and Philosophers*, xv-xvi.

[19] Robert B. Westbrook, *John Dewey and American Democracy* (Ithaca, N.Y.: Cornell
University Press, 1991), ix.

terms of range and primacy of influence, Dewey's standing is not difficult to understand. In 1908, he coauthored the most influential textbook on ethics written by an American philosopher through the first half of the twentieth century.[20] In 1916, he published the most influential American theory of education, which was widely embraced by education leaders and commentators.[21] In 1931, he wrote "the most important contribution to aesthetics that America has yet produced."[22] Meanwhile, Dewey offered the most cogent attempt to address the problem of relating the findings of modern science to judgments of value.[23] Given all this, Dewey's stature and the early prominence of pragmatism are understandable.

By the 1930s, however, the influence of pragmatism was beginning to wane. At least this is the view held by philosophical commentators and by historians of philosophy who follow the doctrinal shifts carefully. In fact, "pragmatism soon ceased to be taken seriously as a philosophy," according to Thayer.[24] The lull extended roughly through the 1940s and

[20] John Dewey and James H. Tufts, *Ethics* (New York: Holt, Rinehart, and Winston, 1908). *See* Douglas Sloan, "The Teaching of Ethics in the American Undergraduate Curriculum, 1876-1976," *Teachers College Record* 82 (1980): 216ff.; Arnold Isenberg, "Editor's Foreword," in Dewey, *Theory of the Moral Life* [1932] (New York: Holt, Rinehart, and Winston, 1960), iii-vi.

[21] John Dewey, *Democracy and Education: An Introduction to the Philosophy of Education* [1916] (New York: Free Press, 1966).

[22] John Dewey, *Art as Experience* (New York: G. P. Putnam's, 1934). *See* Ernest S. Bates, "John Dewey's Aesthetics," *American Mercury* 33 (1934): 253.

[23] John Dewey, *The Quest for Certainty: A Study of the Relation of Knowledge and Action* (New York: Minton, Balch, 1929), *see especially* ch. 10; Dewey, *Theory of the Moral Life*, Part II in Dewey and Tufts, *Ethics*, *see especially* ch. 5. Dewey's attempt is said not to have convinced most observers (see Edward A. Purcell, Jr., *The Crisis of Democratic Theory: Scientific Naturalism and the Problem of Value* [Lexington, Ky.: University of Kentucky Press, 1973], 42-43); Wilson, *Science, Community, and the Transformation of American Philosophy*, 128-29). Nevertheless, that his attempt was more cogent than any other is shown by the fact that two major alternative approaches to the problem over the last two-thirds of the twentieth century essentially beg the question. On the one hand, analytic philosophy dismissed value judgments as not amenable to rational or empirical analysis, and, on the other hand, the postmodern, constructivist approach dismissed the rational and factual conclusions of natural science as "interpretations" suffused with value and power. Each of these two alternatives addresses the problem by dismissing the opposite half of the dilemma.

[24] Thayer, *Meaning and Action*, 561. *See also* Fisch, *Classic American Philosophers*, Pref.; J. O. Urmson, *Philosophical Analysis: Its Development Between the Two World Wars* (Oxford: Oxford University Press, 1956), passim; Kuklick, *Churchmen and Philosophers*, 196; Wilson, *Science, Community, and the Transformation of American Philosophy*, 10, 196. Without specifically addressing pragmatism, Stephen Toulmin placed the rise of rationalism "in the 1930s and '40s" (*Cosmopolis: The Hidden Agenda of Modernity* [Chicago: University of Chicago Press, 1990], 84).

1950s, after which the beginning of a resurgence was signaled by the appearance of Richard J. Bernstein's writings in the early 1960s.[25] In 1961, Richard Rorty observed, "Pragmatism is getting respectable again,"[26] and the number of books and theses addressing "pragmatism" increased rapidly in the subsequent decade and continued growing thereafter, as indicated in the following table.

Total number of books and theses published decennially with "pragmatism" in the title:

1951–1960	49
1961–1970	95
1971–1980	114
1981–1990	136
1991–1994	104

Source: Data compiled from Online Computer Library Center for research libraries, 1994.

In 1969, a critical edition of Dewey's collected works began to appear, followed by one for James in 1975, and one for Peirce in 1982.[27] By that year the resurgence had come so far that Rorty perceived an "anti-prag-matist backlash" in the form of "a reaction in favor of 'realism'—a term which has come to be synonymous with 'anti-pragmatism.'"[28] At nearly the same time, however, Thayer observed in the second edition of his compendious *Meaning and Action* that "the future may well be with Dewey, Lewis, and Mead,"[29] and the "neo-pragmatist" movement has grown with undiminished vigor since that time. In sum, following the philosophical line of discussion, the course of pragmatism seems to have been: a flourishing from the 1890s to the 1930s, a waning in the 1940s and 1950s, and a resurgence from the 1960s onward.

[25] Richard J. Bernstein, ed., *John Dewey on Experience, Nature and Freedom* (New York: Liberal Arts, 1960); R. J. Bernstein, *John Dewey* (Atascadero, Calif.: Ridgeview, 1965).

[26] Richard Rorty, "Pragmatism, Categories, and Language," *Philosophical Review* 70 (1961): 197. *See* John E. Smith, "The Reflexive Turn, the Linguistic Turn, and the Pragmatic Outcome," *Monist* 53 (1969).

[27] John Dewey, *John Dewey: The Early Works, The Middle Works,* and *The Later Works,* ed. Jo Ann Boydston (Carbondale, Ill.: Southern Illinois University Press, 1969-); William James, *The Works of William James,* ed. Frederick H. Burkhardt (Cambridge, Mass.: Harvard University Press, 1975-); Charles S. Peirce, *Writings of Charles S. Peirce: A Chronological Edition,* ed. Max H. Fisch et al. (Bloomington, Ind.: Indiana University Press, 1982).

[28] Richard Rorty, *Consequences of Pragmatism (Essays 1972-1980)* (Minneapolis, Minn.: University of Minnesota Press, 1982), xxi.

[29] Thayer, *Meaning and Action,* 456, 563-66.

Historians tell a somewhat different story, and the turning point is expressed in Commager's often quoted description of pragmatism in 1950.[30] Viewing pragmatism less as "a theory of meaning and truth" than as "a cluster of assertions and hopes about the basis for culture in an age of science, and a range of general images stereotypical of American life," leading historians saw the lull as having begun in the 1950s.[31] Up to that point, stated Edward Purcell, "pragmatic and naturalistic attitudes continued generally to dominate the thought patterns of intellectuals, who at the same time were undergoing a subtle but fundamental shift in their political orientation."[32] It was "middle-ground pragmatists," stated George Cotkin, who "helped to make pragmatism central to the conversation of American culture from the 1920s until the 1940s."[33] As a result, Diggins maintained, "the prestige that pragmatism enjoyed" among intellectuals continued into the 1950s, but this was followed by "its eclipse [in] the following decade," which continued until "neopragmatism...emerged in the early 1980s."[34] In short, the course of pragmatism as depicted by some recent historians of the movement has been: prominence through about 1950, a lull in the 1960s and 1970s, and a resurgence in the 1980s.[35]

The differences in periodization reflected in the narratives offered by commentators emphasizing philosophical doctrines as opposed to those emphasizing historical forces point to different reasons offered for the shifts in the prominence of pragmatism. Consequently, it is difficult to find a full account of these reasons. Nevertheless, by drawing on various collations, a fairly cogent and comprehensive set of explanations for the waning in the influence of pragmatism may be identified.

[30] Pragmatism is "almost the official philosophy of America" (Commager, *The American Mind*, 97-98).

[31] Hollinger, "The Problem of Pragmatism in American History," 106.

[32] Purcell, *The Crisis of Democratic Theory*, 235.

[33] George Cotkin, "Middle-Ground Pragmatists: The Popularization of Philosophy in American Culture," *Journal of the History of Ideas* 55 (1994): 285.

[34] Diggins, *The Promise of Pragmatism*, 401, 11; *see also* ch. 10.

[35] Neither a professional historian nor a professional philosopher, Cornel West, who has written an informative historical overview of pragmatism as a cultural movement, provided an interesting counterpoint to the contrast drawn here between the historical accounts provided by philosophers and historians. Appreciative of philosophical scholarship, West saw pragmatism declining in line with the shift in hegemony among philosophical schools. However, sensitive as well to social and cultural forces, he identified a "motley crew of distinguished pragmatists" who exemplified "the mid-century pragmatic intellectual." All five crew members—C. Wright Mills, W. E. B. Dubois, Sidney Hook, Lionel Trilling, and Reinhold Niebuhr—felt themselves marginalized from the academic elite for various reasons, and the "pragmatism" of each was diluted in some way by another school of thought. Thus, by West's account, pragmatism persevered through the mid-twentieth century—sort of (*The American Evasion of Philosophy*, chs. 4, 5).

The lull may be attributed first to the social and economic crisis of capitalism, which culminated in the Great Depression and led to disillusionment over "the apparent inability of trained intelligence to deal with the Depression."[36] Dewey had written that pragmatism involves "the formation of a faith in intelligence, as the one and indispensable belief necessary to moral and social life."[37] By the 1920s, however, pragmatists such as Mead in Chicago "had grown pessimistic about the reconstructive potential of applying 'intelligence' to politics."[38] As C. Wright Mills wrote in 1944, "Pragmatism...took a rather severe beating from the fashionable left-wing of the thirties and since the latter years of that decade it has obviously been losing out in competition with more religious and tragic views of political and personal life.... Attempts to reinstate pragmatism's emphasis upon the power of man's intelligence to control his destiny have not been taken to heart by American intellectuals."[39]

A second reason for the declining influence of pragmatism was the severe criticism that it received in some of the most respectable circles of philosophy. According to Thayer, even "when pragmatism dominated academic philosophy in the early 1920s...it [was] never an entirely respectable form of thought."[40] In fact, Dewey was subjected to sharp criticism even in *Festschriften* published in 1930, 1940, and 1950, "and in his final years he was constantly fencing with opponents, old and new," observed Robert Westbrook.[41] Early philosophical criticism came most prominently from leading British intellectuals, including Leonard T. Hobhouse, Bertrand Russell, F. H. Bradley, and G. E. Moore,[42] and followed two lines of attack that were prompted particularly by James's playful and often misleading language.

[36] Purcell, *The Crisis of Democratic Theory*, 143.
[37] John Dewey, "*The Development of American Pragmatism*," published originally in French in 1922; English translation reprinted in *Philosophy and Civilization* (New York: Minton, Balch, 1931), 35.
[38] Feffer, *The Chicago Pragmatists and American Progressivism*, 1.
[39] C. Wright Mills, "The Social Role of the Intellectual," in *Power, Politics, and People, The Collected Essays of C. Wright Mills*, ed. Irving L. Horowitz (New York: Oxford University Press, 1963), 292. Diggins's *The Promise of Pragmatism* restated Mills's thesis in light of the crisis in confidence of the late twentieth century. Thayer astutely attributed Dewey's problem in this regard to his failure to address "a practical and analytical question [of] how one proceeds to determine just what are the organic, integrated conditions of growth that make for wise social policy in given cases" (*Meaning and Action*, 446).
[40] H. S. Thayer, "Pragmatism: A Reinterpretation of the Origins and Consequences," in *Pragmatism: Its Sources and Prospects*, 4.
[41] Robert B. Westbrook, *John Dewey and American Democracy* (Ithaca, N.Y.: Cornell University Press, 1991), 379.
[42] *See* Leonard T. Hobhouse, "Faith and the Will to Believe," *Proceedings of the Aristotelian Society* 4 (1909); Bertrand Russell, *Philosophical Essays* (London:

The first attack was directed against what critics understood to be the thorough subjectivity of pragmatism, making truth a matter of individual belief. Although James's emphasis on individualism provided a basis for such criticism, this continuing objection did not accord due weight either to the prominence given by Peirce to the intersubjective judgment of a community of investigators or to Dewey's doctrine of "warranted assertibility" and of analogues between democratic decision making and scientific method. In this regard, a more perspicacious criticism might be that truth, for pragmatism, is a matter of voting, rather than subjectivity.[43]

The second, more damning objection was that self-interest appeared to be the pragmatic criterion by which an individual should decide what to believe. Here again, textual justification for this criticism lay chiefly in James's discussion, wherein language about "useful" or "practical" often wended over to the "gratification," "expediency," or "cash value" of believing something to be true.[44] To complicate matters, "Dewey often used the language of James, saying that 'the true is that which works,' or that which proves 'successful' or 'satisfactory.' He thus became heir to many of the objections that had been made of James's doctrine."[45] And Dewey recognized in 1925 that "it is often said of pragmatism that it...subordinates thought and rational activity to particular ends of interest and profit."[46]

Even so, the pragmatists stated explicitly that "whoever makes his own welfare his object will simply ruin it entirely," in the words of Peirce.[47] Thus, a sympathetic reading discloses that the pragmatists

Longmans, Green, 1910), ch. 5; F. H. Bradley, *Essays on Truth and Reality* (Oxford: Clarendon, 1914), ch. 7; G. E. Moore, *Philosophical Studies* (London: Routledge & Kegan Paul, 1922), 140ff.

[43] John Dewey and Bertrand Russell carried on their exchange over a number of years. *See*, for example, Russell, "Dewey's New Logic," in *The Philosophy of John Dewey*, ed. P. A. Schilpp (Chicago: Northwestern University Press, 1944); Russell, *An Inquiry into Meaning and Truth* (New York: W. W. Norton, 1938), passim. In response to the latter, Dewey made a concerted effort to describe how Russell had misunderstood his ideas both of "warranted assertibility" and of the instrumental character of propositions and their relationship to truth and knowledge ("Propositions, Warranted Assertibility, and Truth," in *Problems of Men* [1941] [New York: Philosophical Library, 1946]). In *Dewey's New Logic: A Reply to Russell* (Chicago: University of Chicago Press, 1944), Tom Burke provided a careful analysis of the debates between Dewey and Russell, particularly following the publication of Dewey's *Logic: The Theory of Inquiry* (New York: Henry Holt, 1938).

[44] William James, *Pragmatism: A New Name for Some Old Ways of Thinking* [1907] (New York: Longmans, Green, 1925), 197-237.

[45] Thayer, *Meaning and Action*, 202.

[46] Dewey, "The Development of American Pragmatism," 15.

[47] Peirce, "[Review of] Clark University," 621.

were arguing that belief depends on whether a proposition is "useful" or "instrumental" in the sense of whether it "fits" the given situation, circumstances, or problem.[48] Dewey's instrumentalism and James's description of ideas, beliefs, and theories as "plans of action" or "modes of adaptation to reality" indicate how, in the words of Thayer, "the primary function of thought and of ideas is that of bringing us to and keeping us in satisfactory relations with the world of persons and things in which we live and move."[49] As James wrote, "A new opinion counts as 'true' just in proportion as it gratifies the individual's desire to assimilate the novel in his experience to his beliefs in stock."[50]

A number of scholars have rebutted these early philosophical critics of pragmatism. Smith observed that "Russell's essay...makes no effort to get 'inside' the pragmatic position...but is content instead to cite some slogans from James supposed to show that for pragmatism, truth is 'made' or manufactured and provides a philosophical justification for believing what one wishes."[51] T. L. S. Sprigge stated, "Moore succeeded in providing an account of truth which can serve as a common-sense foil to James's. However, ...James's view when properly understood...confront[s] what is puzzling about truth in a more profound way than does Moore's account."[52] Wiener concurred, "It is a travesty on American pragmatism to condemn its philosophy as crass opportunism, as subordinating truth to cash value."[53] In response to Max Horkheimer's subsequent attack along the same lines, Westbrook observed that "like the rest of the first generation of the Frankfurt School, Horkheimer did not know what he was talking about when it came to pragmatism."[54] Nevertheless, such "caricatures of the pragmatic doctrine of truth eventually reached a wider audience than the literature being parodied,"

---

[48] It seems preferable to translate the pragmatic idea "use" into "fit," rather than to distinguish between the pragmatists' "use" and either "utilitarian" use or "practical" use, as did Smith, *Purpose and Thought*, 216n., and Thayer, *Meaning and Action*, 5, which only compounds the ambiguity while trying to resolve it.

[49] Thayer, *Meaning and Action*, 140-41, 204.

[50] James, *Pragmatism*, 64-65.

[51] Smith, *America's Philosophical Vision*, 38.

[52] T. L. S. Sprigge, *James and Bradley: American Truth and British Reality* (Chicago: Open Court, 1993), 17.

[53] Philip P. Wiener, *Evolution and the Founders of Pragmatism* [1949] (Philadelphia: University of Pennsylvania Press, 1972), 203.

[54] Westbrook, *John Dewey and American Democracy*, 187. Burke's extensive analysis of the debate between Russell and Dewey suggested that Russell misunderstood key points in Dewey's view of logic (Burke, *Dewey's New Logic: A Reply to Russell*, passim). Smith also observed that F. H. Bradley "more profoundly" criticized pragmatism than did Russell or Moore (*America's Philosophical Vision*, 7).

according to Thayer.[55] Indeed, Smith found that even in 1965 most "British philosophers...were acquainted with James only through the criticism of Russell"; hence, A. J. Ayer, "totally unaware of the thorough-going critique made by the Pragmatists of the classical conception of experience," treated pragmatism as a form of British empiricism.[56] Nevertheless, the early British critics and their criticism continue to be invoked even today,[57] thus demonstrating the extent to which severe criticism by philosophers contributed to the waning of pragmatism.

A third reason for the declining influence of pragmatism was the rise and success of totalitarian regimes, which appeared to be "the logical culmination of the denial of universal values and truth."[58] In 1926, Lewis Mumford sounded one of the earliest warnings that pragmatism offered no resistance to totalitarian philosophies,[59] and the ensuing attack came on two fronts. The "realist" phalanx included Catholic scholars, especially neo-Thomists, fighting against the recently anathematized heresies of Americanism and modernism, as well as neo-Aristotelians led or informed by Robert Hutchins, Mortimer Adler, and Richard McKeon. The seriousness of this contingent is conveyed in an essay penned on his deathbed by a professor of education at the University of Pennsylvania, who argued for absolute commitment to the principle of democracy as a necessary defense against totalitarianism, and suggested, concerning the progressive educators who had formed the John Dewey League in 1936, that "this well-organized and well-armed educational minority may readily become the storm troops through which the public school system as the citadel of democracy is taken and overthrown."[60]

---

[55] Thayer, *Meaning and Action*, 151.

[56] Smith, *America's Philosophical Vision*, 71, 193. See A. J. Ayer, *The Origins of Pragmatism* (San Francisco: Freeman, Cooper, 1968). Hence, John Passmore seemed to regard the view that Dewey was not a good philosopher (shown by Russell's judgment) as a reason for Dewey not being very well understood in Britain, without considering conversely whether the fact that Dewey was not very well understood might explain the view about his philosophy, despite Russell's judgment (Passmore, "Philosophical Scholarship in the United States, 1930-1960," 122-23).

[57] *See* N. C. Bhattacharya, "Demythologizing John Dewey," *Journal of Educational Thought* 8 (1974): 117-19; Ernest Gellner, "Pragmatism and the Importance of Being Earnest," in *Pragmatism: Its Sources and Prospects*, 56; Diggins, *The Promise of Pragmatism*, 134-35, 205, 234-36, 405-6.

[58] Purcell, *The Crisis of Democratic Theory*, 222; *see also* chs. 11, 12. Purcell is the most acute observer on this point.

[59] Robert B. Westbrook, "Lewis Mumford, John Dewey, and the 'Pragmatic Acquiescence,'" in *Lewis Mumford: Public Intellectual*, ed. Thomas P. Hughes and Agatha C. Hughes (New York: Oxford University Press, 1990).

[60] A. Duncan Yocum, "Dr. Dewey's 'Liberalism' in Government and in Public Education," *School and Society* 44 (1936): 1-2. *See also* Sidney Hook, "The New Medievalism," *New Republic* 103 (28 October 1940); Purcell, *The Crisis of Democratic Theory*, ch. 8.

The other phalanx came from the left, because "Marxist critics of pragmatism, like realist critics, attacked the theory of truth as 'subjectivism.'"[61] A version of this less-public objection can be seen in Horkheimer's assessment of the role of pragmatism in the "subjectivation" of reason.[62] Consequently, in the 1930s and early 1940s, various intellectuals accused Dewey of undermining democratic principles with his instrumentalism and of laying the groundwork for totalitarianism. This charge was highly ironic given Dewey's "horror of absolutism and his love of democracy,"[63] for he "had been arguing that philosophical absolutism implied political authoritarianism for over three decades.... Significantly, however, until the middle thirties he was not completely sure what actual governments belonged in which category."[64]

There is a fundamental point here: the criticism that pragmatism abets totalitarianism is a more sophisticated version of the misunderstanding that, in the pragmatic view, belief is defined according to self-interest. Analogous to Russell's early complaint that pragmatism allows individuals to treat as true whatever is in their self-interest, the criticism concerning totalitarianism is that pragmatism allows groups to treat as true whatever is in their self-interest and that ultimately the belief of the stronger will prevail. Hence, if the Nazis wished to believe in Nazism, then pragmatism had nothing to say against it. A form of the same complaint appeared in the recent allegation that Dewey and pragmatism could have said nothing against slavery because slavery "was accepted for centuries as a natural reflection of the order of things."[65]

The pragmatist's response is, of course, that no one listened to the slaves. No warrant exists for believing in Nazism or slavery unless the Jews and the slaves are asked and listened to. If the intersubjective community of inquirers is circumscribed, or the evidence restricted, or the hypothetical order of things not tested against experience, then the experimental method of reflective intelligence has not been followed, and no warrant for belief exists. The problem, thus, is less that pragmatism cannot resist manifestly immoral views, than that embedded within the pragmatic method are presumptions of fairness and equality that are not fully acknowledged by treating it as "scientific" or "naturalistic." This

---

[61] Smith, *America's Philosophical Vision*, 37.
[62] Max Horkheimer, *Eclipse of Reason* [1947] (New York: Seabury, 1974), 42ff. *See also* John E. Smith, "Some Continental and Marxist Responses to Pragmatism," in *Contemporary Marxism*, ed. J. J. O'Rourke (Dordrecht, Netherlands: D. Reidel, 1984).
[63] James Gouinlock, "Philosophy and Moral Values: The Pragmatic Analysis," in *Pragmatism: Its Sources and Prospects*, 101.
[64] Purcell, *The Crisis of Democratic Theory*, 200-201.
[65] Diggins, *The Promise of Pragmatism*, 239-40.

problem of defending the assumptions about "the generic traits of existence which make that [pragmatic] method a fruitful one in revealing
them" is the deepest dilemma for the pragmatists, as suggested earlier.[66]

A fourth reason for the waning of pragmatism was the rise of analytic
philosophy and logical positivism during the 1930s and 1940s. These
schools of thought, stemming from the work of Russell and Ludwig
Wittgenstein that informed the Vienna Circle and the Oxford Movement, held that words and concepts acquire meaning and truth only
insofar as they are or could be verified experimentally or empirically.
Ultimately, this resulted in a "verificationist" definition of meaning.
"[W]e would recognize with Peirce that the meaning of a sentence turns
purely on what would count as evidence for its truth," in the words of
Quine.[67] These two schools had much in common with the Peircean
approach to meaning and belief, and excitement over the newly developed logical and linguistic techniques led analysis and logical positivism to eclipse pragmatism.[68] This eclipse is demonstrated in the
views of Quine, who has repeatedly been called a pragmatist[69] due to his
attack on meanings that are "shadowy, obscure entities," and who concluded his seminal 1951 essay, "Two Dogmas of Empiricism," by stating, "I espouse a more thorough pragmatism."[70] But Quine later sought
to be acquitted of what he called the "soft impeachment" of being
labeled a pragmatist,[71] and this effort confirmed Rorty's contemporaneous judgment that "many philosophers think that everything important
in pragmatism has been preserved and adapted to the needs of analytic

[66] Sidney Hook, *The Metaphyics of Pragmatism* (Chicago: Open Court, 1927), 6. *See also*
Smith, *Purpose and Thought*, 44-45; Thayer, *Meaning and Action*, 454.

[67] William Van Orman Quine, "Epistemology Naturalized," in *Ontological Relativity
and Other Essays* (New York: Columbia University Press, 1969), 80.

[68] *See* Purcell, *The Crisis of Democratic Theory*, ch. 4; Thayer, *Meaning and Action*, 559-
63; Wilson, *Science, Community, and the Transformation of American Philosophy*,
ch. 9. Michael Dummett maintained that what is characteristic of analytic philosophy
is the view that thought can be assessed only through language (*Origins of Analytic
Philosophy* [Cambridge, Mass.: Harvard University Press, 1994], ch. 1, passim). Such a
radical linguistic behaviorism is actually reminiscent of Isocrates's view that "the power
to speak well is taken as the surest index of sound understanding," as is suggested later
in this essay (Isocrates, *Antidosis* [New York: G. P. Putnam's, 1928], 255-56).

[69] Cf. Morton G. White, "Pragmatism and the Scope of Science," in *Paths of American
Thought*, ed. Arthur M. Schlesinger, Jr. and Morton White (Boston: Beacon, 1963), 200;
Ernest Gellner, "The Last Pragmatist: The Philosophy of W. V. Quine," *Times Literary
Supplement* (25 July 1975); Gellner, "Pragmatism and the Importance of Being
Earnest"; West, *The American Evasion of Philosophy*, 182-91.

[70] William Van Orman Quine, "Two Dogmas of Empiricism," in *From a Logical Point of
View* [1951] (Cambridge, Mass.: Harvard University Press, 1953), 46.

[71] Quine, "Pragmatists' Place in Empiricism," 23.

philosophy."[72] Therefore, "among contemporary philosophers, pragmatism is usually regarded as an outdated philosophical movement."[73]

The implicit link made by Quine and Rorty between intellectual judgments, on the one hand, and academic status and attitudes, on the other, was echoed by Thayer in pointing to a fifth and final reason for the waning of pragmatism: "The pragmatic view of philosophy as a continuous effort to develop methods of understanding and effective control of specific human and cultural problems was alien to the [analytic] spirit of the time in which it was increasingly fashionable to regard philosophy as a highly specialized academic discipline."[74]

Thus, the decline in the influence of pragmatism was finally due to "the antiprofessional implications of pragmatism"[75] during a period when the academic profession was asserting its authority over the groups that had previously controlled universities and colleges— trustees, legislators, religious denominations, and presidents.[76] To be sure, Peirce had restricted the community of inquirers employing scientific method to a relatively small group of experts whose consensus would approach truth as if it were a mathematical limit, and Thomas Haskell analyzed the incipient professionalization implied by this restriction to a supposedly disinterested community.[77] James, however, "was quintessentially democratic" and "did not regard philosophy as a specialized, rarified undertaking for experts only," according to David Marcell.[78] In fact, James adopted an "adversarial disposition toward professionalism of any sort."[79] Dewey then made this disposition a cornerstone of his thought through his theory of inquiry. As discussed previously, Dewey held that the reflective experience, method of knowing, or experimental method of the school child was, in its basic contours, no different from that of "the scientific mind."[80] This radically leveling

---

[72] Richard Rorty, "Pragmatism, Relativism, and Irrationalism," in *Consequences of Pragmatism*, 160.

[73] Rorty, *Consequences of Pragmatism*, xvii.

[74] Thayer, *Meaning and Action*, 562.

[75] West, *The American Evasion of Philosophy*, 182.

[76] Christopher Jencks and David Riesman, *The Academic Revolution* (Garden City, N.Y.: Doubleday, 1968), ch. 1.

[77] Thomas L. Haskell, "Professionalism *versus* Capitalism: R. H. Tawney, Emile Durkheim, and C. S. Peirce on the Disinterestedness of Professional Communities," in *The Authority of Experts*, ed. Thomas L. Haskell (Bloomington, Ind.: Indiana University Press, 1984).

[78] David W. Marcell, *Progress and Pragmatism: James, Dewey, Beard, and the American Idea of Progress* (Westport, Conn.: Greenwood, 1974), 146, 147.

[79] West, *The American Evasion of Philosophy*, 54.

[80] John Dewey, *How We Think*, [1910] 2d ed. (New York: Henry Holt, 1933), v.

view was manifest throughout *Democracy and Education* (1916), which appeared contemporaneously with his complaint about the "professionalizing of philosophy" in "The Need for a Recovery of Philosophy" (1917).[81] When this egalitarian approach to method and to doing philosophy is compared to the professionalization implicit in "the cultivation of formal techniques or analytic procedures for dealing with newly resurrected problems of epistemology" that was being promoted by logical positivists and analytic philosophers, it becomes obvious that more than intellectual issues were at stake.[82] In the words of Daniel Wilson, the shift of philosophy "to becoming as esoteric and as unfathomable to the educated public as nuclear physics or molecular biology" went hand in hand with "the shift to a professional, specialized, academic discipline."[83] And these shifts led "academic philosophy" to "relegate pragmatism to a less rigorous, practical philosophy of life, didactic, rhetorical, scarcely distinguishable from journalism," according to Robert Mulvaney and Philip Zeltner.[84]

In sum, academicians' distaste for the antiprofessional and leveling implications of pragmatism was a fifth reason for the decline in its influence, in addition to the loss of faith in trained intelligence to address the crisis of capitalism, the early and prominent philosophical criticism of pragmatism, the fear that pragmatism abets totalitarianism, and the improvements in logical and linguistic techniques that accompanied the development of analytic philosophy and logical positivism.

[81] Dewey, *Democracy and Education* 150, 163, 173, 271-75, 338; Dewey, "The Need for a Recovery of Philosophy," in *Creative Intelligence: Essays in the Pragmatic Attitude* (New York: Henry Holt, 1917), 4-6. According to Arnold Isenberg, it is rarely appreciated that this egalitarianism contributed to the problems in Dewey's writing style, for Dewey "scarcely understood the difference between a book addressed to the profession, another addressed to the laity, and a third intended for the instruction of college freshmen." Thus, his works "represent a student talking to students, a philosopher to philosophers, and a vexed human being to his fellows" ("Editor's Foreword," in John Dewey, *Theory of the Moral Life* [1932] [New York: Holt, Rinehart, and Winston, 1960], iii-iv). By the same token, Dewey's complaint against professionalizing philosophy was directed not only against invidious hierarchies, but also against the isolation of the profession from social, political, and cultural problems. Thus, Dewey's engagement with the world and belief that philosophy should be engaged also contributed to his shifting and inconsistent use of terminology.

[82] Thayer, *Meaning and Action*, 561.

[83] Wilson, *Science, Community, and the Transformation of American Philosophy*, 195, 194; *see also* ch. 8.

[84] Mulvaney and Zeltner, *Pragmatism*, viii. Quine's distaste at being associated with pragmatism is instructive, because his restriction on the innermost community of inquirers to "naturalistic philosophers" is even more restrictive than that of Peirce ("Pragmatists' Place in Empiricism," 33). *See also* West, *The American Evasion of Philosophy*, 186-88.

5/

TURN, TURN, TURN

The resurgence of pragmatism, or the rise of neo-pragmatism, was well recognized by 1980, and had influenced a variety of intellectual fields by 1990.[1] This resurgence constituted yet another revolution among a series of "turns" that have characterized the course of philosophy in the United States. In response to the "reflexive turn" of Descartes that directed philosophical discussion toward questions about the nature of knowledge and the human mind, pragmatists gave what Horace Kallen called "the new turn" to academic thought, which was followed by "the linguistic turn" whereby the central function of philosophy became the analysis of language.[2] By the 1970s some were calling for a "pragmatic turn, which means … the quest for certainty in critical philosophy must be given up and an appeal made instead to the purposes of our inquiries and uses of language rather than to an absolute criterion of meaning or verifiability."[3] Others called this latest shift "the Rortyan turn," sug-

---

[1] *See,* for example, "Symposium on the Renaissance of Pragmatism in American Legal Thought," *Southern California Law Review* 63 (September 1990); Charles W. Anderson, *Pragmatic Liberalism* (Chicago: University of Chicago Press, 1990); Michael Brint and William Weaver, eds., *Pragmatism in Law and Society* (Boulder, Colo.: Westview, 1991); Charlene Haddock, ed., *Feminism and Pragmatism*, special issue of *Hypatia* 8: 2 (Spring 1993).

[2] Horace M. Kallen, "John Dewey and the Spirit of Pragmatism," in *John Dewey: Philosopher of Science and Freedom: A Symposium*, ed. Sidney Hook (New York: Dial, 1950), 16.

[3] John E. Smith, "The Reflexive Turn, the Linguistic Turn, and the Pragmatic Outcome," *Monist* 53 (1969): 594-95. *See also* Richard J. Bernstein, *Praxis and Action: Contemporary Philosophies of Human Activity* (Philadelphia: University of Pennsylvania Press, 1971), 250; Richard Rorty, ed., *The Linguistic Turn: Recent Essays in Philosophical Method* (Chicago, University of Chicago Press, 1967), passim; Daniel J. Wilson, *Science, Community, and the Transformation of American Philosophy, 1860-1930* (Chicago: University of Chicago Press, 1990), ch. 9. The term "linguistic turn" has been attributed to Gustav Bergmann, who noted, "As to *method,* philosophy during the first half of

gesting that the leading figure of neo-pragmatism, Richard Rorty, has infused pragmatism with poststructuralism by imputing concerns for hermeneutics and historicism to the thought of Dewey.[4]

To return to pragmatism without reconstructing it would be ironic, not to say "unpragmatic," as R. J. Bernstein and others have observed.[5] Nevertheless, the claim to be *returning* to pragmatism is one significant reason for its resurgence. To invoke pragmatism is to embrace a tradition that is somewhat antitraditional, and this paradox offers a tactical advantage in intellectual debates much like that gained by the twenti-eth-century commentators on liberal education who advocate what I have called the *artes liberales* accommodation. This accommodation refers to prescribing the reading of traditional texts of critical philoso-phy; a tactical advantage is gained by prescribing an authoritative tex-tual tradition that disavows the authority of a textual tradition.[6] So, too, with the claim to be returning to pragmatism.

Other significant reasons for the resurgence of pragmatism include the increased attention now being directed to questions about "the

the century has taken the linguistic turn. Words are used either philosophically or commonsensically. Philosophical uses are literally unintelligible. The task is to explicate them by talking commonsensically about them. This is the fundamental idea of the turn" ("Physics and Ontology," *Philosophy of Science* 28 [1961]: 1). Michael Dummett maintained that what is specially characteristic of analytic philosophy is precisely this "linguistic turn" (*Origins of Analytic Philosophy* [Cambridge, Mass.: Harvard University Press, 1994], ch. 1, passim).

[4] John Patrick Diggins, *The Promise of Pragmatism: Modernism and the Crisis of Knowledge and Authority* (Chicago: University of Chicago Press, 1992), 416. Certain ironies in these turns are exemplified by the "rationalist turn" taken by the Frankfurt school of critical theory upon the arrival of Max Horkheimer, Herbert Marcuse, and Theodor Adorno, among others, at the Institute for Social Research in the 1930s. In the words of Richard Wolin, these individuals sought "a more theoretical, less narrowly empirical course of research" in a project intended to show the social basis of all thought, belief, and value. This rationalist turn of critical theory reflected "the commitment of certain Institute members to philosophical reason as a new normative ideal," notwithstanding their "predisposition to view the tradition of western rationalism itself as having sown the seeds of modern political despotism" (*The Terms of Cultural Criticism: The Frankfurt School, Existentialism, Poststructuralism* [New York: Columbia University Press, 1992], 25ff.).

[5] Richard J. Bernstein, "The Varieties of Pluralism," *American Journal of Education* 95 (1987): 523. *See also* George P. Schmidt, *The Liberal Arts College: A Chapter in American Cultural History* (New Brunswick, N.J.: Rutgers University Press, 1957), 216; Robert B. Westbrook, *John Dewey and American Democracy* (Ithaca, N.Y.: Cornell University Press, 1991), 552.

[6] *See* Bruce A. Kimball, *Orators and Philosophers: A History of the Idea of Liberal Education*, expanded ed. (New York: College Entrance Examination Board, 1995), 152-53, 176-77, 207-8, 219-23.

nature of action and its relation to thinking and...the relation between natural science and human values."[7] The latter issue looms particularly large in current thought, revealing frustration with the tendency of regnant analytic philosophy to regard ethical statements as unanalyzable "emotive" or "pseudo" concepts.[8] This frustration is confirmed by a complementary resurgence, unmentioned in the neo-pragmatic literature, of philosophical commentary on Socrates. When analytic philosophy was dominant, Socrates was relatively neglected or his central contribution was interpreted as the refinement of a logical "method" for analyzing questions very carefully, as Richard Robinson illuminated.[9] Resurgent Socratic scholarship views the Athenian as laying the foundation for moral philosophy by suggesting "the ideal of moral knowledge."[10]

The characteristics of this resurgent pragmatism, that is to say, of neo-pragmatism, are difficult to assay. Neo-pragmatism is molded in the current intellectual cast named by prefixes: post-, meta-, neo-, anti-, and de-. These prefixes and the associated adjective "critical" signify that these movements are defined in terms of some other view, beyond, after, away,

[7] John E. Smith, *Purpose and Thought: The Meaning of Pragmatism* (Chicago: University of Chicago Press, 1978), 9. See also H. S. Thayer, *Meaning and Action: A Critical History of Pragmatism* [1968] (2d ed. Indianapolis, Ind.: Hackett, 1981), 564-65; Cornel West, *The American Evasion of Philosophy: A Genealogy of Pragmatism* (Madison, Wis.: University of Wisconsin Press, 1989), 4.

[8] Leading statements establishing and assessing this tendency came from, respectively, A. J. Ayer, *Language, Truth, and Logic* (London: Victor Gollancz, 1936), and Charles L. Stevenson, *Ethics and Language* (New Haven, Conn.: Yale University Press, 1944). Dewey addressed this view of "value-expression as ejaculatory" in *Theory of Valuation*, vol. 1, no. 4, in *International Encyclopedia of Unified Science* (Chicago: University of Chicago Press, 1939), 6ff. *See also* Douglas Sloan, "The Teaching of Ethics in the American Undergraduate Curriculum, 1876-1976," *Teachers College Record* 82 (1980): 35-36; Richard Rorty, *Consequences of Pragmatism (Essays 1972-1980)* (Minneapolis, Minn.: University of Minnesota Press, 1982), xlii ff. Arguing that "*emotivism* was long gone by the 1960s" and that this "tendency" has been extinguished, my colleague, philosophy professor Randall Curren, wrote, "Analytic philosophy is still *overwhelmingly* dominant in American *research* universities in the sense that we are nearly all students of people trained in the analytical tradition. We are more eclectic and less preoccupied by science—also more interested in history—but this is an evolution of the [analytical] tradition, not the *dying* of one, and birth of another" (correspondence of October 1994).

[9] *See* Richard Robinson, *Plato's Earlier Dialectic*, 2d ed. (Oxford, England: Clarendon, 1953), chs. 2, 3, 5. I am grateful to Herman Sinaiko for pointing out this trend in Socratic scholarship during a conversation.

[10] R. E. Allen, trans., *The Dialogues of Plato* (New Haven, Conn.: Yale University Press, 1984), 1:3. *See also* Gregory Vlastos, *Socrates: Ironist and Moral Philosopher* (Ithaca, N.Y.: Cornell University Press, 1991), passim.

against which they claim to stand. In this way, the current movements define themselves in terms of some other viewpoint from which they wish to break away. This definitional strategy reveals what will someday be seen as the adolescence of recent thinking—the fierce desire to break away and become independent, coupled with a limited capacity to do so.[11] Not only does the adolescent quality sound a warning about the integrity of such thinking, because the blatant desire to move beyond, after, away, or against something is bound to skew the account of that thing, but it also demonstrates the maturity and fortitude of the pragmatists in their own period, who birthed and named (however reluctantly and uncertainly) a view that sent many critics recoiling and satirizing, yet that lived. In other words, this current groping to get beyond, after, apart, and away—to come up with a new way of thinking, to devise it, name it, make it workable and worthy of being taken seriously by many and for many years—all this should deepen our appreciation of pragmatism, which apparently won't die, notwithstanding analysis, neo-Thomism, and disenchantment with science. The 1980s and 1990s call for the after, beyond, neo, and next, but have not yet taken the step that the pragmatists took. This point is worth emphasizing in preparing to briefly review the turn to neo-pragmatism, because the adolescence of our period makes one wary of the pragmatism found there.

Richard J. Bernstein might be credited with laying the foundation in the 1960s for the return to Dewey. He has nurtured the resurgence of pragmatism while incorporating other perspectives into his thinking, but he does not fail to distinguish what is "unpragmatic." After publishing a collection of Dewey's writings in 1960 and a general assessment of Dewey's thought in 1965,[12] Bernstein by 1971 was explicitly incorporating into his pragmatism insights from Marxism, existentialism, and

[11] The conceptual dilemmas revealed by the prefixes are underscored by the occasional phrasing "Dewey's proto-postpositivist" view, which finds "the postmodern condition in premodern times" (Westbrook, *John Dewey and American Democracy*, 187n.). *See also* Diggins, *The Promise of Pragmatism*, 427-28. Here we define the pragmatists in terms of we who define ourselves in terms of what we think we have surpassed. Feminism is the important exception here, inasmuch as feminism is named as being *about* something, not beyond, after, away, or against something else. It is also telling that feminism, in many quarters, is theoretically suspect compared to the post-, meta-, neo-, anti-, and de- movements that have yet to take the first, semantic step of theoretical independence that feminism has already taken. The perception of theoretical integrity is thus inversely related to semantic independence. Cf. Charlene Haddock, ed., *Feminism and Pragmatism*.

[12] Richard J. Bernstein, ed. *John Dewey on Experience, Nature and Freedom* (New York: Liberal Arts Press, 1960); R. J. Bernstein, *John Dewey* (Atascadero, Calif.: Ridgeview, 1965).

analytic philosophy through consideration of "how the classic dichotomies between thought and action...can be united." By the early 1980s, he was expanding an "early and abiding interest" in the thought of the Frankfurt School, especially that of Jurgen Habermas, who "is very close to the spirit of Peirce, Dewey, and Mead."[13] Consequently, although Bernstein affirmed that "everything that I've written since the early 1950s has been infused and informed by the spirit of Dewey and, more generally, by...the pragmatic tradition," he has been scrupulous in distinguishing that tradition from others and, like Smith, in acknowledging the differences among traditions.[14]

In contrast, certain writings by and about the neo-pragmatists exhibit tendencies of "skipping around," whereby "intellectual history takes on the moves of hopscotch."[15] This tendentiousness appears, for example, in the link that is frequently proposed between Ralph Waldo Emerson and pragmatism. One such proposal is found in the informative "genealogy of pragmatism" of Cornel West, whose "major themes (power, provocation, personality)" attributed to pragmatism and their link to Emerson are not made as clear as the reader might hope. What does emerge clearly is the pragmatic demand to address moral questions, leading West to call for "prophetic pragmatism" as "a form of cultural criticism that attempts to transform linguistic, social, cultural, and political traditions for the purposes of increasing the scope of individual development and democratic operations."[16]

---

[13] Bernstein, *Praxis and Action*, 198; R. J. Bernstein, *Beyond Objectivism and Relativism: Science, Hermeneutics, and Praxis* (Philadelphia: University of Pennsylvania Press, 1983), xv-xvi. Jurgen Habermas drew on American pragmatism, especially Peirce and Mead, in seeking to defend the role of reason in philosophical discourse and the social constitution of the self, respectively. *See* Habermas, *The Philosophical Discourse of Modernity: Twelve Lectures*, trans. Frederick Lawrence (Cambridge, Mass.: Massachusetts Institute of Technology Press, 1987), passim; Habermas, *The Theory of Communicative Action*, vol. 2: *Lifeworld and System: A Critique of Functionalist Reason* [1981] (Boston: Beacon, 1987), ch. 5. See also Maeve Cooke, *Language and Reason: A Study of Habermas's Pragmatics* (Cambridge, Mass.: Massachusetts Institute of Technology Press, 1994).

[14] Bernstein, "Varieties of Pluralism," 509. *See also* the introduction and prefatory comments to the essays included in John E. Smith, *America's Philosophical Vision* (Chicago: University of Chicago Press, 1992).

[15] Diggins, *The Promise of Pragmatism*, 53.

[16] West, *The American Evasion of Philosophy*. 40, 230. West made the link to Emerson by defining pragmatism as "a form of cultural criticism in which the meaning of America is put forward by intellectuals in response to distinct social and cultural crises" (*The American Evasion of Philosophy*, 5). Although Emerson may fit, this definition seems overly broad. In the same vein, West tended to deemphasize Dewey's stress on scientific method and to regard his hallmark as participation "in cultural criticism and cultural

The tendentiousness cropping up in neo-pragmatism induces observers and critics of the movement to follow suit, as Diggins explicitly acknowledged.[17] Rather than Emerson, historian Henry Adams was chosen by Diggins as a touchstone for analyzing pragmatism. Diggins explained that he made this choice "because I am more struck by [pragmatism's] limitations than by its possibilities, because I see pragmatism as having failed to fulfill many of its promises," whereas Adams, as well as Max Weber and Reinhold Niebuhr, "felt the limits of knowledge and the eclipse of authority, and hence registered the crisis of liberalism that had been brought on by the corrosions of modernism." Consequently, although "philosophers and literary critics link American intellectual history to European poststructuralism by returning to the writings of James and Dewey...the deeper link may be with Adams."[18]

The special tendencies characterizing this literature also appear in the writing of the foremost neo-pragmatist, Richard Rorty, who is credited with being "the first philosopher...[who] underscores the broad intellectual affinities [pragmatism] has with the work of Wittgenstein, Heidegger, and Nietzche" and who "first put forth the case for seeing Dewey as a precursor of poststructuralism."[19] Yet these insights are said to be qualified by Rorty's "plausible, yet objectionable readings of Wittgenstein, Heidegger, and Dewey" and his "radical, and disturbing interpretation of pragmatism."[20] Among the "three brief sloganistic characterizations" that Rorty at one point attributed to the "central doctrine" of the pragmatists, most observers probably agree that pragmatism includes "anti-essentialism," or fallibilism, and with the view that there is "no difference between truth and value." However, a number of

creation" (*The American Evasion of Philosophy*, 69, 98ff.). Other works linking Emerson to pragmatism include David Jacobson, *Emerson's Pragmatic Vision: The Dance of the Eye* (University Park, Pa.: Pennsylvania State University Press, 1993); David M. Robinson, *Emerson and the Conduct of Life: Pragmatism and Ethical Purpose in the Later Work* (Cambridge: Cambridge University Press, 1993.

[17] Diggins, *The Promise of Pragmatism*, 53.

[18] Diggins, *The Promise of Pragmatism*, 16, 25. Oddly, Adams receded into the background in the concluding chapter where Diggins presented his central thesis, "that pragmatism represents a decisive break with the past," because the American view, represented by Calvinism, Adams, and Niebuhr, is anything but "cheerful" and recognizes the ubiquity of power and the incapacity of reason to harness power (*The Promise of Pragmatism*, 361, ch. 11).

[19] Garry Brodsky, "Rorty's Interpretation of Pragmatism," *Transactions of the Charles S. Peirce Society* 18 (1982): 320; Diggins, *The Promise of Pragmatism*, 416; Konstantin Kolenda, *Rorty's Humanistic Pragmatism: Philosophy Democratized* (Tampa, Fla.: University of South Florida Press, 1990), xi–xiii.

[20] West, *The American Evasion of Philosophy*, 203; Brodsky, "Rorty's Interpretation of Pragmatism," 320.

objections arise concerning Rorty's third characterization: "that there are no constraints on inquiry save conversational ones—no wholesale constraints derived from the nature of the objects, or of the mind, or of language, but only those retail constraints provided by the remarks of our fellow-inquirers."[21]

Here is the fulcrum for turning pragmatic philosophy into a historical and hermeneutical enterprise, which Rorty proceeded to do in *Philosophy and the Mirror of Nature* (1979). This prominent book called for displacing "systematic" and truth-seeking philosophy, which holds that "questions are to be answered by some new ('metaphysical' or 'transcendental') descriptive or explanatory discourse," with "edifying philosophy," which "aims at continuing a conversation rather than at discovering a truth."[22] The systematic philosopher searching for truth and beauty or for guidelines for the search, in Rorty's program, becomes "the all-purpose intellectual of a post-Philosophical culture" who "feels free to comment on anything at all." Indeed, in *Contingency, Irony, and Solidarity* (1989), Rorty proceeded to argue that works of literature provide a better understanding of social and political justice than do philosophical treatises.[23]

One line of response to Rorty's third characterization of pragmatism is that he was unfaithful to the pragmatists, particularly Dewey, whom he invoked most often and authoritatively. More than one commentator has claimed that "In the face of what Dewey actually says, I find myself baffled by several of Rorty's statements." In fact, some critics consider Rorty to be "availing himself of ideas drawn from the pragmatists, chiefly Dewey, for use in his own agenda, which includes 'overcoming the tradition,' 'the end of Philosophy,' 'literature as the successor of Philosophy' and similar themes."[24] Even Rorty's allies observed that he

[21] Richard Rorty, "Pragmatism, Relativism, and Irrationalism," in *Consequences of Pragmatism (Essays 1972-1980)* Minneapolis, Minn.: University of Minnesota Press, 1982), 162-65.

[22] Richard Rorty, *Philosophy and the Mirror of Nature* (Princeton, N.J.: Princeton University Press, 1979), 383, 373; *see also* ch. 7.

[23] Richard Rorty, *Consequences of Pragmatism*, xl; Rorty, *Contingency, Irony, and Solidarity* (Cambridge: Cambridge University Press, 1989), passim.

[24] John E. Smith, *America's Philosophical Vision* (Chicago: University of Chicago Press, 1992), 11, 9-10. *See also* Wilson, *Science, Community, and the Transformation of American Philosophy*, 192; R. W. Sleeper, "Rorty's Pragmatism: Afloat in Neurath's Boat, But Why Adrift?" *Transactions of the Charles S. Peirce Society* 21 (1985); Richard Rorty, "Comments on Sleeper and Edel," *Transactions of the Charles S. Peirce Society* 21 (1985). An interesting irony stems from the fact that Rorty purposefully neglected Peirce in developing his interpretation of pragmatism. *See* Rorty, *Consequences of Pragmatism*, xlv; Rorty, "Pragmatism, Relativism, and Irrationalism," 160. Although

"wishes Dewey to be a more consistent historicist pragmatist. And I agree."[25] This very phrasing indicates, ironically enough, how Rorty and such allies impute certain essences to the meaning of pragmatism apart from the founders' intentions.

Another line of response is that Rorty's "edifying philosophy" turns philosophy into a meandering and unguided conversation. The resulting danger is expressed stridently by Richard Wolin:

> The central antifoundationalist maneuver of [Philosophy and the Mirror of Nature] is a rejection of all claims to universal and objective value. The logical consequence of this move is the adoption of a thorough-going relativism—which Rorty...freely embraces....[B]y entirely ceding the power of "right" or "normativity" to context, he studiously ignores the context-transcendent powers of reason and critique, and thereby ends up with a de facto endorsement of an essentially neoconservative position: "what is real is rational, what is rational is real"....[A] number of pointed critiques have accused Rorty of implicitly promoting a neoconservative worldview. He has responded...[and] attempted to provide a more favorable account of the political implications of his metaphysical agnosticism, but the results have been less than persuasive.[26]

It should not be forgotten that this kind of criticism can also come from the right, as indicated by the realists' critique of Dewey in the second quarter of the twentieth century.

Still another deeply ironic and overlooked line of criticism, which serves as a bridge between recent discussion of pragmatism and the historical traditions of liberal education, is that Rorty and others addressing neo-pragmatism neglected the long-standing, antiphilosophical tradition in the West. Here is a group of intellectuals discussing pragma-

---

Rorty is occasionally brought to task for his "pragmatism-without-Peirce" (Wilson, Science, Community, and the Transformation of American Philosophy, 1860-1930, 192), the stretch between Peirce and Dewey is so great at points that choosing between the two in some respects cannot be severely reproved. But it is ironic that Peirce, whom Rorty dismisses, may be the exemplar of Rorty's edifying conversationalist philosopher, while Peirce also appears to have shared what West called "Rorty's antiprofessionalism" (Diggins, The Promise of Pragmatism, 11-13, 186; West, The American Evasion of Philosophy, 199). The dismissal of Peirce not only results in the neglect of a potential examplar of edifying philosophy, but also raises the question of whether devotion to approaching-truth-as-a-limit logic precludes edifying philosophy, as Rorty seems to assume.

[25] West, The American Evasion of Philosophy, 96.

[26] Richard Wolin, The Terms of Cultural Criticism: The Frankfurt School, Existentialism, Poststructuralism (New York: Columbia University Press, 1992), 152, 155, 160.

tism in relation to "Post-Philosophical Culture," "the end of Philosophy," or the "evasion of philosophy."[27] Yet there is virtually no appeal to or even recognition of that Western tradition—the rhetorical—that has long opposed the philosophical search for precise truths through rigorous intellectual method. Moreover, in the discussion surrounding neo-pragmatism there are debates concerning the validity of "taking Dewey's scientific-oriented philosophy and reformulating it as a linguistic enterprise,"[28] claims that "a post-philosophical culture" stresses "the ubiquity of language,"[29] and assertions that "The Recovery of Practical Philosophy," in contrast to rationalistic and systematic philosophy, means returning to "the oral...the particular...the local...and the timely."[30] However, despite these intimations and even reflections of the rhetorical tradition, the entire discussion is confined to references to Western philosophers.

The irony, then, lies in the fact that prominent intellectuals, such as Rorty and Stephen Toulmin, who are challenging the rationalistic, epistemological bent of modern philosophy in various ways, confine themselves to the same philosophical tradition in searching for its antidote, apparently unmindful of a long-standing alternative tradition that has periodically eclipsed philosophy while emphasizing many of the same characteristics and propositions for which the challengers now call. This is the lesson that the history of liberal education has to teach neo-pragmatism.

A historiographical version of this oversight appears in Toulmin's recent attempt to overturn "the received view" of intellectual history that fosters our faith in "Modern Science" and "Modern Philosophy—the method of reflection initiated by Descartes."[31] The stance of remaining within the tradition of modern philosophy, while claiming to be outside and to overturn it—and neglecting the rhetorical and Humanist tradition that has long stood outside and periodically overturned it—can also be seen in Rorty's work. Notwithstanding occasional analogues drawn between Rorty and the ancient Sophists or occasional references by Rorty himself to "the opposition between the literary and scientific cultures" or "Poetry and Philosophy,"[32] he looks within philosophy to

---

[27] Rorty, *Consequences of Pragmatism*, xxvii; Smith, *America's Philosophical Vision*, 9-10; West, *The American Evasion of Philosophy*, passim.

[28] Diggins, *The Promise of Pragmatism*, 3.

[29] Rorty, *Consequences of Pragmatism*, xxxix.

[30] Stephen Toulmin, *Cosmopolis: The Hidden Agenda of Modernity* (Chicago: University of Chicago Press, 1990), 186ff.; *See also* Newton Garver and Seung-Chong Lee, *Derrida and Wittgenstein* (Philadelphia: Temple University Press, 1993), passim.

[31] Toulmin, *Cosmopolis*, ix; *see also* the Appendix to this essay.

[32] Wolin, *The Terms of Cultural Criticism*, 5, 153; Rorty, *Consequences of Pragmatism*, xlvii.

discover and demonstrate that language is the counterpoint to reason: the "attack on distinctions between classes of sentences is the special contribution of analytic philosophy to the anti-Platonist insistence on the ubiquity of language. This insistence characterizes both pragmatism and recent 'Continental' philosophizing."[33] In this way, the ubiquity and plasticity of language seem, in Rorty's view, to be the discoveries of modern philosophers, who have also discovered the inseverable links among community, context, valuing, and language, all of which point toward and are to be sustained by "edifying philosophy." Rorty included Dewey among these progenitors of edifying philosophy, although he does not seem to fit very well. To be sure, significant themes are held in common by rhetors and pragmatists, such as concerns for values, community, citizenship, and general education. But the two groups are fundamentally divergent in their respective views that either language or experimental method is the primary conduit and source of knowledge and value. In light of this divergence and its implications, edifying philosophy appears, in fact, to fit the rhetors better than the pragmatists.[34]

The general point in this sketch of the pragmatic turn, the Rortyan turn, or the turn to neo-pragmatism is that certain themes of pragmatism are now resurgent: fallibilism or anti-essentialism; the equivalent status, if not identity, of value claims and knowledge claims; the view that inquiry is a continuing, self-corrective process common to all persons; and the idea that belief is dependent on the intersubjective warrant provided by a community of inquirers. In addition, I have suggested that the resurgence of pragmatism has given rise to appeals by its admirers, fellow travelers, and opponents to a host of figures ranging from Montaigne to Emerson and Henry Adams; these appeals appear somewhat tendentious.[35]

Finally, I have proposed that hovering about the neo-pragmatic attack on modern philosophy are views reminiscent of the long-standing arguments made by rhetors against philosophy. One prominent locus of this

---

[33] Rorty, *Consequences of Pragmatism*, xix.

[34] It is striking that Rorty observed that "pragmatists keep trying to find ways of making antiphilosophical points in nonphilosophical language. For they face a dilemma: if their language is too unphilosophical, too 'literary,' they will be accused of changing the subject; if it is too philosophical it will embody Platonic assumptions which will make it impossible for the pragmatist to state the conclusion he wants to reach" (*Consequences of Pragmatism*, xiv, xix-xx). The long line of rhetors have taken the first route, and have been dismissed by philosophy for being imprecise and unanalytical.

[35] In contrast, the explicit link between Ortega y Gasset and William James confirms the influence. See John T. Graham, *The Pragmatist Philosophy of Life in Ortega y Gasset* (Columbia, Mo.: University of Missouri Press, 1994).

argument has been the historical debate over the nature of liberal education. For example, in Book 7 of the *Republic,* Plato sketched an educational program relying on a number of correlated distinctions:

- in epistemology, between intellection and sensation, truth and appearance (529b–c, 530a, 532a);
- in metaphysics, between being and becoming (521d, 525b, 526d), between permanence and contingency (527b);
- in psychology, between mind and body (529b–c, 532a);
- in valuation, between better and worse, good and bad (532a);
- in society and politics, between the few and the many (527d);
- in curriculum, between axiomatic sciences and language (522a, 525d), between knowledge for its own sake and useful knowledge (527d).[36]

These distinctions were subsequently denied by the Roman orator Cicero, who responded to Plato in his greatest educational treatise, *De Oratore,* rediscovered by the Renaissance Humanists in 1422:

> But just as there have been many who...became eminent in the republic due to their twofold wisdom in action and in speaking (which cannot be separated)...so there have been those who made a deliberate decision to avoid politics and affairs and to censure and condemn oratory, though they themselves had great learning and genius. The foremost of these was Socrates, the one who...in his dialogues ripped the name "philosophy" away from the study and practice of all knowledge and divided two inseparable matters: wise thinking and beautiful speaking....From the writings of Plato then arose that certainly absurd and useless and reprehensible separation of the tongue from the brain, so to speak, such that some among us teach thinking and others teach language....For, as I said earlier, the ancients down to Socrates were accustomed to unite their theory of speech with all knowledge of everything pertaining to life, virtue, and society. These two fields were then separated by Socrates and successively by all the Socratics, so that philosophers despised eloquence and orators learning...although the ancients had wanted there to be a wonderful alliance between speaking and knowing.[37]

Cicero's viewpoint, which is still expressed in twentieth-century discussion of liberal education, looms over the neo-pragmatic arguments, but is not generally recognized or credited by the neo-pragmatists them-

[36] Plato, *The Republic,* trans. Allan Bloom (New York: Basic Books, 1968).
[37] Cicero, *De Oratore* (Cambridge, Mass.: Harvard University Press, 1942), 3:59, 60, 61, 72, 73. Author's translation.

selves. Consequently, the historical debates about liberal education may serve as a helpful corrective or supplement to pragmatic discussion of the end or evasion of philosophy and a postphilosophical culture. Conversely, it is worthwhile to consider whether, in an era of resurgent pragmatism, the ideas and themes of pragmatism are influencing discussions of the reform of liberal education. To be sure, such influence may be quite subtle and indirect, not merely a matter of looking into pragmatists' writings for educational proposals or implications. The influence may lie in providing a deeply rooted rationalization, or intellectual justification, for the various developments in liberal education that appear as disparate responses to particular demographic, economic, or disciplinary changes. Such a rationalization or justification may not be called "pragmatic," or even identified as a coherent philosophy or viewpoint. Nevertheless, it may provide an unstated intellectual framework within which the collection of proposals for the reform of liberal education "makes sense" during the current era.

6

Disjunction, Interlude, Disjunction

There are good reasons to expect that pragmatism would significantly influence thinking and practice concerning liberal education. As a philosophy emphasizing method, pragmatism might have pedagogic implications in the same way that Descartes's emphasis on method reflected his revolutionary intent to educate people to challenge pronouncements based on authority.[1] An additional and, perhaps, related reason is that Dewey is well known for defining philosophy as *"the general theory of education."*[2] James, in a manuscript unpublished at his death, said virtually the same thing in connection with liberal education: "To know the chief rivals...as the history of human thinking has developed them, and to have heard some of the reasons they can give for themselves, ought surely to be considered an essential part of liberal education. Philosophy, indeed, in one sense of the term is only a compendious name for the spirit in education which the word 'college' stands for in America...the graciousness of mind suggested by the term 'liberal culture.'" Without this, a person may be "intellectually pinned down to his one narrow subject, literal, unable to suppose anything different from what he has seen, without imagination, atmosphere or mental perspective."[3] Another reason to expect that pragmatism would influence liberal education is that "the concern for curriculum became the leitmotif of the progressive movement," which may be considered an expression of "the pragmatic vision."[4]

[1] I am grateful to Amelie Oskenberg Rorty for providing this insight in a conversation.
[2] John Dewey, *Democracy and Education: An Introduction to the Philosophy of Education* [1916] (New York: Free Press, 1966), 383.
[3] William James, *Some Problems of Philosophy: A Beginning of an Introduction to Philosophy* [incomplete in 1910], ed. Frederick H. Burkhardt et al., in *The Works of William James*, ed. F. H. Burkhardt (Cambridge, Mass.: Harvard University Press, 1975-), 9-10.
[4] Lawrence A. Cremin, "Curriculum-Making in the United States," *Teachers College Record* 73 (1971): 210; Irwin Unger and Debi Unger, *The Vulnerable Years: The United States 1896-1917* (New York: New York University Press, 1978), 95.

Finally, there were even anticipations of pragmatic themes in discussions of liberal education in the late nineteeth and early twentieth centuries. The word "pragmatism" had not yet appeared in print when the president of the University of Wisconsin warned in 1884 that "the scientific and the practical temper unite" within the university, and pose a threat to "liberal education."[5] Advocating an egalitarian vision of intelligence denying the distinction between thinking and practice, Calvin Woodward in 1887 argued that "A truly liberal education educates equally for all spheres of usefulness."[6]

Near the turn of the century, Peirce observed that "the old ideas which used to cluster about the phrase *Liberal Education* have become scattered," and by 1907 the dean of the Women's College at Brown University, in a historical study of the college curriculum, documented the increasing attention being given to inchoate progressive tenets emphasizing "the *development* of the student…the *liberalizing and equalizing* of studies in the curriculum…*the discovery of the individual*" and the efforts of the college to relate to "the local [and] the wider environment."[7] Holding forth contemporaneously on "Liberal Education in the Twentieth Century," the president of the University of Montana expressed these "cheerful" pragmatic themes:

> We are living in the most wonderful age the world has ever seen.… This is an age of activity and advancement. The one who succeeds will do so because of his ability to enter into competition with others and win success by his own energy and acuteness.… There is not an isolated fact in history. There is not an isolated current event.… History, economics, and sociology are receiving more attention today…[b]ecause men want light on present conditions that will help in the solution of important problems.… The discoveries…in psycho-physics and physiological psychology…coupled with discoveries in natural and physical science…have enabled us to put the philosophy of education on a sure foundation.… Liberal education gives a man control of himself. He knows his own capabilities and his own powers [and] limitations.[8]

---

[5] John Bascom, "The Part which the Study of Language Plays in a Liberal Education," *Journal of Proceedings and Addresses of the National Education Association* (1884): 273.

[6] Calvin M. Woodward, *The Manual Training School* (Boston: D. C. Heath, 1887), 202ff.

[7] Charles S. Peirce, *Reasoning and the Logic of Things: The Cambridge Conferences Lectures of 1898*, ed. Kenneth L. Ketner (Cambridge, Mass.: Harvard University Press, 1992), 181; Louis F. Snow, *The College Curriculum in the United States* (New York: Teachers College, Columbia University, 1907), 106, 173, 174, 14.

[8] Oscar J. Craig, "Liberal Education in the Twentieth Century," *Journal and Proceedings of the National Education Association* (1908): 670, 671, 675. In what Laurence Veysey considered the best early study of the college curriculum, William T. Foster, the new president of Reed College, which was devoted to curricular reform, sounded progressive themes in his call for "a college imbued with that kind of democratic spirit that cooperates for the common good with all the agencies of social progress;…a college that is

The surprising fact is, however, that for much of the twentieth century pragmatism had but limited influence on the discussion about and practice of what has been called "liberal education." Notwithstanding the initial reasons for and anticipation of a close association, there has existed a disjunction between pragmatism and liberal education, except for a period of convergence during the second quarter of the twentieth century, the continuing efforts of certain "Progressive Education Colleges," and a persistent thread of interest in general education.

The foremost pragmatists, in fact, had relatively little to say about liberal education. Peirce appears to have made only a few, though telling, comments on the topic, such as this observation of 1882: "And a liberal education—so far as its relation to the understanding goes—means *logic*....A young man wants a physical education and an aesthetic education, an education in the ways of the world and a moral education, and with all these logic has nothing in particular to do; but so far as he wants an intellectual education, it is precisely logic that he wants."[9] Likewise, James made only passing comments, so far as can be determined by reviewing the most recent edition of his collected works.[10]

More surprising is that Dewey, too, said little about liberal education,[11] and scholars discussing his views on this topic often rely on just

changing because it is living...through daily, practical contact with the many-sided life of city and state, here and now; that looks forward oftener than backward, and yet seeks the wisdom of organized experience...thus supplanting the blind guidance of tradition by the safer guidance of scientific insight" (Foster, *Administration of the College Curriculum* [Boston: Houghton Mifflin, 1911], 340).

[9] Peirce's statement is from the Johns Hopkins University Circulars (1882), and is quoted here from Israel Scheffler, *Four Pragmatists: A Critical Introduction to Peirce, James, Mead, and Dewey* (New York: Humanities, 1974), 87. *See also* comments in Peirce, "[Review of] Clark University, 1889-1899: Decennial Celebration (Worcester, Mass.: Clark University, 1899)," in *Science* n.s. 11 (20 April 1900); Peirce, *Reasoning and the Logic of Things*, 181.

[10] "The Proposed Shortening of the College Course" (1891), in *Essays, Comments, and Reviews*, ed. Frederick H. Burkhardt et al., in *The Works of William James*, dealt little with the nature of college education in this essay, rather focusing on the institutional arrangements concerning its length, especially compared to European standards.

[11] David O. Levine observed that "John Dewey wrote little on higher education specifically" (*The American College and the Culture of Aspiration 1915-1940* [Ithaca, N.Y.: Cornell University Press, 1986], 102). In his magisterial biography, Robert B. Westbrook's discussion of Dewey's views on education made little reference to higher education, aside from Dewey's brief exchange with Robert Hutchins (*John Dewey and American Democracy* [Ithaca, N.Y.: Cornell University Press, 1991], chs. 4, 6, 518-19.

two or three brief writings.[12] For a philosopher who wrote some 40 books and 800 articles, championed education reform, virtually identified philosophy and education, and posited a continuity between the thinking of schoolchildren and that of scientists, it is surprising to find so little on liberal education or, for that matter, postsecondary education. The reasons for this lacuna, given that pragmatism was never warmly embraced in the upper circles of academe, might be attributed to Dewey's concern for his own professional status, or to an incremental strategy of influencing the schools before confronting the leaders of higher education, or to resignation to the neglect of his educational theory given that, as he once complained, his academic critics refused to read *Democracy and Education*, the book in which his educational theory was expressed and in which his philosophy was, for many years, most fully expounded.[13] However, none of these factors seem to have had much influence on Dewey's other work, so perhaps Dewey found liberal education unreconstructible due to its traditionalist, essentialist, status-bound connotations.

Commensurate with the neglect of liberal education in the pragmatists' writings is the disregard of pragmatism on the part of early twentieth-century commentators on liberal education, who kept even

[12] *See* Thomas H. Briggs, "United States," in *The Meaning of Liberal Education in the Twentieth Century, Educational Yearbook of the International Institute of Teachers College, Columbia University 1939*, ed. I. L. Kandel (New York: Teachers College, Columbia University, 1939); George P. Schmidt, *The Liberal Arts College: A Chapter in American Cultural History* (New Brunswick, N.J.: Rutgers University Press, 1957), 213-14, 217-20; Willis Rudy, *The Evolving Liberal Arts Curriculum: A Historical Review of Basic Themes* (New York: Teachers College, Columbia University, 1960), 131-32; Veysey, "Stability and Experiment in the American Undergraduate Curriculum"; Arthur G. Wirth, *Education in the Technological Society: The Vocational-Liberal Studies Controversy in the Early Twentieth Century* (San Francisco: Intext, 1972), 195ff.; Levine, *The American College and the Culture of Aspiration*, 100-102. The writings of Dewey most often cited with reference to liberal education are *The Way Out of Educational Confusion* (Cambridge, Mass.: Harvard University Press, 1931), 19-27; "The Problem of the Liberal Arts College," *The American Scholar* 33 (1944); and, especially, Dewey's brief exchange with Robert Hutchins in the journal *Social Frontier* during 1937: Dewey, "President Hutchins' Proposals to Remake Higher Education," *Social Frontier* 3; Hutchins, "Grammar, Rhetoric, and Mr. Dewey," *Social Frontier* 3; Dewey, "The Higher Learning in America," *Social Frontier* 3. *See also* Dewey, "The Liberal College and Its Enemies," *Independent* 112 (1924); Dewey, "The Prospects of the Liberal College," *Independent* 112 (1924). Further leads into Dewey's discussion of liberal education, along with an extended analysis, can be found in Henry H. Crimmel, *The Liberal Arts College and the Ideal of Liberal Education: The Case for Radical Reform* (Lanham, Md.: University Press of America, 1993), 334-53.

[13] George P. Adams and William P. Montague, *Contemporary American Philosophy: Personal Statements* (New York: Macmillan, 1930), 2:22-23.

remotely pragmatic themes at a distance. In 1905, shortly after Dewey left the University of Chicago, President William Rainey Harper published a collection of addresses on *The Trend in Higher Education in America*, in which not an intimation of pragmatism appeared.[14] Meanwhile, Dean Andrew F. West at Princeton noted that, although "alterations in the content...and in the meaning of the Bachelor's degree" were arising from "the founding of schools of science" and from "the too fierce practicality of American life," these forces could not obliterate "the radical distinction between liberal and utilitarian ideals in education."[15]

Dean West was a somewhat stodgy observer, but reformers and critics of various stripes were equally neglectful of pragmatism. In "The Problem of College Pedagogy" (1909), Abraham Flexner asserted there to be "at bottom a logical incompatibility" between the learning of a college student and the inquiry of a researcher.[16] Such a view was anathema to Dewey, and Peirce had complained about college trustees who viewed the research of professors as contravening the mores of a liberal arts college.[17] In the following decade, Thorstein Veblen wrote dismissively of pragmatism in one of the few explicit references to the movement in early, prominent writings on higher education.[18] Even the biographer of James, Ralph Barton Perry, offered in 1915 a distinctly unpragmatic "Defence of Liberal Education" on behalf of "the old humanistic studies."[19] Conservative critics, such as Alfred E. Stearns, who resisted the "pernicious doctrine" of "the modern educational ideal," identified "the modernists" to be Flexner and Harvard President Charles Eliot, and made no mention of pragmatists.[20] The disjunction between pragmatism and liberal education prevailed through about 1920, prompting the early progressivist David Snedden to wonder, "Can...our teachers of the liberal arts...keep themselves in vital contact with the world of people and of things in which their real work is to be accomplished? Is there any course open to...liberal education which shall meet the modern requirements of pedagogy on the one hand, and of democratic society on the other?"[21]

[14] William Rainey Harper, *The Trend in Higher Education in America* (Chicago: University of Chicago Press, 1905), passim; note especially "The Situation of the Small College" (1900).

[15] Andrew F. West, *Short Papers on American Liberal Education* (New York: Charles Scribner's Sons, 1907), 97-98.

[16] Abraham Flexner, "The Problem of College Pedagogy," *Atlantic Monthly* 103 (1909): 840.

[17] Peirce, "[Review of] *Clark University, 1889-1899*," 621.

[18] Thorstein Veblen, *The Higher Learning in America: A Memorandum on the Conduct of Universities by Business Men* (New York: B. W. Huebsch, 1918), 5n.

[19] Ralph Barton Perry, "A Defence of Liberal Education," *Forum* 53 (1915): 214.

[20] Alfred E. Stearns, "Some Fallacies in the Modern Educational Scheme," *Atlantic Monthly* 118 (1916).

[21] David Snedden, "What of a Liberal Education?" *Atlantic Monthly* 109 (1912): 117.

Over the next two decades, it appeared that Snedden's questions would be answered affirmatively. The 1920s saw "an intensive and concerted effort...to review the idea of liberal education," according to Russell Thomas;[22] and, in the words of David Levine, "most educators' definition of the liberal arts was considerably broadened in the 1920s and 1930s" due in large part to "the ready acceptance of John Dewey's philosophical concept of pragmatism, the application of scientific methods to the study of society, and the continued professionalization of the social scientific disciplines."[23] Indeed, it was during the 1920s that followers of Dewey, such as Thomas Briggs, began explicitly studying and addressing liberal education.[24] At the end of that decade, the Cooperative Study of Changes and Experiments in Liberal-Arts Education, conducted by Kathryn McHale for the American Association of University Women and the National Society for the Study of Education, found that "more changes and experiments have been introduced in the last five years...than in the previous 25 years." Meanwhile, the term "Progressive College" was introduced to refer to the dozens of colleges and universities conducting various curricular experiments in the late 1920s and early 1930s, including Wittenberg, Hamline, Grinnell, Wells, Swarthmore, Franklin and Marshall, Brown, and Johns Hopkins.[25]

In particular, however, "Progressive College" or even "Progressive Education College" was a term applied to a subset of what were called "experimental colleges": the newly founded, refounded, or rejuvenated institutions that were organizing their entire programs around various conceptions of liberal education, and that included Bard, Bennington, Black Mountain, Olivet, Rollins, St. John's, Sarah Lawrence, and

---

[22] Russell Thomas, *The Search for a Common Learning: General Education, 1800-1960* (New York: McGraw-Hill, 1962), 69.

[23] Levine, *The American College and the Culture of Aspiration,* 97-98; *see also* ch. 5.

[24] Thomas H. Briggs, "Interests as Liberal Education," *Teachers College Record* 39 (1928). *See also* Herbert G. Espy, "The Curriculum of the Liberal Arts College" (Ph.D. diss., Harvard Graduate School of Education, 1929), 7-8. In a 1927 editorial, the *Journal of the National Education Association* offered a list of progressive tenets as "The Ideal of a Liberal Education," under the general proposition that, "To educate is to guide growth...until [young people] are able to continue their own development." In 1930, at about the high point of "progressive liberal education," the tenets were reissued on a poster entitled "The Ideal of a Liberal Education," which was offered for purchase in bulk lots for classroom display ("The Ideal of a Liberal Education: A Gift for Graduation," *Journal of the National Education Association* 19 (1930).

[25] Kathryn McHale, "Introduction," in McHale et al., *Changes and Experiments in Liberal-Arts Education, Part II, The Thirty-First Yearbook of the National Society for the Study of Education* (Bloomington, Ill.: Public School Publishing, 1932), 2. *See also* McHale, "Some Progressive College Projects," and "Some Progressive College Projects—II," in McHale et al., *Changes and Experiments in Liberal-Arts Education, Part II.*

Talladega.[26] Among these experimental colleges, the Progressive Education Colleges were a clutch of institutions, such as Reed, said by 1939 to have "lived through all the major phases in the history of the 'progressive education' movement"; Antioch College, rejuvenated in 1920 and led by presidents who invoked Dewey and James; Sarah Lawrence College, chartered in 1926 and organized, according to its first catalogue, "along the lines of progressive education"; Rollins College, which achieved the coup of inducing Dewey to chair its 1931 conference on "The Curriculum for the Liberal Arts College"; and Bennington College, which opened in 1932 under the direct influence of "educational groups from progressive schools and colleges."[27]

Apart from this small group of institutions that deeply imbibed pragmatic, or progressive, thinking and that remained largely on the margin of higher education, the broad range of institutions were less influenced by this philosophy in their programs of liberal education. Briggs, at Teachers College, Columbia University, who had been so hopeful in 1928, observed in 1939, "'progressive' educational philosophy...has had as yet little effect on the practice of liberal arts colleges," even though "the tendency to extend the field of liberal education to include newly discovered knowledge and to make science, even in its utilitarian aspects, respectable, is unmistakable, as also is the tendency to give it a pragmatic responsibility for eventuating in action [based upon] practical values."[28] Thus, a change had occurred in the way liberal education was

[26] *See* Donald P. Cottrell, "General Education in Experimental Liberal Arts Colleges," in *General Education in the American College, Part II, The Thirty-Eighth Yearbook of the National Society for the Study of Education,* ed. Guy Montrose Whipple (Bloomington, Ill.: Public School Publishing, 1939), 217; Ernest H. Wilkins, "What Constitutes a Progressive College?" *Association of American Colleges Bulletin* 19 (1933); Algo D. Henderson, *Vitalizing Liberal Education: A Study of the Liberal Arts Program* (New York: Harper, 1944), 7-8.

[27] Cottrell, "General Education in Experimental Liberal Arts Colleges," 198, 199, 201. *See also* Henderson, *Vitalizing Liberal Education,* 2, 8-13; John Dewey et al., *The Curriculum for the Liberal Arts College: Being the Report of the Curriculum Conference Held at Rollins College, January 19-24, 1931, John Dewey, Chairman* (Winter Park, Fla.: Rollins College, 1931); Robert D. Leigh, "Newer Aspects of College Education," *Progressive Education* 5 (1928); Henderson and Dorothy Hall, *Antioch College: Its Design for Liberal Education* (New York: Harper, 1946); Burton R. Clark, *The Distinctive College: Antioch, Reed, and Swarthmore* (Chicago: Aldine, 1970), chs. 2, 4. Bard College and Goddard were the two other experimental colleges most prominently influenced by progressivism and pragmatism.

[28] Briggs, "United States," 320-21. A leading progressivist assessment came from R. Freeman Butts in *The College Charts Its Course: Historical Conceptions and Current Proposals* (New York, McGraw-Hill, 1939), a 450-page history of the undergraduate curriculum portraying the gradual evolution of the enlightened "progressive" movement in undergraduate education. By the 1930s, in Butts's view, the progressive view had almost gained equal stature with the conservative view, resulting in "a welter of conflicting proposals concerning the American college" that generally concerned the following parallel oppositions: remoteness from versus engagement with social problems, "intellectualism and bookmindedness versus intelligence and personality," "the Great Tradition versus experimental naturalism," "Aristocratic versus Democratic Conception of the College," and "elective system versus prescribed curriculum," 1-9.

conceived of, and by 1940 commentators on the subject often felt obliged to cite pragmatic or Deweyan ideas. But the general cast and practice of liberal education conformed to older traditions, as illustrated by the fact that commentators' obligatory citations of pragmatic ideas were generally not integrated with the rest of their thinking on liberal education. This lack of integration is evident in, for example, Alexander Meiklejohn's writings,[29] Henry Wriston's *The Nature of a Liberal College* (1937), Stewart Cole's *Liberal Education in a Democracy: A Charter for the American College* (1940), Luther Evans's *Essentials of Liberal Education* (1942), and, most notably, *General Education in a Free Society, Report of the Harvard Committee* (1945).[30]

In this interlude during the 1920s and 1930s, the most widespread and enduring influence of pragmatism on liberal education was probably the development of general education. This is not to claim that pragmatism was the original, or sole, force behind general education, although it has repeatedly been said that general education stemmed from the introduction of the "survey course" by Meiklejohn at Amherst College in 1914, based on a 1902 proposal by Dewey. The general education "movement launched by Dewey and Meiklejohn gained momentum after the First World War, with the 'survey course' as its centerpiece."[31] Nevertheless,

[29] *See* Alexander Meiklejohn, *The Liberal College* (Boston: Marshall Jones, 1920); Meiklejohn, *The Experimental College* (New York: Harper, 1932); Meiklejohn, "Required Education for Freedom," *The American Scholar* 33 (1944). This disjunction was noted by observers such as Butts, *The College Charts Its Course*, 305-6, and Hal G. Lewis, "Meiklejohn and Experimentalism," in *Teachers College Record* 44 (1943). Veysey gave a positive spin to what others saw as ambiguity or inconsistency in the views of Meiklejohn, who "more than anyone else...bridged the enormous gap between traditional and progressive versions of liberal education" (Veysey, "Stability and Experiment in the American Undergraduate Curriculum,"44-46).

[30] Paul H. Buck et al., *General Education in a Free Society, Report of the Harvard Committee* (Cambridge, Mass.: Harvard University Press, 1945), 39-40, 46-48, 51, 55. "[F]ew were satisfied with the balance the committee struck," according to John S. Brubacher and Willis Rudy, *Higher Education in Transition: A History of American Colleges and Universities, 1636-1976*, 3d ed. (New York: Harper and Row, 1976), 303. The 11 objectives identified by the President's Commission on Higher Education likewise amalgamated the three traditions that the Harvard Report (Buck et al., 39-40) identified (*Establishing the Goals*, vol. 1, 50-58, in *Higher Education for American Democracy, Report of the President's Commission on Higher Education* [Washington, D.C.: U.S. Government Printing Office, 1947]). *See also* Harold Taylor, "The Philosophical Foundations of General Education," in *General Education, Fifty-First Yearbook, Part I, of the National Society for the Study of Education*, ed. Nelson B. Henry (Chicago: University of Chicago Press, 1952), 39; Schmidt, *The Liberal Arts College*, 217-18.

[31] Ernest L. Boyer and Arthur Levine, *A Quest for Common Learning: The Aims of General Education* (Princeton, N.J.: Carnegie Foundation for the Advancement of Teaching, 1981), 9. *See also* Meiklejohn, *The Liberal College*, 134-37; Thomas, *The Search for a Common Learning*, 52.

the pragmatic idea that knowing is dependent on the general context—that ideas are not understood apart from their practical consequences, that experience involves dynamic interaction with the environment, that one cannot "know something" apart from the temporal, spatial, and other relations of the thing—provided the fundamental rationale not only for introducing general education, but also for claiming to give it equal standing with specialization. In addition, Sloan has observed that general education has always been associated with the teaching of values and ethics,[32] and this can best be explained by the analogous pragmatic idea that value judgments depend on the general context in which they are made. The fact that the first general education movement coincided with the interlude during which pragmatism made its initial impact on liberal education confirms the conceptual link,[33] as does the fact that general education remained the diminutive stepchild of the undergraduate curriculum in subsequent decades, when the influence of pragmatism on liberal education waned.

The disjunction between pragmatism and liberal education gradually reemerged and then widened during the 1940s, coincident with the decline of pragmatism as an academic philosophy. In his 1942 dissertation, C. Wright Mills observed that "our most generic problem consists in explaining the relations between one type of philosophy, pragmatism, and the American social structure." In his view, those relations lay primarily in that "crude but most tangible link...the educational institutions of higher learning."[34] Nevertheless, Mills's study of the institutions constituting that link did not address liberal education, even though, as Irving L. Horowitz observed, Mills was "so fond of criticizing the 'liberal rhetoric.' "[35] Conversely, those who commented on liberal education came no closer to pragmatism than did Mills.

[32] Douglas Sloan, "The Teaching of Ethics in the American Undergraduate Curriculum, 1876-1976," *Teachers College Record* 82 (1980), 237-48.

[33] Boyer and Levine proposed that interest in general education abated between 1930 and 1943 (*A Quest for Common Learning*, Appendix A). However, the writings compiled in W. S. Gray, ed., *General Education: Its Nature, Scope, and Essential Elements* (Chicago: University of Chicago Press, 1934), and Whipple, ed., *General Education in the American College, Part II*, give reason to doubt that there was any such abatement during the 1930s, at which time Alvin C. Eurich of Stanford University even perceived "A Renewed Emphasis upon General Education" (in *General Education in the American College, Part II*).

[34] C. Wright Mills, *Sociology and Pragmatism: The Higher Learning in America*, ed. Irving L. Horowitz (New York: Oxford University Press, 1964), 35. Mills's dissertation (1942) was not published until 1964.

[35] Irving L. Horowitz, "Introduction," in C. Wright Mills, *Sociology and Pragmatism: The Higher Learning in America*, 23.

In 1930, Flexner encouraged universities to remain disengaged from "the actual world" in order to "shelter and develop thinkers ... who, without responsibility for action, will explore the phenomena of social life and endeavor to understand them." To the pragmatists, this proposal was not a matter of being "irresponsible"—an objection Flexner anticipated—but of whether thinkers "without responsibility for action" could even think or understand.[36] Nevertheless, the view that universities and colleges should not enter into "social and moral affairs; [and] must provide merely the factual basis and knowledge that others can somehow use to solve the problems" was widespread, according to R. Freeman Butts.[37] Indeed, at the Southwestern Conference on Higher Education held at the University of Oklahoma in 1935, Isaac Lippincott averred unpragmatically, "there is a clear demarcation between the disciplines engaged in discovery and experiment and those engaged in the applications of the findings."[38] Meanwhile, a 1933 survey of 35 Methodist colleges, largely in the Midwest, found general resistance to progressive proposals for change in liberal education, and, in 1937, Dean Norman Foerster at the State University of Iowa anathematized the "philosophy of education, for which John Dewey and Teachers College are largely responsible" and "in consequence [of which] ... the liberal college is threatened."[39]

By that point, an "absolutist," neo-Aristotelian "counterattack" was arising against "scientific naturalism" and pragmatism,[40] and President Hutchins of the University of Chicago was identified as the leading standard-bearer. Citing Plato, Aristotle, and Thomas Aquinas almost exclusively, Hutchins held in *The Higher Learning in America* (1936) that the central problem of higher education and liberal education was "confusion" and "chaos," stemming fundamentally from an "empirical and experimental and progressive" philosophy "which denies, in effect, that man is a rational animal." In contrast, he prescribed a unified and neo-Thomist vision of intellectual discipline, along with his notorious deduction: "Education implies teaching. Teaching implies knowledge.

---

[36] Abraham Flexner, *Universities, American, English, German* (New York: Oxford University Press, 1930), 15, 10.

[37] Butts, *The College Charts Its Course*, 333.

[38] Isaac Lippincott, "Training the Economist of the Future," in Southwestern Conference on Higher Education, *Higher Education and Society: A Symposium* (Norman, Okla.: University of Oklahoma Press, 1936), 177.

[39] Floyd W. Reeves et al., *The Liberal Arts College, Based Upon Surveys of Thirty-Five Colleges Related to the Methodist Episcopal Church* (Chicago: University of Chicago Press, 1933), see especially ch. 21; Norman Foerster, *The Future of the Liberal College* (New York: Appleton-Century, 1938), 1.

[40] Edward A. Purcell, Jr., *The Crisis of Democratic Theory: Scientific Naturalism and the Problem of Value* (Lexington, Ky.: University of Kentucky Press, 1973), 204; see also ch. 8.

Knowledge is truth. The truth is everywhere the same. Hence education should be everywhere the same."[41]

In 1937, Dewey wrote a critical review of the book; Hutchins responded, and Dewey rejoined.[42] A more extensive, experimentalist critique of Hutchins's book came shortly thereafter from his own university and the pen of Harry Gideonse.[43] By 1938, observers were announcing, "The idealists and the pragmatists have 'squared off' for a fight to the finish."[44] Delighted to see Aristotle and Aquinas embraced by a Protestant president in a Waspish citadel of higher education, a number of Catholic scholars put forth a neo-Thomist interpretation of liberal education. The group included Agatho Zimmer, F.S.C., of Catholic University of America, Samuel Wilson, S.J., of the National Catholic Educational Association, and John Wise, S.J., of Loyola College, Baltimore. But the foremost statement from this quarter was penned by the leading Catholic philosopher in the world, Jacques Maritain, in his Terry Lectures at Yale. Invoking Hutchins's name and criticism of progressive education, Maritain situated liberal education within a neo-Thomist theory of education, and concluded, "With such a philosophy of pragmatism, a great thinker like Professor John Dewey... will naturally lead to a stony positivist or technocratic denial of the objective value of spiritual need." The book of lectures went through six printings over the next 20 years.[45]

In a similar vein, though coming from a different direction, the counterattack continued with statements in 1940 from Mortimer Adler, and in 1941 from President John W. Nason of Swarthmore College, who had more than practicality in mind when observing, "A liberal education is essentially an introduction to intrinsic values and cultural perspectives. It is the purpose of a *liberal*, as contrasted with a *practical* education to

[41] Robert M. Hutchins, *The Higher Learning in America* (New Haven, Conn.: Yale University Press, 1936), 24, 26, 66.

[42] Dewey, "President Hutchins' Proposals to Remake Higher Education"; Hutchins, "Grammar, Rhetoric, and Mr. Dewey"; Dewey, "The Higher Learning in America."

[43] Harry D. Gideonse, *The Higher Learning in a Democracy: A Reply to President Hutchins' Critique of the American University* (New York: Farrar and Rinehart, 1937).

[44] John T. Wahlquist, "The Dilemma of American Education," *Educational Forum* 2 (May 1938): 386. *See also* Butts, *The College Charts Its Course*, 288-329; Abraham F. Citron, "Experimentalism and the Classicism of President Hutchins," *Teachers College Record* 44 (1943).

[45] Jacques Maritain, *Education at the Crossroads* (New Haven, Conn.: Yale University Press, 1943), v, 65n., 115. *See also* Agatho Zimmer, "Changing Concepts of Higher Education in America Since 1700" (Ph.D. diss., Catholic University of America, 1938); Samuel K. Wilson, *The Liberal College in a Democracy* (Washington, D.C.: National Catholic Educational Association, 1946); John E. Wise, *The Nature of the Liberal Arts* (Milwaukee, Wis.: Bruce, 1947).

do just this, and no education which fails...deserves the name *liberal*."[46] The underlying conceptual disagreement here with pragmatism in regard to "intrinsic values and cultural perspectives" became more apparent in a contemporaneous statement sponsored by the American Council of Learned Societies, *Liberal Education Re-examined* (1943), which addressed the role of humanities in liberal education. Whereas pragmatism held that every inquiry for knowledge is value-laden and, for best results, adheres to an experimental method of reflection, these Humanists presented the argument that the understanding of human values, culture, and, indeed, experience, was the special province of one field of inquiry, the humanities.[47] The danger, then, to those on the "value" side of the fact/value distinction, was that pragmatic liberal education would put Humanists and the humanities out of business.

Even commentators attempting to say something nice about pragmatism, about progressive education, or about Dewey, then in his 80s, found ways to dissociate each from liberal education. Mark Van Doren in 1943 averred that progressive education "has hold of a good tradition;...there is nothing in it with which a sensible and humane adult could disagree." But he consigned it to "all those whom education considers before it ascends to become liberal," namely "the students of schools."[48] A decade later, when Theodore Greene, the chair of the committee that had written *Liberal Education Re-examined* (1943), again reconsidered liberal education in a lecture series at a leading graduate school of education, he showered Dewey with praise for "a first-rate philosophical imagination," even asserting that three of the four "fundamental presuppositions, which constitute my frame of reference...I take directly from Dewey." But these three presuppositions were not so much characteristic of Dewey as they were commonplace generalizations phrased in Deweyan terms: "The great complexity and intrinsic value of every human being; his continual interaction with his society and culture; the ubiquity of nature as man's physical base of operations." The fourth principle was the distinctly unpragmatic affirmation of "those depths of ultimate being and ultimate value."[49]

---

[46] Mortimer J. Adler, *How to Read a Book: The Art of Getting a Liberal Education* (New York: Simon and Schuster, 1940); John W. Nason, "The Nature and Content of a Liberal Education," *Association of American Colleges Bulletin* 27 (1941): 53.

[47] Theodore M. Greene, Charles C. Fries, and Henry M. Wriston, *Liberal Education Re-examined: Its Role in a Democracy* [Report for a Committee Appointed by the American Council of Learned Societies] (New York: Harper, 1943), ch. 3.

[48] Mark Van Doren, *Liberal Education* (New York: Henry Holt, 1943), 92, 98.

[49] Theodore M. Greene, *Liberal Education Reconsidered* (Cambridge, Mass.: Harvard University Press, 1953), 4-5, 10.

By the 1950s, those advocating pragmatism, progressivism, or experimentalism appeared resigned to the disjunction of these movements from liberal education, a dissociation that began to seem commonsensical to many, as Harold Taylor observed:

> In the field of contemporary American philosophy there are three main trends which can be distinguished. The first is that of naturalism and instrumentalism, stemming from the work of William James and John Dewey....The second is that of...Greek Philosophy with an emphasis on Aristotle....The third is that of analytic philosophy....[W]hatever significant reforms have occurred [in the schools] were the result of Dewey's ideas....The colleges of liberal arts, with the exception of a half dozen experimental institutions, have been influenced more by the classical humanists and rationalists than by Dewey's philosophy.[50]

Similarly, when John Childs, the author of what Lawrence Cremin called "the clearest restatement of the progressive philosophy,"[51] addressed "Dewey and Education," he referred only to schoolchildren, without mentioning liberal education or even secondary education.[52] Arthur Bestor likewise made no mention of progressive or pragmatic influence in his chapter on liberal education in *Educational Wastelands* (1953), which notably and incisively criticized progressive education.[53]

Meanwhile, the dissociation of pragmatism from liberal education was affirmed by the frequently republished assertion of Yale President A. Whitney Griswold that "instrumentalism" and "pragmatism" were derived from "the Sophists of the fifth century B.C.," whereas "the liberal arts...are expounded in the writings of Plato and Aristotle."[54] Scarcely more charitable than Griswold was philosopher Brand Blanshard, lecturing on liberal education at Swarthmore in 1958:

[50] Taylor, "The Philosophical Foundations of General Education," 23-25. *See also* Karl W. Bigelow, "The Preparation of College Teachers for General Education," in *General Education, Fifty-First Yearbook, Part I, of the National Society for the Study of Education*, ed. Nelson B. Henry (Chicago: University of Chicago Press, 1952), 307; Horace M. Kallen, "John Dewey and the Spirit of Pragmatism," in *John Dewey: Philosopher of Science and Freedom: A Symposium*, ed. Sidney Hook (New York: Dial, 1950), 10.

[51] Lawrence A. Cremin, *The Transformation of the School: Progressivism in American Education, 1876-1957* (New York: Random House, 1961) 333n.

[52] John L. Childs, "John Dewey and Education," in *John Dewey: Philosopher of Science and Freedom: A Symposium*; Childs, *Education and Morals* (New York: Century, 1950).

[53] Arthur Bestor, *Educational Wastelands: The Retreat from Learning in Our Public Schools* [1953] (Urbana, Ill.: University of Illinois Press, 1985), ch. 11.

[54] A. Whitney Griswold, *Liberal Education and the Democratic Ideal and Other Essays*, 2d ed. (New Haven, Conn.: Yale University Press, 1962), 19-20.

"Dewey did much to dispel the dreariness of the little red schoolhouse...; we are all pragmatists from 5 to 10. But I incline to think that a person who is still a pragmatist at 40 is suffering from arrested development."[55] And in a subsequent address on the relation of utility to liberality in "The Uses of a Liberal Education," Blanshard made no reference to pragmatism.[56]

In 1960, a national survey of colleges and universities found that faculty members in arts and sciences departments were moving toward a view that liberal education meant offering "a student an opportunity to prove his intellectual ability by becoming competent in a narrow discipline." In contrast to the heyday of general education and progressive influence, the survey report concluded, "faculties of many departments of the colleges of liberal arts are no longer interested in a *broad* liberal education but rather in specialization in a narrow discipline."[57] In 1965, Lewis Mayhew of Stanford University stated that liberal arts faculties were resisting not only general education, but also "revisions of curricular structure to facilitate the personal development of students, especially their values and their abilities to cope with emotions."[58]

To be sure, the 1960s and 1970s witnessed many reform efforts in undergraduate education, including those "that emphasize ends and purposes that are different from, if not hostile to, the goals of the regnant research universities," such as "communal-expressive" reforms and "activist-radical reforms." Yet those reformers, according to Gerald Grant and David Riesman, apparently gave little or no notice to progressivism or pragmatism, even though these movements were the headwaters of many of the reforms.[59] One prominent advocate of general

[55] Brand Blanshard, "Values: The Polestar of Education," in *The Goals of Higher Education*, ed. Willis D. Weatherford, Jr. (Cambridge, Mass.: Harvard University Press, 1960), 81-82.

[56] Brand Blanshard, "The Uses of a Liberal Education," in *The Uses of a Liberal Education and Other Talks to Students*, ed. Eugene Freeman (La Salle, Ill.: Alcove, 1973).

[57] Paul L. Dressel and Margaret F. Lorimer, *Attitudes of Liberal Arts Faculty Members toward Liberal and Professional Education* (New York: Teachers College, Columbia University, 1960), 37, 54.

[58] Lewis B. Mayhew, "The Liberal Arts and the Changing Structure of Higher Education," *Liberal Education* 51 (1965): 374. *See also* Mayhew, "Destiny of the Liberal Arts College," *Liberal Education* 48 (1962); Mayhew, *The Smaller Liberal Arts College* (New York: Center for Applied Research in Education, 1962); Mayhew and Patrick T. Ford, *Changing the Curriculum* (San Francisco: Jossey-Bass, 1971).

[59] Gerald Grant and David Riesman, *The Perpetual Dream: Reform and Experiment in the American College* (Chicago: University of Chicago Press, 1978), 17, passim. The neglect is made more striking by the fact that Grant and Riesman invoked Dewey sympathetically (15, 16, 21, 36). Invocations of Dewey, progressivism, or pragmatism did appear, however, during this period in Sidney Hook, ed., *The Philosophy of the Curriculum: The Need for General Education* (Buffalo, N.Y.: Prometheus, 1975); Stevens E. Brooks and James E. Althof, eds., *Enriching the Liberal Arts through*

education, Daniel Bell, cited Dewey's ideas sympathetically and offered a quasi-pragmatic definition that "All knowledge...is liberal (that is, it enlarges and liberates the mind) when it is committed to continuing inquiry."[60] However, Bell's attempt at rapprochement between the pragmatist tradition and liberal education "aroused no interest even at his own university," according to Douglas Sloan.[61]

As refulgent pragmatism blossomed in the 1970s and 1980s, its disjunction from liberal education occasionally took on an ironic quality. At a Columbia University symposium on "Liberalism and Liberal Education: Western Perspectives," Charles Frankel offered a paper without citing pragmatism, instrumentalism, or experimentalism, even though the paper was said to exemplify Dewey's thought.[62] And Frankel has been called "one of Dewey's most sympathetic students."[63] Subsequently, a major study of general education programs addressed the "philosophical perspective" of pragmatism in regard to theories of general education. However, this philosophical perspective was defined as having a "practical interest" in making "modest improvements— not...radical restructuring," and Clark Kerr and Riesman were identified as its major proponents.[64] In the 1990s, studies that took as their charge to "discuss knowledge claims recently articulated...and examine their consequences for the undergraduate curriculum" gave no notice to pragmatism or neo-pragmatism.[65] At most, it seems, one might

Experiential Learning (San Francisco: Jossey-Bass, 1979. *See also* Ian Douglass Livingston, "The American Pragmatic Tradition and the Students for a Democratic Society: The Continuity of Thought between John Dewey, C. Wright Mills, and Thomas Hayden, 1900-1962" (unpublished M.A. thesis, Central Washington University, 1992).

[60] Daniel Bell, *The Reforming of General Education: The Columbia College Experience in its National Setting* (New York: Columbia University Press, 1966), 8, 274.

[61] Douglas Sloan, "The Teaching of Ethics in the American Undergraduate Curriculum, 1876-1976," *Teachers College Record* 82 (1980), 246.

[62] David Sidorsky, "Varieties of Liberalism and Liberal Education," *Seminar Reports, Program of General Education in the Humanities, Columbia University* 5 (Spring 1977), 202, 206.

[63] Joe R. Burnett, "Dewey's Educational Thought and His Mature Philosophy," *Educational Theory* 38 (1988), 203. *See also* Charles Frankel, "Intellectual Foundations of Liberalism," *Seminar Reports, Program of General Education in the Humanities, Columbia University* 5 (Fall 1976).

[64] Jerry G. Gaff, *General Education Today: A Critical Analysis of Controversies, Practices, and Reforms* (San Francisco: Jossey-Bass, 1983), 5-6.

[65] Jennifer Grant Haworth and Clifton F. Conrad, "Curricular Transformations: Traditional and Emerging Voices in the Academy," in *Curriculum in Transition: Perspectives on the Undergraduate Experience*, ed. Jennifer Grant Haworth and Clifton F. Conrad (Needham Heights, Mass.: Ginn, 1990), 3. *See also* William G. Tierney, "Cultural Politics and the Curriculum in Post Secondary Education," *Journal of Education* 171 (1989); Frederick S. Weaver, *Liberal Education: Critical Essays on Professions, Pedagogy, and Structure* (New York: Teachers College Press, 1991).

find expressions of regret that the "no longer influential progressive education tradition" could not provide a corrective to the dominant tradition of the liberal arts.[66]

The irony of the disjunction between pragmatism and liberal education is further demonstrated by looking at topics on which we would expect conversations to intersect quite naturally. Given the prominence of the equivalent standing of values and knowledge in Dewey's work, one might expect that his thinking would be addressed amid the recent calls for the teaching of values in liberal education. But such is rarely the case, notwithstanding the fact that the introduction to ethics authored by Dewey and Tufts as well as their approach to teaching values were "to remain standard until the 1950s and 1960s" in U.S. colleges, as Sloan has shown.[67]

Another startling disjunction is the relationship between science and value, which was central to Dewey's thought and which continually arose in discussion of the place of scientific studies in liberal education. On this topic, if any, one would expect to find pragmatism, or experimentalism, intruding. But here too, from the writings in the late 1930s by Hans Zinssner and by Harry Holmes, a chemistry professor at Oberlin College, through a 1945 study funded by the Rockefeller Foundation[68] and in essays by science professors at Rutgers University and the University of Illinois in the 1940s and 1950s, Dewey and pragmatism were not mentioned in discussions on science and liberal education.[69] Pragmatism and Dewey were neglected when the topic was "The Problem of Value in the Age of Science," and even when Dewey wrote on "liberal education" in the *American Scholar*, which described him as the "dean of American philosophers and educators."[70] The foremost

---

[66] Elizabeth Kamarck Minnich, *Transforming Knowledge* (Philadelphia: Temple University Press, 1990), 117-18.

[67] Sloan, "The Teaching of Ethics in the American Undergraduate Curriculum, 1876-1976," 216. *See also* John Dewey and James H. Tufts, *Ethics* (New York, Holt, Rinehart, and Winston, 1908). Recent calls for the teaching of values in liberal education are discussed later in this essay.

[68] Hans Zinssner, "What Is a Liberal Education?" *School and Society* 45 (1937); Harry N. Holmes, "The Contribution of the Physical Sciences," *Association of American Colleges Bulletin* 23 (1937); Fred B. Millett, *The Rebirth of Liberal Education* (New York: Harcourt, Brace, 1945), ch. 1.

[69] Nathan S. Washton, "What Science Course for General Education," *Association of American Colleges Bulletin* 35 (1949); Wayne E. Wantland, "The Role of Science in General Education," *Association of American Colleges Bulletin* 36 (1950). *See also* John H. Randall, Jr., "Which Are the Liberating Arts?" *American Scholar* 13 (1944), 139-45.

[70] Editorial note in *The American Scholar* 33 (1944): 391n. *See also* Schiller Scroggs, "The Problem of Value in the Age of Science," *Association of American Colleges Bulletin* 35 (1949).

exception to this neglect lies in the writings of Joseph Schwab, professor of education and natural sciences at the University of Chicago during the 1950s, 1960s, and 1970s. This is an exception that proves the rule, however. Though associating his concept of scientific inquiry closely with Dewey's "warranted assertibility," Schwab scarcely referred to Dewey in writing on "The Nature of Scientific Knowledge as Related to Liberal Education" and on "What Do Scientists Do?" However, when the topic turned to schools and to the role of the teacher in progressive education, then the term "liberal education" disappeared, the teacher became "she," and the references to Dewey were prominent and numerous.[71]

Finally, it should be observed that not only did the disjunction of pragmatism from liberal education become more pronounced after the 1930s but also that subsequent historiography has gradually wiped away any memory that pragmatism ever influenced liberal education by stimulating dozens of reforms during the 1920s and 1930s, by inspiring and informing the Progressive Education Colleges, and by promoting continuing concern for general education. The historical disjunction thus became a historiographical disjunction of even greater proportion. In the words of David Levine, "Historians have paid little attention to the efforts of those educators who attempted to guide the adjustment of the college curriculum to the modern world without sacrificing their intellectual integrity."[72]

Though not a trained historian, Earl McGrath in 1959 made a significant contribution to this loss of memory. In his capacity as executive officer of the Institute of Higher Education at Teachers College, Columbia University, McGrath wrote a historical essay on the purposes of liberal education that served as the normative statement for an extensive series of reports on liberal education published by the Institute during the 1960s. While citing Alfred North Whitehead, McGrath omitted any reference to pragmatism, progressivism, or progressive colleges, even though he was situated at the very institution that had championed the educational projects associated with these movements.[73] Shortly thereafter, Russell Thomas, professor of humanities at the University of Chicago, wrote a valuable history of the general education movement

[71] Joseph J. Schwab, "The Nature of Scientific Knowledge as Related to Liberal Education," "What Do Scientists Do?" "The 'Impossible' Role of the Teacher in Progressive Education," in Joseph J. Schwab, *Science, Curriculum, and Liberal Education: Selected Essays*, eds. Ian Westbury and Neil J. Wolkof (Chicago: University of Chicago Press, 1978).

[72] David O. Levine, *The American College and the Culture of Aspiration 1915-1940* (Ithaca, N.Y.: Cornell University Press, 1986), 92-93.

[73] Earl J. McGrath, *Liberal Education in the Professions* (New York: Teachers College, Columbia University, 1959), ch. 2.

from 1800 to 1960, in which he succeeded in writing a chapter addressing
"Two Decades of Curricular Reform 1909–1930"—including the experimental and progressive colleges of the time—without making a single reference to pragmatism, pragmatists, or progressive education.[74] Likewise,
the distinguished sociologist Burton Clark in his 1970 study made virtually
no acknowledgment of progressivism or pragmatism in his analysis of the
development of two Progressive Education Colleges, Reed and Antioch.[75]

Among professional historians, Nathan Huggins, in 1976, wrote a brief
essay observing that "the notion...what is useful is good" is one of "three
central features of the American character [that] have given liberal education its peculiar shape in American colleges." Explicating that feature,
Huggins cited the Puritans, Benjamin Franklin, land-grant colleges,
Stuart Sherman, and federal research grants after World War II, but not
pragmatism or pragmatists, although these had usually been included in
similar commentary about the utilitarian "American character."[76] The
following year, Frederick Rudolph's one-volume history of the undergraduate curriculum in America appeared, but included only a passing
reference to the influence of pragmatism and progressivism.[77] Most
recently, the distinguished historian and college president Francis Oakley
published a volume, *Community of Learning: The American College and
the Liberal Arts Tradition*, which reflected a command of the literature
exceeding any other work on the topic. Yet Oakley, too, made no reference
to pragmatism, pragmatists, or progressive education.[78]

Meanwhile, philosopher Eva Brann offered an illuminating historical
interpretation of liberal education that incisively identified three paradoxes characterizing U.S. education, which derive from the nature of the
republic. The first concerned "utility": that Americans treat "learning,
which is naturally an end in itself, as a means." The second concerned
"tradition": that the republic, from its outset, has derogated tradition
even though "insight into origins is essential to a citizen." The third was
"rationality": that the obligation and the need in the republic for citizens
to reason for themselves leads to undermining reason, since all thinking

[74] Russell Thomas, *The Search for a Common Learning: General Education, 1800-1960*
(New York: McGraw-Hill, 1962), ch. 4.
[75] Burton R. Clark, *The Distinctive College: Antioch, Reed, and Swarthmore* (Chicago:
Aldine, 1970), chs. 2, 4.
[76] Nathan I. Huggins, "Aspects of American Character and Liberal Education," *Seminar
Reports, Program of General Education in the Humanities, Columbia University* 5
(Fall 1976), 36.
[77] Frederick Rudolph, *Curriculum: A History of the American Undergraduate Course of
Study Since 1636* (San Francisco: Jossey-Bass, 1977), 275-76.
[78] Francis Oakley, *Community of Learning: The American College and the Liberal Arts
Tradition* (New York: Oxford University Press, 1992).

becomes regarded as subjective opinion. Because the relationships between learning and utility and between subjectivity and thought are prominent topics for pragmatism, which is closely associated with education, democracy, and American culture, one might expect this "classical American philosophy" to be addressed. But Brann did not do so, apart from a few citations of Dewey, whose point of view "is naturally more concerned with the training of children than with higher education."[79]

More recently, the stimulating historical volume by Carnochan expressed a nominalist disavowal of attempting to identify "the abstract ideal" of liberal education. Instead, Carnochan looked for "the purpose of whatever it is, educationally, that we are trying to do," and, quoting Dewey, interpreted purpose in terms of the "*useful*." This approach suggests a pragmatic influence, particularly in this neo-pragmatist era, so it is all the more significant that no reference to pragmatism or progressivism is found in this instructive historical account of twentieth-century liberal education.[80]

Needless to say, this historiographical discussion is not meant to detract from the valuable work of these distinguished scholars who come from a variety of fields, but rather to demonstrate what appears to be a fairly widespread oversight in the historiography of liberal education. Even the handful of exceptions do not appear to address the relationship between pragmatism and liberal education with detachment and cogency. For example, in *The Liberal Arts College: A Chapter in American Cultural History* (1957), George Schmidt distilled the entire twentieth-century discussion into a debate between Robert Hutchins and St. John's College, on one side, and Dewey and the Progressive Education Colleges on the other.[81] A few years later, another rare discussion of "the pragmatist-progressivist" view of liberal education appeared in the concluding four pages of *The Evolving Liberal Arts Curriculum: A Historical Review of Basic Themes*, by Willis Rudy. However, although affirming this view to be historically significant, Rudy made no mention of it throughout the body of the book, and apparently introduced the contrast between "the pragmatist-progressivist and humanist-traditionalist schools of thought" merely as a device to end the book.[82]

[79] Eva T. H. Brann, *Paradoxes of Education in a Republic* (Chicago: University of Chicago Press, 1979), 20-21

[80] W. B. Carnochan, *The Battleground of the Curriculum: Liberal Education and American Experience* (Stanford, Calif.: Stanford University Press, 1993), 6, 115, 23.

[81] Schmidt, *The Liberal Arts College*, 232, chs. 10, 11.

[82] Rudy, *The Evolving Liberal Arts Curriculum*, 129-33. Rudy's assertion that Dewey's philosophy is summed up in a three-page essay on liberal education raises further questions about Rudy's grasp of "the pragmatist-progressivist" view (130-32).

At the opposite pole is an analysis of pragmatism and progressivism that denigrated their influence on liberal education and that appeared in an extensive essay by Laurence Veysey, the eminent historian of the American university. Having been professionally acculturated during the "academic boom" of the 1960s at the crest of the "great elevation of the research-centered ideal in American higher education," Veysey expressed a marked academic elitism: "The bachelor's degree in America has so long been cheapened by the existence of the conventional low-quality fields, and by the similar existence of hundreds of low-quality campuses." In striking contrast to Schmidt and Rudy, Veysey expressly derided pragmatic or progressive influence on undergraduate education. He regarded the "interwar period"—the high tide of progressive influence—as "a long and rather disappointing interregnum....A restless demand for curricular reform, especially in the direction of renewed emphasis upon liberal education, took shape during...these generally dreary decades in the history of American higher education." In keeping with the tone of these remarks, Veysey equated Dewey and progressivism with their least thoughtful proponents:

> The followers of John Dewey...formed a newly visible element reaching a peak of prominence during the 1930s....Courses centering in social and family adjustment and in marriage and the home, indoctrination in John Dewey's liberal civic philosophy, and courses dealing abstractly with the problem of choosing a vocation...were what these reformers put forward....[I]n retrospect the Dewey movement must be judged the least important of the reform crusades. The colleges which it powerfully affected...usually happened to be either girls' schools or else truly obscure, only Antioch was a conspicuous exception. Moreover, the adherents of the Dewey persuasion communicated a tone of belligerent sectarian isolation, offering ritual formulas of low intellectual caliber....Deweyan progressivism...in terms of the wide picture of American higher education...reached...a dead end.[83]

Consequently, while the historiography of liberal education has generally magnified the historical disjunction between pragmatism and liberal education, even the few exceptions to this general pattern

---

[83] Veysey, "Stability and Experiment in the American Undergraduate Curriculum," 8-9, 11-12, 13-17, 18. Writing at the beginning of the 1970s, Veysey may have been reacting against the New Left of the time, which constituted "a cult...far more deeply hostile to the centuries-old tradition of rationality in Western culture than the Dewey movement of the 1930s," 19-20.

demonstrate how difficult it is to provide a balanced and cogent assessment of the relationship between these two movements.[84] Before proceeding to address how and why that disjunction may now be narrowing, it remains to consider the reasons for it.

One explanation may be found in the lag that normally occurs between the introduction of any "new...way of thinking"—to rephrase James—and its institutionalization in the liberal arts curriculum. The incorporation of Aristotle by the medieval universities, the *studia humanitatis* by Renaissance colleges and universities, or the "new science" by colonial and antebellum colleges in America was certainly no more rapid than the century between the coining of the term "pragmatism" and what may be its emerging convergence with liberal education at the present time. A second reason probably lies in the resistance to and criticism of progressive education in the schools. The extent and character of this criticism are subjects of a large scholarly literature, as is the question of whether Dewey's experimentalism was faithfully represented in progressive education and, if it was, whether progressive education was actually institutionalized at more than a few experimental schools.[85] Suffice it to say that if *Life* magazine in 1959 published a warning from the president of the United States that "educators, parents, and students...must be induced to abandon that educational path that, rather blindly, they have been following as a result of John Dewey's teachings," then there probably

[84] One recent book that appears to give due, balanced, historical regard to pragmatism, progressivism, and Dewey concerning the topic of twentieth-century liberal education is that of Charles Wegener, who, however, called his book "not a treatise, a study or a history," although it includes a fair amount of historical analysis. Like Veysey, Wegener is a strong admirer of the disciplined inquiry that he associated with the twentieth-century American university. However, unlike Veysey, Wegener found in Deweyan pragmatism a summative expression of both that inquiry and the spirit of the modern university, which ought, Wegener believed, to characterize liberal education. But it is telling that Wegener's book does not appear to be widely cited in discussion on liberal education or its history (Wegener, *Liberal Education and the Modern University* [Chicago: University of Chicago Press, 1978], vii, 41-42).

[85] This line of recent research is well illustrated by Arthur Zilversmit's judgment that "the educational and philosophical writings of John Dewey...formed the essential core of progressive education," but the essence of progressive education was never widely institutionalized and Dewey's ideas were not fairly or adequately tested (*Changing Schools: Progressive Education Theory and Practice, 1930-1960* [Chicago: University of Chicago Press, 1993], 3, 168, chs. 1, 9).

existed a reservoir of public and political resistance to the adoption of progressive education at U.S. colleges and universities.[86]

A third reason for the disjunction between pragmatism and liberal education is the countervailing criticism of the close relationship that Dewey posited to exist between democracy and science. This relationship was rooted in Dewey's implicit analogy between scientific method and democratic decision making, both of which were said to rely on building a consensus among rational minds attending to evidence and testing their conclusions. What followed from this analogy were two propositions: that science fosters democracy and that democracy encourages science. The former proposition was denied by those on the left, who argued that science fosters reliance on technology and on "experts" seeking to "control" social problems and thereby undermines, rather than fosters, democracy. Less frequently noted was the opposing criticism, often from the right, directed at the second proposition. As Allan Bloom pointed out in his 1967 proto-jeremiad, "The Crisis of Liberal Education": "the launching of Sputnik...resulted in a general belief, probably unjustified, that the United States had fallen behind the Soviet Union in scientific capability. The myth that modern science could flourish only in a democracy was shattered....The alarm...affected the character of the crisis of liberal education in this country.... The easygoing era dominated by the notions of individual 'self-fulfillment' and academic egalitarianism was past."[87] This kind of thinking has been another barrier to the rapprochement of pragmatism and liberal education.

The most significant reason for the disjunction, however, is likely the antiprofessional implications of pragmatism and, in particular, Dewey's radically leveling view of inquiry. This point was discussed earlier as a factor explaining the general academic aversion to pragmatism. But it bears emphasizing here that academics tended to admit or even approve

[86] Quoted in John Patrick Diggins, *The Promise of Pragmatism: Modernism and the Crisis of Knowledge and Authority* (Chicago: University of Chicago Press, 1992), 305. Andrew Feffer offered a nice summary of the pattern: "Conservative educationalists targeted Deweyan relativism and permissiveness during the attacks on progressive education in the 1950s....During the 1960s the direction of attack changed....Writers on the left described Deweyan pragmatism, and particularly Dewey's educational theory, as a thin intellectual veneer over the brute exercise of technocratic corporate power in modern America, reflecting the political and economic authoritarianism ingrained in liberal political culture" (*The Chicago Pragmatists and American Progressivism* [Ithaca, N.Y.: Cornell University Press, 1993], 7-8).

[87] Allan Bloom, "The Crisis of Liberal Education," in *Higher Education and Modern Democracy: The Crisis of the Few and the Many* (Chicago: Rand McNally, 1967), 121.

of Deweyan influence on schools, while denying or dismissing any relevance of pragmatism or experimentalism for liberal education. This position was taken or noted by such varied observers as Van Doren, Taylor, Blanshard, Schwab, and Brann. Indeed, when Dewey's relevance for liberal education has been prominently discussed, as in Arthur Wirth's history of "the vocational-liberal studies controversy in the early twentieth century," the arena of liberal education becomes the schools. Wirth devotes only a few pages to liberal education in colleges or universities.[88] In this regard, it should also be noted that Whitehead, rather than Dewey, increasingly is cited by those who argue against distinguishing between "practical" and "liberal" education or on behalf of the organic and dynamic character of knowledge.[89] Whitehead apparently became the more respectable authority after the decline in the fortunes of pragmatism. When Dewey is cited, as by Schwab or Veysey, the language rapidly shifts from "college" to "school," "professor" to "teacher," "he" to "she," and "liberal arts college" to "girls' school." The implications of this pattern for professional status and authority can scarcely be denied.

[88] Arthur G. Wirth, *Education in the Technological Society: The Vocational-Liberal Studies Controversy in the Early Twentieth Century* (San Francisco: Intext, 1972), 195-96.

[89] *See* Richard Hofstadter and C. DeWitt Hardy, *The Development and Scope of Higher Education in the United States* (New York: Columbia University Press, 1952), ch. 8; McGrath, *Liberal Education in the Professions*, ch. 2; Earl F. Cheit, *The Useful Arts and the Liberal Tradition* (New York: McGraw-Hill, 1975), ch. 1; Jerry G. Gaff, *General Education Today: A Critical Analysis of Controversies, Practices, and Reforms* (San Francisco: Jossey-Bass, 1983), 4, 62. The Wingspread Group on Higher Education, in *An American Imperative: Higher Expectations for Higher Education: An Open Letter to Those Concerned about the American Future* (Racine, Wis.: Johnson Foundation, 1993), also gave prominence to Whitehead, while citing Sidney Hook with reference to "pragmatic liberal education" (19, 165).

7 /

Toward Pragmatic Liberal Education

This essay commenced by reviewing an interpretation of the history of liberal education that identifies two prominent traditions: one emphasizing "reason," the other "speech." This interpretation, it was suggested, relies on a pragmatic historical method that attempts to solve the historiographical problem of entwining descriptive and normative purposes in examining the topic. This method takes the phenomenon of liberal education to mean not an *a priori* conception or purpose, but the use of the term: what people in the past have called "liberal arts" or "liberal education." Based on a review of this use, the method attempts to infer the consequences that attend such use.

With this background, the rise of pragmatism was briefly examined, and a set of six themes was abstracted that appear to characterize the much-debated movement as it was understood in the opening decades of the twentieth century. These themes are (1) that belief and meaning, even truth itself, are fallible and revisable; (2) that an experimental method of inquiry obtains in all science and reflective thought; (3) that belief, meaning, and truth depend on the context and the intersubjective judgment of the community in which they are formed; (4) that experience is the dynamic interaction of organism and environment, resulting in a close interrelationship between thought and action; (5) that the purpose of resolving doubts or solving problems is intrinsic to all thought and inquiry; and (6) that all inquiry and thought are evaluative, and judgments about fact are no different from judgments about value.

The ensuing analysis of the course of pragmatism in twentieth-century America adopted the conventional periodization of an initial flourishing, then a lull or retrenchment, and finally a resurgence. It was emphasized, however, that this conventional periodization is perceived in different ways by different groups of scholars; notably, by philosophers and historians, who have devoted the most attention to the topic.

Hence, the way in which pragmatism is interpreted depends on the context and community within which it is discussed, and this point aids in identifying the reasons that might explain the shifting course of pragmatism over this century. Finally, the turn to pragmatism in recent thought and the rise of neo-pragmatism were discussed, including themes that appear in writings by and about the neo-pragmatists.

The relationship between pragmatism and liberal education was then addressed. Notwithstanding some good reasons to expect that pragmatism would have significantly influenced thinking and practice concerning liberal education, a pattern of disjunction between these two movements appears to have prevailed throughout most of the twentieth century. A period of harmony prevailed during the 1920s and 1930s, when pragmatism stimulated a period of widespread experimentation in the liberal arts as well as the founding or rejuvenation of a small group of what have been called Progressive Education Colleges. In addition, during this period there arose an interest in general education, which was rationalized and justified by the pragmatic idea that all knowing and evaluating depend on context. After the 1930s, however, liberal education again became dissociated, and increasingly so, from pragmatism and progressivism.

Turning to the current situation, I propose that, in this era of resurgent pragmatism, the disjunction is nearing an end: pragmatism and liberal education are converging. By this I mean that pragmatism is exerting an influence on liberal education in a number of ways. The more direct and explicit influence lies in the multiple and varied invocations of, or even protests against, pragmatism, pragmatists, and progressivism by commentators on liberal education.

Philosophical writings from a variety of perspectives exemplify this influence. During the inital resurgence of pragmatism in the 1970s, Stephen Cahn analyzed liberal education in light of a Deweyan conception of the "democratic ideal," while Charles Wegener identified Deweyan pragmatism as a summative expression of both the spirit and the nature of inquiry that ought to prevail in the modern university and in liberal education.[1] As feminist theory developed in the early 1980s, philosopher Jane Roland Martin identified the prevailing view of liberal education with "the now-dominant school of philosophy of education — analytic philosophy of education." Calling for "a New Paradigm for Liberal Education," she assailed the dominant model for its "basic and

---

[1] Steven M. Cahn, *Education and the Democratic Ideal* (Chicago: Nelson-Hall, 1979), chs. 1, 2; Charles Wegener, *Liberal Education and the Modern University* (Chicago: University of Chicago Press, 1978), 41-42.

mistaken assumption that the nature and structure of knowledge determines the nature and structure of a liberal education," and because "it ignores feelings and emotions and other so-called 'non-cognitive' states and processes of mind." Invoking Dewey, Martin then called for "a conception of liberal education as the development of a person" that "integrates thought and action, reason and emotion, education and life," and "does not divorce persons from their social and natural contexts."[2] A decade later, Elizabeth Kamarck Minnich, a professor of philosophy and women's studies, published a prizewinning book in which she observed that "the continuing if no longer very influential progressive education tradition" is allied with "feminist educators" in criticizing the dominant views of the liberal arts, although "feminist educators are attempting to undo the mystifications built even into some progressive views." That undoing included extending the progressive argument that dualisms such as thought/action, mind/body, and leisure/work "derive directly... from old...hierarchies."[3]

The 1992 award-winning book *Undergraduate Education*, by philosopher and university provost Rudolph Weingartner, also demonstrated pragmatic and progressive influence on liberal education through a sympathetic emphasis on practice, populism, heterogeneity, pluralism, localism, and potentiality:

> the philosophy that underlies the *practice* of American undergraduate education is a posteriori and populist....Its logical starting point is the conception of a student as possessing a complex capacity to learn; education is regarded as the process that actualizes this potentiality. Progress is made along a plurality of dimensions and is measured, above all, by what has been added to what existed before....T]here is no single conception of the educated person....If the heterogeneity of the American people makes an a posteriori view of undergraduate education appropriate, the localism of American elementary and secondary education virtually makes it necessary....Thus, if one adds to differing natural endowments the effect of this most variegated system of schooling, uniformity at the undergraduate level would not be achievable either....No shared set of principles exists...that would replace the a posteriori, pluralistic educational philosophy that underlies this discussion of the goals of undergraduate education.[4]

[2] Jane Roland Martin, *Changing the Educational Landscape: Philosophy, Women, and Curriculum* [1984] (New York: Routledge, 1994), 40-47, 172, 173, 179-80, 183.
[3] Elizabeth Kamarck Minnich, *Transforming Knowledge* (Philadelphia: Temple University Press, 1990), 117-18.
[4] Rudolph H. Weingartner, *Undergraduate Education: Goals and Means* (New York: Macmillan, 1992), 7, 5-8, passim.

Explicit evidence of pragmatic influence appeared in other quarters, such as the 1984 conference sponsored by Rollins College, one of the original Progressive Education Colleges, as a sequel to its 1931 conference on "The Curriculum of the Liberal Arts College," which Dewey had chaired.[5] Indeed, Dewey now appears with increasing regularity and prominence in statements about undergraduate education that come from both opponents and proponents. In 1987, Allan Bloom found that the errors of "Dewey's pragmatism" could no longer be ignored, while in 1991, Robert Bellah and his colleagues commended "a rediscovery, conscious or not, of central features in John Dewey's much misunderstood notion of 'progressive education.'"[6] In 1993, philosopher Henry Crimmel published an explicitly "idealist" view of liberal education, while maintaining that "Dewey's...ideal of 'progressive education' is essentially identical with our ideal of liberal education."[7] Thus Dewey's importance for liberal education appears to have grown to such an extent that, while Crimmel argued that "Dewey's ideal coincides with the ideals of Plato and Aristotle, and with the ideal that we have proposed and defended here," others who disavow identifying "a transhistorical value" or "the abstract ideal" of liberal education also quoted Dewey in explaining and justifying their purpose.[8] Meanwhile, out on "the cultural left," as Rorty noted, neo-pragmatism, along with critical theory and various expressions of postmodernism, touched down on liberal education at a 1988 conference on "Liberal Arts Education in the Late Twentieth Century."[9]

Such invocations of, or protests against, pragmatists, pragmatism, or progressivism in regard to liberal education demonstrate the more explicit and straightforward way in which pragmatism and liberal education are converging at the end of the century. But another significant

[5] *The Rollins College Conferences on Progressive Education, 1931 and 1984.* Special Issue of *Liberal Education* 70 (Winter 1984); John Dewey et al., *The Curriculum for the Liberal Arts College: Being the Report of the Curriculum Conference held at Rollins College, January 19-24, John Dewey, Chairman* (Winter Park, Fla.: Rollins College, 1931).

[6] Allan Bloom, *The Closing of the American Mind: How Higher Education Has Failed Democracy and Impoverished the Souls of Today's Students* (New York: Simon and Schuster, 1987) 56; Robert N. Bellah et al., *The Good Society* (New York: Alfred A. Knopf, 1991), 172.

[7] Henry H. Crimmel, *The Liberal Arts College and the Ideal of Liberal Education: The Case for Radical Reform* (Lanham, Md.: University Press of America, 1993), 342, 353.

[8] W. B. Carnochan, *The Battleground of the Curriculum: Liberal Education and American Experience* (Stanford, Calif.: Stanford University Press, 1993), 6, 115, 23.

[9] Richard Rorty, "Two Cheers for the Cultural Left," in *The Politics of Liberal Education,* ed. Darryl J. Gless and Barbara Herrnstein Smith (Durham, N.C.: Duke University Press, 1990). Another recent example of envisioning liberal education from a pragmatist perspective is Charles W. Anderson's *Prescribing the Life of the Mind: An Essay on the Purpose of the University, the Aims of Liberal Education, the Competence of Citizens, and the Cultivation of Practical Reason* (Madison, Wis.: University of Wisconsin Press, 1993).

kind of influence is subtle and indirect, and stems from deep intellectual and cultural roots. Recent developments in liberal education, usually interpreted as responses to demographic, economic, or disciplinary changes, may be construed as "pragmatic" in the sense that such developments are conceptually rooted in pragmatism, or in the sense that they are rationalized or justified in principle by pragmatic conceptions. These demographic and other changes represent challenges to liberal education and demand responses that are justified by some principled rationale, or philosophy, beyond political or economic exigency, a rationale that can legitimate the responses in a basic and fundamental way. This kind of rationale is provided by pragmatism, which has the additional attribute of fitting the historical and cultural context.

The changes that are provoking responses from liberal education include, above all, the phenomenon described by Oakley: "The single most important factor shaping the undergraduate experience in the United States today...is the enormous demographic upheaval of the past 30 years." This upheaval involves "first...unprecedented increases in the numbers of students crowding into colleges and universities....Second,...in terms of their religion, social class, age, gender, race, and ethnicity, the diversity of students today has no historical parallel."[10] A philosophically justifiable response to this upheaval is required, and it is no less true today than early in the twentieth century that "efforts to adjust the college curriculum to the modern world bear [Dewey's] unmistakable imprint," in the words of Levine. This is because "Dewey's philosophy of pragmatism encouraged the incorporation of new subjects for study and new students into American higher education as a means of facilitating individual fulfillment and advancement and ensuring social stability and progress."[11] Pragmatism thus provides a philosophical and historical rationale for the reconstruction of liberal education in light of the current experience whereby diverse perspectives are challenging traditional theories of liberal education.

Another recent change that requires a response justified by some principled rationale is the "cautious vocationalism" expressed by many undergraduates and their parents. This vocationalism derives both from persistent concerns about the strength of the U.S. economy and from expectations of bettering their financial position on the part of many

---

[10] Francis Oakley, *Community of Learning: The American College and the Liberal Arts Tradition* (New York: Oxford University Press, 1992) 106, 107.

[11] David O. Levine, *The American College and the Culture of Aspiration 1915-1940* (Ithaca, N.Y.: Cornell University Press, 1986), 100-101, 102.

students, who are often the first in their families to attend college.[12] As with the demographic upheaval, the effort to make some philosophically grounded accommodation between vocationalism and liberal education leads to pragmatism. This does not mean returning to the British interpretation of pragmatism as emphasizing "crass opportunism" or the "cash value" of truth, criticized earlier. Rather, it means that certain pragmatic conceptions—such as that meaning is determined by practical consequences, that fallible belief must continually be tested against evidence, and that experience involves a close interrelationship between thought and action—contribute to rationalizing and thereby legitimating an accommodation between liberal education and vocationalism.[13] This kind of indirect influence is exemplified by the appeal to cultural "common sense" that is made by the Practical Liberal Arts Education program at Bradford College. In the decade-old Bradford plan, "experience and application are incorporated into the educational process, perhaps more than a 'traditional' liberal arts college would do," and the plan is said to entail "a common-sense approach."[14]

Still another change, frequently neglected in recent reports on higher education, such as the "Wingspread Report," that emphasize the two changes just discussed, is intellectual dissatisfaction with the essentialist, fact/value, theory/practice distinctions that are said to predominate in the academic disciplines. The capacity of pragmatism to explain and justify this dissatisfaction, as well as to respond to the demographic upheaval and to vocationalism, demonstrate the indirect influence of pragmatism on liberal education.

Such indirect influence becomes more significant when recent developments in proposals for the reform of liberal education are considered collectively, rather than individually. These recent developments are usually discussed as separate responses to particular demographic, eco-

[12] Oakley, *Community of Learning*, 5. Such concerns dominate, for example, *An American Imperative: Higher Expectations for Higher Education: An Open Letter to Those Concerned about the American Future* (Racine, Wis.: Johnson Foundation, 1993), by the Wingspread Group on Higher Education.

[13] *See* Stevens E. Brooks and James E. Althof, eds., *Enriching the Liberal Arts through Experiential Learning* (San Francisco: Jossey-Bass, 1979); David Riesman, "Professional Education and Liberal Education: A False Dichotomy," in *Preparation for Life? The Paradox of Education in the Late Twentieth Century*, ed. Joan Burstyn (Philadelphia: Falmer, 1986); Peter T. Marsh, ed., *Contesting the Boundaries of Liberal and Professional Education: The Syracuse Experiment* (Syracuse, N.Y.: Syracuse University Press, 1988); Robert A. Armour and Barbara S. Fuhrmann, eds., *Integrating Liberal Learning and Professional Education* (San Francisco: Jossey-Bass, 1989).

[14] Personal correspondence with Bradford President Joseph Short, March 1995; *see Bradford College* (Bradford, Mass.: Bradford College, 1994), 14.

nomic, or disciplinary changes, and they therefore appear to be unrelated, even disparate. But they may be collectively construed as "pragmatic," either in the sense of being conceptually rooted in pragmatism or in the sense of being rationalized, justified in principle, by pragmatic conceptions. In particular, seven recent developments in liberal education exhibit this collective pattern, which appears to fit pragmatism fairly well. That fit can best be explained as reflecting the influence of the cultural context on those developments during an era of resurgent pragmatism. In other words, pragmatism provides an intellectual and historical framework within which these developments collectively "make sense." It is in this regard that pragmatism is exerting the most widespread and significant influence on liberal education. It might even be said that pragmatism is now infusing liberal education: that pragmatism is pouring over and through the academic dikes that long kept it outside of the liberal arts and that a broad consensus is therefore emerging around a view of liberal education that may be termed "pragmatic."

First among the seven developments is an affirmation of multiculturalism, applying not only to the composition of the student body and faculty but also to the curriculum. Whether the latter implies offering courses or programs addressing a range of cultures (including some that were formerly ignored) or requiring all students to be exposed to different cultures (including some that were formerly excluded), multiculturalism is becoming an article of consensus in discussion of liberal education.[15] This consensus is justified by the pragmatic understanding that belief, meaning, and knowledge depend on perspective and context, as is demonstrated by the fact that "pragmatism has been an inclusive, eclectic, philosophically omnivorous movement in the history of thought," in the words of Robert L. Mulvaney and Philip M. Zeltner.[16] Thus, pragmatism fits the current historical moment when "debate, be it in architecture, literature, painting, photography, criticism, or philosophy, highlights the themes of difference, marginality, otherness, transgression, disruption, and simulation," as Cornel West has observed.[17]

[15] Oakley, *Community of Learning*, 146-48. Richard Bernstein attested to the prominence of the multifaceted and multidimensional topic of multiculturalism in *Dictatorship of Virtue: Multiculturalism and the Battle for America's Future* (New York: Alfred A. Knopf, 1994). Even Dinesh D'Souza, whose *Illiberal Education: The Politics of Race and Sex on Campus* (New York: Free Press, 1991) excoriates "political correctness" in academe, included among his concluding "Three Modest Proposals" that the curriculum should introduce "the basic issues of equality and human difference" and that "non-Western classics belong in this list when they address questions relevant to the subject matter," 254.

[16] Robert J. Mulvaney and Philip M. Zeltner, eds., *Pragmatism: Its Sources and Prospects* (Columbia, S.C.: University of South Carolina Press, 1981), viii.

[17] Cornel West, *The American Evasion of Philosophy: A Genealogy of Pragmatism* (Madison, Wis.: University of Wisconsin Press, 1989), 236.

Second is the new attention being given to values and service in liberal education. In a significant essay, Douglas Sloan has demonstrated how the rise of behaviorism, positivism, analysis, and a pervasive fact/value distinction in academic thought over the first half of the twentieth century meant that by the 1950s, "ethics had become more isolated than ever within the college curriculum." By "the mid-1960s the teaching of ethics was in deep trouble"; few courses were being offered and few students were taking them. Contemporaneous with the resurgence of pragmatism, however: "we are experiencing a rebirth of concern for moral philosophy and the teaching of ethics of an extent and magnitude perhaps unprecedented in modern American education....This renewed attention to the teaching of ethics is manifest at nearly every point in the curriculum."[18] Indeed, a study sponsored by the Society for Values in Higher Education found that "institutions are now willing to accept responsibility, in the curriculum, for helping students to make discriminating moral judgments." And calls for undergraduate education to address "enduring values" and even to require undergraduates to engage in "service" or "philanthropy" can be heard from many sources: the Hastings Center, the Carnegie Foundation for the Advancement of Teaching, the Education Commission of the States, and, most significantly, the National Service Trust Act (1993) and the Corporation for National and Community Service.[19]

The decline and resurgence of an emphasis on values in liberal education are thus correlated with the decline and resurgence of pragmatism. This correlation stems directly from the pragmatic capacity to address,

[18] Douglas Sloan, "The Teaching of Ethics in the American Undergraduate Curriculum, 1876-1976," *Teachers College Record* 82 (1980), 235, 252-53. Derek Bok made a similar point in "On Purposes of Undergraduate Education," *Daedalus* 103 (1974): 171n.

[19] David L. Wee, *On General Education: Guidelines for Reform* (New Haven, Conn.: Society for Values in Higher Education, 1981), 41-42. *See also* Bernard Rosen and Arthur L. Caplan, *Ethics in the Undergraduate Curriculum* (Hastings-on-Hudson, N.Y.: The Hastings Center, 1980); Daniel Callahan and Sissela Bok, eds., *Ethics Teaching in Higher Education* (New York: Plenum, 1980); Derek Bok, "Ethics, the University, and Society," *Harvard Magazine* (May/June 1988); John R. Wilcox and Susan L. Ebbs, *The Leadership Compass: Values and Ethics in Higher Education* (Washington, D.C.: ERIC Clearinghouse on Higher Education, 1992); Bruce Jennings, James Lindemann Nelson, and Erick Parens, *Values on Campus: Ethics and Values Programs in the Undergraduate Program* (Manor, N.Y.: The Hastings Center, 1994). On service or philanthropy, *see*, for example, Ernest L. Boyer, *College: The Undergraduate Experience in America* (New York: Harper and Row, 1987), ch. 13; *Philanthropy in the Undergraduate Curriculum* (special issue of *Liberal Education* 74 (Fall 1988); Thomas Jeavons, *Learning for the Common Good: Liberal Education, Civic Education, and Teaching about Philanthropy* (Washington, D.C.: American Association of Colleges, 1991).

if not to reconcile, the tension between fact and value in an era when "the main problem of modern philosophy" continues to be "that of finding some way of integrating in one conceptual scheme a sound interpretation of natural knowledge and of moral values."[20] As Smith has stated, one of "the reasons for reappraising Pragmatism at the present time" is that "the question of the relation between natural science and human values has been given a sharp and urgent focus."[21]

Linked closely to the attention being given to values and service is a third development in liberal education that suggests the influence of pragmatism: an emphasis on community and citizenship. The link is made explicit in a recent study completed by the Carnegie Foundation for the Advancement of Teaching: "What is needed, we believe, is a larger, more integrative vision of community in higher education.... The goal as we see it...[is] to define with some precision the enduring values that undergird a community of learning."[22] A number of efforts are underway to strengthen these links between values, service, community, and liberal education, including Campus Compact and the Service Learning Program at Rutgers University, which advances "a model that integrates liberal teaching, experiential learning, community service, and citizen education."[23]

This concern for community in liberal education is widespread in academic culture, as is demonstrated in the historical analysis of academic philosophy by Daniel Wilson, who observed that "historians such as David Hollinger, Thomas Bender, and Thomas Haskell, philosophers including Richard Rorty, Hilary Putnam, and Karl-Otto Apel, sociologists such as Magali Sarfatti Larson, and literary critics including Stanley Fish, have placed the notion of community near the center of their analysis of intellectual activity."[24] This scholarship draws from the wellspring of "the pragmatic notions of community and of the communal conceptions of truth and knowledge," including warranted belief

[20] H. S. Thayer, *Meaning and Action: A Critical History of Pragmatism*, 2d ed. (1968) (Indianapolis, Ind.: Hackett, 1981), 454.

[21] John E. Smith, *Purpose and Thought: The Meaning of Pragmatism* (Chicago: University of Chicago Press, 1978), 9. This is not to say, of course, that pragmatism is the only or even predominant form of practical or applied ethics that has appeared during the return of ethics over the past 30 years, prompted, in part, by Stephen Toulmin's *The Place of Reason in Ethics* (Chicago: University of Chicago Press, 1949).

[22] Carnegie Foundation for the Advancement of Teaching, *Campus Life: In Search of Community* (Princeton, N.J.: Carnegie Foundation for the Advancement of Teaching, 1990), 7.

[23] Benjamin R. Barber, *An Aristocracy of Everyone: The Politics of Education and the Future of America* (New York: Oxford University Press, 1992), 260.

[24] Daniel J. Wilson, *Science, Community, and the Transformation of American Philosophy, 1860-1930* (Chicago: University of Chicago Press, 1990), 7-8.

and intersubjective communities of inquiry, as Wilson and R. J. Bernstein have observed.[25] The scholarly emphasis on community, rooted in pragmatic conceptions, is reaching into liberal education, as suggested by Zelda Gamson in 1984, and by Bellah and his colleagues in 1991: "Ultimately the teacher must help the student become a part of a community of interpreters, to use Josiah Royce's phrase, or a community of inquirers, in terms closer to Peirce, which not only carries on the tradition, but constantly amends and expands it in active participation. That is the kind of education that Jane Addams and John Dewey were seeking to embody early in the twentieth century."[26]

A fourth development indicating pragmatic influence on the collective pattern of reform in liberal education is an emphasis on general education. Like the emphasis on community, general education is both historically and conceptually linked to the pragmatic concern with values in liberal education. The historical association between general education and the teaching of ethics was noted by Sloan and revived in the 1980s through efforts such as the Project on General Education Models sponsored by the Society for Values in Higher Education.[27] As discussed earlier, in regard to the origin of the general education movement during the 1920s and 1930s, this historical association with values can be explained by the influence of pragmatism. Arguing against an essentialist view that holds values to be intrinsic, pragmatism maintains that value judgments depend on perspective and context; hence, general education is necessary to understand the context that informs the evaluation. In addition, by maintaining that judgments about fact and value are analogous in their dependence on context and in the method by which they are derived, pragmatism gives equal standing to the formation of values and the search for knowledge. General education, by association with the former, therefore deserves equal rank with specialization, usually associated with the latter. For these reasons, an emphasis on general education would be expected to accompany both an emphasis on values in liberal education and a resurgence of pragmatism.

Consequently, it is not surprising to see that, beginning in the 1970s and continuing into the 1980s and 1990s, "hundreds of individual colleges and universities" have engaged in projects to revitalize general

---

[25] Wilson, *Science, Community, and the Transformation of American Philosophy*, 10. *See also* Richard J. Bernstein, *Philosophical Profiles: Essays in a Pragmatic Mode* (Philadelphia: University of Pennsylvania Press, 1986), 219.

[26] Bellah et al., *The Good Society*, 174. *See* Zelda Gamson et al., *Liberating Education* (San Francisco: Jossey-Bass, 1984), 83.

[27] Sloan, "The Teaching of Ethics in the American Undergraduate Curriculum, 1876-1976," 237-48; Wee, *On General Education: Guidelines for Reform*, passim.

education.[28] The recent advocacy of the departmental major by the Association of American Colleges and Universities (AACU) might appear to be a significant exception, particularly in view of the 1985 AACU report, *Integrity in the College Curriculum*, which severely criticized the major.[29] However, two themes predominate in the AACU advocacy of the major: "educational community" and "integrating education."[30] On the one hand, it is urged that the academic department become the "home" of the student or the "interpretive community" into which the student is inducted.[31] On the other hand, it is advocated that the major become "integrated" and "connected" with other parts of the curriculum and other fields of knowledge. Specialization "must be complemented by deliberately countervailing perspectives, strategies, and experiences" in order to attain a self-critical view.[32] In a similar vein, Boyer has called on departments to "enrich" the major by addressing the larger context of the field.[33] These two themes in the AACU advocacy of the departmental major are among those long associated with general education: enhancing community and providing context. Therefore, this possible exception to the recent emphasis on general education paradoxically confirms the influence of pragmatism on this fourth development in the collective pattern of reforms in liberal education.[34]

[28] Jerry G. Gaff, *General Education Today: A Critical Analysis of Controversies, Practices, and Reforms* (San Francisco: Jossey-Bass, 1983), ix. *See also* Joseph Katz et al., *A New Vitality in General Education: Planning, Teaching, and Supporting Effective Liberal Learning by the Task Group on General Education* (Washington, D.C.: American Association of Colleges, 1988); Jerry G. Gaff, *New Life for the College Curriculum: Assessing Achievements and Furthering Progress in the Reform of General Education* (San Francisco: Jossey-Bass, 1991), 76.

[29] *See The Challenge of Connecting Learning*, vol. 1, from the Project on Liberal Learning, Study-in-Depth, and the Arts and Sciences Major (Washington, D.C.: Association of American Colleges, 1991). Cf. *Integrity in the College Curriculum: A Report to the Academic Community. The Findings and Recommendations of the Project on Redefining the Meaning and Purpose of Baccalaureate Degrees* (Washington, D.C.: Association of American Colleges, 1985), 27-32. Indeed, William Scott Green observed, "To advocate the disciplinary major as the core of liberal education is to flout the conventional wisdom about what is wrong with college learning in the United States" ("The Disciplines of Liberal Learning," in *Strengthening the College Major*, eds. Carol Geary Schneider and William Scott Green [San Francisco: Jossey-Bass, 1993], 101).

[30] Schneider and Green, *Strengthening the College Major*, 5.

[31] *The Challenge of Connecting Learning*, 4; Carol Geary Schneider, "Enculturation or Critical Engagement?" in *Strengthening the College Major*, 52. Elaine P. Maimon, "Unlocking the Doors: From Separate to Connected Knowing," in *Strengthening the College Major*.

[32] Schneider, "Enculturation or Critical Engagement?"p. 52. *see also The Challenge of Connecting Learning*, 14-17.

[33] Boyer, *College: The Undergraduate Experience in America*, ch. 7.

[34] Sheldon Rothblatt would appear skeptical, as am I, of the prospects for departments

The fifth and sixth developments stem from the universality of the experimental method of inquiry, posited by Dewey. The putative universality of, in broad terms, beginning with an experienced doubt or problem, surveying the evidence, making a hypothesis, and testing the hypothesis against the evidence, has been much criticized from the left because of the supposedly technocratic implications of the method; from the right (and, to a lesser extent, from the left) because of Dewey's inference that democratic decision making and scientific thinking are analogous and mutually reinforcing. Notwithstanding the sometimes cacophonous criticism, this egalitarian conception of inquiry supports two developments now gaining widespread support in proposals for reform in liberal education.

On the one hand, the fifth development is the idea that the different levels of the U.S. education system are equally important and engaged in a common enterprise, and that schools and colleges should cooperate closely with each other. This idea, "that we are part of a K-16 continuum" or "a seamless web from pre-kindergarten to post-doctorate" has been promoted by many education leaders, including Frank Newman, president of the Education Commission of the States, and Stanley Katz, president of the American Council of Learned Societies.[35] It is also manifested in the recent, widespread growth of community colleges and of "middle colleges," or high schools, located at community colleges. Against this idea stands the conventional, invidious distinction between "schooling" and "higher" education, rooted in the idea that higher education is qualitatively different from schooling. But Dewey conceived that the same, basic steps of sound inquiry are followed in the elementary school classroom, the library archives, and the scientific laboratory. And it was this conception that led him to view "divisions between higher and lower studies, between theoretical and applied,

enriching, integrating, or connecting the major, inasmuch as the tension between the undergraduate major and general education has long constituted one of the "standing antagonisms" that Rothblatt identified in the state university ("'Standing Antagonisms': The Relationship of Undergraduate to Graduate Education," in *The Future of State Universities*, ed. Leslie W. Koepplin and David Wilson [New Brunswick, N.J.: Rutgers University Press, 1985], 39, 43).

[35] Stanley N. Katz, "Quality and Assessment in Higher Education," draft of an essay prepared for *The Chronicle of Higher Education* (Fall 1994): 4. Katz has sounded a cautionary note about the implications of the metaphor of "a seamless web" (which appeared in the 1993 Report on Achieving National Educational Goals by the National Governors' Association) in S. Katz, "The Scholar-Teacher, the University and Society," unpublished paper presented at the Rutgers Conference on the Politics of Research (New Brunswick, N.J.: 21 October 1994), 6.

between scientific and humanistic, between literary and technological studies" as "devices of convenience at best" and potentially "mischievous."[36] Consequently, "the disjunctions between the different levels of the school system...pained Dewey."[37]

On the other hand, the sixth development, suggesting that pragmatism and liberal education are converging, is the reconceiving of teaching in terms of learning and inquiry. This development has ramifications for both the work of the student and the work of the professor, thereby connecting two seemingly unrelated recent movements. For the work of the professor, this reconceiving implies viewing teaching as a form of learning and inquiry, rather than as the transmission of learning and of the fruits of inquiry. One prominent recent proposal in this regard is Boyer's concept of the "scholarship of teaching."[38] Gerald Graff's noteworthy proposal "to teach the conflicts" also endorses this concept from a somewhat different perspective, in that Graff is proposing to obviate the distinction between what professors teach in their classrooms and what they investigate in their studies.[39] By either approach, the point is for professors to reconceive their teaching as part of their own learning and inquiry, rather than as conveying what they know.

For the work of the student, this reconceiving implies shifting the emphasis in the classroom away from what the faculty member knows

---

[36] Israel Scheffler, *Four Pragmatists: A Critical Introduction to Peirce, James, Mead, and Dewey* (New York: Humanities, 1974) 245. In this regard, it is worth noting that the recent wave of severe criticism directed at the academic profession has likely contributed to the influence of pragmatism on liberal education. The stunning success and maturation of American higher education and the academic profession early in the twentieth century doubtlessly contributed to the disjunction between pragmatism and liberal education, by running counter to the radically leveling implications of Deweyan inquiry and by generally embracing a distinction between theory and practice and between fact and value, which was expressed by Abraham Flexner in 1930 and epitomized in analytic philosophy. Although much of the recent criticism of the universities and the professoriate is venomous and polemical, and the causes and solutions identified for the problems simplistic, it may be providing a check on the self-confidence and autonomy of U.S. professors and stimulating some receptivity to the "antiprofessional tendencies" of pragmatism.

[37] Arthur G. Wirth, *Education in the Technological Society: The Vocational-Liberal Studies Controversy in the Early Twentieth Century* (San Francisco: Intext, 1972), 195. David W. Marcell observed that "Dewey advocated nothing less than making the experimental method the primary lesson of the schools" (*Progress and Pragmatism: James, Dewey, Beard, and the American Idea of Progress* [Westport, Conn.: Greenwood, 1974], 239).

[38] Ernest L. Boyer, *Scholarship Reconsidered: Priorities of the Professoriate* (Princeton, N.J.: Carnegie Foundation for the Advancement of Teaching, 1990), 15-64.

[39] Gerald Graff, *Beyond the Culture Wars: How Teaching the Conflicts Can Revitalize American Education* (New York: W. W. Norton, 1992), 12.

and toward what the student learns, as has been proposed by a great many observers, ranging from Mary Field Belenky to Joseph Katz.[40] Among these proposals, "one of the most interesting, persuasive, and even imaginative educational integrating strategies" is that of "directly introducing undergraduates to research as practiced by faculty in all disciplines."[41] My colleague at the University of Rochester, William Green, has been a thoughtful advocate of this idea, arguing that, "The sharp distinction between teaching and research carries with it a conception of the student as other, as someone whose intellectual life is somehow fundamentally different from, and fundamentally less than, our own."[42] Consequently, the sixth development, like the fifth, stems from the idea that all learning and inquiry follow an experimental pattern. The liberal arts teacher should stimulate and facilitate the student's learning and cannot, in fact, teach in the traditional sense of conveying or informing.[43]

The seventh and final development indicating pragmatic influence on liberal education is to require assessment. To test hypotheses and solutions is a cardinal step in the pragmatic cycle of reflective inquiry. Hence, it is telling that the past decade has witnessed a rising call for assessment in liberal education and, more generally, in all of higher education—assessment of students, assessment of faculty, and assessment of institutions. This call to examine what difference it would practically make to anyone if this rather than that were taught—to paraphrase James—is so loud that it needs no elaboration, although it may require the sage warning of Stanley Katz that mandated standards of assessment mean that "benchmarks could become sledgehammers" leading to the

[40] Mary Field Belenky et al., "Connected Teaching," in *Women's Ways of Knowing: The Development of Self, Voice, and Mind* (New York: Basic Books, 1986); Joseph Katz, *Turning Professors into Teachers: A New Approach to Faculty Development and Student Learning* (Phoenix, Ariz.: Oryx, 1988).

[41] Rothblatt, "'Standing Antagonisms': The Relationship of Undergraduate to Graduate Education," 62.

[42] Green, "The Disciplines of Liberal Learning," 108. I am indebted to Green for discussing this proposal with me, although it is not addressed prominently in the essay cited here.

[43] Note that Peirce maintained a distinction between "institutions of learning" and "institutions of teaching," however distasteful he found it. He observed, "In order that man's whole heart may be in teaching he must be thoroughly imbued with the vital importance and absolute truth of what he has to teach; while in order that he may have any measure of success in learning he must be penetrated with a sense of the unsatisfactoriness of his present condition of knowledge. The two attitudes are almost irreconcilable" (*Collected Papers of Charles Sanders Peirce*, ed. Charles Hartshorne and Paul Weiss (vols. 1-6), with A. Burks (vols. 7-8) [Cambridge, Mass.: Harvard University Press, 1931-58], 5:583).

homogenization of liberal education and diluting the diversity of models that have provided the leaven for undergraduate education over the past century.[44]

In sum, I am proposing that these seven developments are becoming prominent in liberal education, and that they have conceptual and historical roots or find a principled rationale in pragmatism. The seven developments emphasize:

- multiculturalism,
- values and service,
- community and citizenship,
- general education,
- commonality and cooperation between college and other levels of the education system,
- teaching interpreted as learning and inquiry,
- assessment.

To be sure, I do not claim that these seven developments encompass all that goes under the flag of liberal education; nor do I say that they are always found together. I am proposing that sufficient elements of them appear repeatedly and prominently in discussions of liberal education, and that their roots in or justification by pragmatism are strong enough, that it is reasonable to assert that pragmatism and liberal education are converging. The 1993 report of the Wingspread Group provides a prominent example of this convergence.[45]

[44] S. Katz, "Quality and Assessment in Higher Education." The literature on assessment has grown rapidly. *See* Peter Ewell, *Benefits and Costs of Assessment in Higher Education: A Framework for Choicemaking* (Boulder, Colo.: National Center for Higher Education Management Systems, 1991); Alexander W. Astin, *Assessment for Excellence: The Philosophy and Practice of Assessment and Evaluation in Higher Education* (New York: Macmillan, 1991); Dary T. Erwin, *Assessing Student Learning and Development: A Guide to the Principles, Goals, and Methods of Determining College Outcomes* (San Francisco: Jossey-Bass, 1991); Caryn McTighe Musil, ed., *Students at the Center: Feminist Assessment* (Washington, D.C.: Association of American Colleges, 1992).

[45] *An American Imperative: Higher Expectations for Higher Education* opens by employing the conceptual metaphors that gave rise to pragmatism: "Institutions, like organisms, must respond to changes in their environment if they are to survive. Not surprisingly, given higher education's slow adaptation, real problems shadow the real successes of the nation's colleges and universities," 4. The report then calls, first, "for a rigorous liberal education that takes values seriously and acknowledges that value-free education has proven a costly blind alley for society," 7. Second, the report recommends "putting student learning first," which incorporates an emphasis on assessment, 13, 15. The third recommendation is "creating a nation of learners," which means emphasizing the social context of institutions "to align our education enterprise with

In conclusion, I wish to remind readers of the argument in my 1988 FIPSE lecture that discussion in the early and mid-1980s reaffirmed the reemergence of the long-standing oratorical tradition of liberal education[46] in response to the century-old dominance of the philosophical tradition in U.S. higher education. In offering that thesis, I felt quite confident except for one point that now seems enormously significant. Notwithstanding the evident linguistic turn in humanities and social sciences scholarship, I harbored reservations about the emphasis on "the study of language and the textual tradition" that was identified as the first point of consensus, for there appeared to be little more evidence for that point than one might expect to find in any era. Nevertheless, I allowed my reservations in this regard to be overridden by what seemed to be a close fit between the emerging view of liberal education and characteristics of the oratorical tradition.

The significance of these reservations now looms quite large, because there is much overlap between the oratorical tradition and the pragmatic, as previously mentioned. Both maintain that inseverable links exist among evaluation, community, citizenship, and general education. However, the two traditions fundamentally diverge in their respective views that either language or the experimental method is the primary conduit, indeed the source, of knowledge and value.[47] This divergence then leads to other distinctions. Consequently, the chief reservation I had in identifying the oratorical tradition of liberal education in the 1980s corresponded precisely with the fundamental point of its divergence from the pragmatic influence on liberal education. It therefore seems necessary to reconstruct my interpretation and to propose that pragmatism is a better fit for the collective pattern of reform in liberal education that I have outlined.

the personal, civic, and workplace needs of the 21st century," 19. Given the historical course of pragmatism, it is telling that Alfred North Whitehead is named as the exemplar of reconciling "liberal knowledge and practical learning," whereas Sidney Hook is nominated as a representative of "pragmatic liberal learning," 165. Note, however, that the four summative "challenges for higher education" appear redundant and do not correspond precisely with the major points in the body of the report, 23.

[46] I maintained that the reports of the early and mid-1980s addressing undergraduate education most often emphasized these five themes: the study of language and the textual tradition of the culture, the values of students, citizenship and community, the coherence and unity of general education, and teaching. Bruce A. Kimball, "The Historical and Cultural Dimensions of the Recent Reports on Undergraduate Education," *American Journal of Education* 96 (1988), passim.

[47] Thus, in Sandra B. Rosenthal's view, "the model of scientific or experimental method" is "the key to understanding pragmatism" (*Speculative Pragmatism* [Amherst, Mass.: University of Massachusetts Press, 1986], 8).

With all this in mind, I can appreciate the spirit of Rorty's suggestion that "on my view, James and Dewey were not only waiting at the end of the dialectical road which analytic philosophy traveled, but are waiting at the end of the road which, for example, Foucault and Deleuze are currently traveling."[48] However, I am respectfully suggesting that at the end of the road Rorty is traveling are waiting Protagoras, Isocrates and, above all, Cicero—the orators and rhetors who maintained that because language allows and conditions all human interaction and community, human knowledge is shaped by language and cannot be divorced from judgments of value. The questions of what those values are and how they are justified in the absence of a rigorously analytic and logical philosophy remain highly problematic both for the rhetors and for Rorty, as Wolin has noted.[49] But this point only confirms the identity of their destinations.

By the same token, I am proposing here that Peirce, James, and Dewey are waiting at the end of the road on which American liberal education has been traveling during the twentieth century. After a long disjunction, pragmatism and liberal education now appear to be converging. U.S. colleges and universities at the end of the century are thus yielding a view of liberal education that is both new and traditional and that, being rooted in or rationalized by pragmatic conceptions, may be termed "pragmatic."

[48] Richard Rorty, *Consequences of Pragmatism (Essays 1972-1980)* (Minneapolis, Minn.: University of Minnesota Press, 1982), xviii. Cf. Gary Wihl, *The Contingency of Theory: Pragmatism, Expressivism, and Deconstruction* (New Haven, Conn.: Yale University Press, 1994), passim.

[49] Richard Wolin, *The Terms of Cultural Criticism: The Frankfurt School, Existentialism, Poststructuralism* (New York: Columbia University Press, 1992).

Appendix:
A Further Consideration of
Stephen Toulmin

The cardinal tenet of "the received view" of intellectual history that Stephen Toulmin challenged is that "Modernity began with a seventeenth-century commitment to 'rationality'" stemming from "the seventeenth-century rationalists, starting with Descartes." In this way, modern "historians of philosophy and science were...committed to myths about the progressive character of seventeenth-century life and thought which (as they ought to have known in their heart of hearts) falsified the historical record." In response, Toulmin's central claim is that "the contributions of the Renaissance to Modernity" have been neglected, because modernist historiography holds that "[l]acking rational methods," Renaissance Humanists "played fresh variations on medieval themes."[1] Thus Toulmin joins the neo-pragmatists in "dismantling the last timbers of the intellectual scaffolding" of modern philosophy, and his historiographical tactic is "to reappropriate the wisdom of...Renaissance Humanism" in order to balance "the abstract rigor and exactitude of the seventeenth-century 'new philosophy'" that became characteristic of modern philosophy.[2]

Before assessing Toulmin's reappropriation, I should point out that one historiographical tactic significantly ignored by Toulmin and others with similar commitments is to deny that rational method commenced with Descartes or in the seventeenth century. Such a denial would serve to discount even the honor of originating the "modern" viewpoint characterized by a commitment to rational method. This denial would therefore suit those who commonly cite Feyerabend's *Against Method* or Gadamer's *Truth and Method* and stand, with Rorty, "against the very idea of method" and, with R. J. Bernstein, against "the tyranny of

---

[1] Stephen Toulmin, *Cosmopolis: The Hidden Agenda of Modernity* (Chicago: University of Chicago Press, 1990), ix, 80-81, 169.
[2] Toulmin, *Cosmopolis*, 150, xi, x.

Method."[3] Such a denial could be supported by the abundant evidence that reliance on decontextualized, neutral, rational method as a vehicle to attain truth actually stems from the medieval Scholasticism of the thirteenth-century universities. It was the Scholastics who substituted for *modus*, which had prevailed in early medieval Latin, the term *methodus*, which they took from Aristotle along with the syllogism. The Scholastics then employed a supposedly neutral method of deductive reasoning to rationalize the world. To be sure, they appealed to certain authorities for their premises, and Descartes successfully denied the validity of this appeal. But such an appeal, it turned out, was no more invalid than Descartes's introspective identification of first principles. In addition, the denial could be supported by the masterful studies of Neil Gilbert and Walter Ong that pushed back the origins of "method" to an era before Descartes and the seventeenth century.[4] Finally, support may be found in the growing body of scholarship noting the similarities between the arguments of Descartes and the Scholastics. In the words of Peirce, "The University of Paris and that despised scholasticism took Abelard and made him into Descartes."[5]

Again, the merit of this historiographical tactic lies in severing the close association presumed to exist historically between neutral, rational method and modern philosophy. Showing that Scholasticism also embraced neutral, rational method, and embraced it earlier, fundamentally calls into question the absoluteness of modern philosophy. The fact

[3] Paul Feyerabend, *Against Method: Outline of an Anarchistic Theory of Knowledge* (London, England: NLB, 1975); Hans-Georg Gadamer, *Truth and Method*, trans. and eds. Garrett Barden and John Cumming (New York: Seabury, 1975); Richard Rorty, *Philosophy and the Mirror of Nature* (Princeton, N.J.: Princeton University Press, 1979), 358n., 359; Richard J. Bernstein, *Beyond Objectivism and Relativism: Science, Hermeneutics, and Praxis* (Philadelphia: University of Pennsylvania Press, 1983), xi.
[4] That the embrace of neutral, rational method is to be associated as much with the Scholastics as "seventeenth-century rationalists" is evident in Martin Grabmann, *Die Geschichte der scholastischen Methode, nach gedruckten und ungedruckten Quellen,* 2 vols. (Graz, Austria: 1957). Cf. Francis Oakley, *The Medieval Experience: Foundations of Western Cultural Singularity* (Toronto, Canada: University of Toronto Press in association with the Mediaeval Academy of America, 1988). *See also* Neal W. Gilbert, *Renaissance Concepts of Method* (New York: Columbia University Press, 1960); Walter J. Ong, *Ramus Method and the Decay of Dialogue* (Cambridge, Mass.: Harvard University Press, 1958).
[5] Peirce, *Collected Papers*, 5:583; Peirce, "How to Make Our Ideas Clear," in *Collected Papers* 5:406. *See also* Hiram Caton, "Will and Reason in Descartes' Theory of Error," *Journal of Philosophy* 72 (1975); Steven M. Nadler, "Arnauld, Descartes, and Transsubstantiation: Reconciling Cartesian Metaphysics and [the Scholastic doctrine of] Real Presence," *Journal of the History of Ideas* 49 (1988); Tom Sorell, ed., *The Rise of Modern Philosophy: The Tension between the New and Traditional Philosophies from Machiavelli to Leibnitz* (New York: Oxford University Press, 1993).

that Toulmin and others who wish to raise this question do not challenge the seventeenth-century origins of rational method indicates their confinement within the "intellectual scaffolding" that they seek to tear down.[6] While trying to reduce the stature of modern philosophy, these critics accord it too much credit by endorsing the historical account provided by modern philosophy, which attributes to itself the origin of a neutral, rational method.

Nevertheless, Toulmin's reappropriation of "the literary and humanistic phase" of Renaissance Humanism is a promising antidote to historiography enshrining Descartes and the seventeenth century. Toulmin suggested at points that Renaissance Humanism, neglected by modernist historians of philosophy and science, attended to the practical, the concrete, and the particular, and to rhetoric and tolerance, which modern rationality neglected and which the post-1950 world is recovering. These suggestions ultimately led Toulmin to call for "The Recovery of Practical Philosophy"—the return to "the oral...the particular...the local...and the timely."[7]

But something curious happened along the way. Toulmin did not primarily invoke the fourteenth- and fifteenth-century *humanitas*, which "the literary and humanistic phase" of Renaissance Humanism, however uncertainly defined, conventionally brings to mind among leading scholars such as Paul Kristeller.[8] Rather, Toulmin looked primarily to Michel de Montaigne (1533–92) and late Renaissance authors to convey "The Modernity of the Renaissance." Thus he argued that these later figures, exemplified by Montaigne, had as much, perhaps more, of a grasp on critical rationality as did Descartes, and therefore contributed as much to modernity as did "the seventeenth-century rationalists." Indeed, Toulmin suggested that "the opening gambit in the chess game of Modern Philosophy [was], not Descartes' method of systematic doubt, but the skeptical arguments of Montaigne himself," who expressed "a practical concern for human life in its concrete detail," as well as skepticism and tolerance.[9]

Toulmin's reason for choosing Montaigne to exemplify "the literary and humanistic phase" of Renaissance Humanism became apparent when he described "Montaigne's restatement of classical skepticism...with all its anticipations of Wittgenstein" and, conversely,

---

[6] Toulmin, *Cosmopolis*, 30-36.

[7] Toulmin, *Cosmopolis*, 186ff. Toulmin does not address "pragmatism" explicitly.

[8] *See* Paul O. Kristeller, *Renaissance Thought and Its Sources* (New York: Columbia University Press, 1979). Cf. William Kerrigan and Gordon Braden, *The Idea of the Renaissance* (Baltimore, Md.: Johns Hopkins University Press, 1989).

[9] Toulmin, *Cosmopolis*, 22-26, 80-81, x-xi.

how "Wittgenstein presented a skepticism that shared much with that of Montaigne, Pyrrho, and Sextus Empiricus." For Toulmin, "my teacher, Ludwig Wittgenstein," declared the end of epistemology-centered, rationalistic, modern philosophy. Toulmin is looking for a complementary bracket at the beginning of modern philosophy, where the commitment to neutral, rational method supposedly starts.[10] By employing Montaigne to represent Renaissance Humanism and then Wittgenstein to represent Montaigne, Toulmin remained within the tradition of modern philosophy, while claiming to stand outside and overturn it. This paradox of appealing to Renaissance Humanism and then identifying a proto-Wittgensteinian Montaigne as its exemplar is analogous to the paradox of claiming to dispense with the modernist historiography enshrining Descartes while accepting the Cartesian invention of neutral, rational method.

[10] Toulmin, *Cosmopolis*, 42, 190, x, 36.

REFERENCES

Adams, George P., and William P. Montague. 1930. *Contemporary American Philosophy: Personal Statements*. New York: Macmillan.

Adler, Mortimer J. 1940. *How to Read a Book: The Art of Getting a Liberal Education*. New York: Simon and Schuster.

Allen, R. E., trans. 1984. *The Dialogues of Plato*. New Haven, Conn.: Yale University Press.

Anderson, Charles W. 1990. *Pragmatic Liberalism*. Chicago: University of Chicago Press.

Anderson, Charles W. 1993. *Prescribing the Life of the Mind: An Essay on the Purpose of the University, the Aims of Liberal Education, the Competence of Citizens, and the Cultivation of Practical Reason*. Madison, Wis.: University of Wisconsin Press.

Anderson, Margaret L. 1987. "Changing the Curriculum in Higher Education." *Signs: A Journal of Women in Culture and Society* 12: 222–54.

Armour, Robert A., and Barbara S. Fuhrmann, eds. 1989. *Integrating Liberal Learning and Professional Education*. San Francisco: Jossey-Bass.

Association of American Colleges. 1985. *Integrity in the College Curriculum: A Report to the Academic Community, The Findings and Recommendations of the Project on Redefining the Meaning and Purpose of Baccalaureate Degrees*. Washington, D.C.: American Association of Colleges.

Astin, Alexander W. 1991. *Assessment for Excellence: The Philosophy and Practice of Assessment and Evaluation in Higher Education*. New York: Macmillan.

Ayer, A. J. 1936. *Language, Truth, and Logic*. London: Victor Gollancz.

Ayer, A. J. 1968. *The Origins of Pragmatism*. San Francisco: Freeman, Cooper.

Barber, Benjamin R. 1992. *An Aristocracy of Everyone: The Politics of Education and the Future of America*. New York: Oxford University Press.

Bascom, John. 1884. "The Part which the Study of Language Plays in a Liberal Education." *Journal of Proceedings and Addresses of the National Education Association*: 273–81.

Bates, Ernest S. 1934. "John Dewey's Aesthetics." *American Mercury* 33: 252–54.

Belenky, Mary Field et al. 1986. "Connected Teaching." In *Women's Ways of Knowing: The Development of Self, Voice, and Mind*, 214–29. New York: Basic Books.

Bell, Daniel. 1966. *The Reforming of General Education: The Columbia College Experience in its National Setting*. New York: Columbia University Press.

Bellah, Robert N. et al. 1991. *The Good Society*. New York: Alfred A. Knopf.

Bergmann, Gustav. 1961. "Physics and Ontology." *Philosophy of Science* 28: 1–14.

Bernstein, Richard. 1994. *Dictatorship of Virtue: Multiculturalism and the Battle for America's Future*. New York: Alfred A. Knopf.

Bernstein, Richard J., ed. 1960. *John Dewey on Experience, Nature and Freedom*. New York: Liberal Arts Press.

Bernstein, Richard J. 1965. *John Dewey*. Atascadero, Calif.: Ridgeview.

Bernstein, Richard J. 1971. *Praxis and Action: Contemporary Philosophies of Human Activity*. Philadelphia: University of Pennsylvania Press.

Bernstein, Richard J. 1983. *Beyond Objectivism and Relativism: Science, Hermeneutics, and Praxis*. Philadelphia: University of Pennsylvania Press.

Bernstein, Richard J. 1986. "John Dewey on Democracy: The Task Before Us." In *Philosophical Profiles: Essays in a Pragmatic Mode*, 260–72. Philadelphia: University of Pennsylvania Press.

Bernstein, Richard J. 1987. "The Varieties of Pluralism." *American Journal of Education* 95: 509–25.

Bestor, Arthur. [1953] 1985. *Educational Wastelands: The Retreat from Learning in Our Public Schools*. Urbana, Ill.: University of Illinois Press.

Bhattacharya, N. C. 1974. "Demythologizing John Dewey." *Journal of Educational Thought* 8: 117–25.

Bigelow, Karl W. 1952. "The Preparation of College Teachers for General Education." In *General Education, Fifty-First Yearbook, Part 1, of the National Society for the Study of Education*, edited by Nelson B. Henry, 301–28 Chicago: University of Chicago Press.

Blanshard, Brand. 1960. "Values: the Polestar of Education." In *The Goals of Higher Education*, edited by Willis D. Weatherford, Jr., 76–98. Cambridge, Mass.: Harvard University Press.

Blanshard, Brand. 1973. "The Uses of a Liberal Education." In *The Uses of a Liberal Education and Other Talks to Students*, edited by Eugene Freeman, 27–44. La Salle, Ill.: Alcove.

Bloom, Allan. 1967. "The Crisis of Liberal Education." In *Higher Education and Modern Democracy: The Crisis of the Few and the Many*, 129–39. Chicago: Rand McNally.

Bloom, Allan. 1987. *The Closing of the American Mind: How Higher Education Has Failed Democracy and Impoverished the Souls of Today's Students*. New York: Simon and Schuster.

Bok, Derek. 1974. "On Purposes of Undergraduate Education." *Daedalus* 103: 159–72.

Bok, Derek. 1988. "Ethics, the University, and Society." *Harvard Magazine*: 39–50.

Boyer, Ernest L. 1987. *College: The Undergraduate Experience in America*. New York: Harper and Row.

Boyer, Ernest L. 1990. *Scholarship Reconsidered: Priorities of the Professoriate*. Princeton, N. J.: Carnegie Foundation for the Advancement of Teaching.

Boyer, Ernest L., and Arthur Levine. 1981. *A Quest for Common Learning: The Aims of General Education*. Princeton, N. J.: Carnegie Foundation for the Advancement of Teaching.

Bradley, F. H. 1914. *Essays on Truth and Reality*. Oxford: Clarendon.

Bradford College. 1994. Bradford, Mass.: Bradford College.

Brann, Eva T. H. 1979. *Paradoxes of Education in a Republic*. Chicago: University of Chicago Press.

Briggs, Thomas H. 1928. "Interests as Liberal Education." *Teachers College Record* 39: 667–74.

Briggs, Thomas H. 1939. "United States." In *The Meaning of Liberal Education in the Twentieth Century, Educational Yearbook of the International Institute of Teachers College, Columbia University 1939*, edited by I. L. Kandel, 317–29. New York: Teachers College, Columbia University.

Brint, Michael, and William Weaver, eds. 1991. *Pragmatism in Law and Society*. Boulder, Colo.: Westview.

Brodsky, Garry. 1982. "Rorty's Interpretation of Pragmatism." *Transactions of the Charles S. Peirce Society* 18: 311–37.

Brooks, Stevens E., and James E. Althof, eds. 1979. *Enriching the Liberal Arts through Experiential Learning*. San Francisco: Jossey-Bass.

Brubacher, John S., and Willis Rudy. 1976. *Higher Education in Transition: A History of American Colleges and Universities, 1636–1976*, 3d ed. New York: Harper and Row.

Buck, Paul H. et al. 1945. *General Education in a Free Society, Report of the Harvard Committee*. Cambridge, Mass.: Harvard University Press.

Burke, Tom. 1944. *Dewey's New Logic: A Reply to Russell*. Chicago: University of Chicago Press.

Burnett, Joe R. 1988. "Dewey's Educational Thought and His Mature Philosophy." *Educational Theory* 38: 203–11.

Butts, R. Freeman. 1939. *The College Charts Its Course: Historical Conceptions and Current Proposals*. New York: McGraw-Hill.

Cahn, Steven M. 1979. *Education and the Democratic Ideal*. Chicago: Nelson-Hall.

Callahan, Daniel, and Sissela Bok, eds. 1980. *Ethics Teaching in Higher Education*. New York: Plenum.

Carnegie Foundation for the Advancement of Teaching. 1990. *Campus Life: In Search of Community*. Princeton, N. J.: Carnegie Foundation for the Advancement of Teaching.

Carnochan, W. B. 1993. *The Battleground of the Curriculum: Liberal Education and American Experience*. Stanford, Calif.: Stanford University Press.

Caton, Hiram. 1975. "Will and Reason in Descartes' Theory of Error." *Journal of Philosophy* 72: 87–104.

The Challenge of Connecting Learning. 1991. Vol.1 from the Project on Liberal Learning, Study-in-Depth, and the Arts and Sciences Major. Washington, D. C.: Association of American Colleges.

Cheit, Earl F. 1975. *The Useful Arts and the Liberal Tradition*. New York: McGraw-Hill.

Childs, John L. 1950. *Education and Morals*. New York: Century.

Childs, John L. 1950. "John Dewey and Education." In *John Dewey: Philosopher of Science and Freedom: A Symposium*, edited by Sidney Hook, 153–63. New York: Dial.

Cicero, *De Oratore*. 1942. Cambridge, Mass.: Harvard University Press.

Citron, Abraham F. 1943. "Experimentalism and the Classicism of President Hutchins." *Teachers College Record* 44: 544–53.

Clark, Burton R. 1970. *The Distinctive College: Antioch, Reed, and Swarthmore*. Chicago: Aldine.

Cole, Stewart G. 1940. *Liberal Education in a Democracy: A Charter for the American College*. New York: Harper.

Commager, Henry Steele. 1950. *The American Mind: An Interpretation of American Thought and Character Since the 1880s*. New Haven, Conn.: Yale University Press.

Cooke, Maeve. 1994. *Language and Reason: A Study of Habermas's Pragmatics*. Cambridge, Mass.: Massachusetts Institute of Technology Press.

Cotkin, George. 1994. "Middle-Ground Pragmatists: The Popularization of Philosophy in American Culture." *Journal of the History of Ideas* 55: 283–305.

Cottrell, Donald P. 1939. "General Education in Experimental Liberal Arts Colleges." In *General Education in the American College, Part II, The Thirty-Eighth Yearbook of the National Society for the Study of Education*, edited by Guy Montrose Whipple, 193–218. Bloomington, Ill.: Public School Publishing.

Craig, Oscar, J. 1908. "Liberal Education in the Twentieth Century." *Journal and Proceedings of the National Education Association*: 670–75.

Cremin, Lawrence A. 1961. *The Transformation of the School: Progressivism in American Education, 1876–1957*. New York: Random House.

Cremin, Lawrence A. 1971. "Curriculum-Making in the United States." *Teachers College Record* 73: 207–20.

Crimmel, Henry H. 1993. *The Liberal Arts College and the Ideal of Liberal Education: The Case for Radical Reform*. Lanham, Md.: University Press of America.

Dewey, John. 1903. *Studies in Logical Theory*. Chicago: University of Chicago Press.

Dewey, John. 1916. "The Pragmatism of Peirce." *Journal of Philosophy* 13: 709–15.

Dewey, John. 1917. "The Need for a Recovery of Philosophy." In *Creative Intelligence: Essays in the Pragmatic Attitude*, 3–69. New York: Henry Holt.

Dewey, John. 1920. *Reconstruction in Philosophy*. New York: Henry Holt.

Dewey, John. 1922. *Human Nature and Conduct*. New York: Henry Holt.

Dewey, John. 1924. "The Liberal College and Its Enemies." *Independent* 112: 280–82.

Dewey, John. 1924. "The Prospects of the Liberal College." *Independent* 112: 226–27.

Dewey, John. [1925] 1929. *Experience and Nature*, 2d. ed. La Salle, Ill.: Open Court.

Dewey, John. 1929. *The Quest for Certainty: A Study of the Relation of Knowledge and Action*. New York: Minton, Balch.

Dewey, John. [1922] 1931. "The Development of American Pragmatism," published originally in French in 1922. English translation reprinted in *Philosophy and Civilization*, 13–35. New York: Minton, Balch.

Dewey, John. 1931. *Philosophy and Civilization*. New York: Minton, Balch.

Dewey, John. 1931. *The Way Out of Educational Confusion*. Cambridge, Mass.: Harvard University Press.

Dewey, John. [1910] 1933. *How We Think*, 2d ed. New York: Henry Holt.

Dewey, John. 1934. *Art as Experience*. New York: G. P. Putnam's.

Dewey, John. 1937. "The Higher Learning in America." *Social Frontier* 3 March: 167–69.

Dewey, John. 1937. "President Hutchins' Proposals to Remake Higher Education." *Social Frontier* 3 January: 103–4.

Dewey, John. 1938. *Logic: The Theory of Inquiry*. New York: Henry Holt.

Dewey, John. 1939. *Theory of Valuation*, vol. 1, no. 4 in *International Encyclopedia of Unified Science*. Chicago: University of Chicago Press.

Dewey, John. 1944. "The Problem of the Liberal Arts College." *The American Scholar* 33: 391–93.

Dewey, John. [1941] 1946. "Propositions, Warranted Assertibility, and Truth." In *Problems of Men*, 331–53. New York: Philosophical Library.

Dewey, John. [1910] 1954. *Essays in Experimental Logic*. Chicago: University of Chicago Press; New York: Dover.

Dewey, John. [1908] [1916] 1954. "What Pragmatism Means by Practical." [A review of William James, *Pragmatism*] *Journal of Philosophy* 5 (1908): 85–99. Repr. in Dewey, *Essays in Experimental Logic*. Chicago: University of Chicago Press, 1916; New York: Dover, 1954, 303–29.

Dewey, John. [1932] 1960. *Theory of the Moral Life*, Part II in Dewey and James H. Tufts, *Ethics*, rev. ed. New York: Holt, Rinehart, and Winston.

Dewey, John. [1916] 1966. *Democracy and Education: An Introduction to the Philosophy of Education*. New York: Free Press.

Dewey, John. 1969–. *John Dewey: The Early Works, The Middle Works, and The Later Works*, edited by Jo Ann Boydston. Carbondale, Ill.: Southern Illinois University Press.

Dewey, John. [1903] 1969–. "Logical Conditions of a Scientific Treatment of Morality." In *The Middle Works, 1899–1924*, vol. 3, *1903–1906*, 3–39. Carbondale, Ill.: Southern Illinois University Press.

Dewey, John. [1949] 1972. "Foreword" to Philip P. Wiener, *Evolution and the Founders of Pragmatism*. Philadelphia: University of Pennsylvania Press.

Dewey, John et al. 1931. *The Curriculum for the Liberal Arts College: Being the Report of the Curriculum Conference Held at Rollins College, January 19–24, 1931, John Dewey, Chairman*. Winter Park, Fla.: Rollins College.

Dewey, John, and James H. Tufts. 1908. *Ethics*. New York: Holt, Rinehart, and Winston.

Diggins, John Patrick. 1992. *The Promise of Pragmatism: Modernism and the Crisis of Knowledge and Authority*. Chicago: University of Chicago Press.

Dressel, Paul L., and Margaret F. Lorimer. 1960. *Attitudes of Liberal Arts Faculty Members toward Liberal and Professional Education*. New York: Teachers College, Columbia University.

D'Souza, Dinesh. 1991. *Illiberal Education: The Politics of Race and Sex on Campus*. New York: Free Press.

Dummett, Michael. 1994. *Origins of Analytic Philosophy*. Cambridge, Mass.: Harvard University Press.

Erasmus, Desiderius. [1511] 1904. *De Ratione Studii* (ca. 1511), translated in
    Desiderius Erasmus Concerning the Aim and Method of Education, by
    William H. Woodward, 162–78. Cambridge: Cambridge University Press.
Erwin, Dary T. 1991. *Assessing Student Learning and Development: A Guide
    to the Principles, Goals, and Methods of Determining College Outcomes.*
    San Francisco: Jossey-Bass.
Espy, Herbert G. 1929. "The Curriculum of the Liberal Arts College."
    Doctoral dissertation, Harvard Graduate School of Education.
Eurich, Alvin C. 1939. "A Renewed Emphasis upon General Education." In
    *General Education in the American College, Part II, The Thirty-Eighth
    Yearbook of the National Society for the Study of Education*, edited by
    Guy Montrose Whipple, 3–14. Bloomington, Ill.: Public School Publishing.
Evans, D. Luther. 1942. *Essentials of Liberal Education.* Boston: Ginn.
Ewell, Peter. 1991. *Benefits and Costs of Assessment in Higher Education:
    A Framework for Choicemaking.* Boulder, Colo.: National Center for
    Higher Education Management Systems.
Feffer, Andrew. 1993. *The Chicago Pragmatists and American Progressivism.*
    Ithaca, N. Y.: Cornell University Press.
Feyerabend, Paul. 1975. *Against Method: Outline of an Anarchistic Theory
    of Knowledge.* London, England: NLB.
Fisch, Max H., gen. ed. 1951. *Classic American Philosophers: Peirce, James,
    Royce, Santayana, Dewey, Whitehead.* New York: Appleton-Century-Crofts.
Flexner, Abraham. 1909. "The Problem of College Pedagogy." *Atlantic
    Monthly* 103: 838–44.
Flexner, Abraham. 1930. *Universities, American, English, German.* New York:
    Oxford University Press.
Foerster, Norman. 1938. *The Future of the Liberal College.* New York:
    Appleton-Century.
Foster, William T. 1911. *Administration of the College Curriculum.*
    Boston: Houghton Mifflin.
Frankel, Charles. 1976. "Intellectual Foundations of Liberalism." *Seminar
    Reports, Program of General Education in the Humanities, Columbia
    University* 5 Fall: 3–14.
Gadamer, Hans Georg. 1975. *Truth and Method.* Translated and edited
    by Garrett Barden and John Cumming. New York: Seabury.
Gaff, Jerry G. 1983. *General Education Today: A Critical Analysis of
    Controversies, Practices, and Reforms.* San Francisco: Jossey-Bass.
Gaff, Jerry G. 1991. *New Life for the College Curriculum: Assessing
    Achievements and Furthering Progress in the Reform of General Education.*
    San Francisco: Jossey-Bass.
Gamson, Zelda et al. 1984. *Liberating Education.* San Francisco: Jossey-Bass.
Garver, Newton, and Seung-Chong Lee. 1993. *Derrida and Wittgenstein.*
    Philadelphia: Temple University Press.
Gehl, Paul F. 1993. *A Moral Art: Grammar, Society, and Culture in Trecento
    Florence.* Ithaca, N. Y.: Cornell University Press.

Gellner, Ernest. 1975. "The Last Pragmatist: The Philosophy of W. V. Quine."
    Times Literary Supplement 25 July: 23–24.
Gellner, Ernest. 1981. "Pragmatism and the Importance of Being Earnest."
    In *Pragmatism: Its Sources and Prospects,* edited by Robert J. Mulvaney and
    Philip M. Zeltner, 43–65. Columbia, S. C.: University of South Carolina Press.
Gideonse, Harry D. 1937. *The Higher Learning in a Democracy: A Reply to
    President Hutchins' Critique of the American University.* New York:
    Farrar and Rinehart.
Gilbert, Neal W. 1960. *Renaissance Concepts of Method.* New York:
    Columbia University Press.
Gouinlock, James. 1981. "Philosophy and Moral Values: The Pragmatic
    Analysis." In *Pragmatism: Its Sources and Prospects,* edited by Robert J.
    Mulvaney and Philip M. Zeltner, 99–119. Columbia, S. C.: University of
    South Carolina Press.
Gourvish, Terry. 1994. "The Professionals." *History Today* May: 58–60.
Grabmann, Martin. 1957. *Die Geschichte der scholastischen Methode, nach
    gedruckten und ungedruckten Quellen,* 2 vols. Freiburg im Breisgau,
    Germany, 1909–1911; Graz, Austria, 1957.
Graff, Gerald. 1992. *Beyond the Culture Wars: How Teaching the Conflicts
    Can Revitalize American Education.* New York: W. W. Norton.
Grafton, Anthony, and Lisa Jardine. 1986. *From Humanism to the Humanities:
    Education and the Liberal Arts in Fifteenth- and Sixteenth-Century Europe.*
    Cambridge, Mass.: Harvard University Press.
Graham, John T. 1994. *The Pragmatist Philosophy of Life in Ortega y Gasset.*
    Columbia, Mo.: University of Missouri Press.
Grant, Gerald, and David Riesman. 1978. *The Perpetual Dream: Reform and
    Experiment in the American College.* Chicago: University of Chicago Press.
Gray, W. S., ed. 1934. *General Education: Its Nature, Scope, and Essential
    Elements.* Chicago: University of Chicago Press.
Green, Thomas F. 1976. "Liberalism and Liberal Education: The Good Life
    and the Making of the Good Man." *Seminar Reports, Program of General
    Education in the Humanities, Columbia University* 5 Fall: 27–33.
Green, William Scott. 1993. "The Disciplines of Liberal Learning." In
    Strengthening the College Major, edited by Carol Geary Schneider and
    William S. Green, 101–11. San Francisco: Jossey-Bass.
Greene, Theodore M. 1953. *Liberal Education Reconsidered.* Cambridge,
    Mass.: Harvard University Press.
Greene, Theodore M., Charles C. Fries, and Henry M. Wriston. 1943. *Liberal
    Education Re-examined: Its Role in a Democracy.* [Report for a Committee
    Appointed by the American Council of Learned Societies.] New York: Harper.
Griswold, A. Whitney. 1962. *Liberal Education and the Democratic Ideal and
    Other Essays,* 2d ed. New Haven, Conn.: Yale University Press.
Habermas, Jürgen. 1987. *The Philosophical Discourse of Modernity:
    Twelve Lectures,* translated by Frederick Lawrence. Cambridge, Mass.:
    Massachusetts Institute of Technology Press.

Habermas, Jürgen. [1981] 1987. *The Theory of Communicative Action*, vol. 2: *Lifeworld and System: A Critique of Functionalist Reason*. Boston: Beacon.

Haddock, Charlene, ed. 1993. *Feminism and Pragmatism*. Special issue of *Hypatia* 8, no. 2, Spring.

Harding, Sandra. 1986. *The Science Question in Feminism*. Ithaca, N. Y.: Cornell University Press.

Hare, R. M. 1952. *The Language of Morals*. Oxford, England: Clarendon.

Harper, William Rainey. 1905. *The Trend in Higher Education in America*. Chicago: University of Chicago Press.

Haskell, Thomas L. 1984. "Professionalism *versus* Capitalism: R. H. Tawney, Emile Durkheim, and C. S. Peirce on the Disinterestedness of Professional Communities." In *The Authority of Experts*, edited by Thomas L. Haskell. Bloomington, Ind.: Indiana University Press.

Haworth, Jennifer Grant, and Clifton F. Conrad. 1990. "Curricular Transformations: Traditional and Emerging Voices in the Academy." In *Curriculum in Transition: Perspectives on the Undergraduate Experience*, edited by Clifton F. Conrad and Jennifer Grant Haworth, 3–19. Needham Heights, Mass.: Ginn.

Henderson, Algo D. 1944. *Vitalizing Liberal Education: A Study of the Liberal Arts Program*. New York: Harper.

Henderson, Algo D., and Dorothy Hall. 1946. *Antioch College: Its Design for Liberal Education*. New York: Harper.

Higher Education for American Democracy, Report of the President's Commission on Higher Education, vol. 1, *Establishing the Goals*. 1947. Washington, D. C.: U. S. Government Printing Office.

Hirst, Paul H. 1965. "Liberal Education and the Nature of Knowledge." In *Philosophical Analysis and Education*, edited by Reginald D. Archambault, 113–38. London: Routledge and Kegan Paul.

Hobhouse, Leonard T. 1909. "Faith and the Will to Believe." *Proceedings of the Aristotelian Society* 4: 91–109.

Hofstadter, Richard, and C. DeWitt Hardy. 1952. *The Development and Scope of Higher Education in the United States*. New York: Columbia University Press.

Hollinger, David A. 1980. "The Problem of Pragmatism in American History." *Journal of American History* 67: 88–107.

Holmes-Pollock Letters: The Correspondence of Mr. Justice Holmes and Sir Frederick Pollock, 1874–1932. 1941. Edited by Mark DeWolfe Howe, 2 vols. Cambridge, Mass.: Harvard University Press.

Holmes, Harry N. 1937. "The Contribution of the Physical Sciences." *Association of American Colleges Bulletin* 23: 67–71.

Hook, Sidney. 1927. *The Metaphysics of Pragmatism*. Chicago: Open Court.

Hook, Sidney. 1940. "The New Medievalism." *New Republic* 103 (28 October): 602–6.

Hook, Sidney. 1944. "Thirteen Arrows Against Progressive Liberal Education." *The Humanist* 4 (Spring): 1–10.

Hook, Sidney, ed. 1950. *John Dewey: Philosopher of Science and Freedom: A Symposium*. New York: Dial.

Hook, Sidney, ed. 1975. *The Philosophy of the Curriculum: The Need for General Education.* Buffalo, N. Y.: Prometheus.

Horkheimer, Max. [1947] 1974. *Eclipse of Reason.* New York: Seabury.

Huggins, Nathan I. 1976. "Aspects of American Character and Liberal Education." *Seminar Reports, Program of General Education in the Humanities, Columbia University* 5 (Fall): 36–42.

Hutchins, Robert M. 1936. *The Higher Learning in America.* New Haven, Conn.: Yale University Press.

Hutchins, Robert M. 1937. "Grammar, Rhetoric, and Mr. Dewey." *Social Frontier* 3 (February): 137–39.

"The Ideal of a Liberal Education: A Gift for Graduation." 1930. *Journal of the National Education Association* 19: 164.

Integrity in the College Curriculum: A Report to the Academic Community. The Findings and Recommendations of the Project on Redefining the Meaning and Purpose of Baccalaureate Degrees. 1985. Washington, D. C.: Association of American Colleges.

Isenberg, Arnold. [1932] 1960. "Editor's Foreword." In John Dewey, *Theory of the Moral Life.* New York: Holt, Rinehart, and Winston.

Isocrates, *Antidosis.* 1928. New York: G. P. Putnam's.

Jacobson, David. 1993. *Emerson's Pragmatic Vision: The Dance of the Eye.* University Park, Pa.: Pennsylvania State University Press. #123

Jaeger, Werner. 1939–1944. *Paideia: The Ideals of Greek Culture,* translated by Gilbert Highet, 2d ed., 3 vols. Oxford: Basil Blackwell.

James, William. 1890. *The Principles of Psychology,* 2 vols. New York: Henry Holt.

James, William. 1909. *The Meaning of Truth: A Sequel to "Pragmatism."* New York: Longmans, Green.

James, William. 1912. *Essays in Radical Empiricism.* New York: Longmans, Green.

James, William. 1920. *Collected Essays and Reviews,* edited by Ralph Barton Perry. New York: Longmans, Green.

James, William. [1898] 1920. "Philosophical Conceptions and Practical Results." Published in *University of California Chronicle.* Reprinted in *Collected Essays and Reviews,* edited by Ralph Barton Perry, 406–37. New York: Longmans, Green.

James, William. [1907] 1925. *Pragmatism: A New Name for Some Old Ways of Thinking.* New York: Longmans, Green.

James, William. 1975–. *The Works of William James,* ed. Frederick H. Burkhardt. Cambridge, Mass.: Harvard University Press.

James, William. [1910] 1975–. *Some Problems of Philosophy: A Beginning of an Introduction to Philosophy* [incomplete in 1910]. Ed. Frederick H. Burkhardt et al. In *The Works of William James,* ed. Frederick H. Burkhardt. Cambridge, Mass.: Harvard University Press.

James, William. 1975–. *Essays, Comments, and Reviews,* ed. Frederick H. Burkhardt et al. In *The Works of William James,* ed. F. H. Burkhardt. Cambridge, Mass.: Harvard University Press.

Jeavons, Thomas. 1991. *Learning for the Common Good: Liberal Education, Civic Education, and Teaching about Philanthropy.* Washington, D. C.: American Association of Colleges.

Jencks, Christopher, and David Riesman. 1968. *The Academic Revolution.* Garden City, N. Y.: Doubleday.

Jennings, Bruce, James Lindemann Nelson, and Erick Parens. 1994. *Values on Campus: Ethics and Values Programs in the Undergraduate Program.* Manor, N. Y.: The Hastings Center.

John of Salisbury. 1955. *The Metalogicon of John of Salisbury, A Twelfth-Century Defense of the Verbal and Logical Arts of the Trivium.* Translated by Daniel D. McGarry. Berkeley, Calif.: University of California Press.

Kallen, Horace M. 1950. "John Dewey and the Spirit of Pragmatism." In *John Dewey: Philosopher of Science and Freedom: A Symposium,* edited by Sidney Hook, 3–46. New York: Dial.

Katz, Joseph. 1988. *Turning Professors into Teachers: A New Approach to Faculty Development and Student Learning.* Phoenix, Ariz.: Oryx.

Katz, Joseph et al. 1988. *A New Vitality in General Education: Planning, Teaching, and Supporting Effective Liberal Learning by the Task Group on General Education.* Washington, D. C.: American Association of Colleges.

Katz, Stanley N. 1994. "Quality and Assessment in Higher Education." Draft of an essay prepared for *The Chronicle of Higher Education* (Fall).

Katz, Stanley N. 1994. "The Scholar-Teacher, The University and Society." Paper presented at the Rutgers Conference on the Politics of Research, New Brunswick, N. J. 21 October.

Keller, Evelyn Fox. 1985. *Reflections on Gender and Science.* New Haven, Conn.: Yale University Press.

Kerrigan, William, and Gordon Braden. 1989. *The Idea of the Renaissance.* Baltimore, Md.: Johns Hopkins University Press.

Kimball, Bruce A. 1988. "The Historical and Cultural Dimensions of the Recent Reports on Undergraduate Education." *American Journal of Education* 96: 293–322.

Kimball, Bruce A. 1992. *The "True Professional Ideal" in America: A History.* Oxford, England: Basil Blackwell.

Kimball, Bruce A. 1995. *Orators and Philosophers: A History of the Idea of Liberal Education,* expanded ed. New York: College Entrance Examination Board.

Kloppenberg, James T. 1986. *Uncertain Victory: Social Democracy and Progressivism in European and American Thought, 1870–1920.* New York: Oxford University Press.

Kolenda, Konstanin. 1990. *Rorty's Humanistic Pragmatism: Philosophy Democratized.* Tampa, Fla.: University of South Florida Press.

Kristeller, Paul O. 1979. *Renaissance Thought and Its Sources.* New York: Columbia University Press.

Kuhn, Thomas S. [1962] 1970. *The Structure of Scientific Revolutions.* Enlarged edition. (Chicago: University of Chicago Press.)

Kuklick, Bruce. 1985. *Churchmen and Philosophers: From Jonathan Edwards to John Dewey*. New Haven, Conn.: Yale University Press.

Lasch, Christopher. 1990. Personal correspondence with the author, 20 July.

Leigh, Robert D. 1928. "Newer Aspects of College Education." *Progressive Education* 5: 255–60.

Levine, David O. 1986. *The American College and the Culture of Aspiration 1915–1940*. Ithaca, N. Y.: Cornell University Press.

Lewis, Clarence I. 1929. *Mind and the World Order: Outline of a Theory of Knowledge*. New York: Charles Scribner's Sons.

Lewis, Clarence I. 1970. *Collected Papers*, edited by John D. Goheen and John L. Mothershead, Jr. Stanford, Calif.: Stanford University Press.

Lewis, Hal G. 1943. "Meiklejohn and Experimentalism." *Teachers College Record* 44: 563–71.

Lippincott, Isaac. 1936. "Training the Economist of the Future." In Southwestern Conference on Higher Education, *Higher Education and Society: a Symposium*, 175–80. Norman, Okla.: University of Oklahoma Press.

Livingston, Ian Douglass. 1992. "The American Pragmatic Tradition and the Students for a Democratic Society: the Continuity of Thought between John Dewey, C. Wright Mills, and Thomas Hayden, 1900–1962." Unpublished M.A. Thesis, Central Washington University.

McGrath, Earl J. 1959. *Liberal Education in the Professions*. New York: Teachers College, Columbia University.

McHale, Kathryn. 1932. "Introduction." In McHale, Kathryn et al., *Changes and Experiments in Liberal-Arts Education, Part II, The Thirty-First Yearbook of the National Society for the Study of Education*, 1–8. Bloomington, Ill.: Public School Publishing.

Maimon, Elaine P. 1993. "Unlocking the Doors: From Separate to Connected Knowing." In *Strengthening the College Major*, edited by Carol Geary Schneider and William S. Green, 89–100. San Francisco: Jossey-Bass.

Makin, Bathsua Pell. 1985. "An Essay to Revive the Antient Education of Gentlewomen." In *First Feminists, British Women Writers, 1578–1799*, edited by Moira Ferguson. Bloomington, Ind.: Indiana University Press.

Marcell, David W. 1974. *Progress and Pragmatism: James, Dewey, Beard, and the American Idea of Progress*. Westport, Conn.: Greenwood Press.

Maritain, Jacques. 1943. *Education at the Crossroads*. New Haven, Conn.: Yale University Press.

Marsh, Peter T., ed. 1988. *Contesting the Boundaries of Liberal and Professional Education: The Syracuse Experiment*. Syracuse, N. Y.: Syracuse University Press.

Martin, Jane Roland. [1981] 1994. "Needed: A New Paradigm for Liberal Education." In *Changing the Educational Landscape: Philosophy, Women, and Curriculum*, 171–86. New York: Routledge.

Mayhew, Lewis B. 1962. "Destiny of the Liberal Arts College." *Liberal Education* 48: 408–16.

Mayhew, Lewis B. 1962. *The Smaller Liberal Arts College*. New York: Center for Applied Research in Education.

Mayhew, Lewis B. 1965. "The Liberal Arts and the Changing Sructure of Higher Education." *Liberal Education* 51: 366–78.

Mayhew, Lewis B., and Patrick T. Ford. 1971. *Changing the Curriculum*. San Francisco: Jossey-Bass.

Mead, George Herbert. 1964. *Selected Writings*, edited by Andrew J. Reck. New York: Bobbs-Merrill.

Meiklejohn, Alexander. 1920. *The Liberal College*. Boston: Marshall Jones.

Meiklejohn, Alexander. 1932. *The Experimental College*. New York: Harper.

Meiklejohn, Alexander. 1944. "Required Education for Freedom." *American Scholar* 33: 393–95.

Millett, Fred B. 1945. *The Rebirth of Liberal Education*. New York: Harcourt, Brace.

Mills, C. Wright. 1963. "The Social Role of the Intellectual." In *Power, Politics, and People, The Collected Essays of C. Wright Mills*, edited by Irving L. Horowitz, 292–304. New York: Oxford University Press.

Mills, C. Wright. 1964. *Sociology and Pragmatism: The Higher Learning in America*, edited by Irving L. Horowitz. New York: Oxford University Press.

Minnich, Elizabeth Kamarck. 1990. *Transforming Knowledge*. Philadelphia: Temple University Press.

Moore, G. E. 1922. *Philosophical Studies*. London: Routledge & Kegan Paul.

Mulvaney, Robert J., and Philip M. Zeltner, eds. 1981. *Pragmatism: Its Sources and Prospects*. Columbia, S. C.: University of South Carolina Press.

Murphey, Murray G. [1961] 1993. *The Development of Peirce's Philosophy*. Indianapolis, Ind.: Hackett.

Musil, Caryn McTighe, ed. 1992. *Students at the Center: Feminist Assessment*. Washington, D. C.: Association of American Colleges.

Nadler, Steven M. 1988. "Arnauld, Descartes, and Transsubstantiation: Reconciling Cartesian Metaphysics and [the Scholastic doctrine of] Real Presence." *Journal of the History of Ideas* 49: 229–46.

Nagel, Ernest. 1950. "Dewey's Theory of Natural Science." In *John Dewey: Philosopher of Science and Freedom, A Symposium*, edited by Sidney Hook, 231–48. Westport, Conn.: Greenwood Press.

Nason, John W. 1941. "The Nature and Content of a Liberal Education." *Association of American Colleges Bulletin* 27: 53–61.

Oakley, Francis. 1988. *The Medieval Experience: Foundations of Western Cultural Singularity*. Toronto, Canada: University of Toronto Press in association with the Mediaeval Academy of America.

Oakley, Francis. 1992. *Community of Learning: The American College and the Liberal Arts Tradition*. New York: Oxford University Press.

Okrent, Mark. 1988. *Heidegger's Pragmatism: Understanding, Being, and the Critique of Metaphysics*. Ithaca, N. Y.: Cornell University Press.

O'Neil, Robert M. 1992. "Liberal Thoughts on *Illiberal Education*." *Review of Higher Education* 15: 463–71.

Ong, Walter J. 1958. *Ramus, Method, and the Decay of Dialogue*. Cambridge, Mass.: Harvard University Press.

Passmore, John. 1964. "Philosophical Scholarship in the United States, 1930–1960." In *Philosophy*, by Roderick M. Chisolm et al., 1–24. Englewood Cliffs, N. J.: Prentice-Hall.

Peirce, Charles S. 1877. "The Fixation of Belief." *Popular Science Monthly* 12: 1–15. In *Collected Papers*, v. 5: 358–87.

Peirce, Charles S. 1878. "How to Make Our Ideas Clear." *Popular Science Monthly* 12: 286–302. In *Collected Papers* v. 5: 388–410.

Peirce, Charles S. 1893. "Evolutionary Love." *The Monist*: 176–200. In *Collected Papers* v. 6: 287–317.

Peirce, Charles S. [1899] 1900. "[Review of] Clark University, 1889–1899: Decennial Celebration. Worcester, Mass.: Clark University, 1899." In *Science* n.s. 11 (20 April): 620–22.

Peirce, Charles S. 1905. "What Pragmatism Is." *The Monist* 15: 161–81. In *Collected Papers* v. 5: 411–37.

Peirce, Charles S. 1931–58. *Collected Papers of Charles Sanders Peirce*, edited by Charles Hartshorne and Paul Weiss (vols. 1–6), with A. Burks (vols. 7–8). Cambridge, Mass.: Harvard University Press.

Peirce, Charles S. 1982–. *Writings of Charles S. Peirce: A Chronological Edition*, edited by Max H. Fisch et al. Bloomington, Ind.: Indiana University Press.

Peirce, Charles S. [1898] 1992. *Reasoning and the Logic of Things, The Cambridge Conferences Lectures of 1898*, edited by Kenneth L. Ketner. Cambridge, Mass.: Harvard University Press.

Peirce, Charles S. Unpublished. "The Kernel of Pragmatism." In *Collected Papers*, v. 5: 464–68.

Perry, Ralph Barton. 1915. "A Defence of Liberal Education." *Forum* 53: 213–22.

Philanthropy in the Undergraduate Curriculum. 1988. Special issue of *Liberal Education* 74 (Fall).

Plato. 1968. *The Republic*. Translated by Allan Bloom. New York: Basic Books.

Purcell, Jr., Edward A. 1973. *The Crisis of Democratic Theory: Scientific Naturalism and the Problem of Value*. Lexington, Ky.: University of Kentucky Press.

Quine, William Van Orman. [1951] 1953. "Two Dogmas of Empiricism." In *From a Logical Point of View*, 20–46. Cambridge, Mass.: Harvard University Press.

Quine, William Van Orman. 1969. "Epistemology Naturalized." In *Ontological Relativity and Other Essays*, 69–90. New York: Columbia University Press.

Quine, William Van Orman. 1981. "Pragmatists' Place in Empiricism." In *Pragmatism: Its Sources and Prospects*, edited by Robert J. Mulvaney and Philip M. Zeltner, 21–39. Columbia, S. C.: University of South Carolina Press.

Rajna, Pio. 1928. "Le denominazioni *Trivium* e *Quadrivium*." *Studi Medievali* 1: 4–36.

Randall, John H., Jr. 1944. "Which Are the Liberating Arts?" *American Scholar* 13: 135–148.

Reeves, Floyd W. et al. 1933. *The Liberal Arts College, Based Upon Surveys of Thirty-Five Colleges Related to the Methodist Episcopal Church*. Chicago: University of Chicago Press.

Riesman, David. 1986. "Professional Education and Liberal Education: A False Dichotomy." In *Preparation for Life? The Paradox of Education in the Late Twentieth Century*, edited by Joan Burstyn, 35–57. Philadelphia: Falmer Press.

de Rijk, Lambert. 1965. "*Enkuklios Paideia*: A Study of Its Original Meaning." *Vivarium* 3: 24–93.

Robinson, David M. 1993. *Emerson and the Conduct of Life: Pragmatism and Ethical Purpose in the Later Work*. Cambridge: Cambridge University Press.

Robinson, Richard. 1953. *Plato's Earlier Dialectic*, 2d ed. Oxford, England: Clarendon.

The Rollins College Conferences on Progressive Education, 1931 and 1984. 1984. Special issue of *Liberal Education* 70 (Winter).

Rorty, Richard. 1961. "Pragmatism, Categories, and Language." *Philosophical Review* 70: 197–230.

Rorty, Richard, ed. 1967. *The Linguistic Turn: Recent Essays in Philosophical Method*. Chicago: University of Chicago Press.

Rorty, Richard. 1979. *Philosophy and the Mirror of Nature*. Princeton, N. J.: Princeton University Press.

Rorty, Richard. 1982. *Consequences of Pragmatism (Essays 1972–1980)*. Minneapolis, Minn.: University of Minnesota Press.

Rorty, Richard. 1982. "Pragmatism, Relativism, and Irrationalism." In *Consequences of Pragmatism (Essays 1972–1980)*, 160–75. Minneapolis, Minn.: University of Minnesota Press.

Rorty, Richard. 1985. "Comments on Sleeper and Edel." *Transactions of the Charles S. Peirce Society* 21: 39–48.

Rorty, Richard. 1989. *Contingency, Irony, and Solidarity*. Cambridge, England: Cambridge University Press.

Rorty, Richard. 1990. "Two Cheers for the Cultural Left." In *The Politics of Liberal Education*, edited by Darryl J. Gless and Barbara Herrnstein Smith, 222–33. Durham, N. C.: Duke University Press.

Rosen, Bernard, and Arthur L. Caplan. 1980. *Ethics in the Undergraduate Curriculum*. Hastings-on-Hudson, N. Y.: The Hastings Center.

Rosenthal, Sandra B. 1981. "John Dewey: Scientific Method and Lived Immediacy." *Transactions of the Charles S. Peirce Society* 17: 358–68.

Rosenthal, Sandra B. 1984. "Pragmatism and Scientific Method: A Revisit." *Southwest Philosophy Review* 1: 5–29.

Rosenthal, Sandra B. 1986. *Speculative Pragmatism*. Amherst, Mass.: University of Massachusetts Press. Paperback edition 1990, Peru, Ill.: Open Court.

Rothblatt, Sheldon. 1985. "'Standing Antagonisms': The Relationship of Undergraduate to Graduate Education." In *The Future of State Universities*, edited by Leslie W. Koepplin and David Wilson, 39–66. New Brunswick, N. J.: Rutgers University Press.

Rudolph, Frederick, ed. 1965. *Essays on Education in the Early Republic*. Cambridge, Mass.: Harvard University Press.

Rudolph, Frederick. 1977. *Curriculum: A History of the American Undergraduate Course of Study Since 1636*. San Francisco: Jossey-Bass.

Rudy, Willis. 1960. *The Evolving Liberal Arts Curriculum: A Historical Review of Basic Themes*. New York: Teachers College, Columbia University.

Russell, Bertrand. 1910. *Philosophical Essays*. London: Longmans, Green.

Russell, Bertrand. 1938. *An Inquiry into Meaning and Truth*. New York: W. W. Norton.

Russell, Bertrand. 1944. "Dewey's New Logic." In *The Philosophy of John Dewey*, edited by P. A. Schilpp, 135–56. Chicago: Northwestern University Press.

Scheffler, Israel. 1974. *Four Pragmatists: A Critical Introduction to Peirce, James, Mead, and Dewey*. New York: Humanities.

Schmidt, George P. 1957. *The Liberal Arts College: A Chapter in American Cultural History*. New Brunswick, N. J.: Rutgers University Press.

Schneider, Carol Geary. 1993. "Enculturation or Critical Engagement?" In *Strengthening the College Major*, edited by Carol Geary Schneider and William Scott Green, 43–54. San Francisco: Jossey-Bass.

Schneider, Carol Geary, and William Scott Green, eds. 1993. *Strengthening the College Major*. San Francisco: Jossey-Bass.

Schwab, Joseph J. 1978. *Science, Curriculum, and Liberal Education: Selected Essays*, edited by Ian Westbury and Neil J. Wolkof. Chicago: University of Chicago Press.

Scroggs, Schiller. 1949. "The Problem of Value in the Age of Science." *Association of American Colleges Bulletin* 35: 519–25.

Searle, John. 1990. "The Storm Over the University." *New York Review of Books* (6 December): 34–39, 42.

Short, Joseph. Personal correspondence, March 1995.

Sidorsky, David. 1977. "Varieties of Liberalism and Liberal Education." *Seminar Reports, Program of General Education in the Humanities, Columbia University* 5 (Spring): 202, 206.

Sleeper, R. W. 1985. "Rorty's Pragmatism: Afloat in Neurath's Boat, But Why Adrift?" *Transactions of the Charles S. Peirce Society* 21: 9–20.

Sloan, Douglas. 1980. "The Teaching of Ethics in the American Undergraduate Curriculum, 1876–1976." *Teachers College Record* 82: 191–255. Also in *Ethics Teaching in Higher Education*, edited by Daniel Callahan and Sissela Bok, 1–60. New York: Plenum.

Smith, John E. 1969. "The Reflexive Turn, the Linguistic Turn, and the Pragmatic Outcome." *Monist* 53: 588–605.

Smith, John E. 1971. "Purpose in American Philosophy." In *Themes in American Philosophy*, 7–25. New York: Harper & Row.

Smith, John E. 1978. *Purpose and Thought: The Meaning of Pragmatism*. Chicago: University of Chicago Press.

Smith, John E. 1984. "Some Continental and Marxist Responses to Pragmatism." In *Contemporary Marxism*, edited by J. J. O'Rourke, 199–214. Dordrecht, Netherlands: D. Reidel.

Smith, John E. 1992. *America's Philosophical Vision*. Chicago: University of Chicago Press.

Snedden, David. 1912. "What of a Liberal Education?" *Atlantic Monthly* 109 (January): 111–17.

Snow, Louis F. 1907. *The College Curriculum in the United States*. New York: Teachers College, Columbia University.

"Some Progressive College Projects." 1931. *Association of American Colleges Bulletin* 17: 312–21.

"Some Progressive College Projects—II." 1931. *Association of American Colleges Bulletin* 17: 480–87.

Sorell, Tom, ed. 1993. *The Rise of Modern Philosophy: The Tension between the New and Traditional Philosophies from Machiavelli to Leibnitz*. New York: Oxford University Press.

Sprigge, T. L. S. 1993. *James and Bradley: American Truth and British Reality*. Chicago: Open Court.

Stearns, Alfred E. 1916. "Some Fallacies in the Modern Educational Scheme." *Atlantic Monthly* 118: 641–55.

Stevenson, Charles L. 1944. *Ethics and Language*. New Haven, Conn.: Yale University Press.

Stuhr, John J., ed. 1987. *Classical American Philosophy: Essential Readings and Interpretive Essays*. New York: Oxford University Press.

"Symposium on the Renaissance of Pragmatism in American Legal Thought." 1990. *Southern California Law Review* 63 (September).

Taylor, Harold. 1952. "The Philosophical Foundations of General Education." In *General Education, Fifty-First Yearbook, Part 1, of the National Society for the Study of Education*, edited by Nelson B. Henry, 20–45. Chicago: University of Chicago Press.

Thayer, H. S. [1968] 1981. *Meaning and Action: A Critical History of Pragmatism*, 2d ed. Indianapolis, Ind.: Hackett.

Thayer, H. S. 1981. "Pragmatism: A Reinterpretation of the Origins and Consequences." In *Pragmatism: Its Sources and Prospects*, edited by Robert J. Mulvaney and Philip M. Zeltner, 3–20. Columbia, S. C.: University of South Carolina Press.

Thomas, Russell. 1962. *The Search for a Common Learning: General Education, 1800–1960*. New York: McGraw-Hill.

Tierney, William G. 1989. "Cultural Politics and the Curriculum in Post Secondary Education." *Journal of Education* 171: 72–89.

Toulmin, Stephen. 1949. *The Place of Reason in Ethics*. Chicago: University of Chicago Press.

Toulmin, Stephen. 1990. *Cosmopolis: The Hidden Agenda of Modernity*. Chicago: University of Chicago Press.

Unger, Irwin, and Debi Unger. 1978. *The Vulnerable Years: The United States 1896–1917*. New York: New York University Press.

Urmson, J. O. 1956. *Philosophical Analysis: Its Development Between the Two World Wars*. Oxford: Oxford University Press.

Van Doren, Mark. 1943. *Liberal Education*. New York: Henry Holt.

Veblen, Thorstein. 1918. *The Higher Learning in America: A Memorandum on the Conduct of Universities by Business Men.* New York: B. W. Huebsch.

Veysey, Laurence. 1973. "Stability and Experiment in the American Undergraduate Curriculum." In *Content and Context,* edited by Carl Keysen, 1–63. New York: McGraw-Hill.

Vlastos, Gregory. 1991. *Socrates: Ironist and Moral Philosopher.* Ithaca, N. Y.: Cornell University Press.

Wahlquist, John T. 1938. "The Dilemma of American Education." *Educational Forum* 2 (May): 378–88.

Wantland, Wayne E. 1950. "The Role of Science in General Education." *Association of American Colleges Bulletin* 36: 257–65.

Washton, Nathan S. 1949. "What Science Course for General Education?" *Association of American Colleges Bulletin* 35: 509–18.

Weaver, Frederick S. 1991. *Liberal Education: Critical Essays on Professions, Pedagogy, and Structure.* New York: Teachers College Press.

Wee, David L. 1981. *On General Education: Guidelines for Reform.* New Haven, Conn.: Society for Values in Higher Education.

Wegener, Charles. 1978. *Liberal Education and the Modern University.* Chicago: University of Chicago Press.

Weingartner, Rudolph H. 1992. *Undergraduate Education: Goals and Means.* New York: Macmillan.

West, Andrew F. 1907. *Short Papers on American Liberal Education.* New York: Charles Scribner's Sons.

West, Cornel. 1989. *The American Evasion of Philosophy: A Genealogy of Pragmatism.* Madison, Wis.: University of Wisconsin Press.

Westbrook, Robert B. 1990. "Lewis Mumford, John Dewey, and the 'Pragmatic Acquiescence.'" In *Lewis Mumford: Public Intellectual,* edited by Thomas P. Hughes and Agatha C. Hughes, 301–22. New York: Oxford University Press.

Westbrook, Robert B. 1991. *John Dewey and American Democracy.* Ithaca, N. Y.: Cornell University Press.

Whipple, Guy Montrose, ed. 1939. *General Education in the American College, Part II, The Thirty-Eighth Yearbook of the National Society for the Study of Education.* Bloomington, Ill.: Public School Publishing.

White, Morton G. 1963. "Pragmatism and the Scope of Science." In *Paths of American Thought,* edited by Arthur M. Schlesinger, Jr. and Morton White, 190–202. Boston: Beacon.

White, Morton G. 1973. *Pragmatism and the American Mind.* New York: Oxford University Press.

Wiener, Philip P. [1949] 1972. *Evolution and the Founders of Pragmatism.* Philadelphia: University of Pennsylvania Press.

Wihl, Gary. 1994. *The Contingency of Theory: Pragmatism, Expressivism, and Deconstruction.* New Haven, Conn.: Yale University Press.

Wilcox, John R., and Susan L. Ebbs. 1992. *The Leadership Compass: Values and Ethics in Higher Education.* Washington, D. C.: ERIC Clearinghouse on Higher Education.

Wilkins, Ernest H. 1933. "What Constitutes a Progressive College?" *Association of American Colleges Bulletin* 19: 108–11.

Wilson, Daniel J. 1990. *Science, Community, and the Transformation of American Philosophy, 1860–1930.* Chicago: University of Chicago Press.

Wilson, Samuel K. 1946. *The Liberal College in a Democracy.* Washington, D. C.: National Catholic Educational Association.

Wingspread Group on Higher Education. 1993. *An American Imperative: Higher Expectations for Higher Education: An Open Letter to Those Concerned about the American Future.* Racine, Wis.: Johnson Foundation.

Wirth, Arthur G. 1972. *Education in the Technological Society: The Vocational-Liberal Studies Controversy in the Early Twentieth Century.* San Francisco: Intext.

Wise, John E. 1947. *The Nature of the Liberal Arts.* Milwaukee, Wis.: Bruce.

Wittgenstein, Ludwig. 1958. *Preliminary Studies for "Philosophical Investigations Generally Known as 'The Blue and Brown Books."* Oxford, England: Basil Blackwell.

Wolin, Richard. 1992. *The Terms of Cultural Criticism: The Frankfurt School, Existentialism, Poststructuralism.* New York: Columbia University Press.

Woodward, Calvin M. 1887. *The Manual Training School.* Boston: D. C. Heath.

Wriston, Henry M. 1937. *The Nature of a Liberal College.* Appleton, Wis.: Lawrence College Press.

Yocum, A. Duncan. 1936. "Dr. Dewey's `Liberalism' in Government and in Public Education." *School and Society* 44: 1–4.

Zilversmit, Arthur. 1993. *Changing Schools: Progressive Education Theory and Practice, 1930–1960* Chicago: University of Chicago Press.

Zimmer, Agatho. 1938. "Changing Concepts of Higher Education in America since 1700," Ph.D. dissertation, Catholic University of America.

Zinssner, Hans. 1937. "What Is a Liberal Education?" *School and Society* 45: 801–7.

Part 2/

The Condition of American Liberal Education

Contents

126

Seeking Pragmatic Essentialism
Douglas W. Foard

Pragmatism, Liberal Education, and the Transformation of Knowing
Douglas Sloan

Pragmatism, Scientific Method, and Liberal Education
Sandra B. Rosenthal

Wishful Thinking: On the Convergence of Pragmatism and Liberal Education
Robert B. Westbrook

Funeral Rites
David M. Steiner

Needed: A Pedagogy Please!
Thomas F. Green

No Consensus in Sight
Alan Ryan

Because I Like the Questions
Arturo Madrid

Prognostication and Doubt
Ellen T. Harris

Reckoning versus Reasoning: A Struggle for the Soul of Mathematics
Susan L. Forman and Lynn Arthur Steen

The Educated Person, Curriculum Content Standards, and Pragmatic Liberal Education
Miles Myers

Possibilities for Remaking Liberal Education at the Century's End

Stanley N. Katz

Before speculating on the ways in which liberal education can be adapted to the needs and circumstances of the fin de siècle, we must be clear about where higher education is now. The best starting point for thinking about the possibilities for the remaking of liberal education is former Williams College President Francis Oakley's observations about the current situation of liberal education in U.S. colleges and universities. To summarize, Oakley contended: (1) We really have no "system" of higher education in this country, since our education institutions are so "vast, sprawling, markedly variegated, and extremely decentralized,"[1] and include public and private, secular and religious, single-purpose and multi-purpose schools of all sizes. (2) The number of students actually attending institutions of higher education (and their percentage of the relevant age cohort) has increased at an unprecedented rate—unprecedented not only in this country but elsewhere in the world as well. It might also be noted that the average age of university students has risen sharply, as the number of nontraditional (part-time or adult) students has increased. (3) Nationally the student population is strikingly diverse with respect to religion, social class, gender, age, race, and ethnicity; college students are truly a sample of the populace at large. (4) Although increasingly the object of criticism, U.S. higher education has been remarkably effective in responding to these developmental shocks, especially when contrasted with the experience of other national education systems in transition. Our institutions have answered with a dazzling variety of organizational and pedagogical efforts. (5) The principal unacknowledged factor in the transformation of U.S. higher education has been the knowledge explosion—the exponential increase in the range and quantity of new knowledge in all fields that must be covered in curricular plans and research programs.

Liberal, or general, education is widely acknowledged to be one of the central tasks of almost all institutions of higher education. Why then should we worry about the situation of liberal education in our colleges

---

[1] Francis Oakley, "Discontents in American Higher Education," in *The Politics of Liberal Education*, ed. Darryl J. Gless and Barbara Herrnstein Smith (Durham, N.C.: Duke University Press, 1992).

and universities, if we agree with Oakley, as I do, about the fundamental (or at least comparative) health of higher education in this country? I believe the answer is (as Bruce Kimball shows so clearly) that liberal education has evolved to serve specific goals throughout modern history. In the United States, the most recent iteration of this development was the general education movement that took root after World War I. It was designed to give the new American elite (largely white, male, and European in origin) a broad and shared cultural experience prior to entering the increasingly requisite graduate professional training.

General education was revivified after World War II in the more democratic circumstances of the postwar era. The underlying theory of the new approach was nowhere better articulated than in James Bryant Conant's Introduction to the Harvard Red Book (quoting from his 1943 report to the Board of Overseers):

> The heart of the problem of a general education is the continuance of the liberal and humane tradition. Neither the mere acquisition of information nor the development of special skills and talents can give the broad basis of understanding which is essential if our civilization is to be preserved.... Unless the educational process includes...some continuing contact with those fields in which value judgments are of prime importance, it must fall far short of the ideal.... There is nothing new in such educational goals; what is new in this century in the United States is their application to a system of universal education....[T]oday, we are concerned with a general education—a liberal education—not for the relatively few, but for a multitude.[2]

Across the country, in colleges and universities, in public as well as private institutions, attempts were made to find locally relevant and effective adaptations of liberal education in the form of general education.

But the tradition has by now weakened at most institutions and disappeared at some. There are no doubt many reasons for this phenomenon, ranging from a lack of a sense of novelty to rejection of liberal education in favor of vocationalism. Over the past decade, however, even the postwar version of liberal education has increasingly been rejected by significant numbers of faculty and students as being antidemocratic in its pro-Western, intellectually elitist assumptions. The vanguard of this attack has been led by those who describe themselves as multiculturalists, those who believe that undergraduate curricula must more nearly reflect the newly pluralistic character of faculty and under

---

[2] James Bryant Conant, *General Education in a Free Society* (Cambridge, Mass.: Harvard University Press, 1945), viii-ix.

graduate students. I think, however, that most multiculturalists still share many of the objectives of liberal education, including the notion that education for citizenship in contemporary democracy requires a common core of intellectual experience. But the multiculturalists define that core entirely differently than did the founders of Contemporary Civilization at Columbia, the General Education program at Harvard, or Integrated Liberal Studies at the University of Wisconsin.

Kimball's powerful argument that Deweyan pragmatism forms the underlying rationale for contemporary liberal education in the United States gives me hope that there is a core of common understanding that may form the basis for a reconsideration and reformulation of liberal education in these last years of the century. I, for one, share John Dewey's views on the relationship of education to democracy. But I am less sure than Kimball that a consensus on the meaning of liberal education is emerging. For I see few signs of awareness among education leaders that a clear vision of the goals of education is feasible or desirable.

The increasing complexity of the undergraduate sector as described by Oakley works against even a common language of educational practice, and acts more powerfully against the specification of common goals. Since World War II we have attempted to achieve commonality amidst diversity by the segmentation of the institutional structure of higher education. The Carnegie classifications of colleges and universities are the clearest embodiment of that strategy, but there are such differences even within the Carnegie classifications these days that commonality within segments is difficult to define. Oakley's Williams College is in important ways quite different from other "liberal arts" colleges of approximately the same size, just as Princeton University (on whose faculty I serve) is significantly different from Yale or Pennsylvania and from Wisconsin or Chicago. Diversity is one of the glories of U.S. higher education, but this very diversity has made it difficult to think about higher education in large parts, much less as a whole. And that is one of the principal reasons why there is so little writing about "education" by education leaders.

Another reason for the absence of intellectual debate about liberal education is that "higher ed" does not attract scholarly attention. We no longer have persuasive paradigmatic frameworks in which to situate our thinking about the reform of postsecondary education. And, alas, academic contempt for schools of education and writing on education serves as a continuing disincentive to informed speculation about education. Small wonder, then, that the critics of higher education have had a field day for more than a decade. Much of their writing, and that most frequently rehearsed in the popular media, is factually inaccurate, but at least the ideological conservatives among the critics have had the great advantage of building their negative analyses on a logically structured view of the world.

The leaders of our universities (less so the presidents of our colleges) have been unwilling or unable to respond, in part because they no longer seem to have an intellectually coherent view of the enterprises they purport to lead. We may today reject the pronouncements of Robert Maynard Hutchins and Conant as simplistic and out-of-date, but we do not have anything with which to replace them. We thus live in a state of educational anomie, and, for the moment, I fear that we shall simply have to make the best of it. That, in my judgment, requires at least that each institution (and each component segment) undertake the task of self-analysis to articulate its own goals and values. Perhaps induction will work when deduction is no longer feasible.

This is why the emerging debate about "national standards" for higher education offers an important perspective on the current dilemma of institutional identity and purpose. So far as I can tell, most academics oppose the idea of externally imposed standards, whether federal or state in origin, largely on the ground that it is the prerogative of each institution to determine its own education standards. But when we set aside the turf question and ask whether a particular institution has specified its own standards, the response is usually an embarrassed silence. And even when education goals are clearly laid out, relatively few colleges and universities attempt to systematically assess their ultimate fulfillment. I have discussed this problem at greater length elsewhere. Here I simply want to make the point that developing an institutional attitude toward standards of educational accomplishment is not simply a question of determining the content of the curriculum, but one of specifying the basic education goals of the institution. It is much easier to identify the education goals of vocationalism than of liberal education, since most U.S. educators are much less sure than Kimball of the essence of liberality.

At our research universities, the problem of institutional definition has been intensified by the sheer size and complexity of the contemporary multiversity. The origins of this problem lie in the opportunities for expansion during the 1960s, when universities competed for students and funds without much strategic educational planning. When I complained in the late 1960s that we were neglecting undergraduates in our unexamined quest for research funding and graduate students at the University of Wisconsin, where I was then an assistant professor of history, I was invariably (and with impatience) told that the opportunity for such growth might not come again. And so we grew from an institution of 18,000 students to one of 33,000, with a corresponding increase in bricks and mortar and research capacity, and an inversely diminished capacity and commitment to instruct undergraduates. That process has haltingly continued for the past quarter century, with the result that research (and some general) universities have become less coherent than the sum of their parts. An analogous process has gone on in smaller universities and colleges, especially with respect to the provision of those human and physical resources deemed necessary to compete in an era of student scarcity.

Hostile critics of higher education have made much of the trend toward overemphasizing research and graduate education, the tendency to overbuild plants, and the consequent financial dependency of our universities, contrasting these with a half-imagined golden age of close faculty-student relations, institutional symmetry, and parsimony. The critics are not all wrong, of course, but they fail to see the powerful reasons (scientific as well as economic) for building research capacity, although most defenders of the multiversity justify their efforts in just such terms. We have done less well in responding to the charges of undergraduate neglect, probably because we have little to say on the subject. The universities were able to explain how they served liberal education in the 1940s and 1950s, but they have seldom troubled themselves to do so over the last generation. It will not do to say that liberal education is simply one element of undergraduate education, because *it is the essence of educational liberality that it must be the organizing principle of education.*

Is it still possible, as Kimball contends, to aspire to organize undergraduate education according to the principles of liberal education? I am not as sure as Kimball that it is. It seems to me that the competing pressures of vocationalism on the one hand, and disciplinarity on the other, make it difficult for general education to compete as an operational theory. The context of higher education has changed so dramatically from that which confronted the authors of the Red Book in 1945 that it is inappropriate to apply old education strategies to the conduct of contemporary liberal education, at least at the research universities. I have already indicated that I concur with Oakley's optimism about the resilience of our institutions of higher education, but my optimism is based on the university's success in coping with changed material circumstances, not on its pedagogical vitality.

I am less optimistic about our capacity to rise to the challenge of adapting liberal education to the intellectual circumstances of the late twentieth century. Here the principal obstacles are the knowledge explosion, the breakdown of the nineteenth- and early twentieth-century sociology

of knowledge, and the new pluralism (which is how I interpret multiculturalism). We have learned so much in every field of thought, especially
in the sciences, since the end of World War II that it is less and less clear
how to represent all this new knowledge in our universities, much less
how to present it to undergraduate students. New knowledge is not only
the result of conceptual and experimental breakthroughs, however. It
is also the result of the dramatic growth in the number of trained
researchers and, correspondingly, in the enlargement of the detail in
which we understand relatively familiar subjects. The power of the
microscope lenses in all fields has geometrically increased. The result is
that we can examine subject matters in infinite detail and in so doing
perceive patterns and activities that were previously shielded from our
sight. As a matter of *Wissenschaft* this is enormously exciting, but we do
not know how to handle our newfound power pedagogically.

The rapidly expanding quantity of knowledge causes problems
enough, but these are in turn exacerbated by our inability to reorganize
the structure of the university to cope with the intellectual challenge of
new knowledge. I have in mind here the departmental structure, based
on disciplinary departments founded on the sociology of knowledge that
predominated during the first half of this century. While the traditional
disciplines continue to have analytical and methodological power, they
no longer constitute the organizing principles for much cutting-edge
research. Similarly, they no longer constitute the divisions of thought
most important for drawing undergraduates into the excitement of the
new knowledge. We have responded to this problem with the creation of
off-budget units ("centers" and "programs"), but these are precisely the
parts of the university most likely to fall to the budgetary axe in this
period of financial stringency and "downsizing."

The new pluralism intersects with the expansion of knowledge and
the need to reorganize the taxonomy of knowledge. We are now aware of
the global context of knowledge in all fields, especially in the humanities and social sciences. It is less feasible these days to focus almost
exclusively on the European and North American situation, both from
the point of view of student (and faculty) demand and from that of intellectual rigor. The world is smaller and our need for global understanding
is greater. The demands of multiculturalism create an urgent need for
both new bodies of evidence and new modes of understanding, and these
needs arise in the context of an ever-expanding universe of knowledge
and an increasingly rigid intellectual organization of the university.

How can traditional notions of liberal education guide us in the formulation of new approaches to the general education of our undergraduate students? Surely we do not want to throw up our hands and surrender

to the particularism of a free elective system, in the mode of the Brown program. Nor should we settle for the mechanical distribution system that so frequently passes for general education these days, such as the ineffective system at my own university, Princeton. We know the alternatives, mostly "core" programs such as the one at Harvard, and we also know how lightly these are taken by the best students. There will not be simple or universal solutions in the next century, for each institution will have to work out a program that is suitable to its own circumstances. But, at the research universities at least, it is not likely that liberal education in a genuinely pluralistic society can be introduced without significant reform of institutional and intellectual structures. I see few signs today of the imminence of reform.

Thus, the pessimist in me is discouraged by the absence of discussion, much less action, in the direction of structural reform. The optimist in me, however, believes that there is hope for the continued centrality of liberal education. I agree with Kimball that John Dewey's emphases on the relationship between learning and experience, sense and sensibility, fact and value, democracy and education offer a promising basis for the organization of undergraduate education. I also agree with Kimball that liberal education cannot prosper as a backward-looking set of principles, but must constantly adapt itself to social change. What could be more pragmatic? But the question remains—are university faculty and administrators up to the challenge?

STANLEY N. KATZ *is the president of the American Council of Learned Societies.*

Historical Perspective and Our Current Educational Discontents

FRANCIS OAKLEY

One of the frustrating features of the great battle of the books about U.S. higher education that broke out in the mid-1980s, peaked with the onset of the 1990s, and appears now to be sputtering out in a series of inconclusive marginal skirmishes, has been the gap in perception between those engaged in the debate (many of them writing from vantage points outside the academy or at its margins) and those fully engaged on a day-to-day basis in teaching, research, and administration. The mood of apocalyptic foreboding so often evinced by the "cultural warriors" (of whatever stripe) has not, at least from my observation, been commonly prevalent among those laboring in the libraries, laboratories, and pedagogic trenches on our nation's campuses. If the latter have followed the debate at all, and many have not (a prayerful daily reading of the editorial pages of *The Wall Street Journal* is not part of the customary academic liturgy), their response to the hyperbolic onslaughts of the more vituperative critics has often taken the form of a genuine (if wounded) puzzlement, of a failure to recognize in their own attitudes or those of their colleagues, in the daily challenges they have to confront, or in the extremely varied conditions prevalent on their campuses, any unambiguous signs or portents of that great fall from intellectual and educational grace that has loomed so very large in the cultural theologies of the critics.

That that should be so, however, should come as no surprise. Even the critics of more conservative bent who might, after all, have been expected to evince a genuine interest in the past and its accumulated wisdom, have characteristically mounted their onslaughts in a contextual void—historical no less than institutional and statistical.[1] That is to say, they have betrayed few signs of being conscious of the sheer scale and enormous variety of the U.S. higher education enterprise (on any comparison extraordinary in the reach of its ambition and the pluralism of its goals), almost no interest in probing the statistical data that might be expected to yield some insight into what that enterprise actually

---

[1] For a more extended comment on this issue, *see* Francis Oakley, *Community of Learning: The American College and the Liberal Arts Tradition* (New York: Oxford University Press, 1992), 105-36.

involves, not a great deal more in its particular history, and still less in the longer history of liberal education in Europe and North America. For any genuine attempt to come to terms with this last, indeed, they have tended to substitute a sort of cultural *Heilsgeschichte,* moving from the evocation of a golden age of educational coherence, curricular integrity, and pedagogical commitment (sometimes, and oddly, located in the 1950s),[2] via a catastrophic fall from grace during the countercultural upheavals of the late 1960s, to the proclamation during the 1980s of the Good News, the salvific call to effect a redemptive reattachment of the curriculum to a hallowed norm, by reinstituting and generalizing the "western civilization" and "great books of the western tradition" approaches to undergraduate education.

To a surprising and damaging degree the recent battle of the books has been waged within the terms set by this ahistorical and highly tendentious framework, and it would be hard to overemphasize the extent to which the success of any attempt to come to terms with our present educational discontents will depend on the tenacity with which we are willing to pursue the prior effort to acquire a deeper, richer, more accurate, and much more nuanced historical understanding of where we come from, educationally speaking, and how, exactly, we got to be where we are. To that prior effort Bruce Kimball has made a whole series of impressive contributions. And, whether attacking from the right or counterattacking from the left, the failure of the cultural warriors to attend to the lessons emerging from his prize-winning *Orators and Philosophers* (1986) stands out as one of the more discouraging features of our decade-long debate about the undergraduate curriculum. Among those lessons, and one strongly reinforced by W. B. Carnochan's *Battleground of the Curriculum,*[3] the most important may well be that of the sheer untenability of any claim that the educational turmoil of recent years represents a departure from a more favored and tranquil past characterized by curricular agreement and educational harmony. Far from it. As Kimball and such earlier scholars as Vernon Jaeger, H. I. Marrou, Paul Kristeller,

[2] *See* Allan Bloom, *The Closing of the American Mind: How Higher Education Has Failed Democracy and Impoverished the Souls of Today's Students* (New York: Simon and Schuster, 1987); Martin Anderson, *Imposters in the Temple: American Intellectuals Are Destroying Our Universities and Cheating Our Students of Their Future* (New York: Simon and Schuster, 1992).

[3] Carnochan's primary focus on the modern American education scene nicely complements Kimball's wide-ranging survey of the longer European past.

and Sheldon Rothblatt have made clear,[4] the liberal arts tradition has been a tension-ridden one ever since its inception in classical antiquity. Whatever their novelties and characteristically modern twists and turns, the educational debates and disagreements of the recent American past have witnessed powerfully to the age-old conflictedness of that tradition, and especially to the historic tension between competing rhetorical and philosophico-scientific ideals, which, over the centuries, has imparted to it much of its vitality.

That much, I believe, is clear. The insistence that the liberal arts tradition has always been tension-ridden is well grounded in the historical evidence. It affords us an illuminating historical perspective on the confusions of the present, and the quality of our contemporary discourse about higher education would be mightily improved if it were to succeed in nudging to one side the type of dyspeptic presentism that, of recent years, has characterized so much of that discourse.

I find myself more agnostic, however, about the success of Kimball's subsequent moves, both his 1988 lecture sponsored by the Fund for the Improvement of Post-Secondary Education and his most impressive contribution to the present volume. In both he has attempted to identify a core of coherence in the tangled array of reportage, exhortation, commentary, and critique that has shaped and informed the discourse about higher education and to tease out from it the lineaments of an emerging consensus about the direction that higher education in general and the undergraduate course of study in particular should commit themselves to taking. That attempt is undoubtedly worth making. And there are few among our current education commentators as well equipped as Kimball is to make it. But I myself believe that we are almost certainly too close to the debates and disagreements of the recent past to be able to discern, in anything but the most tentative and provisional of fashions, the direction in which the intellectual and political currents of the day are sweeping us. That being so, I incline to the further belief that any confidence about an emerging consensus (and *a fortiori* a consensus linked with so elusive a philosophic posture as pragmatism) is almost certainly premature.

[4] Werner Jaeger, *Paideia: The Ideals of Greek Culture*, trans. Gilbert Highet, 2d ed. (Oxford, England: Basil Blackwell, 1939-1945); H. I. Marrou, *A History of Education in Antiquity*, trans. George Lamb (New York: Sheed and Ward, 1956); Paul O. Kristeller, *Renaissance Thought: The Classic, Scholastic, and Humanist Strains*, rev. ed. (New York: Harper and Row, 1960); Sheldon Rothblatt, *Tradition and Change in English Liberal Education: An Essay in History and Culture* (London: Faber & Faber, 1976).

Such craven scruples duly recorded, I should confess myself, nonetheless, to having been both stimulated and (uneasily) intrigued by Kimball's 1988 suggestion to the effect that the series of reports on undergraduate education published in the years immediately preceding (including those of more conservative bent), however disparate they might at first seem, were in fact converging on the reassertion in modified form of some of the central values embedded in the old rhetorical understanding of liberal education, and doing so at the end of a period during which the philosophico-scientific version of the liberal arts ideal, with its stress on the free, skeptical, and unending pursuit of truth by the individual critical intellect, had been dominant. I was also, at a deeper level, stimulated by his related suggestion to the effect that characteristic concerns of the neo-rhetoricians themselves paralleled or reflected the great wave of questioning so evident in contemporary intellectual life in general. That questioning has been generated by the anxious preoccupation of our century with language, interpretation, and the very grounding of knowledge, and it has posed a severe challenge to the philosophico-scientific ideal that lies so close to the very heart of the modern university. One of the more intriguing aspects of these twin suggestions is their evocation of the ironic possibility that the more conservative among the new rhetoricians, sworn enemies of the post-structuralist tendencies that they see as altogether too well entrenched in the faculties of our leading colleges and universities, may themselves be responding at some level to the great "linguistic turn" shaping so very much of our contemporary intellectual discourse.

The pragmatic educational ideal, moreover, whether rightly or wrongly understood, has long been a favorite whipping boy for those convinced that American education has taken a wrong turn. The ironies will deepen, then, should Kimball prove to be correct in his current claim that, while the two overlap, pragmatism is "a better fit" than the old rhetorical tradition for the sort of consensus he believes to be emerging in our recent debates about liberal education, a consensus in which the more vociferous conservative critics presumably share. But should that indeed prove to be the case, such critics would surely be able to draw a measure of solace from the fact that what they were witnessing (and participating in) would be the emergence of a new and distinctively *American* tradition of liberal education. And if that were the case, there would, I believe, be some real grounds for satisfaction.

Of the seven developments suggesting the emergence of pragmatic liberal education that Kimball specifies, two deserve particular emphasis because they speak so directly to a truly neuralgic point in the recent spate of criticism directed at U.S. higher education. These developments, he argues, "stem from the universality of the experimental method of inquiry, posited notably by Dewey" (94), support "the idea that the different levels of the U.S. education system are equally important and engaged in a common enterprise" (94), and, by "viewing teaching as [itself] a form of learning and inquiry" (95), challenge the sharp distinction commonly made between research or scholarship as a process of investigation, and teaching as a process simply of transmitting the fruits of prior scholarly investigation. The emergence of a consensus around these happily demystifying attitudes would represent a consummation devoutly to be wished.

The last decade has seen a great deal of nonsense written about the active hostility of "the academic culture" to teaching,[5] about "the inescapable incompatibility of teaching and research,"[6] and about the triviality and irrelevance of most academic research—most recently by Martin Anderson who, in *Imposters in the Temple: American Intellectuals Are Destroying Our Universities and Cheating Our Students of Their Future*, contemptuously dismisses such research as a cognate of Hermann Hesse's "glass bead game," as something clearly destructive of the quality of undergraduate teaching, and even as "the greatest intellectual fraud of the twentieth century."[7] But, as I have written elsewhere,[8] what is actually known about the attitudes of the American professoriate and about its actual scholarly activity and productivity in aggregate conveys a very different story—or, at least, *can* do so if we are willing to listen to it and forgo the joys of anecdotal polemic and slipshod innuendo.[9] Most U.S. academics, it turns out, and *pace* the overheated claims of the critics, view themselves primarily as teachers; less than a fourth publish extensively; a clear majority publish little or nothing. Moreover, it is not at all clear that, as a group, the more active researchers at our leading research universities are any less attentive to teaching than their less active colleagues. And the postulation of the sharp division between teaching and research that the pragmatic view of liberal education happily challenges is very much at odds with one of the

[5] Thus Charles T. Sykes, *Profscam: Professors and the Demise of Higher Education* (New York: Kampmann, 1988), 54.
[6] Thus Brian Barnett, "Teaching and Research Are Inescapably Incompatible," *Chronicle of Higher Education* (June 3, 1992): A40.
[7] Anderson, *Imposters in the Temple*, 85, 103-6, 112; cf. Page Smith, *Killing the Spirit: Higher Education in America* (New York:

established (if largely unrecognized) strengths of that quintessentially *American* contribution to the vitality of higher education, the free-standing undergraduate liberal arts college—an institution geologically embedded in the oldest stratum of our higher education system. For a truly impressive scholarly track record has long since been achieved by the faculty teaching at our leading colleges, in which the quality of teaching is very high, student expectations for teaching are even higher, and the institutional commitment to the central importance of good teaching has remained clear, consistent, unwavering, unambiguous. And proudly so.

FRANCIS OAKLEY *is the Edward Dorr Griffin Professor of the History of Ideas at Williams College and president emeritus of the college.*

Marketing Postmodernism

Louis Menand

Bruce Kimball's subject is the philosophical legitimation of higher education. He believes that many of the elements that once composed this legitimation have been changing, and he proposes "pragmatism" as a synthetic term for what those changes add up to. I agree with Kimball that the consensus philosophy of liberal education is undergoing an alteration; I admire the clarity of his account of the pragmatist contribution to this process; and I am sympathetic, in general, to pragmatism as a philosophical (or, as it is sometimes termed, a postphilosophical) position. But I do not think that pragmatism, as Kimball has defined it, is entirely adequate as a description of what is going on inside the academy, and I am skeptical about its usefulness in meeting challenges from outside the academy. I think, in other words, that the philosophical crisis is less easily resolved than Kimball believes, and I think that the social crisis is more urgent.

Whether accidentally or not, it is at least a misfortune that uncertainty about the intellectual foundations of higher education is pervasive among academics at the very moment that institutions of higher education have become subject to external pressures, both economic and political, to retrench. The sponsor of this volume, the College Board, is right in assuming that it is crucial for educators to put a coherent and plausible face on their enterprise, and it is right, as well, in assuming that this will involve some re-self-definition. The intellectual value of a liberal arts education is something Americans no longer take entirely for granted: it does require a fresh legitimation. Are educators currently in a position to provide one?

My picture of the situation Kimball is addressing looks like this: there are these things called the disciplines—English, philosophy, sociology, biology, and so forth—that operate as more or less autonomous, self-regulating departments of knowledge, but that all float in a kind of fluid. This fluid is "the philosophy of liberal education"; it is the foundational ideology, the metarationale, of the whole enterprise, an account of what higher education "does for you," or what higher education "is all about," that is subscribed to by English professors, sociology professors, philosophy professors, and biology professors alike. Different liberal arts colleges find different ways of expressing their commitment to this philosophy: by distribution requirements, by core courses in "Western

Civilization" or "World Cultures," by required classes in methods of study or in composition and rhetoric. Even within the disciplines, specialized undergraduate study is ordinarily understood to take place against the background of this metarationale, which gets reflected in things like the design of the major, the nature of the prerequisites to advanced study, and the emphasis on translatable skills, such as "research techniques" and "critical analysis." The idea is that a liberal arts education is not merely the sum of the knowledge acquired over four years (or 32 credits, or some other measure), but the acquisition of the general intellectual equipment necessary to live a productive and fulfilled life in the modern world.

This ambient fluid is the stuff Kimball is attempting, with admirable learning and lucidity, to describe. Once, it was possible to describe what higher education is all about by using words such as "disinterestedness," "objectivity," "reason," and "knowledge," and by talking about things such as "the scientific method" and "the fact-value distinction." Today, that vocabulary is in relative disrepute. Academics tend to talk about "interpretations" (rather than "facts"), "perspectives" (rather than "objectivity"), and "understanding" (rather than "reason" or "analysis"). An emphasis on universalism has been largely replaced by an emphasis on difference and diversity; the scientistic norms that once prevailed in many of the "soft" disciplines are viewed with skepticism; context and contingency are everywhere emphasized; attention to "objects" has given way to attention to "representations."

"Pragmatism" is Kimball's term for these (and allied) developments. It's a friendly sounding term. "Postmodernism" has, to many ears, a less genial sound; but the developments Kimball calls pragmatic might just as easily be called postmodernist. It is worth remembering that pragmatism, as a contemporary academic movement, owes its reemergence to the work of, essentially, one man, Richard Rorty, and that Rorty succeeded by equating the thought of William James and John Dewey with that of Jacques Derrida and Michel Foucault, by assimilating pragmatism into poststructuralism. Rorty defined pragmatism as anti-foundationalist, "textualist" (by which he meant taking the position that all truths are language-relative), and historicist. And he directed the force of the pragmatist critique of scientistic knowledge-claims against the academic disciplines—specifically against his own discipline, philosophy. For pragmatism is, at bottom, much less another way of doing philosophy than it is an attack on the traditional ways of doing philosophy, just as postmodernism (or poststructuralism) is less a new mode of inquiry than it is an assault on traditional modes of inquiry, on the ways knowledge has conventionally been conceived. Postmodernism does not, in other words, look like a development within the philosophy of liberal education so much as it looks like a reaction against the philosophy of liberal education. This is certainly the way it is perceived by its opponents, both within and outside the university.

The postmodernist position has two elements that seem to me to be insufficiently acknowledged in Kimball's account. First, most postmodernists (and, indeed, many *soi-disant* pragmatists) regard the university as a political site. The belief informing attacks on disinterestedness, objectivity, and universalism is that these terms mask the fundamentally political character of education and scholarship. Thus the current emphasis on interpretation is, generally, an emphasis on the *politics* of interpretation. Thus multiculturalism draws its persuasiveness, for many of its adherents, from the belief that the traditional academic culture has been not merely oblivious of, but antagonistic to, nontraditional ways of understanding and expression. And thus skepticism about the "Enlightenment values" of rationality and universalism is often yoked to revisionist accounts of Western expansionism. A political animus sustains, for many people, the postmodernist attitude toward knowledge, and I don't see how it is possible to fillet out that animus in the interests of putting a neutral face on what it is that now goes on in higher education.

The second element of the postmodernist dispensation, the implications of which need to be more seriously scrutinized is anti-essentialism, for anti-essentialism is subversive of the integrity of the disciplines. The critique Rorty used pragmatism to make of the discipline of philosophy is a critique that postmodernist theory generally makes of disciplinarity *tout court*. The disciplines were established, and developed, on a formalist premise: that each field of study had its own discriminable subject matter and its own theoretical assumptions and methodological equipment. Assumptions and equipment might be borrowed (ordinarily with considerable fanfare, signaling the daringly imaginative character of the transaction) across disciplines; but scholarly and educational activity within each discipline was understood to be self-contained and coherent on its own terms. There was something called "literature," teachable as literature, something called "history," teachable as history, and so forth. This formalism has now broken down—partly for theoretical reasons and partly because it cannot accommodate many growing areas of interest. At the graduate level, much of the action is in areas that are interdisciplinary (or "postdisciplinary") by definition, such as women's studies, African American studies, gay and lesbian studies, and cultural studies. The most important force keeping the disciplines together is the job market, which continues to require that candidates present themselves as scholars working in some recognized specialty. But eventually, interdisciplinarity (and postdisciplinarity and even antidisciplinarity) will trickle down into the undergraduate curriculum and challenge the standard organization of liberal arts education—that is, a major field of study, organized as protoprofessional training in a scholarly discipline, complemented by a smattering of general education requirements.

The threats these two elements—the new emphasis on the fundamentally political character of education and scholarship, and anti-essentialism—pose to the future of liberal arts education are not primarily philosophical. The problem is, to put it crudely, a marketing one. Public universities are heavily subsidized. Private universities are very expensive. If we say universities are places in which academics possess knowledge about the world—indeed, in many respects, possess a monopoly on knowledge about the world—and they will impart this knowledge to you for a fee, which you may pay in taxes or tuition, then you can decide that the knowledge is worth acquiring and pay to support the knowers. But if we say universities are places in which academics, each according to his or her political bent, come up with competing interpretations of texts, none of which can claim to be true in any ultimate sense, and people can go to hear these academics argue with one another about their interpretations and learn how to argue about them, too, I think people will wonder what they are paying for. (This is why I find Gerald Graff's "teach the conflicts" proposal,[1] for example, a recipe for public relations disaster, though it is frequently invoked as a *via media* among conflicting views.) It has been suggested that what people are paying to learn is "how to think critically." This strikes me as a weak selling point, considering the price tag; but even if it's not, what are those professors doing with all that research time? Are they simply sharpening their wits? Once the concept of knowledge production is abandoned as a legitimating idea, a fairly cold light gets thrown on academic activity in the humanistic disciplines.

There is a further danger, also practical, which has to do with the collapse of disciplinarity authority. It is not a fluke that it is the job market that is currently holding the traditional disciplines together, for the disciplines are professional organizations. They regulate themselves (after the manner of all professional groups) by setting their own standards for employment, advancement, and tenure. There are all kinds of pedagogical and intellectual reasons for wishing that the disciplines would

[1] Gerald Graff, *Beyond the Culture Wars: How Teaching the Conflicts Can Revitalize American Education* (New York: W. W. Norton, 1992).

wither away, but they perform two functions most people would not wish withered. One is that they ensure that standards for professors, and thus for curricula and scholarship, are universal, so that a student at a state institution and a student at an Ivy League college will be taught by professors whose training is virtually identical. Professors identify with their disciplines first and with their campuses second—they define themselves nationally, not locally—and this helps to prevent the development of a two-tiered education system (or a more sharply two-tiered education system than we already have) in the United States, with all the social invidiousness that would imply. The other function performed by the disciplines is the preservation of academic freedom. The discipline acts as a community that judges the merit of its members' work by community standards. When professors are hired on an ad hoc basis by academic administrators, or when they are not professionally situated in a particular department, they lose this protection. Their status becomes a function of lines in a budget.

It has taken a long time for academic postmodernists to see that the ultimate target of their criticism of traditional forms of knowledge is the institution in which they work, and that postmodernist thinking does not merely redefine that institution philosophically, but also undermines its very structure. Seeing this much, contemporary academics ought to see as well how serendipitously this undermining meets the interests of those who are not friends of liberal arts education and scholarship, particularly when the latter are subsidized by public money. Administrators financially answerable to state legislatures would love to melt down the disciplines, since that would allow them to deploy faculty more efficiently, and the claim that disciplinarity represents a factitious organization of knowledge is as good an excuse as any. Further, there are many people who would love, on political as well as financial grounds, to dispense with the protection of academic freedom. For these people, too, the argument that disinterestedness is a false standard serves their purposes very nicely. My analysis may sound like an expression of nostalgia for the old justifications for academic study. It is not. It is only a note of warning about the uses to which some of the new justifications can be put.

LOUIS MENAND *is professor of English at the Graduate Center of the City University of New York.*

Knowledge, America, and Liberal Education

JULIE THOMPSON KLEIN

Answers to the core question asked at the College Board seminar—is there a uniquely American tradition of liberal education?—depend a great deal on the starting points. Beginning from philosophy or history yields one perspective; starting from cultural theory or institutional practices another. My own answer is shaped by two themes that were undercurrents at the seminar—knowledge about America and the structure of knowledge. Aspects of these themes are not inconsistent with pragmatism, but they are not entirely encompassed by it either. They are lenses that heighten awareness of the extent to which liberal education in the United States is shaped by the relationship among disciplinary, general, and interdisciplinary claims about knowledge.

Concerning the first theme, to argue that there is an *American* tradition begs the question of what is meant by "America." Despite Francis Oakley's call for more cross-cultural comparison,[1] the international perspective was relatively absent from the seminar. However, when international comparisons are made, several characteristics of the U.S. system of higher education loom large. The most obvious is institutional structure. Students in the United States encounter the concept of liberal education at a particular point in their social and intellectual development, primarily as undergraduates from 18 to 21 years of age. The form of specialization that took root in the United States is a major reason for this. In the transformation of the traditional "American college" into the modern U.S. research university, "pure research" was emphasized over "pure learning." This narrow methodological connotation overlooked the broad, contemplative element of the German model of *Wissenschaft*, while privileging the expanding scientific dimension of knowledge.[2] Over the course of the twentieth century, the time and place for liberal learning narrowed to particular sectors of the academy, especially the humanities, institutions where the idea of the traditional college was preserved, and, for the greatest number of students, general education and the core curriculum.

---

[1] Francis Oakley, "Against Nostalgia: Reflections on Our Present Discontents in American Higher Education," in *The Politics of Liberal Education*, eds. Darryl J. Gless and Barbara Herrnstein Smith (Durham, N.C.: Duke University Press, 1992), 271.

[2] Hans Flexner, "The Curriculum, the Disciplines, and Interdisciplinarity in Higher Education," in *Interdisciplinarity and Higher Education*, ed. Joseph Kockelmans (University Park, Pa.: University of Pennsylvania Press, 1979), 103.

Cultural styles also influence the selection of subject matter and the drawing of disciplinary lines. The U.S. distinction between humanities and social sciences, for example, has not been a major organizing principle in European higher education. The current use of the term "human sciences" by American academics is read as yet another turn to Europe, to theory, in order to legitimate new practices. This usage, however, is also related to a much longer history of efforts to study American subjects, objects, problems, and themes that do not fit neatly into traditional domains of inquiry. Over the course of the twentieth century, the number of specialties that focus on the United States has grown significantly and fostered new fields. The most obvious examples are the older field of American studies, an outgrowth of hybrid interests in history and English departments, and the more recent turn into American cultural studies.

The turn into cultural studies has inserted both the contemporary world and American subjects into research and assumptions about what every American ought to know. International comparison, again, is illuminating. In both Britain and the United States, debates over mass culture and the mass media's place in cultural life promoted the growth of a heterogeneous field of interests. In Britain, though, the question of ideology emerged sooner and more sharply than it did in the United States, where Marxism has a different status in the larger social and political culture. The notion of "popular culture" also occupies a different place within the dominant culture in the United States.[3] In addition, feminism and the cultural epistemologies of particular groups have played a prominent role, resulting in the variegated institutional topography of Indian Studies in Minnesota, Native American Studies in the Southwest, Latino Studies in California, Appalachian Studies in North Carolina, Africana Studies in Detroit, and border studies in El Paso and San Diego.

Over time, the inclusion of knowledge about America has blurred traditional demarcations. The notion of disciplinary "coverage" has expanded to include new content and material as well as broader social, political, historical, and economic explanations once considered outside the parameters of departmentalized categories of knowledge. At the same time, the notion of "liberal learning" has expanded to incorporate the shift from a consensus view of history and culture to a pluralistic view. This shift was propelled by developments both in the disciplines

[3] Norma K. Denzen, *Symbolic Interaction and Culture Studies: The Politics of Interpretation* (Cambridge, England: Basil Blackwell), 1992, 75; Patrick Brantlinger, *Crusoe's Footprints: Cultural Studies in Britain and America* (New York: Routledge, 1990), 117-19.

and in new hybrid fields. Furthermore, all areas of the curriculum—departments, cross-departmental programs, and interdisciplinary fields—are assuming a measure of responsibility for training students in generic skills in a country and a world where work and knowledge have become fluid. The result is greater intellectual traffic in and out of traditional compartments of specialization, breadth, and integrative capacity. This traffic is marked by a widening gap between traditional organizational charts and what faculty are actually doing.

This changing presence of America in research and in the curriculum is related to the second theme, the comprehensive set of changes that have altered the structure of knowledge. The disciplines that dominate standard taxonomies date back to the nineteenth century. Many specialties and fields, however, are of more recent origin, and a significant number of them evolved from cross-fertilizations of hierarchically unrelated fields of knowledge, new mission-oriented fields, and new interdisciplinary subject fields.[4] By the year 1987, there were 8,530 definable fields of knowledge.[5] The shadow taxonomy of new knowledge spans molecular biology and cognitive science, medical anthropology and gerontology, critical legal studies and historical sociology. Part of the reason for the oft-noted "knowledge explosion" is the increase in problem-focused and mission-oriented research. Yet the narrow pragmatism of instrumentality is not the only reason. Complexity and hybridity have become prominent characteristics of the production of knowledge. The inner development of the sciences has posed ever broader tasks, leading to interconnections among the natural, social, and technical sciences. Classically framed objects, concepts, and problems in the humanities and social sciences have also been reconceived. Reformulations of concepts once regarded as discrete to particular domains—organism, text, behavior, culture, mind—have made "boundary" a new keyword for describing knowledge, and boundary blurring has become commonplace.

The institutional landscape of knowledge is being further reconfigured by an increase in the number and kinds of organizations in which knowledge is produced and transmitted. This trend includes the growth of academic alliances with industry and government. The demand for new skills and new instrumentation has fostered a heightened need for

---

[4] Ingetraut Dahlberg, "Domain Interaction: Theory and Practice," *Advances in Knowledge Organization* 4 (1994): 60.

[5] Diana Crane and Henry Small, "American Sociology since the Seventies: The Emerging Crisis in the Discipline," in *Sociology and its Publics: The Forms and Fates of Disciplinary Organization*, eds. Terence Halliday and Morris Janowitz (Chicago: University of Chicago Press, 1992), 197.

continuing education outside the academy, at work sites and in the community, as well as inside the academy, especially in scientific fields, technology, and the professions. As colleges and universities serve a greater number of functions, ranging from abstract research to utilitarian training, older distinctions of campus core and periphery are blurring and institutional missions are becoming fuzzier. The broadening social base of students also means that the core skills and values of the older tradition of liberal education are being reinterpreted by students and teachers who are bringing into the academy the cultural and political currents and conflicts of the larger society.[6]

These developments have had direct and specific effects on the entire epistemological domain. Each of the approximately 3,400 postsecondary institutions in the United States is an institutional realization of selected parts of a crowded whole that is more sum than unity. What gets taught is the result of a selection shaped by local personnel and resources, institutional mission, and the extent to which the recommendations of learned societies and policy groups create and sustain commonalty. One of the prominent developments over the past two decades has been increased interest in interdisciplinary approaches. Basil Bernstein, who has written on the sociology of education, predicted that as society became more fragmented and specialized, there would be a greater movement toward integrated codes that foster new forms of interdependence and cooperation in education.[7]

This trend is not unique to the United States. In Europe, renewed calls for coherence and connectedness are being heard in the professions and across university subjects. Nevertheless, despite continuing impediments and the widely noted observation that disciplinary walls are often higher in the United States, the U.S. system of education has a striking number and diversity of interdisciplinary forms. In a recent special issue of the *European Journal of Education* devoted to "Interdisciplinary Studies," the editor, Ludwig Huber of the University of Bielefeld, dubbed the United States the "eldorado of interdisciplinary studies." In contrast to European institutions, Huber pointed out, the "liberal arts college" not only protects the value of general education, but also encourages diversity while offering a remarkable scope for curricular flexibility. Teaching and learning are thus guided along multiple lines of canon and subjects, interdisciplinary themes and problems.[8] The strongest growth

---

[6] Michael Gibbons et al., *The New Production of Knowledge: The Dynamics of Science and Research in Contemporary Societies* (Thousand Oaks, Calif.: Sage, 1994), 76-80.

[7] Basil Bernstein, *The Structuring of Pedagogic Discourse. Volume IV. Class, Codes, and Control* (London: Routledge, 1990).

[8] Ludwig Huber, "Editorial," *European Journal of Education* 27 (1992): 197. Special issue on "Interdisciplinary Studies."

in subject-matter areas of general education encourages interdisciplinary approaches in fields such as international studies, American multicultural and gender studies, and the inherently synoptic areas of historical and ethical understanding.[9]

Increased interest in interdisciplinary approaches would be misunderstood, however, if equated solely with the general education sector of the curriculum. The results of the Association of American Colleges and Universities' mammoth three-year study of the major, collected in *Reports from the Fields*, revealed that the individual disciplines are equally significant sites.[10] The variety of integrative devices in disciplinary curricula is striking: the use of portfolios and process-oriented learning, integrative seminars and course components, capstone courses that draw connections to the "real world" and other disciplines, the incorporation of new interdisciplinary research into disciplinary courses, the reformulation of science as a liberal art for nonmajors, and the growing inclusion of new elements in preprofessional education. Interdisciplinary approaches are also being mainstreamed in the form of topical first-year seminars, core courses in all fields, advanced courses on intellectual problems, and senior projects involving research, seminars, or artistic productions.[11]

Significantly, the shift in models from the traditional American college to the research university to the plurality of roughly 3,400 postsecondary institutions is paralleled by a shift in the classical triangular relationship of content-teacher-student that placed learning at the center. The rhetoric of teaching has shifted from metaphors of prescription, product, control, performance, and classroom to dialogue, process, alliance, growth, and learning community. The theory of pedagogy has shifted, in kind, from universal strategies to situational strategies focusing on the unique needs of particular students. While not restricted to the United States, the expanding network of teaching and learning centers is a striking feature of U.S. higher education at this particular historical moment. This movement has promoted the belief that teaching and learning are shared responsibilities of the professoriate, thus widening interest in the undergraduate curriculum and emphasizing the importance of liberal education. Cultivation of the skills of teaching and learning gain primacy in a system in which the need for specialized knowledge, breadth, and integrative capacity are simultaneous, not restricted to particular ages or confined to particular sectors.

[9] Beth A. Casey, "The Administration and Governance of Interdisciplinary Programs," in *Interdisciplinary Studies Today*, eds. Julie Thompson Klein and William Doty, Vol. 58 in the New Directions in Teaching and Learning series (San Francisco: Jossey-Bass, 1994), 56.

[10] *Reports from the Fields*, vol. 2 of *Liberal Learning and the Arts and Science Major* (Washington, D.C.: Association of American Colleges and Universities, 1991).

[11] Marilyn Stember, "Advancing the Social Sciences through the Interdisciplinary Enterprise," *Social Science Journal* 28 (1991): 3.

A loyal reading of John Dewey would suggest that none of these developments is inconsistent with pragmatism. I would be the first to argue that the fuller, enlightened reading of Dewey that Bruce Kimball provides is in order. The inclusion of knowledge of America and changes in the structure of knowledge underscore the dynamic interaction of organization and environment, the close interrelationship between thought and action, the intrinsic role of purpose in thought and inquiry, the perpetually reconstructive nature of science and inquiry, and the role that context and intersubjective judgment play in shaping belief, meaning, and truth. "Consensus," though, is too strong a word for an emergent agreement that, Kimball himself admits, is not explicitly or directly acknowledged in much of contemporary writing about liberal education. The notion of "fit," though, is rich. The central tenets of pragmatism provide a unifying focal point for a dialogue in which "America," "liberal," and "education" will continue to be the loci of both uncertainty and certitude about how to get on in a world defined by the traits of complexity, hybridity, heterogeneity, and globality.

JULIE THOMPSON KLEIN *is professor of Humanities at Wayne State University, Detroit, Michigan.*

Pragmatic Missions and the Struggle for Liberal Education in State Colleges and Universities

JUNE K. PHILLIPS

In his lead essay, Bruce Kimball suggests that higher education is moving toward pragmatic liberal education. Faculty and administrators who have spent significant amounts of their professional lives in the public sector of higher education, especially at the institutions that are not included in the research classification, might have been startled by Kimball's characterization of pragmatic liberal education as a destination not yet reached. Educators at public colleges and universities find themselves already well "within" the pragmatic paradigm, whether or not they have consciously placed themselves in that philosophical context. In public education, the struggle to preserve a "liberal education" does constitute a constant concern, given the strength of pragmatism as an organizing principle. The very establishment of the state college system in the mid-nineteenth century was rooted in pragmatism, tied to missions that served an expanding population of students, and attentive to the requirements of society for professionals with specialized, career-oriented skills built on a base of general knowledge.

I have no official mandate to speak for public four-year colleges and universities, but I cannot help but note that there are few contributors to this volume from the public sector, which currently enrolls 67 percent of all undergraduate students in four-year institutions. Only in Massachusetts and the District of Columbia are fewer than 50 percent of college students in public institutions. When public research universities and land-grant universities are factored out, the primarily undergraduate public colleges grant between one-fourth and one-third of all baccalaureate degrees.[1] This group of higher education institutions might be designated the "invisible universities," for in spite of the numbers of students they educate, they are often ignored by writers and critics concerned with higher education.

For students at public universities, the context, the content, and the practice of their higher education experience reverberate with the elements Kimball describes as influential in a pragmatic framework.

---

[1] These statistics were drawn from student enrollment data in *Chronicle of Higher Education Almanac* (1 September 1994): 5, 9.

Faculty and administrators challenged to serve the multiple masters of students, legislators, and taxpayers, in addition to adhering to disciplinary and accreditation standards, have long acknowledged the tenets of a pragmatic philosophy as the basis for their efforts. Therefore, this response addresses the ways in which pragmatic liberal education is quite clearly manifested at many of today's public four-year colleges and universities. (The diversity among these institutions precludes a comprehensive account.) It further suggests that the strength of pragmatism sometimes threatens the liberal arts; thus, faculty members must be constantly vigilant in an age of accountability to justify the "liberal" in a pragmatic education.

As long as only a small number of Americans had access to higher education, colleges and universities could enjoy defining their missions, as Bardo wrote, for "a variety of intellectual, political, religious, and social reasons."[2] From the end of World War II to the present, the number of students claiming access to higher education has increased dramatically. Oakley considered demographic changes to be "the single most important set of factors shaping the American undergraduate experience today."[3] The majority of these new students, often the first in their families to pursue higher education, entered public colleges and universities, and their presence was a major spur to the expansion of state colleges beyond their traditional emphasis on teacher preparation.

Research institutions and the selective liberal arts colleges were able to plan and control their own growth, thereby enjoying the luxury of discussing and analyzing the directions that higher education might take in their future, but the state institutions had to provide access and meet enrollment and curricular demands quickly. Public institutions are more closely bound to the changing exigencies of the political forces that have monitored, and at times patently interfered with, core academic issues such as credit hours, program offerings, faculty workloads, number of tenure appointments, and promotions. The constant thread that runs through the postwar development of state colleges and universities is pragmatic education built on the concept of "general education" and designed to fulfill the goals of a liberal education. The fact that these institutions must directly answer to the public and policymakers means that their priorities reflect the kind of education U.S. taxpayers are willing to support; that translates to pragmatic, realistic preparation

---

[2] John W. Bardo, ed., *Defining the Missions of AASCU Institutions* (Washington, D.C.: American Association of State Colleges and Universities, 1990), 7.

[3] Francis Oakley, "Discontents in American Higher Education," in *The Politics of Liberal Education*, eds. Darryl J. Gless and Barbara Herrnstein Smith (Durham, N.C.: Duke University Press, 1992), 271.

for work in the larger community. Fortunately, thus far most institutions have managed to accommodate students in pursuit of scholarship in the humanities and natural sciences as well.

The 1985 mission statement of the American Association of State Colleges and Universities (AASCU) quite clearly embodies characteristics Kimball attributes to pragmatic liberal education:

Academic Mission Statement

The typically American institutions that compose the American Association of State Colleges and Universities play a distinct role in the higher education system of this democratic nation. Their mission is to create an integrative yet dynamic balance among diverse and often conflicting demands on contemporary public colleges and universities. A balance is sought between access for all who can profit from an education and the quality of instruction necessary for maximal development of each student; between theory and application in the instructional process, so that teaching, research, and service can all be appropriately emphasized; between liberal education for the student's personal lifelong growth and professional education for career preparation; between internal institutional needs and increasing demands of external forces; between regional service on the one side and national and international views on the other. Each institution, in determining the balance point appropriate to its individual mission, its resources, and its constituencies, can serve both academic values and the changing needs of society.[4]

If we highlight and match key words or concepts in this statement with the seven developments indicating pragmatic influence on liberal education as summarized by Kimball (97), there is compelling overlap (e.g., values, service, community and citizenship/constituencies). This does not imply that only public institutions draw on uplifting concepts for mission statements, but the primary mission of state colleges is the provision of education for a broad base of students. The return to the state for its financial investment is presumed to be a more highly educated citizen who will contribute to a more competent and productive workforce. Toward that end, public universities have historically concentrated, and continue to concentrate, a preponderance of resources in professional and preprofessional fields such as agriculture, education, business and management, health professions, and technological areas. To distinguish themselves from vocational schools, four-year public institutions sometimes embrace and at other times barely tolerate the general education program that permits them to offer the baccalaureate

[4] Drafted in 1985 at the Academic Affairs Resource Center and later refined by committee; cited in Bardo, ed., *Defining the Missions of AASCU Institutions*, 13.

to their students. The tension revolves around the recognition that general education provides a broader perspective beyond the narrow skill orientation of vocational schooling, and the reluctance of some students and faculty in professional programs to meet the time and credit requirements of study for which they perceive no immediate application. Pragmatism was and remains at the heart of the system.

The diversity of the U.S. higher education system may mitigate against ever being able to define it under a single rubric, even one as broad and encompassing as pragmatic liberal education. In fact, the panoply of differences in our colleges and universities may be the dynamic that allows such a high percentage of students to pursue higher education and consequently a large number of faculty to be employed in both teaching and research. One of the major intersections between research universities on the one hand and comprehensive universities and four-year undergraduate colleges on the other might lie in their progress *toward* or their status *within* the context of pragmatic liberal education.

One of Kimball's theses seems to be that higher education is moving in the direction of pragmatism while avoiding the term, that John Dewey's principles are taking hold while little reference is made to his name or philosophy. This may be true for research institutions, which generate much of the new knowledge in the disciplines and in pedagogy. It is less valid for public colleges and universities that openly acknowledge their applied role and their philosophical ties to Dewey-inspired educational objectives. The bias against curricular innovation, pedagogy as scholarship, or faculty development based on common curricular issues, encountered at research institutions, is absent at most public undergraduate institutions. Instruction today at many such institutions has readily incorporated pedagogical processes initially generated by research faculties whose own institutions are reticent to accept the implied changes.

Several of the developments identified by Kimball as reflective of pragmatic liberal education constitute the core of initiatives underway at many of the nation's public four-year colleges and universities, which have the ability, even the mandate, to focus their energies almost exclusively on instruction at the undergraduate level. Faculty members assume responsibility for both general education and specialized courses for majors. Thus, the K to 16 seamless curriculum is part of the explicit mission of most state colleges and universities, and it dominates their interactions with the schools.

Formal and informal alliances between faculty from public colleges and universities and from the schools promote discussion of concepts such as Rudolph Weingartner's proficiencies and conversancies and their application to curricula.[5] For example, Weingartner described proficiencies in writing, foreign languages, and mathematics that he posited as desirable outcomes of undergraduate education. The concepts of writing as process and of foreign language goals that aim for communicative competence arose from new theories of first- and second-language acquisition largely formulated and researched at prestigious institutions. The professoriate in the scholarly disciplines at many, although not all, of these institutions, primarily in departments of English and foreign languages, continue to debate and argue against adopting such a pragmatic orientation in their own curricula. At many of the state colleges and universities, however, we see in practice quite innovative demonstrations of programs such as Writing across the Curriculum, specialized tenure-track faculty teaching composition, and requirements and assessments for foreign languages stated in terms of proficiency in functional contexts. Similarly, other pedagogically oriented practices that fall into categories Kimball describes as pragmatic, such as collaborative learning and learning communities, are thriving and providing focus for faculty development at state colleges and universities.

Another idea that is gaining a prominent role in undergraduate programs is the infusion of community service into the curriculum. The range of involvement extends from informal programs that encourage student participation in volunteerism sponsored by campus organizations to more formally constructed combinations of service and study. Among the best of the latter are programs in which students receive academic credit for doing background research on issues relevant to their volunteer work, and for writing papers or reflective journals on their service. (These programs work especially well in medium-sized colleges located in towns where one community depends greatly on the other. The new federally established program has provided even more visibility and reward for community service.)

Assessment of education outcomes, another characteristic of Kimball's pragmatic liberal education, has been mandated by state higher education boards for public institutions. Mixed progress is reported as faculties struggle to implement meaningful measures that are academically sound and adequately reflect both knowledge and performance.

[5] Rudolph H. Weingartner in *Undergraduate Education: Goals and Means* (Phoenix, Ariz.: American Council on Education and Oryx, 1993), described *proficiencies* as skills that can be measured by doing in academic areas such as literacy, foreign languages, mathematics, and computers. He defined *conversancies* as goals of familiarity with basic information and modes of thinking within disciplines such as the sciences, history, and art.

State governments, as does the federal government, frequently mandate unfunded programs, and assessment has fallen into that trap. Assessing computer literacy or math competency has posed fewer problems than, for example, assessing a general education program. For many faculty, the general education program is a de facto responsibility of all departments, so identifying outcomes raises more questions than it answers. Many faculty members lived through the period when behavioral objectives dominated school assessment. Hence mandated assessments arouse anxiety because it is feared they will promulgate a similar concentration on low-level competencies because these are easier to measure than is more sophisticated knowledge. Pragmatism of this sort could seriously undermine the contribution of the liberal arts to professional programs at public institutions.

Publicly supported undergraduate colleges and universities are also emphasizing two other developments that Kimball identifies as indicating a pragmatic influence on liberal education: multiculturalism and teaching as learning and inquiry. These institutions, often the choice for the multicultural population in a particular region, are going beyond demographics and creating cross-disciplinary and interdisciplinary curricula that adopt multiculturalism as a focus. The reward system for faculty in undergraduate institutions encourages development of interdisciplinary and innovative programs. Creation of new courses, collaboration with faculty from other departments, even participation in seminars sponsored by agencies such as the National Endowment for the Humanities, lie within the criteria for teaching and scholarship for purposes of tenure and promotion. On balance, budgets at state institutions encourage faculty development more heavily than they do travel to present papers. Scholarship with the goal of improving the ability of the undergraduate curriculum to address contemporary issues, e.g., multiculturalism, is rewarded in the same way as scholarship that advances a discipline or an individual faculty member's professional reputation. In addition, many state colleges and universities devote significant internal research funds to projects that focus on teaching and learning. Further, institutional policy does not view pedagogy as a negative when used to describe a liberal arts faculty member, although that rift still exists in practice in many departments.

None of this is intended to glorify public colleges and universities, for they face problems both similar to and different from those in other sectors of higher education. Each time a new state legislature meets, the agenda may shift. One concern always in the fore entails the search for an equilibrium between a pragmatism that lawmakers equate with "jobs" and the liberal education that faculty value as essential to a thinking, thoughtful, and useful citizen.

The research institutions, as Kimball suggests, may well be tilting toward his construct of liberal education, but they will avoid at all costs embracing the label of pragmatism. In contrast, the vocational and the community colleges sell their programs to the public by citing the employability of their graduates. Nestled in between these types of institutions, the comprehensive universities and four-year undergraduate colleges are positioned to carry forward within the model of pragmatic liberal education.

JUNE K. PHILLIPS *is the dean of Arts and Humanities at Weber State University, Ogden, Utah.*

Pragmatism Won't Save Us—But It Can Help[1]

RICHARD M. FREELAND

For historians and philosophers, the question of whether the United States has developed a distinct tradition of liberal education possesses intrinsic interest and merits consideration in scholarly terms. At a time, however, when the nation's academic enterprise faces substantive and political challenges as daunting as any in this century, a purely intellectual approach to this subject seems an indulgence. It is more important to concentrate on the potential of the question to clarify our thinking about the essential purposes of our institutions and thereby to help us define a basis for responding to the pressures for change that bear so insistently upon us.

Bruce Kimball's provocative essay argues that the United States has, indeed, evolved an original version of liberal learning. Citing seven contemporary developments in higher education—including multiculturalism, assessment, general education, an interest in teaching, and intensified links to the schools—Kimball asserts that all share a common bond with pragmatism—one of the nation's few contributions to philosophic thought. Kimball's central concern is the intellectual rationale for the trends he cites, and he is ingenious in showing how pragmatism, with its emphasis on the contextual nature of meaning and the relationship of thought to action, can be used to justify each of them.

This short commentary will sidestep the invitation to debate the scholarly merits of Kimball's claims and instead—in a true spirit of pragmatism—will ask a more utilitarian question: of what use is the idea of "pragmatic liberal education"? Can Kimball's formulation help us answer any of the urgent questions that we currently face?

Kimball's seven developments in fact constitute a subset of higher education's most important contemporary challenges. Indeed, most of them can more accurately be characterized as issues or movements rather than developments. For one thing, it is far from clear that most have gained significant acceptance at the operational level within the academy—that is, among faculties that will ultimately make the vital judgments about curriculum and personnel. (Multiculturalism is probably the only one of these movements that has gained wide acceptance

---

[1] The author acknowledges the assistance of Dr. Robert Picken in drafting this commentary.

among faculties.) Even more important, Kimball's developments all correspond to current critiques of higher education that have arisen from one or another quarter. To assess the usefulness of pragmatism in ordering our thinking about liberal education, it is necessary to understand more precisely the sources of these critiques and the pattern of academic responses to them.

The demand for a multicultural approach to curriculum comes largely from internal academic constituencies, especially the faculty. Professorial interest in this subject is rooted in the changed demography of the college-going population as well as of the academic professions, though ultimately, of course, these changes reflect the evolving social structure of the country itself. The call for more rigorous assessment, by contrast, is an outside pressure that comes most urgently from the insistence by those who pay our bills, especially government agencies, that we demonstrate the actual results and benefits of our work. Pleas for a greater emphasis on general education—a venerable jeremiad that has been repeated in recommendations from distinguished commissions on a regular basis for 30 years—is a favorite theme of administrative leaders and stirs little interest among most faculty and students.

These critiques—and the others on Kimball's list as well—are, of course, part of a larger phenomenon of questioning, skepticism, and appeals for reform that currently besets much of higher education and extends far beyond the boundaries of liberal learning. This atmosphere is by no means new. On the contrary, we have been wrestling with disenchantment among nonacademics since the late 1960s, when we began to lose the public confidence that sustained academia's expansion during the 25 years following World War II. In recent years, however, the external complaints have grown more insistent and have merged with a broader societal impatience with large institutions, especially agencies of government, that has become increasingly evident in political trends at both the national and state levels. For higher education, the most significant manifestation of this deteriorated climate has been the devastating decline in financial support by the states combined with the growing aggressiveness of government entities in regulating our institutions.

Why are we in so much trouble? Kimball's essay draws attention to a number of social forces that are at the root of the problem. The first and most important is that higher education has yet to come fully to terms with the fact that the enrollment increases of the past 40 years have brought into the postsecondary system a student population infinitely more diverse—both academically and socially—than the cohorts we served prior to World War II. The educational challenges posed by this expansion have been especially acute for faculty in the liberal arts and sciences, a form of education developed to nurture elites bound for advanced training that we have too often replicated rather mechanically in institutions serving large numbers of poorly prepared students, most of whom are unlikely to pursue graduate degrees. We should hardly be surprised that the results have been mixed and that the public has grown skeptical of the social return on its investment.

The changed economic circumstances of the country constitute a second factor contributing to our current difficulties. During the 1950s and 1960s, when the United States was unchallenged as the preeminent economic power on the globe, students, parents, and government leaders did not find it necessary to ask too many hard questions about the practical value of the education we were providing. The country was thriving; jobs were plentiful; standards of living were rising. Recently, however, as Europe and Asia have recovered from the war and as new centers of economic energy have emerged in the developing world, we have found our position challenged and our future far less sure. In this context, the stakes for our educational enterprise have been greatly raised and the country is truly—and properly—frightened by evidence of nonperformance by students at both the secondary and postsecondary levels.

How responsive has academia been to these mounting pressures over the past 25 years? An honest answer would have to be ambivalent. We have clearly done an excellent job of expanding our institutions to afford greater access, not only by adding seats but by creating more flexible structures to facilitate attendance by nontraditional students. We have enlarged our system of graduate education to provide teachers for colleges and universities—though the character of advanced training often has little to do with preparation for the role of teacher. We have developed a research enterprise unrivaled in the world for quality and productivity. We have enriched the undergraduate curriculum, discipline by discipline, to take account of changes in knowledge and social interests, including those—as Kimball points out—out advanced under the banners of diversity and multiculturalism. We have evolved new forms of academic organization—most notably interdisciplinary centers and institutes—to assist industry and government in addressing social and technological problems.

Academia has done less well, however, in responding to other claims arising from our broadened social role. I am less impressed than Kimball by the recent reemphasis on general education, since few faculties, in my observation, have done much more than patch together distribution requirements that force students to take some course or other from a set of categories based on fairly standard combinations of the academic disciplines. I also see less evidence than does Kimball that most faculties are seriously addressing issues of values and citizenship in the formal curriculum. Similarly, it is far from clear that efforts to link higher education and the schools in a true K to 16 system, or to recognize a stronger link between teaching and scholarship, have yet gotten very far beyond the aspirations of a minority of reform-minded administrators and well-motivated professors. I recite these skeptical impressions reluctantly, since I believe we should be doing much more on all these fronts.

The pattern of academic response to recent critiques reflects, as it must, the underlying structures and dynamics of the academic enterprise. What drives change in our decentralized system of higher education, ultimately, is less the compelling power of ideas, such as pragmatism, than the interaction of institutional and professional interests within a market-oriented system dominated by competition among colleges and universities for prestige and resources. Our campuses have repeatedly demonstrated their capacity to adapt to new social needs, but they do so within the conventions of interinstitutional competition that are dominant at a given historical moment.

For most of the post–World War II period, the terms of interinstitutional competition in higher education have been determined by the model and values of the research university. As lower-ranking institutions have sought to improve their positions, they have tended to do so by becoming more like the major universities that occupy the upper echelons of the status hierarchy. Changes that advanced that kind of institutional agenda—such as the development of research-oriented graduate programs, the strengthening of scholarly standards, even the addition of new fields to the curriculum—have tended to gain support; changes that did not advance this agenda—including most of the ideas on Kimball's list of "trends"—have fared less well. Indeed, in the competitive context that has existed since the 1950s, little institutional or professional advancement has been gained by placing a greater emphasis on teaching, or building new programs of general education, or attending to questions of value in the curriculum, or working more closely with the schools—despite the evident importance of all of these matters. It is, in fact, precisely because these important issues have been neglected for so long that they are receiving so much attention from our critics.

The idea of pragmatic liberal education—that is, an approach that is evolutionary and responsive to context, that attempts to address the real needs of our students, that avoids ideology and especially the tendency to espouse a pure vision of liberal learning based on traditions established when higher education was restricted to elites—can be useful in opening up our thinking about how we can better serve the country. It can't, of course, do the whole job. We need new paradigms of institutional excellence that enable colleges and universities to compete with each other on the basis of the quality of teaching and learning that they foster rather than the scholarly output of their faculties. We need definitions of scholarship that acknowledge instructional effectiveness and mastery of disciplinary traditions as much as technical brilliance and productivity in an academic specialty. And we need to supplement Kimball's concept of pragmatic liberal education by encouraging faculties of arts and sciences that serve large numbers of modestly or poorly prepared students to offer something more compelling than a diluted version of the offerings available at our most selective colleges.

Three items, in particular, need to be added to Kimball's list. First, we should recognize that a large percentage of liberal arts graduates at many of our colleges and universities will not pursue advanced degrees. Such students need curricular options that enable them to develop useful occupational skills while simultaneously engaging them in the riches of liberal learning. A second thing we must do is address the issue of basic skills more honestly. At too many of our institutions we are passing students through programs that represent the traditional forms of liberal education without their underlying intellectual rigor, while looking the other way at skill levels among our graduates that are grossly inadequate for the challenges they face. Finally, we have for too long been complacent about majors that are little more than scaled-down graduate programs, with all the narrowness of perspective that that implies. We should be doing much more to utilize the major as a vehicle for exploring interdisciplinary relationships and thus for helping students develop the habit, so crucial in nonacademic problem solving, of thinking across conventional boundaries.

We have much work to do in recasting our system to tackle the challenges we currently face. The country needs us to address the task of reform with the utmost seriousness. The attitudes associated with pragmatism—and an approach to liberal education informed by those attitudes—can be an asset in this critical endeavor.

RICHARD M. FREELAND *is Vice Chancellor for Academic Affairs at the City University of New York.*

Pragmatism, Liberal Education, and Multiculturalism: Utilizing the "Master's Tools" to Restructure the "Master's House" for Diversity[1]

SHIRLEY HUNE

To use Clark Kerr's words, from 1960 to 1980 U.S. higher education underwent its second "great transformation." Higher education grew in numbers of students and types of institutions. It became more public than private, with state institutions providing universal access to those high school graduates who wished to attend. It became strongly linked to national economic and social policy through federal expenditures funding research and development and student aid. It experienced a significant shift in student interest and enrollment from the traditional liberal arts to professional studies. Compounding these changes were the student revolts of the late 1960s, which contributed to a more diverse student body, faculty, and curriculum. The results have been various efforts at academic and institutional reform that have managed to dissatisfy both those who sought increased equality of opportunity and those who opposed the modification of standards.[2]

The changes have been challenging and generally unwelcome to those who view liberal education as the training ground for the reproduction of the governing elite and for the cultural production, preservation, and transmission of appropriate knowledge and culture. The litany of popular best-sellers countering the changes, and the intensity of public debates that led to the terminology "the culture wars," suggest that many Americans no longer feel that their house is their home. But for those formerly closed out of higher education, the transformation is a much desired step toward democratizing U.S. society. As historic outsiders to higher education, students of color, women, older students, members of the working class, and those with disabilities are now seeking entry into the "master's house." Increasingly, supporters of the new diversity have also sought to restructure the master's house to make it

---

[1] I have borrowed the concepts of the "master's tools" and the "master's house" from Audre Lorde. *See Sister Outsider: Essays and Speeches* (Trumansburg, N.Y.: Crossing, 1984), 99.
[2] Clark Kerr, *The Great Transformation in Higher Education 1960–1980* (Albany, N.Y.: State University of New York Press, 1991), xii-xiii.

their home as well. Their renovations include the recruitment of faculty of diverse background, the establishment of multicultural curricula, and the revision of policies and practices to reduce barriers to access and ensure equity.

Bruce Kimball's essay on pragmatic liberal education offers us an opportunity to rethink liberal education. For Kimball, the recent developments in higher education have required a response beyond political or economic exigency and are reflected in changes in liberal education. That response, he argues, is grounded in the philosophy of pragmatism. His central argument is that liberal education, formerly disconnected from pragmatism, is at the end of this century strongly influenced by it.

In surveying current writings on liberal education, what strikes Kimball is the intersection of liberal education and pragmatism. Discussions about liberal education have shifted recently, and as Kimball notes, now center on at least seven concerns that are repeatedly highlighted in the literature. These include the affirmation of multiculturalism, the incorporation of values and service into liberal education, an emphasis on community and citizenship, attention to general education, identifying commonality and cooperation between college and other levels of the education system, the interpretation of teaching as learning and inquiry, and the need for assessment. Each of these aspects of liberal education, he argues, is deeply rooted in pragmatism, although not openly identified as such.

Kimball gives two significant reasons to explain the new influence of pragmatism on liberal education. The first, he suggests, could be termed "problems" in pragmatic terms. They are the cluster of recent changes in higher education that have challenged universities and colleges— Kerr's second great transformation. Kimball specifically notes the unprecedented growth in the numbers of undergraduates, the variety of backgrounds students bring to college, the need for curriculum reform, and what he terms "cautious vocationalism" on the part of students and their parents. Given the uncertainty of the U.S. economy and the escalating costs of attending college, there is an increased concern that a liberal education be linked to and serve the realities of the world of work.

The second reason Kimball offers for the return to pragmatism is the growing strength of U.S. universities and the academic profession. American intellectuals, in their increasing self-confidence and autonomy, have begun to redirect higher education away from European norms and to center it and liberal education within American culture.

Kimball concludes that the reemergence of pragmatism and its linkage with liberal education is the result of the confluence of the maturity and independence of academics and the need for higher education to respond to the most demanding set of challenges it has had to face. Clearly, Kimball has deep empathy for the new developments in liberal education, particularly the seven articulated previously. Hence, he utilizes an established and respected philosophical tradition to support current discussions about liberal education, some of which are hotly contested. In linking current developments in liberal education to pragmatism, Kimball establishes legitimate and historical claims to what many view as radical change in U.S. higher education. By grounding change in something familiar and revered, Kimball seeks to authenticate educational innovations that challenge the status quo and thus to make them more acceptable. In other words, if the master's house no longer feels like home to its original occupants, they should nonetheless feel secure knowing that the renovations are utilizing the "master's tools."

I do not concern myself here with whether or not Kimball has proved his point that "pragmatic liberal education" is emerging as we approach the twenty-first century. What he has done is to open the door to rethinking liberal education. In this context, I will add to the discussion with some remarks on liberal education in general and on multiculturalism.

Kimball says little about liberal education itself. Does liberal education as it is presently constituted and delivered meet the needs of current students and prepare them for the twenty-first century? Liberal education has traditionally been based on a privileged lifestyle. The typical undergraduate has been a white male who, with the financial support of his family, attended college full time after high school, lived on campus, and finished within four years without a debt. The undergraduate experience took place in a relatively closed and controlled environment. Students were provided with a defined liberal arts curriculum purported to be the "best" that had been written or said and one that remained relatively unchanged from one generation to another.[3] Graduates had little difficulty in finding gainful employment and those from elite institutions took their "proper places" in the economic, political, intellectual, and cultural leadership of the nation.

The master's house has changed in many respects. The G. I. Bill broke the class hegemony of higher education by opening the doors to the working and lower-middle classes. It also broke the age barrier as institutions adapted programs to educate the older student. The student revolts of the late 1960s further diversified the student body by social

---

[3] *See* Elizabeth Fox-Genovese, "The Claims of a Common Culture: Gender, Race, Class and the Canon," *Salmagundi* 72 (Fall 1986): 133.

class and age, but especially by race and gender. Today's undergraduates are predominantly female, include more students of color, and are older. Higher education has also diversified itself through the creation of different levels and types of institutions.

What has not changed in the master's house is the intellectual hegemony of liberal education as it has been traditionally defined. As I will discuss in greater detail later, the resistance to sharing the ownership of liberal education persists. The historic occupants continue to hold on to their privilege of determining what it means to be an educated person and a responsible and informed citizen in the 1990s. The value system, curriculum, and knowledge base of liberal education have yet to reflect the experiences and perspectives of the new diversity—minorities, women, the working class, and others. Nor do they do justice to global realities and to the influence of non-Western societies, their economies, religions, and cultures. What is the purpose and content of a liberal education in a multicultural and global world? To what extent is a liberal education fixed and immutable or dynamic, contextual, and situational?

The democratization of the student body, their lived experiences, and technological changes in the postmodern world also raise questions about the traditional delivery system of liberal education. The concept of a liberal education has assumed a controlled environment populated with students sharing similar backgrounds and values. Today's undergraduates have a distinctly different educational experience than had students of previous generations. They work, often attend college part time, and take longer to complete their degrees. Commuting to college from home is as common as living in residence. Even at elite institutions, students take developmental courses to prepare them for college-level work. They transfer from and to institutions. They step out of college for a time and return. They live in a world of technology in which the printed text, on which traditional liberal education was based, no longer dominates. Liberal education needs to address the vast explosion in information, as well as the relationship between a college education and a work world that is undergoing its own restructuring and transformation.

In short, a student's learning environment is no longer defined and controlled by the college or university, nor is it confined in time and space to four years on a campus. Higher education competes with work, home, the media, and the information superhighway for the student's attention. Hence the design of pragmatic liberal education must take into consideration the life experiences of undergraduates and the preparation they need for the future, as well as the *process* and *purpose* of such an education.

Kimball also identifies the affirmation of multiculturalism as a recurring theme in liberal education today. Multiculturalism is probably the most controversial aspect of current education reform. It was born out of protest and is part of a larger struggle for equity in the United States. I do not agree with Kimball that there is an "article of consensus" with regard to multiculturalism as an element of liberal education. And, for those who recognize the need for liberal education to incorporate multiculturalism, there is a lack of consensus and considerable contention over the meaning of multiculturalism itself and the extent to which it is to be incorporated.

I would argue that liberal education is far from being multicultural at this point. Higher education is increasingly attracting a diverse student body, but many racial and ethnic groups are still underrepresented. And students of diverse backgrounds, including women, are also concentrated in the community colleges. Furthermore, the increase in the diversity of students over the past 25 years is not reflected in the faculty, particularly at elite liberal arts colleges and research universities. In 1991, faculty of color were only 12 percent of all full-time faculty, an increase of just 3 percent in 10 years. Women of color were only 4 percent in 1991, a gain of merely 1 percent from 1981. In short, the diversification of the faculty has been exceedingly modest.[4] Minorities and women have entered the master's house, but they are transitory and do not hold positions of influence and power in it.

Multiculturalism means more than diversity of students and faculty. It includes multicultural education, which is a complexity of concepts including the integration of multicultural content, the construction of knowledge, and pedagogy.[5] The content of multicultural courses, their theoretical perspectives and methodologies, and their research findings are still suspect and devalued in the master's house. Those who teach and conduct research in these areas are similarly suspect, devalued, and less likely to obtain tenure.[6] To date, the majority of institutions of higher education have limited their curriculum reform to the adoption of a few ethnic-studies and gender-studies courses. Only a small number

---

[4] *See* Deborah J. Carter and Eileen M. O'Brien, "Employment and Hiring Patterns for Faculty of Color," Washington, D.C.: American Council on Education, *Research Briefs* 4 (1993): 9.

[5] *See* James A. Banks, "Multicultural Education: Historical Development, Dimensions, and Practice," in *Review of Research in Education*, ed. Linda Darling-Hammond (Washington, D.C.: American Educational Research Association, 1993), vol. 19.

[6] *See* Bernice R. Sandler, *The Campus Climate Revisited: Chilly for Women Faculty, Administrators, and Graduate Students* (Washington, D.C.: Project on the Status and Education of Women, Association of American Colleges, 1986); Marian J. Swoboda, ed. *Retaining and Promoting Women and Minority Faculty Members: Problems and Possibilities* (Madison, Wis.: University of Wisconsin System, 1990).

have instituted requirements in these areas for *all* students. Furthermore, the infusion of new content across the curriculum is generally restricted to one or two topics or readings, with no change in the overall approach or narrative, and is almost nonexistent outside of the humanities and social sciences. Consequently, multicultural content remains marginalized in the curriculum and largely dependent on the few minority and women faculty recruited to teach in these areas. Multicultural studies are yet to be viewed as central to the core curriculum, to general education, or to the requirements of a given major. For most students, the content of liberal education remains largely unchanged.

Assuring a place for multiculturalism in liberal education goes beyond content integration. Even more challenging is the concept of knowledge construction. Scholars in ethnic studies, women's studies, and more recently, cultural studies, have drawn attention to the ways in which knowledge is produced and legitimated. Multicultural studies identified how race, gender, class, religion, and other influences, as well as culture-based assumptions, worldviews, and biases within academic disciplines influence knowledge construction. They have also questioned the Enlightenment paradigm of liberal education and its exclusivity as defined by European and American male heterosexual experiences and interests.[7] The recognition that the knowledge-base of the liberal arts is socially constructed and neither value-free nor unbiased is thus far limited. At the same time, the reconstruction of this knowledge base to reflect multiple frames of reference remains a challenge even for those involved in multicultural studies. These problems result from the fact that even those who seek to restructure the master's house have been trained with the master's tools.

In addition, multicultural studies address pedagogy, which is noticeably absent from discussions about liberal education. Embedded in liberal education are pedagogical practices that mirror the power structure of American society by silencing the disadvantaged and privileging particular ways of knowing, being, learning, and thinking. While some attention has been given to transforming teaching methodologies at the K to 12 level, in higher education the dominance of the lecture method,

---

[7] *See*, for example, Sandra Harding, *Whose Science? Whose Knowledge?* (Ithaca, N.Y.: Cornell University Press, 1991); bell hooks, *Yearning* (Boston: South End, 1990); Elizabeth Kamarck Minnich, *Transforming Knowledge* (Philadelphia: Temple University Press, 1990); Renato Rosaldo, *Culture and Truth* (Boston: Beacon, 1989); Steven Seidman, *Contested Knowledge* (Oxford, England: Basil Blackwell, 1994); and Dorothy E. Smith, *The Everyday World as Problematic* (Boston: Northeastern University Press, 1987);

with teacher as expert and student as empty vessel, is rarely questioned. This method has been described by Paulo Freire as a passive and oppressive form of educational practice.[8] It is a practice that is contrary to the premise of liberal education to prepare citizens capable of thinking for and informing themselves. Embedded in multicultural studies is a critical pedagogy that seeks to empower the less advantaged, to respect different experiences and ways of knowing, and to enhance the active engagement of citizens in a democratic society.[9] Multicultural studies offer an opportunity to rethink the ways in which we teach and learn and how we involve a diverse student body in becoming full and active participants in society.

In its fullest definition, multiculturalism is a social movement to democratize American society and its institutions. Those involved in it have sought to transform liberal education and liberate it from its elitist standpoint. Pragmatic liberal education may facilitate this effort.

Pragmatic liberal education proposes using the master's tools to restructure the master's house. Audre Lorde has stated that "The Master's tools will never dismantle the master's house. They may allow us temporarily to beat him at his own game, but they will never enable us to bring about genuine change."[10] Hence pragmatic liberal education would address education reform rather than transformation. But then reform is very much in the philosophical tradition of social change in the United States.

SHIRLEY HUNE *is professor of Urban Planning in the School of Public Policy and Social Research and associate dean for Graduate Programs, Graduate Division at the University of California, Los Angeles.*

[8] Paulo Freire, *Pedagogy of the Oppressed* (New York: Continuum, 1990), 57-74.
[9] *See,* for example, Mary Field Belenky et al., *Women's Ways of Knowing: The Development of Self, Voice, and Mind* (New York: Basic Books, 1986); Kenyon S. Chan and Shirley Hune, "Racialization and Panethnicity: From Asians in America to Asian Americans," in *Toward a Common Destiny: Improving Race and Ethnic Relations in America,* ed. Willis D. Hawley and Anthony Jackson (San Francisco: Jossey-Bass, forthcoming); Henry A. Giroux, "Liberal Arts Education and the Struggle for Public Life: Dreaming About Democracy," in *The Politics of Liberal Education,* ed. Darryl J. Gless and Barbara Herrnstein Smith (Durham, N.C.: Duke University Press, 1992); Keith Osajima, "The Hidden Injuries of Race," in *Bearing Dreams, Shaping Visions,* eds. Linda A. Revilla et al. (Pullman, Wash.: Washington State University Press, 1993).
[10] Lorde, *Sister Outsider: Essays and Speeches,* 99.

Four Appreciative Queries

EVA T. H. BRANN

Don Quixote recants his chivalrous quest for the disenchantment of the Lady Dulcinea at the end of his book. Bruce Kimball, on the other hand, begins his essay with a recantation of the disillusioning claim that American liberal education has no indigenous tradition and then sets out on his beguiling search for a unifying theory, which he finds in pragmatism.

While an initial effect of Kimball's thesis on the participants at the seminar was to unite them in the view that there is no unifying American theory of education—any more than there is an American system of education—the pragmatist solution provides an excellent springboard from which to consider American liberal education in the context of a positive intellectual proposal. For me, reading Kimball's essay was invigorating. I shall, consequently, set aside his partial recantation of his recantation at the seminar and proceed to do his remarkable effort the best honor I know of, which is to bring forward four queries that seem to me to take the essay's thesis seriously and to invite a second round of clarifying discussion.

My first query addresses the fact that none of us who are responsible for the institutional health of a liberal arts college can these days get our minds off the chief menace of the moment (apart from regulation, which is not really an educational issue), namely, the so-called "new vocationalism," the opinion, attributed to a broad public, that higher education is chiefly vocational training. At first sight it seemed that Kimball might be providing a rationalization of our apparent nemesis—for pragmatism is, through John Dewey, an educational theory that links schooling to work. In fact Kimball presents no such direct connection to or disjunction from contemporary vocationalism, which means that his pragmatist account omits this influential recent phenomenon.

Let me give a brief description of it. The new vocationalism speaks of education in the language of the factory and the marketplace. It speaks of customers, products, quality control. It is born of the unhappy conjunction of the rising costs of college, falling prospects for employment, and the business community's discovery that the workforce is undertrained. The consequence is a loud call for the displacement of liberal education by vocational training in higher education (usually accompanied by a cursory bow to service, self-fulfillment, and values).

Now pragmatism as a philosophy of education has a certain surface relation to the vocational perspective, since it eschews the liberality of liberal education as originally understood, for example, by Aristotle. He construed "free pursuits" in opposition to the "useful arts," so that which was liberal or free was that which was done not for use but for its own sake. Kimball, however, reveals certain strange truths about pragmatism. For one, pragmatism is not exactly an all-American theory; at least the American education establishment has managed to ignore it as its underlying philosophy (61ff.). It is not clear that Americans, who tend to be nonphilosophical, would in fact welcome pragmatism's theoretical practicality, since their popular pragmatism shows a continual urge to flip into sheerest idealism. (Margaret Mead in her contribution to the war effort, *And Keep Your Powder Dry* [1942], notes a similar tendency for that much vaunted American materialism to etherialize itself into a form of idealism.) To add to the confusion, it seems that the present-day, real-life practicality of philosophical pragmatism is tenuous, since its cognitive version addresses the disciplined experience of a scientific elite (Charles S. Peirce), and its social version applies to a vanishing species, the conforming citizenry of a progressive democracy (John Dewey). I might even argue that pragmatism is in fact preeminently impractical, since in real life nothing gets done unless truth is out-front as an incentive, not emerging as a construct. But in this last point my prejudices speak.

My first query thus amounts to a desire for clarification: How is philosophical pragmatism related to ordinary pragmatism? How are both related to the current call for a severely practical higher education? What has the pragmatist theory of liberal education to say about this potent movement?

My second query concerns Kimball's method. At this point he might argue that the pragmatists' position would be antivocational, because they take so liberal and so sophisticated a stance on practicality in learning as to make its effects indistinguishable from those of the Aristotelian view. And that argument causes me some uneasiness. Kimball calls his method "pragmatic historical" (11)—pragmatic because it avoids essentialism and looks for the use and the logical consequences of the terms in question, historical because it is temporally longitudinal.

By its means, protean pragmatism must be made to yield up its descriptive nonessence. The method has the intellectual charm of being self-referential: a pragmatic procedure applied to the discovery of pragmatism. That is another way of saying that Kimball is friendly to his subject, a good thing, since it requires him to survey a vast field critically. One of the profitable pleasures in reading Kimball's work comes from his

widely absorptive study of texts of every conceivable quality; his essay is
a treasure trove of judicious references. For Kimball's procedure is to
make a collage of utterances, or better, to find their intersections and
produce a list of family resemblances.

Now this method seems to succeed in delineating what ancient
philosophers called "opinion" in the slightly pejorative sense. It is what
like-minded people think insofar as they *don't* think. It yields those curiously drained intellectual vessels called "abstracted propositions" or
"general frames of reference." This use of texts is not, it seems to me,
necessarily illegitimate, first, because once the word is made paper it has
to subject itself to anonymous restatement, and second, because the
resulting abstraction is somehow recognizable. Whether a contextless
and an authorless thought is more than an intellectual ghost is precisely
my query.

While scanning the six themes Kimball so derived (29), it seemed to
me that pragmatism-in-general is an aggregate that is less than the original parts, and that exists in a mist in which all cats are grey. To give a
perhaps somewhat contrived example, I amused myself by asking which
of the six themes Plato, the aboriginal anti-pragmatist, might take issue
with, and found myself replying for him, "Of course *X*—but in addition
also *Y.*" Thus the first theme of general pragmatism is "that belief and
meaning, even truth itself, are fallible and revisible" (29). To which
Socrates would say, "You are telling me, who invented dialectical refu-
tation—but also, there is truth ahead, which we are seeking." And the
sixth theme says "that all inquiry and thought are evaluative, and judgments about fact are not different from judgments about value" (29). To
which Plato might respond, "Where's the news to me who thought that
the source of intelligibility and of goodness is one?—but also, we may
sometimes come on truths that run quite counter to our human interests." The neatest case is Kimball's identification of pragmatic goodness
with fitness. The Greek word for excellence, *areté*, comes from the verb
ararisko, to fit or be suitable.

So the pragmatic historical method produces a pragmatism-in-
general, which, because it is based on comparisons of usages more than
on intended meaning, and on longitudinal readings more than on
individual authors, is a somewhat flaccid collage, which no particular
pragmatist might wish to acknowledge.

Yet the method yields something useful to be aware of, a recognizable
opinion scheme, a definable intellectual atmosphere.

My third query addresses the question of whether it is this opinion
complex that does in fact govern some large part of American thinking
on liberal education.

The schema that the pragmatist solution caused Kimball to retract was a very persuasive one, not as describing any institution but as providing two pretty perspicuous rubrics under which we could profitably try to range most conceptions of liberal education: the rhetorical and the philosophical. Kimball recapitulates his older dualistic theory (iii), which goes back to antiquity, and insofar as it fits the American scene shows that liberal education is rooted in Europe and has no purely American intellectual foundation (as what does?). These two models with all their historical vicissitudes and accommodations, the one centered on speaking well and all its concomitants and the other on thinking deeply and all its requirements, can be useful in clarifying what a particular education plan is getting at. To be sure, the abstracted dualistic schema suffers from a difficulty that is the opposite of the one faced by pragmatists. Where the latter melds all the different pragmatisms, the former disjoins modes that are in practice usually closely related. For example, my own institution, St. John's College, would certainly fall within the philosophical model, since it institutionally and unabashedly encourages the search for truth, but in its incessant attention to speech not only as telling truth but also as producing persuasion and touching the sensibility, it certainly has a stake in the rhetorical model as well.

Nonetheless, Kimball succeeds in showing that these two elements of education have been discernible from the earliest divergence of the signification of *logos* into speech and reason. Is the dual European model really superseded by the unitary American pragmatist model? My query is whether Kimball does not rather prove implicitly that pragmatism tends to reinforce the rhetorical side, since it is an antiphilosophical philosophy. Is pragmatism-in-general not a new element in his rhetorical model, especially in view of the pragmatist "linguistic turn"? (47). Might we not set up contrasting descriptive complexes in these terms?

Philosophical (speech as truth telling)	Rhetorical (speech as persuasive)
Liberal (learning as an end in itself)	Vocational (learning for social use)
Contemplative (truth as discovered object)	Pragmatist (truth as emerging construct)

The only purpose of my schema is to ask whether Kimball's pragmatist theory of liberal education does not perhaps in effect simply establish his previous rhetorical tradition as preferentially American?

My fourth query addresses Kimball's emphasis on the pragmatist collapse of the fact-value distinction, but that, at least, is not an element of his own pragmatic method. It yields a list of seven developments that characterize a pragmatist approach to liberal education (97) with which, I imagine, Kimball has sympathy, but which his descriptive mode does not judge. One might, as it happens, interpret the seven developments as a register of educational disasters. Let me give two examples, the first and the last developments. The others all seem to me to pose subtle but documentable threats to liberal education, but it would take more space to set out these arguments than I am allowed here.

First on the list is multiculturalism. The seminar seemed to regard the success of this movement as a given, though I wondered why. As a social policy, multiculturalism is highly deleterious to the minorities involved, and it is by no means clear that they want it. For example, recent studies in Hispanic communities have shown that it is more the leadership than the public in general who support multiculturalism; the immigrants by and large want what immigrants have always wanted— integration into the mainstream and economic opportunity. As a form of educational separatism, it is bound to lead to resentment because even the largest institutions cannot support departments or centers for all minorities, and as a form of educational integration, it will lead to disappointment because no course of study can do real justice to all the cultures from which Americans come. Meanwhile the more extreme multiculturalists, in attempting to break down the national community, leave the spheres of commerce and entertainment as the only common ground. Consequently the complement and reaction to this multiculturalism is apt to be fierce vocationalism, a serious assault on all liberal education even in its most diluted form.

Last on the list of developments is assessment. The harm that the assessment movement will do to liberal education is enormous. We now have a blessedly diverse *non*system (as all the participants agreed), capable of absorbing students of all degrees of talent and preparation. There are hundreds of small institutions that do essential work on the margins of higher education—historically black schools, Christian schools, "alternative schools." With national assessment these institutions will be endangered, or at least denigrated. Even if the standards are so vapid as to threaten no one, there will be yet another expensive and threatening bureaucracy. There will be teaching to the test and consequent homogenization. That there will be better learning we do not know, because no one can tell whether assessed schools and students are better schools and students. In any case, there will be yet another externality influencing learning. Whatever else assessment will do, it will impair liberal education. Take a concrete example: the "critical thinking" movement, largely a private enterprise, stands ready to take over the training for and testing of this illiberally defined skill.

To my mind—and I am not alone—liberal education is facing a severe crisis, and some of its features are those fairly neutrally described by Kimball as "pragmatist." My question is what method, if any, is now to be used for making the necessary critical judgments?

What is the good of all this fancy theorizing in the face of such a critical condition, one might ask. There *is* an answer, enforced by the consensus of the seminar, that institutions of liberal education must speak up to the public for themselves, not with one voice but with determinately diverse voices. Unified utterance about liberal education is evidently not achievable because there is, even after Kimball's essay, no agreement on a theory. One might even say that the essay focused the resistance to such a theory. Moreover, consensual speech about liberal education, were it achievable, would still be undesirable, because it would be—indeed insofar as it now exists, it is—flabby beyond bearing.

Liberal education has its concrete seat in institutional communities, and it is they, severally, who have to achieve a brisk, clear, persuasive language about themselves. While no sensible representative of such a community is likely to burden the public with much education philosophy, it seems to me that it is next to impossible for us to develop the power of suasion we yearn for without having honed our wits on theory of the sort Kimball has provided. These inversions of the quixotic quest serve a very practical purpose in our disenchanted world.

EVA T. H. BRANN *is dean at St. John's College, Annapolis, Maryland.*

Beyond Disciplinary Hierarchies in Higher Education

GREGSON DAVIS

On display in Bruce Kimball's essay are at least three recurrent issues that he manages to keep aloft, like so many juggling pins, with considerable dexterity: the perennial debate about the adequacy and relevance of the liberal arts in an age and a society increasingly dominated by science; the rise, fall, and resurgence of the homegrown American philosophical movement known as "pragmatism"; and the putative relationship ("convergence") between the trajectories of the current neo-pragmatic revival, on the one hand, and the ongoing moves to refigure undergraduate curricula, on the other. Within the circumscribed space of this response, I shall set forth briefly what I see as the major conceptual clouds that hover above and around these three horizons, and offer reflections on some of the risks, as well as rewards, involved in manipulating such an array of ideas and values.

First, with commendable concern for the longer, historical perspective, Kimball provides a cogent account of the dichotomies that have marked the debate over liberal education through the ages. From the ancient Greek "quarrel" between philosophy and rhetoric (famously represented as such by Plato in terms of the Socratic versus the Sophistic approaches to education) to polarizations of more recent vintage, such as fact versus value, Kimball's excursions into the history of educational ideals vividly remind us that we are probably dealing with perennial pendulum swings that owe as much to ephemeral polemical stances as to deep substance. Like the recurrent pseudo-opposition between "hard" and "soft" disciplines, for instance, the ostensible cleavage between the liberal arts, on one side, and science, on the other (compare C. P. Snow's "two cultures"), is by no means as profound and unbridgeable as the most fervent advocates on either side have insisted on portraying it.

My own conversations over the years at several major universities with undergraduate science majors who have expressed frustration at their encounter with "fuzzy studies" have made me realize that terms like "fuzzy" say much more about the speakers' anxieties in the face of cross-disciplinary exposure to the humanities than about the epistemological bases of the differing disciplines involved. In the long history of the polemic in its various transformations and reincarnations there have been, needless to say, intermittent voices proposing ways of mediating (and thereby transcending) the dichotomy, e.g., Cicero's well-known definition of the ideal orator as *vir bonus dicendi peritus* ("a good man skilled in speaking"). A prime task of those of us who wish to improve the quality of dialogue among the warring disciplines, then, is to overcome such reductive oppositions by pointing out that neither the sciences nor the humanities have a monopoly on fuzziness or lucidity.

Second, despite Kimball's express intent to circumvent what he himself calls "the problem of relating normative and descriptive purposes" in his quest for a "pragmatic historical method" (11), he eventually comes close to proposing (and, by extension, prescribing) a philosophy of education that he derives mainly from pragmatism à la John Dewey as a cure for the historical dichotomies mentioned earlier. This prescriptive undercurrent, though somewhat occluded in the main historical narrative, comes to the fore in the chapter significantly entitled "*Toward* Pragmatic Liberal Education" (emphasis mine), where Kimball concludes, *inter alia*, that a renascent pragmatism is the best foundation on which to build "an emerging consensus" in current discussions about the future of liberal education.

Whether we accept Kimball's viewpoint as primarily descriptive of an actual historical convergence or prescriptive of a consensus that will repair the disjunction of the past, it is important to raise the issue of his implicit privileging of a single discipline, philosophy, in his laudable effort to transcend the crippling dichotomies. On the face of it, philosophy might seem to be the obvious choice for a disciplinary model destined to sponsor a large-scale revitalization of the threatened concept of a liberal education. Similar totalizing claims, however, can readily be made on behalf of other disciplines. I myself have recently renewed my sponsorship of the claims of cultural anthropology as the all-inclusive discipline that will most efficiently engender nonhierarchical approaches to the study of diverse cultural traditions.[1] Others have constructed equally plausible cases for the privileging of, say, mathematics, on the grounds of the overwhelming impact of science and technology on contemporary society. The point I wish to stress here is that pragmatism, despite the disclaimers of its proponents, is no more or less "universalist" than other schools of philosophy with which it is in competition as a totalizing system.[2] An agenda that is truly

[1] *See* Gregson Davis, "Between Cultures: Toward a Redefinition of Liberal Education," in *African Studies and the Undergraduate Curriculum*, eds. P. Alden, D. Lloyd, and A. Samatar (Boulder, Colo. and London: Lynne Reicher, 1994); cp. W. B. Carnochan, *The Battleground of the Curriculum: Liberal Education and American Experience* (Stanford, Calif.: Stanford University Press, 1993), 104.

[2] *See* Charles S. Peirce, *Philosophical Writings of Peirce*, ed. Justus Buchler (New York: Dover, 1955), 42-43.

transdisciplinary must ipso facto eschew any seeming allegiance to a favored discipline (let alone a particular school within such a discipline) if it is not to appear arbitrary in its choice of prescriptive instrumentality.

Third, behind Kimball's approval of the neo-pragmatic "return to Dewey" (as formulated most influentially by Richard Rorty) lies a desire he shares with most educators, myself included, to redefine for our time what constitutes the ideal undergraduate education. Here I am fully in sympathy with Kimball's endorsement of the movement that used to be called "general education." As a direct and grateful beneficiary of that approach, which I experienced at Harvard in the late 1950s in the form of a salutary broadening of disciplinary horizons, I am strongly in favor of reinstating this earlier concept, and even of replacing the term liberal education with general education, especially in view of the elitist accretions that cling to the former designation. One of the chief advantages of the older general education model was the way in which it maintained the integrity of the disciplines while at the same time initiating students into the habit of thinking across disciplines. To use my own case as an illustration, I am convinced that, had I gone from a British colonial "sixth form" directly to Oxbridge and, irrevocably, to further overspecialization in the minutiae of classical philology, I would have received a far narrower education at the university level than I experienced during the heyday of James Conant's vision of general education at Harvard, where, though I "concentrated" in classics, I nonetheless was obliged to round out my academic perspectives with courses in the social and natural sciences.

At its best, then, the ideal of a general education, to which I, perhaps nostalgically, continue to subscribe, goes beyond a viewpoint that would posit a particular discipline, such as philosophy, as a neutral zone for opposing troops in the "battleground of the curriculum" (to borrow the apt phrase from the title of W. B. Carnochan's recent book).[3] Rather, philosophical discourse would be presented to undergraduate initiates on equal terms with the other major disciplinary discourses to which they would be exposed as a matter of principle. To be sure, something akin to what may be labeled, *faute de mieux*, the "scientific method," may be said to underlie all disciplines that value research in the higher reaches of academia, but *pace* Dewey and his nostrums, there is no easily formulated consensus on what that method is. As a matter of effective strategy, therefore, the promotion of critical thinking (even the innocuous "fallibilist" approaches described by the more stimulating pragmatists, such as William James and Charles S. Peirce) might more

---

[3] Carnochan, *The Battleground of the Curriculum*.

persuasively be couched in terms of a standard that is perceived to be truly transdisciplinary. In this regard, "experimentalism" certainly fits the bill, but it does not need to be packaged as part of a specifically (neo-)pragmatist platform.

Fourth, in promoting the egalitarian ends he ascribes to the pragmatist world view, Kimball directs our attention to the current vogue of "multiculturalism." This concept, which is no longer a mere buzzword but a rallying cry of curricular reformists at various levels of instruction, he rightly regards as a central component in whatever consensus can be discerned, even tentatively, in the current ideological cacophony. In this respect, I would like to sound a note of solidarity as well as caution. To the extent that a multicultural agenda refers principally to the dethronement of Eurocentric representations of culture, it is clearly an idea whose time is woefully overdue. I vividly recall a conversation with a former colleague in which I was pointedly asked to justify my emphasis on Haitian culture in a symposium I had organized on Caribbean studies. My interlocutor wanted to know about cathedrals and other symbols of European culture in the context of judging Haitian accomplishments; with some impatience I responded that a culture that had produced the only successful slave revolt in history needed no special pleading.

My temptation now, as then, is to favor legislation of a required course in cultural anthropology that would confront learners with their own unexamined assumptions about what constitutes culture or civilization. Multiculturalism, however, need not be the monopoly of any one discipline in the humanities. Furthermore, it is important for advocates of what I prefer to call an "intercultural" perspective not to fall into the trap of sounding defensive about the dethronement of Europe. Literary studies may serve as a telling example. Anyone who has kept up with the genre of the novel in this century cannot fail to be struck by the non-European provenance of some of its major practitioners (Gabriel Garcia Marquez, Toni Morrison, and V. S. Naipaul spring immediately to mind). And in the domain of poetry, Pablo Neruda, Audre Lorde, and Derek Walcott can surely hold their own in the company of the best contemporary European poets. In fine, those who would dismiss multiculturalism as lacking in intellectual justification have simply not been paying attention to the expanded geographical horizons of superior literary achievement in our era. I suspect that some of the negative reactions to multiculturalism stem from its political genesis in the protests of minority students rather than from a thoughtful examination of its intrinsic worth.

Kimball's narrative culminates in a distillation of seven developments (of which multiculturalism is only one) of a putative consensus on broad educational desiderata. Rather than attempting to comment on each of these in turn, I shall treat the case of the multiculturalist movement as representative in pursuing further the tangential issue of whether the ongoing conversation it has so far provoked is marked as much by assent as by dissent. It is worth pointing out, in passing, that there are whole areas of the college curriculum that are virtually unaffected by the ferment sparked by the movement. It is hard to conceive, for instance, in what fundamental sense fields like mathematics or the physical sciences are implicated in the "culture wars," except in very attenuated and marginal ways (e.g., the increased respect for, and assimilation of, ethnoscientific data in the medical sciences).

The humanities, it must be conceded, are the authentic arena for the multicultural agon, most strenuously so in the disciplines of literature and history. Here it is by no means transparent to most observers of the academic scene that a consensus is emerging from behind the clouds. Take the conspicuous instance of the debate over the enlargement of the literary canon alluded to previously. From this more focused angle of vision, multiculturalism may be regarded simply as the latest phase in the evolution of a debate that first took shape in the battles over the reorganization of "Great Books" and "Western Civilization" courses close to a decade ago. This debate was typified most memorably in the oratorical conflicts that gripped Stanford University surrounding the merits of a required course for undergraduates in Western Culture. Adherents of the prior (now dethroned) Eurocentric model are still to be heard, though what has emerged in practice is better described as compromise rather than consensus.[4] Assimilation of marginal or previously excluded voices, then, is emblematic and more accurately predictive of the kind of accommodation that, in my view, is likely to occur in the future as far as reform of the undergraduate humanities curricula in our leading institutions is concerned. We are certainly now more inclined to treat Sappho, for instance, as a major figure in general literature courses—a development, it needs to be stressed, that restores her to the level of renown she formerly enjoyed in antiquity as an acknowledged member of the supreme canon of the "nine lyric poets."

A stable consensus in matters educational, whether we are dealing with curriculum content or pedagogy, or even student attitudes such as altruism or preprofessionalism, may turn out to be an elusive goal. This very elusiveness, however, may prove to be a sign of health rather than decadence, if we truly subscribe to a revivification of the Socratic

---

[4] Cp., Herbert Lindenberger, "The Western Culture Debate at Stanford University," *Comparative Criticism* 11 (1989).

approach to the search for truth and knowledge. Was it not by challenging the established order and its cherished, but sclerotic and unexamined assumptions, that Socrates succeeded as an educator of "transnational," if not "transhistorical" value?

GREGSON DAVIS *is the Andrew W. Mellon professor of Humanities at Duke University, Durham, North Carolina.*

On the "Purposes" of Liberal Education

In *The Battleground of the Curriculum: Liberal Education and American Experience*[1] I proposed that we could perform the offices of "liberal education" better if we could better establish the purpose of what we are trying to do. It was an unwary proposition, open to reservations that ought to be taken into account, all of them reservations from what can roughly be described as a pragmatist point of view. Though I largely subscribe to an educational pragmatism, albeit (as Bruce Kimball perceives) without hanging out the banner of an allegiance that could well have been made more explicit, I don't doubt the existence, the usefulness, or the necessity of what can be called a self-corrective or an "autopoetic" reason. In denying the traditional claims of overriding principles and deductively generated programs, pragmatists sometimes blur reason's narrower capacity to make midcourse adjustments, to decide to come up higher or lower into the wind in order to make more headway. I want instead to highlight this narrower capacity of reason in connection with the questions: How does change happen? How can it?

I will begin with two philosophers of quite a different stripe, namely Michael Oakeshott (the Burkean pragmatist) and Richard Rorty (the "neo"-pragmatist) who, whatever their differences, each begin by doubting the primacy of principles or purposes. Then I will add a word about Kimball's critique of "the criteria of purposefulness" before trying to clarify what I had and still have in mind when I talk about specifying "whatever it is, educationally, that we are trying to do."

I turn first to Oakeshott, who wrote in a 1950 piece called, after Newman, "The Idea of a University": "It is a favourite theory of mine that what people call 'ideals' and 'purposes' are never themselves the source of human activity; they are shorthand expressions for the real spring of conduct, which is a disposition to do certain things and a knowledge of how to do them."[2] Therefore it follows, in Oakeshott's dry comment on a habit even more common today than in 1950, that "the current talk about the 'mission' and the 'function' goes rather over my

[1] W. B. Carnochan, *The Battleground of the Curriculum: Liberal Education and American Experience* (Stanford, Calif.: Stanford University Press, 1993).

[2] Michael Oakeshott, "The Idea of a University" [1950], in *The Voice of Liberal Learning: Michael Oakeshott on Education*, ed. Timothy Fuller (New Haven, Conn.: Yale University Press, 1989), 95.

head; I think I can understand what is intended, but it seems to me an unfortunate way of talking."[3] To which I would add a firm assent. Anyone who has suffered (as I occasionally have) through meetings when so-called mission statements have been up for discussion will recognize the strangeness of the exercise. To come back to the nautical metaphor, it feels like trying to blow wind into one's own sails. The boat is probably not really becalmed, of course, but during the time one is laboring over a "mission statement," it certainly feels that way.

Yet as Timothy Fuller made too plain in his introduction to a volume of Oakeshott's writings on education, it is easy to turn a mistrust of mission statements and even of missions into what looks like a defense of tradition for tradition's own sake. Of the contemporary education scene, Fuller said, "What has been obscured, if not lost, is the *idea* of a school, a college, a university."[4] He continued, "It is important to emphasize the danger this loss entails. Many mistakenly assume that what is missing is an organizing, energizing purpose or goal for education. It is characteristic of our time to look for ulterior purposes, and to design programmes to achieve them, rather than to recall what we have already learned how to do and to take that as our guide."[5] It seems not far from here to Matthew Arnold's Oxford with its Gothic spires, its lost causes, and its habits of elegy. Or, to recast my complaint in the more pointed language of Samuel Coleman, whose essay "Is There Reason in Tradition?" (included in a volume presented to Oakeshott on his retirement) paid Oakeshott the tribute of dissent, "traditional practices can be shown to have 'reason': they provide satisfactions to some, at least. Yet, in time, they usually fall short of the criterion of 'rationality' made more volatile by our racing science and technology."[6] At the point where traditional practices are felt to fall short, whether for reasons of technological change or otherwise, the question will necessarily be: what now?

Before coming to a particular case of "what now?" I want to consider the example of Rorty, a pragmatist with as firm a distrust as Oakeshott of mission statements (in any form), a conservative in the sense of seeing no clearly better alternative to the social order of bourgeois liberalism, but nonetheless dramatically, even melodramatically, alert to the structures of change. Rorty on change, however, is not always an easy

[3] Oakeshott, "The Idea of a University," 96.

[4] Timothy Fuller, "Introduction: A Philosophical Understanding of Education," in Oakeshott, *The Voice of Liberal Learning*, 3.

[5] Fuller, "Introduction," in Oakeshott, *The Voice of Liberal Learning*, 3-4.

[6] Samuel Coleman, "Is There Reason in Tradition?" in *Politics and Experience: Essays Presented to Professor Michael Oakeshott on the Occasion of His Retirement*, eds. Preston King and B. C. Parekh (Cambridge: Cambridge University Press, 1968), 282.

thinker to grasp, and it is with this question in sight that I want to look at his *Contingency, Irony, and Solidarity*.

In the first place, Rorty rejected traditional modes of philosophic investigation: "Any argument to the effect that our familiar use of a familiar term is incoherent, or empty, or confused, or vague, or 'merely metaphorical' is bound to be inconclusive and question-begging." And why? Because "such arguments are always parasitic upon, and abbreviations for, claims that a better vocabulary is available."[7]

By inference, therefore, to claim that our understanding of liberal education is not fully coherent, as I do, amounts to an abbreviated version of the claim that a better vocabulary is available; let's say the new vocabulary of multiculturalism or some other vocabulary as yet unknown or but dimly perceived. This is actually a radical proposition, even a revolutionary one, for it implies that real change, being dependent on paradigm shifts or, in Rorty's language, on basic metaphorical reconfigurations, demands the sort of conceptual turn that Rorty associates with the assorted names of Galileo, Hegel, and the later Yeats. Real change "cannot be reached by an inferential process."[8] Rorty's argument here effectively dismisses as irrelevant (or worse) the middle ground of a practical reason; and yet that middle ground is where, pragmatically speaking, most of us spend a good part of our daily lives.

But there is another side to Rorty, too, namely his knowledge that paradigm shifts and metaphorical reconfigurations are themselves past-dependent: "Metaphors are unfamiliar uses of old words, but such uses are possible only against the background of other old words being used in old familiar ways"—old words, that is, like "liberal education," on which the new idea of "multicultural education" is self-evidently dependent. "Even the strongest poet, " said Rorty, following Harold Bloom, "is parasitic on her precursors."[9] So even the late Yeats is no revolutionary except in a colloquial sense. Does it not follow that, if in fact the difference between strong poets and others, say quotidian philosophers who argue about the coherence of a familiar terminology, is a difference only in degree, then we have reason to take heart when forced to choose between doing the best we can with what we have and doing nothing? There are not many strong poets like Galileo or Hegel or Yeats, but there are quite a few of us, philosophers and others, who can carry on an argument. Rorty himself is one of that number. Because we are not

[7] Richard Rorty, *Contingency, Irony, and Solidarity* (Cambridge: Cambridge University Press, 1989), 8-9, 9.
[8] Rorty, *Contingency, Irony, and Solidarity*, 12.
[9] Rorty, *Contingency, Irony, and Solidarity*, 41.

Galileo or Hegel or Yeats, does it follow that we should give up hope of contributing something to the process of historical change—even if that something only happens to enforce a gathering recognition that old paradigms are wearing thin and need to be replaced, when the right strong poet comes along, with new ones? Is the way not open to the utility of a practical reason, "parasitic" or not?

In fact, that is the real character of Rorty's own project in *Contingency, Irony, and Solidarity*; namely an effort not to establish new foundations of liberal democracy, much less to overturn it, but to redescribe it. To redescribe cannot be an ungrounded exercise, if only because the very idea of liberal democracy rests on a foundation laid not necessarily by Locke or Jefferson, but on a history that has incorporated the description of liberal democracy as *having* such foundations as those that Locke and Jefferson once offered. That brings me back to my proposition that we could do better by better understanding what it is we're trying to do.

It also brings me to Kimball's concern that by seeking criteria of the purposeful I have fallen into the Serbonian bog of essentialism—where whole armies of philosophers, I agree, have sunk. What I intended to claim was this: when it comes to liberal education as embodied in particular requirements in particular universities in particular places with particular students, it makes sense to redescribe what we are doing and why we are doing it as carefully as possible. That is what I actually thought I *had* said, but no doubt not clearly enough. Nothing in the world could induce me to prescribe the essence of a Liberal Education. All I hope for is attention to what our liberal education, in certain of its aspects, specifically aims to do. If U.S. education still requires some grand metaphorical reconfiguration, no doubt it will come in time. In the meanwhile, patient redescription and analysis will serve better than the disorderly scuffling of the recent past.

Now I want to bring the case down to cases, in particular to the kind of required courses, not in existence everywhere but much contested where they do exist, that have provided an arena for those wishing to change the education agenda, on the one hand, or those wishing to rescue Western Civilization from its would-be destroyers on the other. By no means could such courses be construed as amounting to a liberal education *tout court*, which is why they make a good laboratory case. Even if we shouldn't expect, or don't need, a definition of the mission of liberal education, that hardly means we should give up all scrutiny of the curriculum. Surely nobody believes we should drop the sails and tiller and just drift helplessly.

And, coming to the exemplary case of requirements in Western Civilization, which can be regarded as the product of a specifically

American curriculum, I start by pointing to just three things, among many others, that have been claimed as providing the course's pedagogical justification: preparing students for assuming civic responsibilities in the American democracy; understanding our own cultural genealogy—or, as it is more often named by those I will call for convenience conservatives, our cultural heritage; and understanding diversity in the American "multiculture." I single out these three claims because they represent in outline a chronological history of American liberal education, in its most visible aspect, since somewhere near the turn of the century. First came "civics" as a school discipline in the late nineteenth century, which in turn generated the post—World War I flowering of courses in "Contemporary Civilization" and "Western Civilization"; then the withering of civics as a respectable influence in the university, along with a new concern for "great books" and their "cultural heritage"; and, most recently, a new and compensatory multiculturalism.

The thing to notice about this mini-history and its evolving descriptions of what Western Civilization requirements are for is the underlying consistency of concern with who we as Americans are and what our responsibilities to the society are. Furthermore, all three versions of the case assume, even when they do not explicitly specify, the values of a common social bond achieved through the shared experience of U.S. education itself. As is obvious, such a commonalty of value assures no unity of opinion about what the curriculum should contain. But should we therefore judge such statements as empty vessels, statements of purpose detached from any verifiable reality, or merely anxious codifications of whatever it is that happens to be being done? And if we judge multiculturalism as approaching the condition of strong poetry, should we nonetheless dismiss it on grounds that, since even strong poetry cannot escape its own past, we do better to take shelter in a tradition-based skepticism?

I think these would be the counsels of unjustified despair, if only because looking attentively at the several pedagogical justifications of Western Civilization reveals an oddly common discrepancy between supposed ends and actual means, especially when it comes to number two (cultural heritage) and number three (diversity). It turns out that we do *not* know very well what we have been doing recently, given the purposes that, on a pragmatic view, can be taken to derive from the force of practice and of desire. Even if that accurately describes how, in fact, the intentional statements were achieved, their very existence highlights a gap that could not be measured in their absence. And, as Oakeshott said, even if "the act precedes the reflection," that should not be construed to mean that reflection therefore need or should be subordinate to action.[10]

[10] Michael Oakeshott, "Historical Change: Identity and Continuity," in Michael Oakeshott, *On History and Other Essays* (Oxford, England: Basil Blackwell, 1983), 118.

The gap I have in mind lies in the failure of some programs with traditional cultural or not-so-traditional multicultural aims to examine sufficiently the logic of what is and what is not to be included. For if the desire is on the one hand to offer students the experience of our cultural heritage, or on the other to offer them the experience of our cultural diversity, it follows in either case that, as things now go, something is often missing—and that something is an adequate sampling of American culture itself. Have the William Bennetts and the Allan Blooms not noticed that Western Civilization as sometimes taught simply excludes classic American texts, probably in the implicit but untrue belief that students will come upon them sometime anyhow? Have the advocates of the multicultural not noticed or ignored the same exclusion, as damaging to them as to the conservatives because, if diversity is the desideratum, it is hardly furthered by the omission from the curriculum of, say, Franklin, Hamilton, Melville, Wharton, and DuBois? An incoherence lies at the heart of some of our fondest curricular commitments.

By way of evidence, I will describe what it would be grossly generous to call a survey that I ran in a small undergraduate seminar at Stanford last year—despite misgivings about E. D. Hirsch-like inquests into cultural literacy—with an eye to confirming my sense that an acquaintance with classic American culture was not something generally shared by Stanford undergraduates. It was a thoroughly nonrandom survey, comprised almost wholly of English majors, largely seniors. And to the question, had they ever read Franklin's autobiography or de Tocqueville or any novel of Wharton or DuBois's *The Souls of Black Folk* or a number of other canonical texts, the answers were in fact often "yes," but only, I was told, because as English majors many of them had taken a popular course on American literature and culture before 1855. Otherwise they agreed their answers would have been mostly "no," since neither in any introductory requirement nor in high school had the material been assigned. Of the texts I named, only *The Souls of Black Folk*, crazily enough in a time of multiculturalism but perhaps not surprisingly, pretty much drew a blank; multicultural requirements often mean a novel here, another novel there, but little more. Of U.S. university students, how many will ever have heard of DuBois by the time they graduate?

I also took the chance to inquire into these students' acquaintance with three classical names in nineteenth-century American art: Homer, Eakins, and Cassatt. Here I expected lower returns, since art has never found its way into a canon dominated by "great books," but I was (naively?) surprised by just how much lower the returns really were. Of the 13 students responding, 8 had heard of none of the three painters, and no one had heard of all three. Without suggesting an equivalence of painterly value, it's worth pondering how 13 French university students would respond if asked whether they had ever heard of Manet, Monet, and Renoir. Of course, it's likely that the 13 American students I polled would also have known the French Impressionists, and that's part of my point. If America suffers from a culture deficiency, as the Bennetts and the Blooms would claim, it's quite as much because we have not yet truly learned to value our own culture as because we have drifted away from reading only dead white European males. Despite all our patriotic utterance and despite the accomplishments of American culture (whether "high" or in the vernacular), we have never outgrown the inferiority complex vis-à-vis Europe that has bedeviled us since the founding of the Republic. And, in any case, you need not believe that Mary Cassatt was as significant a painter as Renoir (though it is not a totally preposterous claim, even granting Renoir's formative influence) in order to believe that American university students would be well served by learning who she was and what she painted.

Lest I be misunderstood, I am not saying that everybody absolutely has to know about Mary Cassatt, because that kind of prescriptiveness is among other things utterly impractical. What I am saying is that when questions of the curriculum, its inclusions and its exclusions, are debated, it is typically within too narrow a band of possibilities simply because the logic of opposing positions has not been fully thought out. Perhaps this might go to prove that principles and purposes and even descriptions and redescriptions are wholly to be avoided because they are bound to be jury rigged and saturated by self-interest. I think, on the contrary but by all means pragmatically, that it proves that statements or descriptions of purpose (which I now lump together because there is generally less rhetorical difference between them than the effort to distinguish each from the other might imply) can serve as good tools of measurement, useful heuristic devices rather than prefabricated decrees.

Finally, why is pragmatism both so pervasive and so regularly taken for granted? My answer is, because pragmatism is a philosophy that at best *demands* to be taken for granted—and that this, philosophically speaking, is probably its greatest virtue. A pragmatism such as John Dewey's tells us to get on briskly with ordinary tasks, whatever exactly they may be. This is a welcome piece of advice in the American context, for however we may worry about how much we lack in culture, we like to think we make it all up when it comes to matters practical. Whether this self-image is accurate or not could be doubted, but none of the counterevidence, which after all is in considerable supply, has yet been sufficient to dislodge it. In such a climate, pragmatism flourishes like a flower unseen.

W. B. CARNOCHAN *is Richard W. Lyman professor of the Humanities, emeritus, at Stanford University, Stanford, California.*

Response to Bruce Kimball's "Toward Pragmatic Liberal Education"

EDMUND W. GORDON

Kimball has presented us with an essay that is almost as frustrating as it is brilliant. His conceptual analysis is richly descriptive of the intellectual currents and political cross-currents that have intermingled to form the fabric of liberal education. This is an informative and very useful essay, but it is frustrating in the sense that Kimball has used descriptive analysis not only to generate a conceptually driven history but also to make normative statements about liberal education. Although Kimball acknowledges the tensions inherent in efforts to move from data that are descriptive of what is to normative statements concerning what will or should be, his essay contributes little to the reduction of these tensions. In fact, I find that this work contributes to these tensions rather than reducing them. I think Kimball's essay points us in the wrong direction. He seems to look at the form rather than at the substance of what the academy is about. From his description of those manifested forms, he attempts to understand, predict, and to some extent prescribe. I agree that there are prominent pragmatic elements in the history of higher education, but there also have been ideas and implicit, even if unstated, purposes. These tend to get overlooked in the context of Kimball's efforts to support his thesis that pragmatism is the driving force. I contend that his use of these descriptive data in support of his thesis provides insufficient evidence with which to address the normative questions, if by normative we mean what should and can be.

I have less need to contest Kimball's descriptive analysis of the concepts, issues, and pressures that have shaped U.S. higher education than to challenge his interpretation of these phenomena. Kimball gives considerable attention in his descriptions, classification, and labeling of developments in the history of higher education to their correspondence to philosophical currents extant at the time. Because either these developments meet criteria for being called pragmatic or their emergence was contemporaneous with the prominence of pragmatic philosophy, he appears to also argue that the developments derive from pragmatism, and thus that pragmatism has guided and should and will guide the future development of higher education. This logic seems to me to be tautological. I find the seven developments he identifies in modern higher education consistent with, even reflective of, pragmatic thought, but they are not necessarily grounded or rooted in pragmatism. Nor is this correspondence between pragmatism and developments in the field sufficient evidence to support his assertion of a causal relationship between them.

Kimball's appropriately acknowledged tensions between descriptive and normative statements are procedural with respect to his essay. Of more substantive concern are the essential tensions between the purpose of the academy as an institution of conservation and its purpose as an institution of reformation or revolution—conserving what is considered to be the best, the seed, the yeast, yet preserving space for and nurturing of the mutant, the maverick, and the new. The academy may be pragmatic with respect to how these tensions have been managed, but that history should not cloud the fact that this historical path is strewn with the remnants of conceptual, epistemological, and ideological struggles. I prefer to read this history of higher education as indicative of continuing human efforts at the preservation of knowledge even as new knowledge is produced; at sense making and transformation of things in the interest of problem solving; at the interpretation and transfer of knowledge, understanding, and technique; and fundamentally at the development and refinement of human intellective capacities. Jean Paul Sartre has reminded us that intellectuals and universities, in their roles as nurturers of intellect, are caught in a paradox of contradiction because they are, by their very nature, conservative of the traditions, the collective experience, the accumulated knowledge of humankind. Paradoxically, however, one who has acquired or developed intellect has, in the process, become committed to criticism, which is a primary condition for change and transformation. Rather than being characterized as pragmatic, I see this movement as purposeful, but directed at paradoxical purposes, i.e., both conservation and transformation. At the extremes these efforts are alternatingly reactionary and revolutionary, and sometimes bidirectional at one and the same time. The search is not so much for what works or for a response to the bell that is ringing at the moment, but for the reconciliation of the demands of the contradictory purposes of the academy.

Now why is my challenge to Kimball's claims for pragmatism so important? It becomes clearer when we turn to his treatment of the demographic changes of the present, and the debates concerning the integrity of the canon. If we follow Kimball's argument, the debates to which higher education is responding are the demands of the changing demographics of the society and the academy as we struggle with multicultural education. He seems to see these debates as an argument over whose culture, whose history, whose voice will be privileged. According to this view, it is the presence of new players and the recognition of diverse identities that are reshaping the academy. The pragmatic response is then guided by judgments as to what is necessary to appease contending claimants to control of the curriculum. I see these debates as peripheral political skirmishes. The substantive struggles have to do with changing notions concerning the nature and sources of knowledge; with changing notions concerning what it means to know and understand; with changing conceptions of the processes by which teaching and learning are mediated; with changing conceptions of the affective and cognitive mechanisms and meanings of human mental activity. While on the surface, curriculum decisions are being influenced by the heat of the political debates, behind discipline-based councils' deliberations I see scholars worrying about more accurate representations of knowledge, about the protean nature of the relationships among most phenomena, and about the critical roles of appreciation of relational adjudication, contextual analysis, and perspectivist interpretation in the intellective behavior of learning persons. Now these are the seeds, the yeast, the new, the revolutionary elements in the academy. Yet the same scholars are struggling to maintain respect for knowledge anchors, that which is independent of context and perspective, and to assert the cruciality of the disciplines as the lenses through which experience and knowledge—new and old—must be mediated. The underlying questions are not the pragmatics of canonical politics but the epistemologic and pedagogic implications of humans' continuing efforts at making sense of and changing the phenomena of the world through the one institution that, at one and the same time, has responsibility for both their conservation and their transformation.

While I appreciate the fact that Kimball's essay has created an occasion for the discussion of what the academy is and should be about, I wish that he had moved us to think, more broadly, about the bidirectional purposes that define the primary context for the pragmatism with which he sees the academy as being preoccupied, as well as the context in which this institution must be understood.

EDMUND W. GORDON *is distinguished professor of Educational Psychology at the City University of New York and John M. Musser professor of Psychology, emeritus at Yale University.*

After Pragmatism, What?

Nicholas H. Farnham

I have long advocated reforms such as those that Bruce Kimball identifies as characteristic of contemporary liberal education, and yet I do not consider myself a pragmatist. Therefore I find it surprising that he identifies pragmatism as the place where liberal education is heading.

In this commentary I shall argue that one significant theme of pragmatism—the belief that learning is experiential—continues to influence education reform in this country. But as a coherent philosophy, pragmatism has failed to take root in our education system. The reforms Kimball identifies are not experimental; neither do they contain other important pragmatic ideas. In fact, pragmatism was tried in education—in the form of the progressive education movement—and failed. The new reforms he speaks about represent efforts to find alternative ways of eliciting understanding from experience, ways that go beyond pragmatism. Their purpose is to structure the educational experience to help students understand their own natures, each other, their communities, and the world. This is not a pragmatic purpose, because it conflicts in part with the individualistic philosophy on which pragmatism has been based.

As Kimball suggests, it is difficult to study or discuss liberal education because of the entwining of normative and descriptive purposes. Nevertheless, that should not prevent us from trying; otherwise we may lose our way in the analysis. I shall posit at the outset that fundamentally, liberal education is grounded in experience, not in a set of facts or ideas. It is not a particular epistemological framework, theory of knowing, mode of understanding, set of books on the shelf, series of courses, or the same thing as "liberal arts," even though theologians and philosophers have linked these to it at various times. As John Dewey argued, education lies in the quality and nature of the experience it provides rather than in the tools used to convey it. This means the focus for describing it should be what goes into the experience and its outcome. For the most part that is the way the term "liberal education" is used today, and that is the predominant way Kimball used the term in his book, *Orators and Philosophers*.

In this earlier work, Kimball explained the difference between Humanist liberal education in the Renaissance and the post-Enlightenment model of liberal education. The Humanists urged the study of classical texts, the recapturing of ancient tradition, and the appreciation of ancient literary achievements. This emphasis on *artes liberales* was the result of their interest in the bond that cultures hold in common, understanding their own membership in a universal *res publica*. Outside the Humanist tradition, the new science gradually gathered strength during the Renaissance, eventually providing the basis for the philosophy of the Enlightenment.

The Enlightenment had the effect of replacing the Humanist focus on *artes liberales* with a new focus on philosophic principles, according to Kimball. These principles have been with us ever since, supporting the growth of research in the universities and ultimately the evils of specialization. Among the principles that Kimball showed coming down to us are the concepts of individual freedom (which replaced a Humanist sense of *liberale* connected to cultural conventions), tolerance, and egalitarianism—i.e., an "emphasis upon volition rather than obligations of citizenship."[1] He called the Enlightenment principles the "liberal-free ideal" to stress the different sense of the term "liberal" they contained.[2]

I return to these points in Kimball's first work because I believe I am not alone in thinking that he was heading toward a critique of the liberal-free ideal that would in some way help us to circle back to earlier views, particularly views of community that were implicit in pre-Enlightenment education. Joseph Featherstone certainly thought so in his foreword to the work:

> The liberal-free conviction that intellectual mold breaking was the highest good made excellent sense when the philosophers and their friends were on the outside of a hostile society looking in; now that they are insiders, they must ask whether their sovereign ideal amounts to a complete educational vision or not. The answer is, for all its obvious and heroic glories, no. The splendid liberal-free vision of learning all by itself—so rare in an illiberal world—leads to anarchy and nihilism in the end.... That is why today we badly need to restate the position of the orators....[3]

Kimball, however, now proposes to help us not by restating the position of the orators but by reembracing the liberal-free ideal. Pragmatism, as he made clear in his first work, is an offshoot of the liberal-free ideal. My discomfort with this new direction is not that I find pragmatism objectionable. It is simply that I find in pragmatism too little that is new

[1] Bruce A. Kimball, *Orators and Philosophers: A History of the Idea of Liberal Education*, 2d ed. (New York: College Entrance Examination Board, 1995), 122.
[2] Kimball, *Orators and Philosophers*, ch. 5.
[3] Joseph Featherstone, "Foreword," in Kimball, *Orators and Philosophers*, xiii.

and too much that is peripheral to make it the focus of my hopes for revitalizing higher education. Fortunately, I am relieved to think, the case Kimball makes for moving pragmatism into the driver's seat is not overwhelming.

Kimball makes the connection between pragmatism and contemporary liberal education through the adoption of a pragmatic method influenced by Charles S. Peirce (13). This approach tries to follow the words "liberal education" through history, and to infer the logical consequences that have attended its usage. In Kimball's survey of what has been written on liberal education, he admits that almost no writer has specifically connected liberal education, or for that matter higher education generally, to pragmatism. The connection, therefore, must lie, if anywhere, in the logical consequences that can be inferred from the reforms now underway.

I have no quarrel with the seven developments leading to reforms in liberal education that Kimball identifies or with his definition of pragmatism, which he says has six themes. I do, however, see serious flaws in the way he fits them together. For example, Kimball discerns one of the reforms, the trend toward general education, as an application of the pragmatic principle that knowing is dependent on context and the intersubjective judgment of the community. I see in general education the application of the idea that what can be known in one field can be sharpened or expanded by relating it to what can be known in another. But that is not a pragmatic idea. General education is encouraged today in a number of institutions through the development of core requirements represented by a set of courses, or a program of activities, in different fields, usually highlighted by broad surveys and interdisciplinary perspectives. The avowed aim is to provide an integrated view of knowledge, not contextual knowledge. This brand of general education is certainly not meant to demonstrate that what may be true in one discipline may not be true in another, as the pragmatic principle Kimball points to suggests. It is meant to demonstrate that truth is not necessarily discipline-based.

I also have difficulty fitting pragmatism into the reform characterized as the affirmation of multiculturalism. While it is surely possible to believe in pragmatic ideas such as the fallible nature of truth or its contextual origin and to affirm multiculturalism at the same time, it is not necessary to do so. It is possible, for example, to believe strongly in a single absolute truth or set of truths and to believe at the same time that different roads lead there from different cultural perspectives. Including such avenues in the academy to accommodate diverse student populations involves believing in principles of fairness that likewise do not necessarily derive from pragmatic ideas. Of course neo-pragmatists such as

Richard Rorty and Stanley Fish may write frequently about multiculturalism, but there are other proponents making reasoned arguments as well.

I do not think that pragmatism fits with the reform Kimball identifies
as the new emphasis on community and citizenship, either. It is not
clear to me from the examples he uses whether he means the communities inside institutions of higher education or service to the outside
community, or both. Assuming he means both, I am hard put to see a
connection to pragmatism in either one. It is especially hard to see the
connection with respect to a curricular emphasis tying course work to
outside community service. Although the aim may be to instill values,
as Kimball suggests, it is not to instill pragmatic values. The aim is to get
students to care about community and be concerned for others.
Historically, pragmatic concern was not for the community qua community but chiefly for the community's capacity to disentangle truth
from false opinion.

As for communities inside the institution, a possible connection is
suggested by Kimball's description of the pragmatic idea that truth is
connected to context and the intersubjective judgment of the community. However, the new movement toward emphasizing the communities inside the institution is directed toward improving opportunities for
learning, not toward verifying truth. Its aim is mostly pedagogical, not
epistemological.

Another of Kimball's points is the renewed emphasis on values and
service. Here the connection he makes is a historical one between the
decline and resurgence of emphasizing values in the curriculum and the
decline and resurgence of interest among philosophers and historians in
pragmatism. But mere correlation does not prove causation. Without
other compelling evidence, the pattern of both movements might be
assumed to be the result of some third historical phenomenon. In connection with the renewed emphasis on values, Kimball cites the greater
stress on the teaching of ethics. Yet, as he himself footnotes, pragmatism
is not the predominant form of ethics that has recently emerged.

Despite these difficulties, I find that one of Kimball's postulates for
pragmatism connects strikingly with the reforms of liberal education. I
refer to the belief in the importance of experience for learning, i.e., the
belief that there is a dynamic interaction between what goes on in our
heads (thinking) and what goes on around us (environment), out of which
comes understanding. This theme seems to me easily linked to the way
many general education programs are set up, to the way multicultural
studies plans are implemented, and to community service objectives. It
also connects well to two of Kimball's points that I have not covered—
cooperation with schools and reconceiving teaching in terms of learn-

ing. This relates to Kimball's final point, assessment, as well, since the assessment movement in higher education today does not mean simply testing students' cognitive development, but rather a general evaluation of their performance.

We can understand the role Dewey envisioned for experience in education by looking at how he summarized the modern age's dilemma in *Democracy and Education*. The modern age, he said, revolted against the classical view that reason and experience are complete opposites. "But various circumstances led to considering experience as pure cognition, leaving out of account its intrinsic active and emotional phases, and to identifying it with a passive reception of isolated 'sensations' [as empiricists tend to do]. Hence the education reform effected by the new theory…did not accomplish a consistent reorganization."[4]

Dewey wanted a reorganization along his own principles, of course. He thought he could reconcile the "intrinsic active and emotional phases" with cognition, in a way that would not do violence to individualism and other principles of the Enlightenment, by uniting a focus on experience with the experimental method of inquiry that obtains in pragmatism. Here I believe the new reforms part company with Dewey and with pragmatism as well. The idea that the experimental method of inquiry obtains in all reflective thought is not a feature of today's reforms. Multicultural studies, community service, cooperation with schools, reconceiving teaching as learning, the formation of communities of learning, and assessment of performance are not innovations conceived of as experimental models; neither does the experimental approach to learning figure much in how they work. Thus Dewey's plan has not been followed. The reforms we see today attempt in various ways to integrate cognition with the active and emotional sides of experience, but none of them attempts to do so through experimentation.

One clue to where the new reforms may be headed is their tendency to be nonindividualistic and yet student-centered. They seem grounded in the idea that by bringing students together in collaborative action, both inside and outside the institution, personal reconciliation of the three phases of experience will be realized by everyone. There is also the tendency to emphasize interpersonal relationships, as seen in the effort to reconceive teaching and learning and also in some reforms that emphasize the power of stories and narrative teaching. These are certainly not pragmatic tendencies. Whether they signal a turning toward a new sense of community reminiscent of the tradition of the orators is not clear.

[4] John Dewey, *Democracy and Education: An Introduction to the Philosophy of Education* (New York: Free Press, 1966), 276.

They do, however, provide hope that the experiential predicament Dewey set out for us may yet be surmounted, even though not on his terms.

NICHOLAS H. FARNHAM *is the director of the Educational Leadership Program at the Christian A. Johnson Endeavor Foundation.*

Pragmatism: Plausible or Panacean?

JOHN H. MORROW, JR.

Bruce Kimball's essay on pragmatic liberal education asserts that a resurgent pragmatism is presently shaping a new consensus in American liberal education. This pragmatism will rescue the curriculum from fragmentation and incoherence and will reunite elements that seem adversarial, such as multiculturalism and common national identity, and science and the humanities. In our present condition of demographic upheaval, Kimball's pragmatism, an "inclusive, eclectic, philosophically omnivorous movement" (89), encourages incorporation of new students and subjects into U.S. higher education to promote individual advancement and ensure social stability and progress.

Kimball's pragmatic liberal education is characterized by the following: a multiculturalism in curriculum and student body that "is becoming an article of consensus" (89); the incorporation of values and service into liberal education; an emphasis on a larger, more integrative vision of community and citizenship; an emphasis on general education linked to values; the recognition of a K to 16 continuum in which the different levels of our education system are considered equally important and cooperate in a common enterprise; the reconceptualization of teaching in terms of learning and inquiry rather than as the transmission of learning and the fruits of inquiry; and the importance of assessment.

These are admirable goals, although I certainly do not perceive the consensus or even the potential for it that Kimball does, nor am I convinced that pragmatism can achieve that consensus. Lynn Cheney's and Rush Limbaugh's recent objections to historian Gary Nash's national history standards for grades 5 to 12, national standards that Cheney herself commissioned and now attacks as too multicultural, suggest no such consensus. Even Kimball's earnest desire for an emerging consensus on pragmatism cannot conjure up such a chimera.

In labeling himself a pragmatist in the tradition of Charles S. Peirce, Kimball notes that Peirce hoped that a community of individual inquirers using the experimental method would secure a community consensus that approached truth, an opinion that would not be "broken down." This notion of consensus seems reminiscent of the mechanistic positivism prevalent in the late nineteenth century and essentially discredited by the world wars and the Fascist and totalitarian movements of the twentieth century. Returning to attitudes so thoroughly eviscerated by history holds little merit or potential.

Within the narrower philosophical context, can we resurrect and revert to a philosophy that has supposedly been superseded by other philosophies? I would leave such questions to the philosophers, though I would note that there were disagreements about the nature and staying power of pragmatism even within our seminar.

The seminar seemed to confirm a sense of the positive nature of pragmatism, but also of its inability to convince even those present of its efficacy. Sandra Rosenthal emphasized John Dewey's focus on the growth of the self, which necessarily includes the perspective of the other. Dewey's analogy of the close association between the scientific and democratic processes smacks of an egalitarianism that many scientists would probably eschew in the late twentieth century. The antiprofessional implications of pragmatism pose a serious hurdle for an elitist professoriate, however liberal it may be, that is concerned about credentials.

Does a philosophical justification carry sufficient weight in the broader society to be effective? Certainly pragmatism must be capable of convincing at the very least the philosophers, yet even at its height in the early years of the century it seemed to have been incapable of converting the more elitist realms of higher education.

Shirley Hune suggested that Kimball is trying to project a nineteenth-century model into the twenty-first century, and that his emphasis on the commonalities of K to 16 education contradicts the present experience of disjunction between secondary and college education. David Steiner doubted pragmatism's pedagogical or political effectiveness in this era of tribalism.

Ultimately, Stanley Katz suggested that we may be engaged in the wrong discussion, because seeking a single philosophy for education could be destructive in our uniquely diverse education environment. We need to focus on more concrete education goals, such as the integration of high school and college curricula, the reconfiguration of knowledge free from the constraints of departmental boundaries, the implications of downsizing and budgetary constrictions for educational quality, and the role of technology.

Alan Ryan considered the search for consensus likely to fail and found it implausible to appeal to pragmatism to elicit that consensus. Should we not expect multiple perspectives in our complex society, which renders the very declaration of a consensus artificial? Historians' proclamations of past eras of consensus have been founded on the omission of significant groups of people and have proved to be an artificial construct of a particular historian's mind rather than an accurate depiction of the complex reality of American society. Ryan also pointed out Dewey's optimism and assumption of a latent, better American nature, yet such attitudes seem naive and out of place in an increasingly conservative, and consequently pessimistic, United States.

In his essay, Kimball attributes "lulls" in pragmatism to social and economic crises of capitalism, and to pessimism about the potential of applying intelligence to politics. This suggests that the context of education—political, social, cultural, and economic—is critical to the acceptance and success of his educational philosophy. Yet his essay does not discuss the present circumstances or context at all. And if that present context is fraught with economic and social crises that give rise to irrational political currents, then it may not be conducive to the acceptance of pragmatism.

Pragmatic philosophy might fulfill Kimball's hopes for integration, but present circumstances prompt me to doubt its efficacy in this role. The ascendance of the Republican party to power just prior to our seminar crystallizes my sense that the present currents flow in a direction opposite to that of pragmatism, which lacks the power to dam or reverse them.

The context is the United States at the end of the twentieth century, a society riven with class, gender, ethnic, and racial divisions and open to exploitation by the unscrupulous; a country in which powerful interest groups dominate an increasingly polarized political process; a country in which single-issue movements care little for the commonweal in their obsessive devotion to one cause; a country in which an enormous national debt and inadequate provision of health care for all citizens loom as unsurmounted and perhaps insurmountable problems.

American society declares itself, undifferentiatedly and misguidedly, as middle class. Yet in fact a small percentage of our society is concentrating most of the wealth in its hands and cloaking the increasingly hourglass shape of our society with appeals to patriotism and the free market. Unfortunately, in times of disarray, of crisis—whether real, perceived, or even self-made—a buffeted U.S. middle class, like its European counterparts, seeks scapegoats for its condition among those whom it defines to be "outsiders," those different or less fortunate and most unprotected—in the United States the poor, the black, and the brown.

The context is a United States in which a resurgent South and California set the pace. Yet it is a South that for all its change remains fundamentally racist, a South that never surmounted segregation, a South whose suburbs are unabashedly founded on white flight and toward which the rest of the country appears to be rapidly regressing. And it is this suburban South that the Republican party, the new party of white supremacy, represents. This is very old wine in new bottles.

It is a South, for example, that persists in the practice of overassigning minorities to special education classes, while the rest of the country has eliminated this overtly racist practice. The NAACP has lost court cases because it cannot prove intentional discrimination, although evidence confirms the disproportionate placement of black students in these classes. The misclassification of black children continues.[1] The inability to prove intent does not mean the absence of discrimination.

Southerners and westerners also love their firearms, so much in fact that they want to make certain that everyone has them. Georgia exports not only Newt Gingrich, but also guns, leading the nation in supplying illegal weapons to other states.[2] The difficulties of enacting gun control in the face of a powerful gun lobby when the majority of U.S. citizens desire such control, when a murder rate fueled by guns is skyrocketing, and when the United States alone of the industrialized nations has no gun control, is typical of the irrationality of the present circumstances.

The South enforces laws in such a fashion that black males receive harsher punishments than do white males for the same crimes. The racial imbalance in the application of the death penalty epitomizes this injustice. Southerners prefer the violence and expense of punishment to prevention, in part because historically they have resorted to violence to control the poor and black. As politicians everywhere join the rush to punish rather than prevent crime, we should recall that there are presently more black males in prison than in college, and a callous elimination of social programs will combine with the declining availability of industrial jobs to worsen those statistics.

California generates reactionary "revolts," first in taxes with Proposition 13, the results of which still threaten the stability of the state education system. Now Proposition 187 exemplifies measures that scapegoat minorities. It blames illegal immigrants for the ills of California, which would probably have no illegal alien "problem" if it were not for the businesses and individuals who exploit their labor at cheap wages and pay no Social Security tax for them. California Governor Pete Wilson is already preparing to unleash the next assault, on affirmative action. The Republican vision of a multicultural society is apparently one of constant race-baiting and scapegoating attacks on minorities, not their inclusion to promote individual advancement and ensure social stability and progress.

[1] See "Separate and Unequal," *Atlanta Constitution* (Sun., 11 December 1994): F1, 3; "Sidetracked into Special Education," *Atlanta Constitution* (Sun., 11 December 1994): G1, 4, 5
[2] See "Georgia's Deadly Export," *Atlanta Constitution* (Tues., 13 December 1994): A22.

In this context, the irrational in politics thrives, as evidenced by the rise of opportunistic right-wing politicians such as Georgian Newt Gingrich, who firmly believes that politics is war, and the internally incoherent posturing of the Republicans' "Contract with America." Gingrich's penchant for blaming U.S. society's ills on social programs that attempt to cure them, while ignoring the more fundamental cause, the evolving economic system of U.S. capitalism, may be popular, but it is also illogical and superficial.

The conservatives' unabashed worship of an unbridled free market manifests a combination of a short historical memory that does not extend even to the Great Depression and a celebration of an idealized American past that bears little connection to historical reality. The retreat to laissez-faire is an unvarnished attempt to revert to a time before the New Deal. The era of U.S. history that conservatives apparently wish to restore is the turn of the twentieth century, which was also, and not coincidentally, a time of rampant racism, corruption, and the exploitation of labor.

America's fundamental anti-intellectualism and ideological naïveté lend themselves to irrational appeals and impede a clear understanding of the true nature of politicians such as Gingrich. He is variously labeled a conservative, a revolutionary, even a conservative futurist. In fact, Gingrich is a former untenured and unpublished history professor at West Georgia College, a historian with more interest in the future than in the past, a hawk who avoided military service during the Vietnam War. His vision of the country's past is formed as much by movies as by history, the latter of which is useful only insofar as it furthers his ideological causes. He has assumed the guise of the history professor in his course "Renewing Western Civilization" and in assigning reading lists to Congress and the American public. Perhaps it is the ultimate and deserved fate of an anti-intellectual country to be led by professorial mediocrities.

Conservatives constantly cloak themselves in the mantle of high standards. Yet Gingrich's recent appointment/retraction of sycophant Christina Jeffrey, a professor of political science at Kennesaw State College, to be the House historian shows an utter disregard for standards and quality. Gingrich purportedly did not know that Jeffrey opposed an educational program on the Holocaust for eighth and ninth graders because it did not adequately present the views of Nazis or the Ku Klux Klan. Jeffrey acknowledged that she knew as little about the Holocaust as she does about Congress.[3]

---

[3] See "Evaluation of Holocaust Course Outraged Jews," Atlanta Constitution (Tues., 10 January 1995): A6.

Perhaps the best indication of the reign of irrationalism is the Republican Contract with America, which will purportedly balance the budget while lowering taxes and increasing defense spending for Star Wars. The Contract will more likely repeat the fiscally irresponsible Reagan Republican policies of increased military spending without commensurate tax increases that drove the deficit into the trillions of dollars in the 1980s.

Republican welfare plans are likely to drop six million low-income Americans, most of them children, from food-stamp rolls in 1996, throwing the burden back on the states, or private charities, which are already in dire straits. Gingrich suggests orphanages (modeled on a 1938 movie) as a solution, yet he cannot logically endorse a tremendously more expensive child-care system concomitant with severe budget reductions. Welfare specialists contend that ill-conceived Republican welfare plans could have grave consequences—including explosions of poverty, homelessness, and crime so severe that the middle class will not be able to build walls high enough or move to suburbs remote enough to escape them, or build sufficient prisons to house all the criminals.[4] "Sesame Street" poses the elementary question—what happens next?—to its youthful viewers. Their parents seem incapable of posing or answering this essential question when conservative policies are concerned.

It is not just this political, social, and economic context that militates against pragmatism; it is the cultural context as well. This is the age of Rush Limbaugh's "dittoheads," of the Christian Coalition, of fin de siècle millennialism, of assaults against the National Endowment for the Humanities, the National Endowment for the Arts, and the Corporation for Public Broadcasting, and of attempts to undermine confidence in public schools and higher education.

The movement toward privatization may well ultimately threaten the very foundations of public primary and secondary education. Proponents of privatization proclaim panacean solutions, such as absurdly simplistic voucher schemes, to counter the complex welter of problems facing public education. Few pause to reflect that the nation's problems are more social and economic than educational. Ironically, a leading proponent of privatization of education, entrepreneur Chris Whittle of Knoxville, Tennessee, has become as bankrupt as his proposals.

Conservatives attack university education primarily because they view it as controlled by liberals. Yet what do we plan to substitute for liberalism? Conservatism? I cannot recall when any society has set for

[4] *See* "Welfare Specialists Contend GOP Plan Rests on Too Many 'False Assumptions,'" *Athens (Ga.) Banner-Herald* (Thurs., 29 December 1994): 8.

itself the overt aim of a "conservative education." Is this perhaps because a "conservative education" would be an oxymoron, a mind-closing experience, as opposed to the expansive and open process we associate with the term liberal? A liberal environment allows the existence of conservative and a variety of other views; a conservative environment will tend to crush divergent opinion.

It is also the era of Richard Herrnstein and Charles Murray's book, *The Bell Curve: Intelligence and Class Structure in American Life*, illustrative of contemporary exhumations of the pseudo-scientific justifications of racism that were once in vogue at the end of the nineteenth century in the United States and Europe. The book relied heavily on research supported by the Pioneer Fund, an organization that advocates eugenics. Despite Murray's protestations that he knew "very little" about the Fund, and the Fund's assertions that it did not support Murray's research, *The Bell Curve*'s conclusions "mirror the philosophy of the Pioneer Fund: that intelligence is determined by heredity, not environment; that blacks tend to be less intelligent than whites; and that, therefore, remedial education programs aimed at improving the education and job prospects of black people are doomed to fail."[5] Such attitudes are certainly not conducive to efforts at inclusion in education.

The Pioneer Fund's supported research includes psychologist Arthur Jensen's writings that African Americans may be genetically less intelligent than whites, psychologist Philippe Rushton's attempts to show that small genitalia must be a sign of superior intelligence, and philosophy professor Michael Levin's assertions not only that IQ differences are genetic but also that blacks are less intelligent and therefore more likely to be criminals. Critics accuse the Fund of being racist and elitist, while admirers praise it for shedding light on long-tabooed subjects.[6]

The recent book *In Defense of Elitism* by the late William A. Henry III, who insisted that he was a Democrat with liberal credentials, opposes current efforts to extend the opportunity for a college education to a wider and more diverse clientele. Henry proposed to reduce the number of high school graduates going to college from nearly 60 percent to 33 percent and to stop watering down curricula to accommodate youth who do not measure up. He suggested that we should close many community colleges and former state teachers colleges that cater to the "academically marginal" and instead offer them vocational courses in high school and job training. In Henry's view, this would improve the quality

---

[5] "'Bell Curve' Research Tied to Supremacist Group," *Atlanta Constitution* (Wed., 23 November 1994): A1, 4.
[6] See *Chronicle of Higher Education* (12 December 1994): A28-29.

of college education, reduce its public costs, and increase competition and achievement in high schools.[7] Henry would thus oppose not only the recent burgeoning of community colleges, but also Kimball's incorporation of new students and subjects into U.S. higher education under the banner of pragmatic liberal education.

The optimism, egalitarianism, and inclusiveness of Dewey's pragmatism starkly contrast with the pessimistic, elitist, and exclusive character of conservative ideas about human nature and society. The fear of modernity lies at the root of these conservative attitudes. The prediction that the United States will gradually grow to become a "majority-minority" country has essentially unleashed a preemptive strike of conservative policies to forestall these developments and to ensure the preservation of white male power for as long as possible and by any means necessary, as indicated by the existence of angry white males and armed white militias.

Robert Orrill has asked whether pragmatic philosophy really is sufficiently animating to be up to the task of integrating and mediating divisions that it failed to mend in the first two-thirds of the twentieth century. In the context of U.S. education at the end of the twentieth century, I would have to answer no. Our condition will require stronger medicine than pragmatism has provided in the past and is probably capable of offering now, though it might be a small part of a far larger solution.

These are critical times for American society. It can move forward constructively to a multicultural world, or retreat into a tribalistic, martial, and racist past. To understand the nature of our contemporary circumstances, we must ask where increasing conservatism and polarization have led societies historically. In general the political polarization, the right's strident attacks on liberalism, and the domination of political life by powerful interest groups are reminiscent of Western Europe in the 1920s and 1930s.

Newt Gingrich was a student of European history, an admirer of Bismarck, and has been quoted as saying that he is all that stands between America and Auschwitz, an ominously hubristic and equivocal statement. For my reading list on understanding Gingrich, I would recommend studying some modern German history from 1870 to 1945, with concentration on Otto von Bismarck, who was sometimes labeled the red reactionary, and on Adolf Hitler, who opportunistically lied to gain his political ends, and their effect on democracy in Germany. The fact that some audiences love Gingrich's and Rush Limbaugh's vituper-

---

[7] *See* "A Deft Blow to Thorny PC Causes," *Athens (Ga.) Banner-Herald* (26 December 1994): 4A.

ative and irresponsible attacks on the government and liberals is dangerously reminiscent of the political cynicism, viciousness, and desperation of German politics in the early thirties.

I find particularly instructive the events in pre–World War I imperial Germany, a society rapidly industrializing and urbanizing and consequently under severe stress similar to our society as we move into the postindustrial information age. After 1870, German universities experienced a substantial enrollment expansion analogous to if not commensurate with the demographic explosion in U.S. education that began in the 1960s. The liberal German professoriate, ambivalent about educational modernization and viewing the influx of lower-middle-class students as a threat to their elite status, abandoned liberalism for more conservative ideas. Student subculture also moved to the right, as student fraternities became increasingly anti-Semitic and xenophobic. Ultimately, these changes were an essential precondition for Germany's postwar susceptibility to Nazism.[8]

American society and its education system are certainly more diverse than those of imperial Germany. Furthermore, our democratic tradition should certainly be stronger, although present apathy and low voter turnout might give cause for concern. Awareness of German developments suggests that we need to be careful to contain rightward movements within the bounds of reasonableness. Given the present strength of the conservative tide, such containment will necessitate the forceful articulation of a broad-based conception of society that embraces the role and nature of the education system and incorporates the philosophical approach of Kimball as well as the more practical one of Katz.

JOHN H. MORROW, JR. *is the Franklin Professor of History at the Franklin College of Arts and Sciences at the University of Georgia, Athens.*

[8] *See* Konrad H. Jarausch, *Students, Society, and Politics in Imperial Germany. The Rise of Academic Illiberalism* (Princeton, N.J.: Princeton University Press, 1982); Fritz Stern, *The Failure of Illiberalism: Essays on the Political Culture of Modern Germany* (Chicago: University of Chicago Press, 1971).

Phi Beta Kappa: Seeking Pragmatic Essentialism

Once every three years, a group of distinguished academic members of Phi Beta Kappa gather at the society's headquarters in Washington, D.C., to sort through an imposing stack of chapter applications. The intention is to locate among the extraordinary variety of institutions described in those documents, colleges and universities whose education goals and programs most closely approximate the society's notions of what constitutes excellence in the liberal arts.

Many institutions that have already attained Phi Beta Kappa distinction appear in Bruce Kimball's essay on pragmatic liberal education. Distressingly, the society itself is not mentioned, even though it has been seeking to delineate excellence in liberal education in this country for more than two centuries. The experience has been instructive in terms of Kimball's subject, and was well described in Richard Current's 1989 volume, *Phi Beta Kappa in American Life.*

The society's origins are coincident with the movement Kimball describes as beginning when "The ideas of scientists and *philosophes* began to inform discussion of liberal education in the late eighteenth and early nineteenth centuries" (7). The young men who formed their secret society at the College of William and Mary in 1776 penned the following words with which Phi Beta Kappa's president was to greet new members of the organization, "Here...you are to indulge in matters of speculation that freedom of inquiry that ever dispels the clouds of falsehood by the radiant sunshine of truth."

"Freedom of inquiry," therefore, has been fundamental to Phi Beta Kappa's definition of liberal learning from its inception at Williamsburg. Kimball might maintain that it is also a hallmark of the scientific method exalted by the pragmatists. It can be argued as well that the idea is an ancient one; always essential to liberal education regardless of the cultural context in which it is offered.

The tensions that eventually developed between the liberal arts and the natural sciences, described so well by Kimball, are reflected in Phi Beta Kappa's own history. Just as its scattered chapters were moving to create a national organization to foster liberal education, in 1886 the faculty at Cornell founded its own honors organization for student researchers in the sciences and named it Sigma Xi. It was to be one of the first of many such honor societies employing the Phi Beta Kappa model to recognize excellence in a host of disciplines and an increasing variety of institutions of higher education in the United States.

Phi Beta Kappa, meanwhile, continued to insist on the vitality of the liberal arts ideal, and in the 1930s, established a systematic method of recognizing quality undergraduate programs that embraced that concept. This is the mechanism that every triennium brings together a dozen scholars, elected by the society's leadership, to decide which of the institutions seeking a chapter truly value and exemplify the concept of liberal learning. To that extent, at least, it may be argued that Phi Beta Kappa clings to the notion that there are essentials in higher education and in the common human experience that it seeks to illuminate.

Kimball cites Francis Oakley's book, *Community of Learning: The American College and the Liberal Arts Tradition*,[1] on the vast forces in society at work altering the nature and mission of postsecondary education in the United States (87). Certainly, Phi Beta Kappa, even with its commitment to "essentials," has not ignored those changes. During the past triennium, the society's leadership was engaged in an intense dialogue with representatives of the American Association of State Colleges and Universities (AASCU) on the subject of how Phi Beta Kappa might better comprehend and appreciate the nature of liberal arts education within the context of a contemporary, comprehensive university. At this writing, the discussion continues within the organization as it seeks to extend its eighteenth-century ideals into the twenty-first century.

Regardless of the changing demographics and the "cautious vocationalism" of the moment, which Kimball mentions, distinguished scholars continue to assist the society in defining liberal education by defining itself. There are essentials, and foremost among them remains freedom of inquiry. On this point, pragmatism, with its emphasis on process, falters as a guide. Great and celebrated institutions approach Phi Beta Kappa each triennium, seeking to gain chapters by marshaling impressive statistics on endowments, student enrollment, distinguished alumni, and even noteworthy faculty. Relying exclusively on its own resources, the society assesses these applications and in so doing publicly attests to what it believes are the enduring qualities of liberal education.

DOUGLAS W. FOARD *is executive secretary of Phi Beta Kappa.*

---

[1] Francis Oakley, *Community of Learning: The American College and the Liberal Arts Tradition* (New York: Oxford University Press, 1992), 118-19.

Pragmatism, Liberal Education, and the Transformation of Knowing

Douglas Sloan

It is a privilege to write in response to Bruce Kimball's rich and percep-
tive account of the history of pragmatism within U.S. higher education
and of its particular relationship to changing views of liberal education.
He makes clear the dimensions of pragmatism, traces in illuminating
details its pulsing cycles of influence within higher education, and
argues, convincingly I think, that there is emerging, in his words,
"recent developments in liberal education...may be construed as 'pragmatic' in the sense that such developments are conceptually rooted in
pragmatism, or...rationalized...by pragmatic conceptions." (87).

While many aspects of Kimball's account invite response, I want to
focus my comments on what he shows to have been one of the major concerns, if not the central and guiding concern, of all the leading pragmatists;
namely, overcoming the split in modern education and culture between
our dominant modern ways of knowing, as these find expression preeminently in modern science, and the need and quest for human meaning and
value, the split between, as the catchphrase has it, fact and value.

I will first note what seem to me to be some key aspects and consequences of the knowledge-value dualism. I will then explore whether pragmatism as the rationale for a conception of liberal education can actually
provide what is needed to overcome this dualism. I will suggest that pragmatism in itself is not adequate to the task, and that, indeed, without some
deeper, fundamental transformations in our ways of knowing, pragmatism
could very well in the end deepen the gulf between knowledge and values
(and much else that this troublesome term "values" usually includes).[1]

I choose this focus because, as Kimball points out, John Dewey himself
saw the split between modern scientific knowledge, on the one hand, and
the realm of ethics, morality, and meaning on the other, as the major problem of the modern world, and I think that Dewey was correct in this.
"Certainly," wrote Dewey, "one of the most genuine problems of modern
life is the reconciliation of the scientific view of the universe with the claims
of the moral life."[2] Or, again in the words of Dewey quoted by Kimball: "the

---

[1] Whether what would remain after these transformations could still rightly be called
pragmatism in essential continuity with the tradition is not a question that I will address.
[2] John Dewey, *Philosophy and Civilization* (New York: Capricorn, 1963), 43.

problem of restoring integration and cooperation between man's beliefs about the world in which he lives and his beliefs about the values and purposes that should direct his conduct is the deepest problem of modern life" (26).

Dewey and the other early pragmatists saw this knowledge-value split at the heart of all the other dualisms of modern life that they set themselves to overcome: the dualisms of theory and practice, science and the humanities, thought and action, and so forth. Kimball makes clear that the renewed interest in pragmatism owes much to the possibilities it seems to offer for overcoming these dualisms, and to the fact that in our time, as Kimball quotes John Smith, "the question of the relation between natural science and human values has been given a sharp and urgent focus" (91). Assuming, as I do in this response, that the knowledge-value split is the central modern problem, overcoming this separation would be a sine qua non of a liberal education. An education that fosters or does nothing to heal such a fundamental rupture within society and the individual cannot be liberating. It becomes of crucial importance, therefore, to ask whether the newly emerging pragmatic rationale for liberal education can provide the one thing most needed.

This central modern dualism has arisen from certain assumptions about knowing and knowable reality. During the nineteenth and early twentieth centuries, three of these assumptions in particular became increasingly dominant in modern thinking and consciousness. All three are today coming under question. Nevertheless, these assumptions are peculiarly modern and their influence still remains strong and often determinative for modern knowledge and experience.[3]

The first of these assumptions has been described as the objectivistic assumption of knowing that derives from the now notorious Cartesian split between subject and object. It has also been called the assumption of the "onlooker consciousness." This view of knowing is that of a detached onlooker standing over and describing a world of mind-independent objects as though neither knower nor known were fundamentally interrelated and mutually affected in the process.

The second assumption is the epistemological one that we can know only that which is given through our ordinary physical senses and abstractions from sense experience. Realities within or behind the veil of appearances may, indeed, exist, but in this view they cannot be known; they can at best be more or less blindly experienced.

---

[3] Indeed, these assumptions are rooted in the depths of our modern psyches, and, in fact, probably still constitute our real and most powerful modern, collective unconscious. Even when we contemplate change, these assumptions repeatedly reassert themselves in manifold and unexpected ways.

The third assumption is the related metaphysical one that ultimate reality is quantitative, without consciousness, life, or qualities, and is to be understood mechanistically, that is, primarily in terms of physical cause-and-effect and external relationships. This may be called the mechanistic assumption.

With the development of modern science, these assumptions proved enormously powerful. They provided humanity with a hitherto unknown power of analysis, discovery, and manipulation of the mechanical and quantitative dimensions of reality. They also helped give rise in the nineteenth century to the so-called scientific-technological view of the universe as dead, mechanistic, and meaningless.

A good deal of naive realism attended this view of the world, a naive realism that went hand in hand with the assumption of the onlooker consciousness. Already in the nineteenth century, however, this view of the onlooker consciousness and its attendant naive realism were beginning to be called into question. Even then it was clear to many that a strict separation between the knower and the known is spurious, that the knower and the known are always in a relationship of participation and interaction with one another.

A prominent response to this realization has been to adopt an instrumentalist view of knowing that denies that our knowing can reveal anything about the nature of reality, but is, instead, only a means for manipulating and controlling the world. Knowing in this view is redefined, and instead of meaning "insight into the nature and truth of things" it becomes "that which works." This instrumental rationalism can be seen as essentially an attempt to take into account the difficulties in assuming a naive realism and nonparticipative objectivism without giving up the manipulative power of a reductionist and quantitative way of knowing.

As the assumptions of an exclusively mechanistic, quantitative, and instrumentalist conception of knowing and of knowable reality have increasingly permeated modern education and culture, the results have been momentous. One consequence has been the propensity to attempt to reduce the whole of reality to what is taken to be a more real, underlying quantitative and mechanistic substratum, and to explain everything in terms of social, economic, and biological theories based entirely on material and mechanistic assumptions. This has, of course, proved totally inadequate for meeting the actual social and ethical needs of human beings, to say nothing of their religious needs. Nor has it been adequate for understanding life and quality in nature.

A second consequence has been that, since these deeper social, ethical, and religious needs of the human being do not go away (in spite of attempts to define them away), a great split has developed between the realm of knowable reality provided by our instrumentalist, sense-bound ways of knowing and the extra- or non-sensory realms of meaning, values, qualities, freedom, selves, and spirit. These latter realms have traditionally figured in the substance of a liberal education, though they have had no grounding in the view of knowing and of knowable reality that has dominated modern education and culture. The nonsensory has been pushed inexorably toward the unknowable, the irrational, and often, finally, the unreal. Religion, ethics, the arts, and personal-communal meanings and values—all the realms having to do primarily with the qualitative—are constantly placed on the defensive and forced to justify their place in our lives and in our curricula, or increasingly to assert themselves arbitrarily and dogmatically.

A third consequence of these modern assumptions has been that, all the while, qualitative nature—the nature around and in us, the nature of beauty and life in which we live and move and find our being and meaning—continues relentlessly to be torn apart by a purely quantitative, reductionist, instrumental rationalism.

All these consequences are manifest in higher education. For the past 200 years, the subjects that deal primarily with the qualitative—literature, the arts, philosophy, the humanities—have had to fight a continual rearguard action to preserve a place for themselves within a curriculum in which no doubts are raised about the place of those subjects that deal with the quantitative. And since the humanities, even when they remain in the curriculum, are not usually regarded as genuine sources of knowledge, but rather merely as cultural ornaments, as repositories of traditional lore, or as ideology, they devolve increasingly into counters, rationalizations, and battle cries in a raw administrative and cultural struggle for power—witness the war over "the canon." And in our laboratories and classrooms, truncated, mechanistic images of the human being abound, guiding our research and teaching. The results are wrenching ethical, medical, and cultural dilemmas as the full nature of the human being is pressured to conform to the less-than-human realities generated in the laboratory and then released upon a hapless public.

And while a quantitative, instrumental rationalism is often presented as value-free, it has its own values written in: it values knowledge exclusively as power. This rationalism, therefore, has an affinity for power and control, and for the powerful and those in control. The increasingly close ties between higher education and the corporate world—the electronic, genetic, pharmaceutical, agribusiness, military industries, and so on—does not bode well for the development within higher education of a robust medical, ecological, or cultural ethic. The growing university-industrial connection renders the view of higher education as a primary source of radical, creative cultural criticism, surely one mark of a liberal education, increasingly anachronistic, even quaint.

Now the question is, can a resurgent pragmatism adequately address and overcome this modern split between knowledge, on the one side, and values, meaning, and qualities, on the other, and the unfortunate consequences of this split? It was just this hope that motivated the early pragmatists, and accounts again, according to Kimball, for the current resurgence of pragmatism. One way, indeed, of understanding the origin of pragmatism is as an attempt on the part of persons such as William James, Charles S. Peirce, and Dewey to affirm the clarity and power of science and at the same time maintain the significance of values, meaning, and quality as central and guiding in true scientific inquiry, and, by extension, central in all knowing. In other words, from this perspective, pragmatism promised the ability to affirm the instrumentalism of science (hence Dewey's term "instrumentalism" to describe his own pragmatism) while preventing it from degenerating into a speciously value-free instrumental rationalism. Certainly the varieties of pragmatism developed by James, Peirce, and Dewey were suffused with their own values and ethical, even religious, concerns and commitments.

Whether any of these three ever really overcame the knowledge-value/quality split by affirming that genuine qualitative knowledge was a full equal with quantitative knowledge is a complex and controversial question, and space does not permit pursuing it here.[4] What I want to do instead is simply ask whether a pragmatism not grounded in the larger context of genuine nonsensory, qualitative ways of knowing can fulfill its promise; whether without this epistemological grounding and context pragmatism is not, in fact, peculiarly in danger of reinforcing some of the worst consequences of instrumental rationalism.

---

[4] Elsewhere I argued that Dewey, in his metaphysics and aesthetics of experience, pushed very far toward the development of qualitative, nonsensory ways of knowing, but in the end pulled back, reserving the term "knowledge" exclusively for control (and sometimes even for an extremely formal, strict operationalism), maintaining that we cannot know, we can only experience qualities. (This did not prevent him from talking a lot about qualities, which suggests something Dewey surely did not intend; namely, that we can talk cogently about that which we cannot know in some real sense.) I also suggested that Dewey offered rich resources for the development of qualitative, nonsensory ways of knowing, but that these resources have to be liberated from the strictures of Dewey's other assumptions. *See* Douglas Sloan, "John Dewey's Project for 'Saving the Appearances': Exploring Some of Its Implications for Education and Ethics," *Revision* 13 (Spring 1991, 23–41).

Let us look at some of the main themes of pragmatism as Kimball describes them, with respect to both the origins of pragmatism and its current resurgence.[5]

First, consider fallibilism. This theme of pragmatism has the virtue of pointing to the limitations of the knower, the complexity of all phenomena, and the infinity of perspectives that may be brought to bear on any subject. It provides a salutary warning against dogmatism and against claims to a full grasp of truth. Fallibilism can be interpreted as a perspectival view of truth, in which no single claims for truth can ever have the final word, but also within which a heightened sense of truth and the capacities of perception and discrimination are all the more, not less, important. If fallibilism, however, is unaccompanied by a heightened sense of truth, it easily falls prey to the currently modish, putatively postmodern doctrine that there is no truth. A radical relativism thus begins to arise. (Although the fact that the doctrine that there is no truth is itself usually embedded in a thick tissue of unexamined, conventional truisms is often overlooked.)

And since radical relativism is difficult to live with for very long, two temptations arise with it. The first, the temptation to rely as a guide for action on that which works at the moment, becomes ever stronger, as does the desire to seek security and stability in the community. A crass instrumentalism of the most uncritical kind becomes the test of truth, the very conclusion the leading pragmatists tried most to avoid. And with convention as the only other available test of truth, the second temptation, dogmatism, raises its head again, also a major concern of the original pragmatists. This tendency toward conventionalism, as I note later, also feeds into and distorts the role of the community in the quest for knowledge. Ironically, the fallibilism of pragmatism seems especially vulnerable in these putatively postmodern times to reinforcement of some of the very dangers it was intended to guard against.

Let us now look at a second theme of pragmatism, the centrality of the experimental method in all inquiry. In our time, the experimental method is of crucial importance. What happens, however, when experiment is made the defining and primary mode of all knowing? Experiment makes control—problem solving and the resolution of doubt—the beginning and end of all knowledge. With this, a radical historical-philosophical displacement has occurred. Wonder and reverence, once regarded as the sources of all knowledge ultimately worth having, are set aside and replaced by problem solving and doubt. All of intelligence and all of education are then likewise defined in the same terms.

[5] I do not discuss these themes in exactly the same order as Kimball presents them.

A deeper and more encompassing way of knowing that seeks an understanding and contemplation of reality disappears. Openness to the fullness of reality is sacrificed to the desire for control. Without a knowing grounded in wonder and reverence, however, without a knowledge that seeks the largest possible sense and appreciation of our actual situation—quantitative and qualitative—we cannot even begin to know what our real problems are. Pragmatism is itself lamed and becomes aberrant. Our problems are then set for us not by understanding and respect for reality, but increasingly by the narrowest demands of immediate expediency, inner obsession, and ignorance, and, finally, not even by a valid utility. Moreover, all human tasks come to be seen as problems to be solved, and in the current context most likely as technological problems, with everything human that cannot be cast in technological terms eliminated. Finally, making experiment, with the control it seeks, definitive for all knowing drastically narrows the possibilities of knowledge about persons to management, control, and use of the other—not a desirable basis for liberal education, to say nothing of friendship.

Experiment is important, but separated from a context of qualitative knowledge that alone can provide the necessary understanding, direction, and restraint, experiment becomes its own context, hypertrophies, and begins to devour rather than to generate meaning.

A third theme of pragmatism, the dependence of belief, meaning, and truth on community judgment, points to the social dimensions of all knowledge, to its communal grounding, interconnections, and purposes, to the centrality of language in shaping and communicating knowledge, and to the essential participatory nature of knowledge. In Dewey's view, for instance, community and communication, along with experimental method, were almost basal categories.[6] In the modern world, however, the participatory, communal nature of knowledge is more and more interpreted to mean that all knowledge is entirely a social construction of the community and that language, the means of communicating knowledge, is only an expression of the life-forms of the community.[7]

This denial of a larger qualitative, prelinguistic, and nonsensory reality transcending, even as it nourishes, community, begins to result in a kind of communal positivism or communal emotivism. Truth and value become what the group, the communal convention, says they are. As already noted, when convention is the test of truth, dogmatism is quick

[6] In this, it seems to me, Dewey did have a firm foot in Kimball's rhetorical/oratorical tradition.
[7] Kimball points out that Dewey tended strongly toward this view.

to follow. And especially important for education, when convention is the test of truth, the possibilities for creativity and the discovery of genuine newness become more and more problematic.

Although the notion of the communal construction and testing of knowledge is in part actually intended to prevent the control of knowledge by certain segments of the community and to ensure that claims to knowledge are adequately tested, the tendency to see nothing beyond the community and the language and life-forms of the community can have just the opposite effects.

In education, for example, when convention becomes the test of truth, knowing is viewed more and more as primarily communal problem solving. Any conception of an act of fundamentally radical insight that pierces the given, that runs counter to the traditional and the mainstream, becomes suspect. Creativity is conceived more and more as trial-and-error problem solving, which, to be sure, can have a kind of novelty to it, but which works always within the given framework, never calling that framework itself into question. Less and less provision is made for attending to the lonely voice within the community—the political, the religious, the artistic, the scientific creator, the dissident— who resists and breaks through the pressures of convention. An education emphasizing freely determined, liberating, individual insight and action is apt to be increasingly neglected, sometimes suppressed.

In the process, the emergence of incommensurate communities of discourse is accentuated, and the tendency toward social balkanization and communal conflict grows unchecked. It is difficult to see how a pragmatism that is not grounded in a larger qualitative way of knowing can counter these tendencies toward communal convention and insularity, indeed, how it cannot help but reinforce them.

Finally, let us consider a fourth theme of pragmatism, the dynamic interaction of organism and environment and the interrelationship of thought and action. Suffice it to note that pragmatism has tended to accept uncritically the conception of environment and organism provided by science, in both its realistic and its purely operational modes. But the problematic character and status of scientific concepts of organism and environment have become apparent in the twentieth century and a major point of contention within the philosophy of science. It has become increasingly evident, for example, that the dominant mechanistic assumption of science, while a useful abstraction for certain purposes, is extremely limited. A mechanistic mode of thought, for example, is patently inadequate for dealing with the phenomena of living organisms—growth, form, development, and metamorphosis through time—and it can handle the environment of culture and consciousness not at all. Yet the tendency of pragmatists from the beginning, when talking about the interaction of organism and environment, has often been to employ uncritically, as though they were wholly unproblematic, some of the most naïve conceptions, images, and assumptions of a mechanistic science. These conceptions, images, and assumptions also often constitute the major, unexamined truisms of a fallibilism that says there is no truth.

At this point, basic epistemological work needs to be done if pragmatism is to free itself from the shackles of narrow ways of knowing that by their nature perpetuate the knowledge/value split. Such work would entail the development of ways of knowing, in science and elsewhere, whereby the qualitative is as much a source and goal of knowledge as the quantitative. The pragmatist emphasis on the relation between the nature and quality of thought and action itself demands that this work be done.

These questions are not intended to deny the importance of pragmatism, but simply to ask whether the resurgence of pragmatism can provide a basis for liberal education without some deeper changes in our ways of knowing and dominant assumptions about knowable reality. Of course, we are unavoidably all pragmatists a good deal of the time. Much of our lives is spent in trying to solve the myriad utilitarian problems with which our ordinary daily existence confronts us.

There is also another level of pragmatism, however, which Peirce pointed to in appealing to the scriptural wisdom, "By their fruits ye shall know them." It is crucial here to realize that the fruit of which the Scriptures speak is not the solving of discrete problems—whether political, technological, economic, or curricular. The fruit spoken of in this context is the fruit of the spirit—love, joy, peace, patience, kindness, goodness, faithfulness, gentleness, self-control, and perhaps we can add others such as wonder, reverence, gratitude, and courage. Genuine knowledge of these becomes essential for the pragmatic judgment of which the Scriptures speak. Knowledge of these also becomes essential for all pragmatisms that serve the fullness of human purpose and meaning. Such knowledge, however, demands self-transformation, for we cannot come to know the qualities in the world without being able to bring those qualities to birth within ourselves.

Such a self-transformation would seem to lie at the heart and marrow of a liberal and liberating education. Pragmatism could be a strong support for such an education; it could also, without its own inner transformations, be a mighty obstacle.

Douglas Sloan *is professor of History and Education, Teachers College, Columbia University, New York City.*

Pragmatism, Scientific Method, and Liberal Education

SANDRA B. ROSENTHAL

One of the key points in Bruce Kimball's proposal that a resurgent prag-matism is shaping a new tradition in American liberal education is his insight that the incorporation of a scientific or experimental method separates pragmatism from the new linguistic turn. While Kimball him-self affirms the pragmatic emphasis on scientific method, his essay sketches several objections raised by others, and in the seminar discus-sion these objections, rather than his own affirmations, were reinforced. The major concern of the present commentary is further exploration and expansion of the link between pragmatism and scientific method as the key to understanding pragmatism as a philosophy of liberal education. First, however, to clear the path for my response, I offer some very brief critical remarks concerning Kimball's methodology for dealing with the meaning of liberal education.

Kimball follows what he calls a general Peircean method of determin-ing meaning, to which, as he acknowledges, he has given a nominalistic and linguistic twist. In so doing, he traces the words "liberal education" or "liberal arts" through history to determine the way these words have been used. This reduction of "meaning" to "use" gives Charles S. Peirce's understanding of meaning a decidedly un-Peircean twist that conflates meaning and truth. For Peirce, a meaning, which is instru-mental in organizing experience and which incorporates a network of conceivable consequences, is legislative for its correct or incorrect appli-cation. To view it as reducible to or derivative from its applications puts the cart before the horse.

There is of course no requirement that Kimball follow Peirce's under-standing of the nature and function of meaning. It may well be that the descriptive methodology Kimball used in conducting his historical, empirical investigation can best be understood as drawing from a different philosophical interpretation of meaning. And his essay does indeed stand as a fine exemplification of a very important historical approach to the issue. But I think there are key insights to be gained by proceeding as well with a philosophical, normative approach, and it is this latter that directs my remaining critical remarks, as well as the analysis that I then develop.

The consequences of following Kimball's linguistic and nominalistic twist of Peirce's position result in some confounding of issues, for this twist is in large part responsible for the conflation, throughout the essay, of liberal education and what transpires in liberal arts colleges. Whatever liberal arts colleges hold forth as education then becomes a meaning of liberal education. This, in turn, involves a further and related conflation of liberal education and general education. From the perspective of a normative approach, however, the question becomes: Under what conditions can it be said that liberal arts colleges, or more generally, undergraduate institutions of higher education, do in fact supply the student with a liberal education, and when should it be said that they abrogate this in favor of specialization and/or a general education that is not a liberal education? To answer this question, I must go out on a limb, so to speak, and offer a definition of liberal education. In defining liberal education as a prelude to discussing the role of pragmatic experimentalism, this commentary is following Peirce in taking a view of meaning that is neither essentialist nor nominalist, and is legislative yet fallible.

Liberal education, like general education, can be contrasted with specialization, but they are not the same. General education may be met by a distribution requirement in which the student takes one or more courses within each of several discipline areas. In this way the student gets isolated assortments, a collection of fragments. A liberal education, in contrast, is concerned by its very nature with the education of the whole person, and this cannot be achieved by the accumulation of fragments.

Liberal education is meant to liberalize or liberate the individual as a full human being, to liberate the individual from the bonds of tunnel vision, of uncritical acceptance, of limited perspective, of fragmented life. Liberal education programs offer courses specifically thought out and drawn up around the explicit rationale of educating the whole person, thus giving that person a certain integrity, unity, coherence. Courses have to fit into the whole, not simply by accumulation of variety as with a general education program, but rather as part of an integrated whole. Each course, though representing a particular discipline, deals from its unique perspective with the enrichment of the whole person and introduces, from its unique perspective, a critical reflection on value. The aim is to integrate and develop individuals in their fullness and richness and to prepare them for examining, and reconstructing when necessary, society's values, goals, and structures. Integration is not achieved through the tunnel vision of overspecialization, and neither is it attained by an accumulation of fragments.

With the above understanding of liberal education in mind, my response now turns to the pragmatic understanding of scientific or experimental method, which Kimball insightfully points to as a key feature in distinguishing American pragmatism in the classical vein[1] from the Rortyian linguistic, or the rhetorical, opposition to reason. Indeed, it will be seen that pragmatism, in focusing on experimental method, is treading a path that undercuts these two extreme alternatives just as it does so many others.[2]

Exploring the way in which experimental inquiry within pragmatic philosophy is intertwined with liberal education as the education of the entire person requires a brief sketch of the way experimental method permeates various features of pragmatism, for in a sense it can be said that pragmatic philosophy *is* a philosophy of education that prepares individuals for participation in a democratic way of life.

Science, as the *method* of experimental inquiry, provides the model for understanding all knowledge. This method involves a meaningful, creative organization of experience—a theory or interpretive structure—that directs the way individuals act, the truth of which is tested by its ongoing workability in guiding them through experience in ways anticipated by its claims. The theory itself is constituted by possible ways of acting toward the data and the anticipated consequences of such theory-laden activity. The process is self-corrective, for if anticipated consequences do not occur, a reconstructed interpretive context is developed. Experimental method must provide ongoing reconstruction of continually emerging problematic situations by expanding them through a reorganization and reintegration that now incorporates previously excluded or conflicting data.[3] From this point, our discussion should turn to an examination of this function in relation to self and community. To have a self, according to pragmatism, is to have a particular type of ability, the ability to be aware of one's behavior as part of the social proc-

---

[1] By classical American pragmatism I mean the position incorporating the works of its five major contributors: Charles S. Peirce, William James, John Dewey, Clarence I. Lewis, and George Herbert Mead. That these philosophers provided a unified perspective is assumed in this commentary, but this claim is defended at some length in my book, *Speculative Pragmatism* (Amherst, Mass.: University of Massachusetts Press, 1986; paperback edition (Peru, Ill.: Open Court, 1990). While Kimball usually refers to Dewey's pragmatism, he states that this type of pragmatism includes, for him, the other four classical American pragmatists as well. In the remainder of this commentary, any unqualified reference to pragmatism is a reference to the general framework provided by the classical American pragmatists, and my discussion draws from the collective corpus of their writings.

[2] The rejection by pragmatism of traditional dichotomies is well noted at various points throughout Kimball's essay.

[3] Interest in this aspect of pragmatism was expressed by several participants when I briefly introduced it during the seminar.

ess of adjustment, as an acting agent within the context of other acting agents. Selves exist only in relationship to other selves, and no absolute line can be drawn between our own selves and the selves of others, because our own selves are there for and in our experience only insofar as others exist and enter into our experience. The origins and foundation of the self, like those of the mind, are social or inter-subjective.

In incorporating the perspective of the other, the developing self comes to take the perspective of others as representing the group as a whole. In this way, the self comes to incorporate the standards and authority of the group; there is a passive dimension to the self. Yet, in responding to the perspective of the other, it is this individual as a unique center of activity that responds; there is a creative dimension to the self. Any self thus incorporates, by its very nature, both the conformity of the group perspective and the creativity of its unique individual perspective. And, when the individual selects a novel perspective, this novelty in turn enters into the common perspective that is now "there" as incorporating this novelty. The unique individual both reflects and reacts to the common perspective in its own peculiar manner. This novel perspective is an emergent because of its relation to the institutions, traditions, and patterns of life that conditioned its novel emergence, and it gains its significance in light of the new common perspectives to which it gives rise. In this continual interplay of adjustments between the common perspective as the condition for the novel emergent perspective and the novel emergent as it conditions the common perspective, the dynamic of community is to be found. When problematic situations arise, they must be creatively reconstructed in ways that work in integrating the conflicting demands through an expanded context. In brief, the ongoing process of adjustment reflects the dynamics of experimental method.

Our moral beliefs, as is true of all beliefs, do not come ready-made; they are not something that we passively find, but rather are the results of effort, of intelligent inquiry through experimental method. Our moral "oughts" are not rules handed down from on high, but rather are workable hypotheses for the organization of valuing experiences, which lead to the enhancement of value for all. Ongoing dialogue about values and debate about what is valuable must be ultimately attuned to the valuings of humans, or there is nothing for the debate to be about. Reconstruction of the moral situation, as involving authentic growth, thus requires a deepening attunement to the pulse of human existence, for this is where we find the data needing organization and integration through the dynamics of experimental method.

The pragmatic understanding of scientific method is very much intertwined with its understanding of democracy. This tie, however, cannot be broken by something like the advent of Sputnik,[4] for it has nothing to do with achievement in the technical sciences. Rather, the tie has to do with the way the process of democracy reflects the model of scientific method discussed earlier. Pragmatism stresses that democracy is not a particular body of institutions or a particular form of government, but the political expression of the functioning of experimental method. Any social structure or institution can be brought into question through the use of social intelligence guided by universalizing ideals, leading to reconstructive activity that enlarges and reintegrates the situation and the selves involved, providing at once a greater degree of authentic self-expression and a greater degree of social participation. The development of the ability both to create and to respond constructively to the creation of novel perspectives, as well as to incorporate the perspective of the other, not as something totally alien but as something sympathetically understood, is at once growth of community and growth of self. Scientific method, in providing the model for the ongoing process of democracy, also provides the model for inclusiveness, fairness, and equality.[5] Indeed, scientific endeavor best reflects impartial intelligence and universal inclusiveness as the "working character" of its claims, claims that are always subject to reconstructive change. In this way, science and democracy alike provide for a society that controls its own evolution under the ideal of universal inclusiveness or the rational resolution of conflict. Thus, the ultimate "goal" is ongoing growth or development, not completion.

   This, in turn, means that neither democracy nor the working ideal of universality can imply that differences should be eliminated or melted down, for these differences provide the necessary materials by which a society can continue to grow. Though society indeed represents social meanings and social norms, social development is possible only through the dynamic interrelation of this dimension with the unique, creative individual. That which will solve present problems and provide the means for ongoing growth of the self and the community is human intelligence, with its creativity, sensitivity, imagination, and moral awareness, geared to the human condition in all its qualitative richness and the possibilities contained therein for betterment. It is these human

[4] That this criticism has been put forth in the past was noted in Kimball's essay, and it was voiced again by participants during the seminar. My response at the seminar is placed in a broader context in this commentary.

[5] Kimball, while highly supportive of the pragmatic focus on scientific method, does indicate that he thinks there are embedded within the pragmatic method presumptions of fairness and equality that are not fully acknowledged by treating it as "scientific."

skills that must be developed. This, in turn, requires the education of the entire person.

A true community, then, to maintain itself *as* a community, requires an understanding of the educational process as concerned with the whole person. Education must provide the skills of experimental inquiry needed not just for the adequate exploration of specific subject matter, but for the possibility of the interrelated ongoing reconstruction and expansion of the self, values, and the institutions and practices of the community. This pragmatic focus on method does not ignore content, but rather provides a unifying thread for dealing with the vastly varied and huge amount of content to which the student is exposed. Indeed, creative intelligence can extend and reintegrate experience in productive ways only if it is not capricious, but rather seizes on real possibilities that a dynamic past has embedded in the changing present. Students thus must learn to live in the present through the appropriation of a living tradition that they creatively orient in light of a projected future.

The proper method of education is in fact, for pragmatism, the road to freedom. To the extent that we intelligently participate and independently think, rather than passively respond, we are free, for we, not external factors, determine the nature of our responses. We are free when our activity is guided by the outcome of intelligent reflection, when we do not let ourselves be passively pushed this way and that by the external factors bombarding us, but can take what comes to us, reconstruct it through intelligent inquiry, and direct our activity in terms of the unique synthesis of the data brought about by our unique creativity. The ultimate goal of liberal education is the development of free individuals with the ability for ongoing reintegration of problematic situations in ways that lead to widening horizons of self, of community, and of the relation between the two. In this way growth, and hence liberal education itself, have an inherently moral and aesthetic quality.

The above understanding of the role of scientific method in fostering a liberal education has implications for the issue of multiculturalism facing American education today, and for the broader issue of fragmentation versus unification.[6] The United States seems to be moving from the ideal of the grand melting pot to the ideal of the grand accumulator of aggregates. Within the context of today's multiculturalism, there are many who want not to assimilate but to isolate in terms of their heritage

[6] While Kimball's essay expresses the congeniality and compatibility of pragmatism and multiculturalism, it does not pursue this issue to any marked extent. The following provides an expanded context for my own response during the seminar to the objection that the link between pragmatism and multiculturalism seemed somewhat elusive.

and customs. Yet the debates and arguments over these alternatives are wrongheaded in both directions, for both extremes are destructive of the dynamics of true community. And neither alternative is what is called for by the insights of pragmatism. The multiculturalism of today offers the opportunity for the enrichment of all, but only if the collection of aggregates is woven into the dynamic interplay of a pluralistic community. The uniqueness of diverse cultures, as representative of the individual perspective, must be maintained not through separation from, but through a dynamic interplay with, the common perspective, bringing about a resultant enrichment of each.

The pragmatic understanding of the method of experimental inquiry can come into play here in a fruitful way. Because the method of experimental inquiry calls on individual creativity, and because students vary in their individuality, problems will "speak" to different students in different ways. The common endeavor of identifying, and evaluating the relevancy of, problems, issues, and possible alternative solutions can bring forth culturally diverse, historically rooted sensitivities to these problems and issues, as well as to possible solutions. In this way, the experimental method can foster the expression, and sympathetic understanding, of diverse cultures. For the diverse senses of value operating in diverse ways to mark the significance of the problems and issues within the content dealt with, as well as in the evaluation of the consequences of the proposed solutions, can lead to a sympathetic understanding of diverse perspectives and sensitivities within a common context. What is brought to various issues by the cultural diversity of students is a diversity of concrete ways of being situated in a world, and this carries with it the potential for bringing about at once both the enrichment and enlargement of the selves involved and a heightened attunement to the human condition and the felt value dimensions of existence.

Liberal education can provide the vehicle by which the sympathetic understanding of diverse cultures, through the incorporation of diverse perspectives, leads to the internalized tolerance of enlarged selves. In this way, liberal education can use the enriching potential of multiculturalism to move beyond the destructive alternatives of assimilation or factional isolation and toward a truly pluralistic community in which the creative diversity of perspectives operates in constructive and ongoing dialogue, adjustment, and growth within a common perspective of national identity.

The pragmatic focus on experimental method indicates that liberal education need not be in conflict with the undergraduate major as an area of specialization. Indeed, no person *is* an engineer, an accountant, a historian, a literary critic, or a physicist, but is first and foremost a concrete human being. Liberal education provides enrichment of the latter as the anchor for and context of the pursuit of a particular area of specialized functioning. The development of the skills of experimental inquiry requires utmost rigor. The relationship among pragmatism, practice, and science indicates not that reason is sacrificed to practice, but rather that rationality is "brought down to earth," so to speak, and encompasses the entire human being as active agent engrossed in the world, and the rigorous method of experimental inquiry is applicable to the entire gamut of its interests. In this way, pragmatism undercuts the alternatives offered by the traditions of reason and speech, and allows us to view liberal education and the pursuit of specialization through a major as mutually enriching rather than conflicting endeavors.

SANDRA B. ROSENTHAL *is professor of Philosophy, Loyola University of New Orleans, Louisiana.*

Wishful Thinking: On the Convergence of Pragmatism and Liberal Education

Bruce Kimball claims that "a new tradition of liberal education is emerging" in the United States, a tradition "rooted in the resurgent intellectual tradition of pragmatism" (iii). Philosophical pragmatism, he says, has come to "influence liberal education in the closing decades of the twentieth century" (iii). This is a startling claim, a claim that, if warranted, would warm the hearts of those of us who have taken part in the revival of sympathetic interest in pragmatism in the last 15 years. Unfortunately, the case Kimball makes for this assertion is weak.

And remarkably brief. One of the disappointments of Kimball's essay is how little effort he makes to convince us of his original and surprising contention that American liberal education has become philosophically pragmatic. His argument for this assertion is made only in fleeting fashion at the end of a lengthy essay, most of which is given over to rehearsing the oft-told story of the emergence, eclipse, and reemergence of pragmatism. Kimball moves in long-winded fashion over familiar trails blazed by others and then becomes distressingly short of breath when he finally leads us onto unexplored terrain. Ironically, he is far more convincing when he seeks to establish the limited impact of pragmatism on American higher education for most of the twentieth century than when he tries to demonstrate that this situation has changed of late.

But, as I say, it is the latter argument that commands attention—and critical scrutiny. Perhaps the most efficient way to consider it is to unpack and interrogate Kimball's own summary statement of its essentials. "The long-delayed influence of pragmatism upon dominant conceptions of liberal education," he says, "is coming to pass." Such influence, he further states, is especially significant "when recent developments in proposals for the reform of liberal education are considered collectively rather than individually." Moreover:

> These recent developments are usually discussed as separate responses to particular demographic, economic, or disciplinary changes, and they therefore appear to be unrelated, even disparate. But they may be collectively construed as "pragmatic," either in the sense of being conceptually rooted in pragmatism or in the sense of being rationalized, justified in principle, by pragmatic conceptions. In particular, seven recent developments in liberal education exhibit this collective pattern, which appears to fit

> pragmatism fairly well. That fit can best be explained as reflecting the influence of the cultural context on those developments during an era of resurgent pragmatism. In other words, pragmatism provides an intellectual and historical framework within which these developments collectively "make sense." It is in this regard that pragmatism is exerting the most widespread and significant, albeit indirect, influence on liberal education. It might even be said that pragmatism is now infusing liberal education: that pragmatism is pouring over and through the academic dikes that long kept it outside of the liberal arts and that a broad consensus is therefore emerging around a view of liberal education that may be termed "pragmatic." (88-89)

This argument requires Kimball to establish that the dominant, or at least a prominent, view of liberal education is emerging that is clearly and distinctively pragmatist, though it does not require those who have articulated this view to recognize it as such. Whether they know it or not, Kimball claims, liberal educators are now speaking the language of pragmatism, and they are doing so because pragmatism has "infused" the liberal arts.

Let me begin with the causal argument. That is, assume for the moment that the pragmatist view of liberal education Kimball describes exists. Can it be explained by an infusion of pragmatic thought into the liberal arts?

Kimball offers no convincing evidence of such an infusion, and I think he would be hard pressed to find much. His weakest argument is one that simply notes the chronological coincidence of the renewal of interest in pragmatism with the emergence of certain ostensibly pragmatic themes in discussions of liberal education. Kimball then characterizes this coincidence as a "correlation," and goes on to treat it as a *causal* relationship (with the arrows running from neo-pragmatism to liberal education). I know of no way of rescuing this line of reasoning from logical perdition. A bit more persuasively, Kimball cites three books on liberal education published in the last 15 years that acknowledge an explicit debt to John Dewey's pragmatism, two others in which he finds what he takes to be pragmatist language, and a scattering of further Deweyan references in recent work on undergraduate education, including Allan Bloom's offhand trashing of Deweyan pragmatism.[1] Now it seems to me that even the most generous critic would find it difficult to say that this evidence amounts to much. It certainly does not establish the flooding of pragmatism into discussions of liberal education, especially when we consider the counterevidence Kimball himself offers: a roughly equal literature on liberal education produced in the same period that ignores or slights pragmatism.

What about Kimball's broader claim that pragmatism has infused not only writings about liberal education but the liberal arts generally? He offers no evidence whatsoever to substantiate this assertion. My own view, the view of one who has tried to do a bit of this infusing, is that the "pragmatism revival" has as yet had very limited effects on most of the liberal arts. It can claim two extraordinary and powerful philosophical voices, those of Richard Rorty and Hilary Putnam, and one exceptional public intellectual, Cornel West. It has provided a context for some important developments in political and legal theory and some first-rate intellectual history. Neo-pragmatism has also taken root in literary theory as a kind of home-grown poststructuralism, though many pragmatists regard this as a perverse development. But in its "home" discipline, philosophy, neo-pragmatism has had little impact, and the same could be said for most other disciplines as well.[2] In the fierce debates waged during the last two decades over the undergraduate curriculum in the humanities, efforts of pragmatists to establish a "third camp" apart from the dead certainties of "traditionalists" and the corrosive skepticism of "postmodernists" have made little headway. The long-standing academic bulwarks of positivism and rationalism remain firmly in place in the sciences and social sciences, and in the humanities equally formidable levees of a quite different sort have been built from French manuals by black-clad academic engineers. Kimball's pragmatist flood has yet to occur; we continue to live in antediluvian times.

Nonetheless, a lot of water might have conceivably leaked through the dikes. This sort of leakage seems to be what Kimball posits in his most extended argument for an emergent pragmatist conception of liberal education. Even though few people realize it, he says, a recognizably pragmatic program for liberal education has emerged, comprised of seven developments: multiculturalism, values and service, community and citizenship, general education, commonality and cooperation between college and other levels of the education "system," teaching interpreted as learning and inquiry, and assessment. Here pragmatism has not so much breached the bulwarks erected against it in the liberal arts as snuck incognito into current discourse about liberal education.

---

[1] *See* Allan Bloom, *The Closing of the American Mind: How Higher Education Has Failed Democracy and Impoverished the Souls of Today's Students* (New York: Simon and Schuster, 1987).

[2] Here Kimball would have done well to heed the observation of his colleague, Randall Curren, that the hegemony of analytic philosophy in American philosophy departments remains firm (49 n. 8). Rorty, after all, has not been a member of a philosophy department for years, and his appreciative audiences are not among philosophers.

Let me leave aside the question of how it is that academics, who are usually very self-conscious about the language they use, have come to "speak pragmatism" without recognizing it. Let me bracket as well the question of whether Kimball's seven developments form a coherent program for liberal education. Let me instead ask whether in analyzing each of these developments he makes the case for an (unwitting) pragmatist grounding for them.

In each case, Kimball employs a dubious logic. In the instance of the incorporation of values and service into liberal education, he transforms contemporaneity into causation, an illicit practice on which I have already commented. In the instances of multiculturalism, general education, community and service, teaching as learning and inquiry, and assessment, he points to some more or less plausible connections between a particular aspect of pragmatism and these developments. But in none of these instances does he take account of the fact that equally (and in some instances more) plausible connections could be made between these education reforms and other philosophical traditions. For example, in the cases of multiculturalism and general education, Kimball traces the pragmatist aspect of these themes to their grounding in the pragmatic conception that belief, meaning, and knowledge depend on perspective and context. But there is nothing peculiarly pragmatist about this conception. Hegel or Nietzsche would serve as well as Dewey here. Finally, in the case of the integration of different levels of schooling, Kimball draws an analogy between Dewey's efforts to break down rigid distinctions between common sense and scientific reasoning and the efforts of reformers to more tightly link higher education and schooling. This is a nifty analogy (as Dewey saw), but Kimball offers no evidence that anyone other than Dewey has made use of it.

In general, Kimball makes no effort to show that advocates of these various proposals for a reconstructed liberal education are in fact speaking pragmatism; at best he demonstrates that they could. He seems to be saying that because these proposals are "objectively" pragmatist, there is no need to investigate whether they are empirically so. But since they could easily be "objectively" rendered a lot of other things, philosophically speaking, this is not an argument that convinces. I suspect that were Kimball to investigate matters empirically, he would find that some advocates of the sort of liberal education he describes are speaking pragmatism (some knowingly), but that most are not.

Since I do not think Kimball has made the case for the extensive influence of pragmatism on the liberal arts that he posits, I suppose it is unnecessary to say much about his explanation for this putative influence.

Suffice it to say that while the "problems" he identifies in higher education—demographic upheaval, "cautious vocationalism," and dissatisfaction with rigid distinctions between fact and value, theory and
practice—might conceivably evoke a response couched in pragmatist
terms, there is nothing about these problems that requires or necessi-
tates such a response. It is not enough to say that these problems might
logically elicit a pragmatist reply; Kimball would have to establish that
they have, as a matter of empirical fact, done so. This he fails to do.
Similarly, it might logically follow that the growing professional self-
confidence of American academics would lead them to entertain a
heretofore threatening pragmatist philosophy, but whether they have in
fact done so has to be established empirically, which Kimball does not
do. In both instances, Kimball's logic leads him to testable hypotheses,
which he then neglects to test adequately. Moreover, these hypotheses
are designed to explain the existence of a state of affairs that Kimball
never convincingly establishes in the first place.

For all Kimball's talk of moving toward a pragmatic liberal education,
we get very little sense from his essay of what that would mean. As he
says, the leading pragmatist philosophers, both past and present, are not
much help since they had little to say about higher education. He takes
note of experiments in liberal education in the 1920s and 1930s that
fashioned themselves "Deweyan," but he does not tell us what these
experiments involved, and we are left wondering if they any more
closely approximated Dewey's ideas and ideals than other ventures in
"progressive education" launched in his name.

The best effort that I have encountered to describe the sort of liberal
education that a pragmatist might envision for American colleges and
universities is Charles Anderson's *Prescribing the Life of the Mind*, a
book that Kimball overlooks. Anderson argued forcefully that if discussion of the aims of higher education is pressed hard enough, it will take
an epistemological turn toward questions of what we know, what we
can know, and how we can know it. Anderson's own epistemological
position is in many respects explicitly pragmatist, and he set out to
imagine the sort of liberal education for undergraduates that this epistemology might entail. He concluded that for a pragmatist, the purpose
of a liberal education is to develop the capacity of undergraduates for
"practical reason." This is the purpose, he argued, that should transform
the university from a holding company for disparate disciplines into a

common enterprise with an integrated curriculum.[3]

This is not the place fully to engage Anderson's argument, but I will sketch some of its essentials. By practical reason, he meant "the activity of examining a pattern of practice, and criticizing it, analytically, reflectively, with an eye to its improvement. Practical reason is a matter of distinguishing excellence and error. It also implies mastery, the effort to do something as well as it can be done."[4] The essential purpose of the university is to "find out what can be done with the powers of mind,"[5] that is, the practice that practical reason engages in at the university is reason, thinking, inquiry itself. In a university "the very *object* of inquiry should be to find out how thought can do better. The core educational aim of the university then is to teach those thoughtways, those habits of mind, that it can show work well in comprehending the world and deciding what to do in it."[6] With this object in mind, Anderson laid out an imaginative curriculum integrating the sciences, social sciences, and humanities as well as "practical studies," which he contends would lead undergraduates from an understanding and mastery of prevailing modes of inquiry to a critical assessment of these thoughtways, and then on to the cultivation of the arts of judgment, the fostering of creativity and innovation, and finally to a point of transcendence where students are pressed to ask essentially religious questions about "what mind is supposed to be doing in the world."[7]

I do not mean to endorse Anderson's vision of a pragmatic liberal education, but merely to suggest that it manifests a much more compelling, coherent, and undeniably pragmatist conception of liberal education than the hodgepodge that Kimball puts together at the end of his essay. In many significant respects, I can well imagine *Prescribing the Life of the Mind* as the sort of book Dewey might have written had he gotten around to providing a sequel—a higher education supplement, so to speak—to *How We Think* and *Democracy and Education*.

---

[3] Charles Anderson, *Prescribing the Life of the Mind: An Essay on the Purpose of the University, the Aims of Liberal Education, the Competence of Citizens, and the Cultivation of Practical Reason* (Madison, Wis.: University of Wisconsin Press, 1993). As Anderson said, his book was an effort to apply the method of practical political reason that he developed in an earlier book, *Pragmatic Liberalism* (Chicago: University of Chicago Press, 1990), to a concrete problem. *Pragmatic Liberalism* is one of the most important of several recent ventures in neo-pragmatist political theory.

[4] Anderson, *Prescribing the Life of the Mind*, 97.

[5] Anderson, *Prescribing the Life of the Mind*, 54.

[6] Anderson, *Prescribing the Life of the Mind*, 59.

[7] Anderson, *Prescribing the Life of the Mind*, 117.

But Anderson was under no illusions that he was describing prevailing practice or even prevailing theory. He did, to be sure, propose in good Deweyan fashion to reconstruct rather than to revolutionize higher education, but he left no doubt that he was not talking about minor repairs. For him, pragmatic liberal education is at this point a matter of wishful thinking. Kimball, on the other hand, asserts that the influence of pragmatism on American higher education is "unmistakable." But, as it turns out, this influence is quite mistakable, and he has mistaken it.

ROBERT B. WESTBROOK *is associate professor of History, University of Rochester, New York.*

Funeral Rites

David M. Steiner

Vertigo is not the sensation I would have expected to associate with Bruce Kimball's measured, splendidly synoptic, descriptive essay on the resurgence of pragmatism in U.S. higher education. Certainly, I might quibble at the margins; as my co-respondent Eva Brann would attest, there remain colleges and universities in which *paideia* owes more to Plato and Shakespeare than to John Dewey and Alfred North Whitehead. Kimball's empirical claim that "values and service" or "community and citizenship" constitute the core of, say, the university preparation of the premedical student, can only be based on the evidence of institutional rhetoric. The confidence with which Kimball employs a pragmatic test for the evidence of a pragmatic triumph in contemporary education has a faintly circular quality to it. But each of these three objections is gently anticipated and deflected in the text itself. Kimball's claim is for evidence of a pragmatic pattern in higher education, not proof that it constitutes a universal condition. His use and defense of a "nominalist" pragmatic standard (measuring the importance of a phenomenon by evidence of its verbal usage), is overt. Finally, Kimball offers a reasoned account of why he chose pragmatism as the guiding *ratio* of his investigation.

Kimball's self-professed intention is simply to discover how the term "liberal education" is used in higher education. He discovers an affinity between the contemporary employment of the term and essential characteristics of the philosophy of pragmatism, and rests his case. At most, we might ungenerously charge the author with normative modesty. After all, to describe rather than to evaluate in the context of higher education sets the stage for a debate but leaves the key judgments to others. Nevertheless, description alone can be important. If true, it is surely interesting that U.S. institutions of higher learning are embracing Dewey's teachings once again. Kimball persuades me that this is indeed the case, and offers some compelling explanations, at the level of both demography and epistemology, as to why.

From whence then my vertigo? First, in the discovery that Kimball's pragmatic approach is curiously allied to the modesty of his essay. To put the matter bluntly, Kimball's method is taken (with exaggeration) from Peircean nominalism, while his empirical data are validated on Deweyan grounds. The result of this odd synthesis is to free Kimball of the ethical responsibility that Dewey argued was incumbent upon all inquiry. In

Human Nature and Conduct Dewey wrote, "The problem of delibera-
tion is...to appraise present proposed actions....It is our business to
watch the course of our actions so as to see what is the significance, the
import, of our habits and dispositions."[1] By restricting himself to "the
logical consequences that attend the use of the term" (13), Kimball takes
refuge in a pragmatism freed from its own consequentialist logic and
one that is utterly disconnected from the pragmatic method he discovers pervading higher education. I would like Kimball to take up the
Deweyan challenge to think through the ends of our current activity.

A further source of vertigo comes from the discussion that took place
about Kimball's essay at the seminar. What this participant heard (or
projected?) in the conversations was a reluctance to take up Dewey's
challenge in almost every respect. It was, for example, difficult to animate a debate on the central issue: Is pragmatism as Kimball identifies it
a worthy and exciting pedagogic project? What kind of citizenry would it
foster, what kind of lives would it enable? I say in almost every respect
because one consequence that was exhaustively debated—almost to the
exclusion of all others—was the market value of pragmatism. The constant questions: How could we make pragmatism more attractive to the
education consumer? What balance of multiculturalism, of testing by
results, of vocationalism, of interdisciplinary inquiry, would assure the
continuance of the education dollar?

As the seminar proceeded, it became clearer that the success of pragmatism to date rests largely on the professional practice it enables and
protects. Thus multiculturalism may actually be attractive to an English professor because of the work of the postmodernist Jacques Derrida,
but the approach can be packaged as a sop to tribalism or a gesture to the
liberal fantasy of *e pluribus unum*. Vocationalism may strike the academic as the last refuge of the weak student, but universities can remind
parents that "big business" still wants the imaginative as opposed to the
robotic mind (capitalism having discovered that robots make better
robots). Thus our institutions of higher learning can defend the production of imaginative minds on vocational grounds while protecting the
employment of traditionalists teaching Latin, Greek, or European history. What of the rest? While Kimball points to the increasing popularity
of interdisciplinary studies, the problem is that many education con-
sumers don't understand the point of interdisciplinary inquiry. (In that
regard they are no more obtuse than the authors of some of our recent
national standards in education.) Many large grant-giving foundations,

---

[1] John Dewey, *Human Nature and Conduct*, in *John Dewey: The Middle Works*, 1899-1924,
ed. Jo Ann Boydston (Carbondale, Ill: Southern Illinois University Press, 1969-), 14:206.

by contrast, certainly do. Thus the pragmatic epistemology of organic connectivity (as evidenced in Dewey's *Experience and Nature*) not only offers philosophical support for cross-boundary conferences and projects, but becomes a financial necessity. To summarize my point, the refrain was that the academy better get its act together and agree to champion something, and that something might as well be a flexible, rather mushy, but very American theory of pragmatism, which offers so much justification for the practices of so many.

I exaggerate, somewhat. There were those at the seminar for whom Dewey's pragmatism constitutes at least part of a compelling pedagogic vision in its own right. There were participants ready to champion the virtues of multiculturalism come what may, as a vital gamble on behalf of a humane politics. A few spoke from the urban trenches, toughened by the demands of slashed budgets and harried students. Pragmatism struck such teachers as a necessity, not a choice.

Nevertheless, before we decide that liberal arts education can be subsumed under the demands of academic professionalism and political exigency, we might remind ourselves of what it is we are abandoning. No doubt we can trace liberal arts education back to Plato, to Cicero, to Erasmus, or to subsequent models derived from what Kimball terms Christian gentility. But the model that contemporary pragmatism most soundly destroys belongs to the sensibility of the literate imagination, to minds steeped in the fabric of *literae humaniores*, to those who can hear in a Shakespearean passage the echoes of Plutarch, Ovid, and Homer; those for whom Troilus, Thisbe, Medea, and Nestor are more than footnotes. It need not of course be Shakespeare, though it cannot be just anybody. Essential is the joy of the tapestry, the wealth of colors embodied in each of the multiple strands of the whole, a furnishing worth "minding," as Dewey might have put it. Liberal democracy might have promised that that which had been the treasure of a few could be offered to the many. So it has not proved, and for a multitude of historical reasons. In presiding over the funeral rites, I should not sentimentalize, but it is at least unclear to me whether the gray pragmatism on offer to the American academy can elicit the passion in students and teachers alike that liberal arts education at its problematic best could so evidently arouse. My own teacher cited a remark of Kafka's at the close of a discussion of education. Its tone and message, so distant from the vocabulary I heard at the seminar, might prompt reflection: "If the book we are reading does not wake us, as with a fist hammering on our skull, why then do we read it? So that it shall make us happy? Good God, we should also be happy if we had no books, and such books as make us happy we could, if need be write ourselves.... A book must be like an ice-axe to break the sea frozen inside us."[2] Is what is at stake here only another metaphor?

Can a pragmatic higher education represent something beyond the gray funeral of liberal arts education? As I have argued elsewhere, changes in demography and the economic market do suggest fresh challenges for the inescapable task of rethinking the educational curriculum. Rather than complaining that our 18-year-olds don't know anything, we need to ask what they do know, why they know it, and how we might create the incentives to reengage a demanding investment of their energies. To date there is too little discussion of what schooling should mean to millions of future citizens who will engage in essentially menial jobs; nor do we know what to teach the future economic elite beyond calculus, computer skills, and good manners. The pragmatism of Dewey has much to offer us in this task, not because he argues for measuring success in a certain way, but because of his thinking about consummation in learning and the aesthetics of investigation. Dewey's absolute debt to Hegelian aesthetics should remind us that pragmatism is a path of experience in which experience, temporality, ethics, and judgment are all implicated. A rereading of Dewey's *Art as Experience* might even suggest that elements of the older liberal arts curriculum could find a place in a pragmatic education for democratic citizens.

My sense, imperfectly formulated, is that the new pragmatism of the academy has little patience with such difficult issues. An academy committed to what I might term a "depth pragmatism" would, for example, be deeply concerned with the previous schooling of its incoming students. The world of public secondary education is currently split: the profession, through procedures of national licensing, certification, and new pupil and teacher testing methods, is trying to "rationalize" American schooling. On the other side, strong populist energies are trying to return education to the most local level of control, in part through rescinding key elements of the Goals 2000 legislation. Universities dedicated to a depth pragmatism have a large and inescapable stake in this debate. We might have expected, for example, that the academy would push hard for a national curriculum with an interdisciplinary focus, or make the case for testing standards that moved toward project-based learning and away from the SAT. But instead, a widespread silence.[3]

---

[2] From a letter Franz Kafka wrote at the age of 20, quoted in George Steiner, *A Reader* (Oxford: Oxford University Press, 1984), 36.

[3] There are exceptions. Ironically, some of the more interesting thinking about the new role of higher education is coming from our poorly funded urban public universities, which are having to ask difficult questions about the relationship between learning, community, politics, and democracy. These are questions Dewey would have regarded as fundamental.

To the extent Kimball is right, the universities are focused on a new pragmatism, but I believe that it is a pragmatism barely worthy of the name. Imagine what Dewey would have said about the disjunction between the practices of secondary and tertiary education, or the rush to embrace a narrow vocationalism. While he might have been a more sympathetic advocate of multiculturalism, Dewey would surely have heeded Stanley Fish's warning (in the *London Review of Books*) that "an interdisciplinary map, a map of routes going in and out of disciplines, will be incapable of indicating just why any particular discipline is there, what it does, why anyone would take it seriously." Replacing Matthew Arnold's collection of all the best that is thought with dictates of political correctness, mistranslations of European postmodernism, and the demands of last year's workplace is no way to break that sea frozen inside us.

DAVID M. STEINER *is assistant professor of Political Science, Vanderbilt University, Nashville, Tennessee.*

Needed: A Pedagogy Please!

Thomas F. Green

Even after several readings, it remains unclear—at least to me—just what Bruce Kimball has accomplished in the remarkably inclusive, extended, and suggestive essay that constitutes the first portion of this book. Despite his talk of "pragmatic liberal education," he offers no account of a distinctive kind of liberal education, no theory or philosophy of liberal learning. And this, it seems to me, is a good thing because, and here again I speak for myself alone, it isn't at all clear what we would have if we had such a theory, how we would recognize it, or how it might help us. Neither does Kimball offer any hope that some extension of pragmatism, some fresh version of that tradition, might illumine the nature of liberal education. It may be a good thing here, too, that he stops just short of such a venture. That "liberal education" is any more than a term of art or craft, that there is such a thing, in other words, as the *nature* of liberal education, may be merely another of those seductive yet enduring intellectual mirages, the vision of a possibility that simply vanishes at every approach. Kimball offers us no philosophy.

What then, does he accomplish? Just this. He describes a situation and the elements of a consensus in response to that situation, and then he gives that consensus a name. The situation is that for demographic and other reasons, settled conceptions of liberal education have supposedly become unsettled, a circumstance in response to which he says there is an emerging consensus on what ought to be done, a consensus that can itself be called "pragmatic" or at least be discerned as an expression of "pragmatism." The U.S. system of higher education has become more nearly universal and hence it must become multicultural. It has to become more receptive to dealing with varieties of value; it must accord greater prominence to ideals of community and citizenship; it must give more attention to forms of general education and to a coherent concern for learning among the different levels of the education system, from precollege to postgraduate. Kimball believes that if not the roots of, then at least the rationalization for these tendencies will be found in pragmatism. And this rationalization is what he wants to call "pragmatic liberal education."

My own doubts are strong that what Kimball sees as responses to the current situation ought to be described as rooted in pragmatism in any sense. Consider an analogy. Claims of John Dewey's influence on U.S.

elementary and secondary schools usually reach far beyond any reasonable belief. Except for some few of those who have had graduate courses in philosophy of education, I have yet to discover a teacher or school administrator with more than the most rudimentary knowledge of what Dewey had to say on any matter vital to the conduct of education. I am tempted to conclude that the extraordinary reach of his influence, much less its beneficence, is the stuff of mythology. Still, even though teachers typically know very little about Dewey's thought, and for that reason can hardly be described as "followers," or even as influenced by Dewey any more than by the climate, nonetheless, there is hardly a teacher or school administrator who, when invited to think deeply and with discipline about the actual *situated* problems of their practice, will not find in Dewey's ideas helpful hints to understanding the problems that they actually face.

In short, Dewey often seems to be the one philosopher who actually talks to teachers in ways that they recognize, the one who, more than any other, seems to answer questions that they are actually ready to ask. It is not, therefore, that they seek in their practice an application of pragmatism, but more simply that certain paths of reflection offer a recognizable interpretation of their practice and in that respect offer them self-understanding. To attach the name "pragmatism" to those reflections, after the fact, is, to them, a matter of slight importance, a mere curiosity.

As I reflected on this perspective while reading Kimball's essay, I thought it useful to think again about the philosophical situation at the turn of the century in which the movement called pragmatism found its strength. That setting, I believe, was stated nowhere better than by Arthur Murphy in a lengthy study, completed in 1940 but only recently published.[1] In describing the "philosophical crisis" out of which pragmatism emerged, Murphy wrote:

> A felt discrepancy between the principles and leading ideas that are employed in practice, and justify themselves by their usability for the particular purpose in question, and those which, by accepted standards, ought to serve as models for truth and reality, will naturally generate philosophical disquiet. The standards of formal or ceremonial authenticity then conflict with those of relevance and workable reliability....If philosophy is thought of as the spokesman for ultimate truth and validity,[2] philosophy,

---

[1] Arthur E. Murphy, "Pragmatism and the Context of Rationality," ed. Marcus G. Singer, *Transactions of the Charles S. Peirce Society* 29 (Spring 1993): 123-78; 29 (Summer 1993): 329-68; 29 (Fall 1993): 687-721.

[2] It is worth noting that philosophy is still thought of in this way (however rarely) by some, but almost never by philosophers themselves. Nowadays, whenever philosophy is presented in this way we may be sure it is usually to proclaim its irrelevance to the practical affairs of human beings.

under such conditions, will appear peculiarly remote from practice and from life, as, in non-philosophical inquiries, we encounter them....In philosophy the Idealists at this time performed a function comparable to that of the 'statesman' in politics.[3] They recalled men's minds to the fundamental soundness of the eternal verities without being able to connect their 'Reality' in any reliable way with what passes for true, reliable, and valuable in non-philosophic circles. In Bradley's Absolute the combination of complete authority for "the demands of thought" and very nearly complete irrelevance of thought to the ordinary criteria of good thinking is strikingly manifest.[4]

If we now consider this hiatus between the presumed canons of thought and the undoubted testimony of practical life as Murphy described it, and for "philosophy" substitute something like "formalism in ethics, history, and law," then we shall have in hand a fair account not only of the pragmatists' project, but also of the circumstances producing what Morton White called *The Revolt Against Formalism*.[5] In this way we can discern in these circumstances, as White did, the conditions producing kindred intellectual movements in history, law, and economics, i.e., Charles Beard, Justice Oliver Wendell Holmes, and Thorstein Veblen.

Indeed, *any* attempt to address such a philosophical discontinuity as Murphy described is, quite understandably, going to bear a strong resemblance to the movement that we have come to call pragmatism, whether that movement stems from pragmatism or can be called pragmatism. For precisely the same reasons, however, *any* philosophical venture whatever aimed at bridging such a manufactured chasm between theory and practice is also bound to show a strong kinship to the various traditions of "common sense" in philosophy. We shall find ourselves thus recovering the sensibilities of G. E. Moore, Thomas Reid, and more likely, Henry Sidgwick, none of whom could conceivably be described as pragmatists. Faced with an intellectual situation of the sort that Murphy described, *any* effort to recover the legitimacy of philosophical governance in practical affairs would cause us to pay serious attention to the contingencies of ordinary life. In a world governed by contract and liability, for example, it would force us not to search for the rule that will

---

[3] Murphy here drew on the distinction between the "statesman" and the "politician" as described by Thurmon Arnold in *The Folklore of Capitalism* (New Haven, Conn.: Yale University Press, 1937).

[4] Murphy, "Pragmatism and the Context of Rationality," 29 (Spring 1993): 145-46.

[5] Morton G. White, *Social Thought in America: The Revolt Against Formalism* (Boston: Beacon, 1957).

cover all contingencies, since that is bound to be far removed from actual life and real human interests. No, in such a world, we shall be driven to actually examine the texture of "reasonable prudence," and thus to reexamine the undoubted claim of both reason and common sense that circumstances alter things. Context matters, matters a lot, in fact, and matters differently for different persons. We shall find ourselves returning with renewed interest to Aristotle—at least to the Aristotle of the *Ethics* and the *Politics*. And so, along with the resurgence of pragmatism noted by Kimball, we would have to take into account an equally strong revival of various forms of common sense in philosophy together with a vigorous renewal of Aristotle's "studies" and both Jewish forms of rhetoric and Catholic concerns with casuistry. These are movements every bit as strong in contemporary philosophy as the pragmatic tendencies that Kimball notes. All arise from the same conditions that gave rebirth to pragmatism, yet none could be described as "pragmatic."

Murphy went on to describe the "reforming spirit" of the pragmatists in confronting this philosophical situation. On the view of the pragmatists, said Murphy, it is:

> a false standard of philosophical adequacy which has led men to treat practice as 'narrow,' empirical inquiry as 'merely' an unintelligent respect for particular matters of fact and the application of ideas to specific situations as a makeshift and hand-to-mouth affair. Viewed from the standpoint of a false philosophy such activities have been robbed of their full significance and the men who pursue them encouraged to take a narrow and distorted view of the meaning of what they were doing. To raise the tests of 'experience' and 'practice' to the level of philosophical criteria would be to enable us to discern the meaning of what we say and the worth of what we do in all aspects of experience and in all types of practice by the use of standards appropriate to the ideas and activities in question and pertinent therefore to a 'life' in which a reasonable man makes the most of his experience and enlightens his practice by a just estimate of what he really wants. It was in this sense, and with this end in view, that the pragmatists, in their reforming moments, denounced the absolutes of traditional philosophy and sought to substitute 'experience' and 'practice' as the ultimate criteria of truth and validity.[6]

In his description of the "situation" from which pragmatism emerged, Murphy began by speaking of a *felt* discrepancy between what philosophers advanced as the principles of thought and what everyone knows in common life to be reasonable principles of practice. To speak of the felt

---

[6] Murphy, "Pragmatism and the Context of Rationality," 29 (Spring 1993): 147.

discrepancy and its consequent disquietude is an explicitly Deweyan way of talking. It echoes of Dewey's notion that thought is initiated when we are confronted with a "problematic" or "indeterminate" situation; when certainties fall away, something interrupts the accustomed flow of interest into action and thus forces reflection. First comes a hypothesis on how to resolve the problematic situation and then comes a testing of it. If all this is so, as it appears for the most part to be, then we should be able to fathom the indeterminate state of affairs and the disquiet it produces by asking, in effect, what is the hiatus, the uncertainty for which this hypothesis is supposed to yield a solution? In like manner we might also ask: "What is the question for which 'liberal learning' purports to provide the answer?" or "What are the questions of practice for which Dewey seems to offer sympathetic and discerning answers?" or "How have our settled ways of talking to one another about 'liberal learning' come unraveled?"

Along the path of such a heuristic, we may surmise that the circumstances of liberal learning that Kimball sees as disquieting are its undue limitation to a narrow range of cultural traditions, including perhaps a kind of tired "essentialism"; its limitation to the nonvocational, forsaking any understanding of the liberal aspects of vocational preparation; its neglect of civic and communal values; and finally its abandonment of general education in favor of specialization. These are the features of the disquieting situation, the hiatus between our talk of liberal education and our enactment of it. That is to say, these are the problematic aspects of current practice. These are the uncertainties for which some pragmatic consensus, according to Kimball, provides the calming resolution.

There is here no pragmatic theory of liberal education, but simply a renewed search for a literally more engaging way of explaining to others and to one another what we are doing when we claim to uphold the cause of something that we call liberal learning. But we shall not find an answer to this hiatus, this problem, this indeterminate situation, by looking for another underlying doctrine that can, in turn, serve up another set of settled answers. It is worth recalling that pragmatism is not, at heart, so much a doctrine as it is an attitude, a method. But when we give it a name, it immediately becomes a doctrine, a thesis demanding defense.

In like manner I suggest that most of the difficulties surrounding liberal education in a multicultural, highly administrative world arise because we have tended to identify liberal learning by its content and then are bound to try defending education of such content by all kinds of doubtful claims about its effects. It is this that no longer engages. If we take the philosophical situation seriously, however, we may be able to catch a glimmer of the fact that learning of certain sorts aims at cultivating those powers of human beings that are theirs by virtue of being human but that cannot be fully possessed without the intervention of others. I have in mind the necessity of a capacity for the exercise of craft, judgment, and taste, the necessity of a social memory and hence some social identity, a memory and attachment that extend far beyond the lifetime of any individual. Economy, polity, literature (as the contextualized narrative of such explorations), religion (as narratives of meaning), and the arts become the substance of such an education not because they contain the canonical statements of liberal learning, but because they engage these human capacities. So what is needed for a resurgence of liberal education is not a fresh way of justifying a given body of content as framed by some philosophical tradition. We need, rather, an engaging pedagogy, a way of talking about what paths of learning are best suited to stir these capacities and bring them farther along a path toward maturity. Give me not a theory, but a pedagogy, please!

This call for a pedagogy, that is, for a more considered attention to how these human capacities might be nurtured, is just the sort of call that Dewey might have issued. But knowing that does not warrant our branding it pragmatic, nor does assigning such a label advance our understanding.

THOMAS F. GREEN *is professor emeritus of Cultural Foundations of Education and Curriculum at Syracuse University, Syracuse, New York.*

No Consensus in Sight

Alan Ryan

This response is not a commentary on Bruce Kimball's wonderfully interesting essay, or on the equally interesting book to which it is a coda. It is a reflection on the two issues his essay raises: whether there is an emerging consensus on the aims and purposes of liberal education, and whether pragmatism is intrinsically well adapted to provide the basis of such a consensus. I have less authority than most to pronounce on these matters, but a somewhat foreign perspective on the U.S. scene may be of interest. I was educated at an English boarding school and at Balliol College, Oxford. I subsequently taught philosophy and politics for 18 years at another Oxford college. I have only taught in the United States for 10 years in total, and have seen only one child through only one, a typical, U.S. public school. The effects of my foreignness will surely be evident in what follows, but most interestingly evident in ways of which I am largely unconscious, and I will not say more about it.

It is a commonplace that a liberal education was formerly so-called because it was an education in the "liberal arts," and that these were *liberal* because they provided the intellectual accomplishments of a free man, not the technical skills of a mechanic or a laborer. In English parlance, this became the thought that they provided the education of a "gentleman." It is worth noticing that Cardinal Newman insisted, in *The Idea of a University*, that the purpose of a university education was not to make students cleverer or morally better, not to save their souls or to make them more apt to the service of the state, but to make them gentlemen. This has never been an easy idea to naturalize in an American context. The wish to produce gentlemen—or its functional equivalent— was a common aspiration among college teachers in the nineteenth century and earlier, but it was always under threat.

On the one side, the wish to save the souls of the young was always strong; revivals were a standing feature of the spring semester at New England colleges throughout the nineteenth century, moral philosophy was always taught by a minister, and the college president was expected to specialize in moral uplift.[1] The social pressures that these phenomena reflected are still strong in the United States, the least secularized of modern industrial societies. On the other side, a hearty contempt for the

---

[1] *See*, for instance, George Marsden, *The Soul of the American University* (New York: Oxford University Press, 1994), for some rather surprising examples.

"college-educated man" was part of the psychological equipment of the self-made man from Andrew Carnegie downward. Even so good-natured a representative of the "plain man" tendency as John Dewey's father remarked that he didn't much mind whether his boys went to college, but did hope one might be a good mechanic. The first would have sacrificed liberal education to "getting Jesus," while the second would have sacrificed *liberal* education to more narrowly utilitarian ends.

The infuriated attacks on the American college leveled by Thorstein Veblen, Abraham Flexner, and Robert Hutchins[2] complained of the utilitarianism that had reduced American colleges to "service stations"; but when Matthew Arnold wrote *Culture and Anarchy*, and lectured on "American Civilization"—the lecture's subject was the absence of its subject—it was American Calvinism that he took aim at, not American utilitarianism. Indeed, one oddity of the history of liberal education is that at the end of the twentieth century, conservatives discuss Arnold as though he had wished high culture to *be* a religion, when he rather wished it to be an antidote to the religiosity epitomized in American Protestantism.

We cannot today say with a straight face that we are engaged in producing gentlemen; few of us wish to see ourselves as the handmaids of religious indoctrination. And those of us who take undergraduate teaching seriously are equally eager not to see it dismissed as "preprofessional education." Too many academics believe that everything important happens only after we have passed our students on to postgraduate training. But what can we say? I find the idea that we are approaching a consensus on the answer to what is a liberal education implausible. We are not even of one mind on the question whether a liberal curriculum is a proper thing for a high school to teach, and therefore not of one mind about *who* is responsible for the liberal education of the young. It is a disaster that most discussion takes for granted that liberal education is what liberal arts colleges and the colleges of arts and sciences in most universities provide. High schools, in this view, just do what it takes to get their students into college; and that is increasingly a matter of polishing their test-taking skills.

The state of students when they arrive even at distinguished colleges such as Princeton suggests that 80 or 90 percent of contemporary high schools neglect liberal education. Students can pass E. D. Hirsch's tests

---

[2] Thorstein Veblen, *The Higher Learning in America: A Memorandum on the Conduct of Universities by Business Men* (New York: B.W. Huebsch, 1918); Abraham Flexner, *Universities, American, English, German* (New York: Oxford University Press, 1930); Robert M. Hutchins, *The Higher Learning in America* (New Haven, Conn.: Yale University Press, 1936).

of "cultural literacy," but are strikingly uncultivated; they have the computational skills that their science teachers will require, but are unable to discuss the history and philosophy of science, its place in contemporary culture, or its promise and its dangers in a democratic society. Their ability to argue cogently and write interestingly is largely unawakened. This is an indictment of a system in which students waste half the time they spend in K to 12 education, teachers are too unambitious for their charges, and colleges therefore must engage in remedial education. As with the tale of *Sleeping Beauty*, there is a happy outcome—sometimes.[3] Colleges do a terrific job on the raw material they are offered, and the liveliness of American intellectual life in all its branches is proof of the quality of that raw material.

Still, the deficiencies of American intellectual life reflect the fact that we leave young people so untutored for so long. Contemporary American literature is strikingly insular, surely to some degree the result of the neglect of languages, teaching, history, and geography in the earlier years of education. Most contemporary novels are obsessed with the inner life narcissistically conceived; their authors have learned a lot about creative writing and something about themselves, but have not learned to look outward. The insularity of U.S. political science is equally striking and a consequence of the same failures. The low level of political and cultural discussion outside three or four charmed circles on the coasts and around Chicago reflects the same insularity and isolation. Pragmatism as practiced by William James and John Dewey was utterly hostile to all insularity, whether psychological, cultural, or geographic. Pragmatism emphasized that the self is an object in the world, and that the world is an infinitely varied object of experience, and urged us to look outward. It is therefore hard to see contemporary culture as a satisfactory implementation of the hopes of pragmatism.

In the absence of consensus, I can only say that my view is that liberal education should begin when a student is 6 or 7 years old, able to learn languages quickly and to enjoy poetry and history. To my mind, the aim of liberal education today must be to make its possessor a citizen of the intellectual world, and the earlier this training starts, the better. The freedom at which liberal education aims is the freedom that comes from understanding our own intellectual resources and being fully in possession of them. This is an ideal that animated Aristotle as well as Arnold and John Stuart Mill; James displayed it in person. It was not something that Dewey had much feeling for. I will argue for it by discussing understandings of the aims of liberal education other than my own.

[3] Francis Oakley gave a sensible but upbeat account of the state of liberal education in the better colleges in *Community of Learning: The American College and the Liberal Arts Tradition* (New York: Oxford University Press, 1992).

My view is individualist, present-centered, and combative. The point of engaging with a tradition of thought is to *engage* with it: to assess its strengths and weaknesses; to learn what can and cannot be said, thought, and felt within it; to compare its strengths and weaknesses with those of other traditions of thought. We need a period of apprenticeship to a tradition, but we hope to master it. One obvious alternative to this view is the view that we should surrender to tradition; we should not master it, but allow it to transform us. I must not exaggerate the opposition between these views, nor deny that adherents of both sides can converge on a middle ground. Unless we are capable of an initial surrender to authors and texts, we shall not discover the inwardness of a tradition of thought and sentiment; unless we are capable of going on to work in that tradition for ourselves, *we* have not grasped it. But if there is a middle ground, there are extremes: one is a conservative attachment to the classics and the canon that suggests that the peaks of human attainment have been reached already, and that our task is to appreciate and (perhaps) emulate them; the other the radicalism of the *bricoleur* who thinks we should approach the past as plunderers, raiding the tombs of the glorious departed for whatever we can use. My view represents the middle ground.

I now suggest two things: first, that pragmatism, at any rate Dewey's pragmatism, is far closer to the radical position than to the conservative position; second, that most contemporary defenders of liberal education are closer to the conservative position than to the radical position. I espouse the virtues of the middle ground, but the mere existence of a middle ground does not guarantee a consensus on the virtue of occupying it. I will argue for these thoughts very briefly indeed.

Dewey was extremely hostile to the conservative belief in the superiority of the past to the present. He was, as his daughter recorded, bored to death during his high school years, and for all that he remarked in his autobiography that Plato remained his favorite reading, the driving force behind much of his educational writing was hostility to the frame of mind that placed the classics on a pedestal and confused education with servility to the achievements of the past. He was himself well educated in the classics, but thought of traditions as something to be *used*. *Use* was an all-embracing term, and not narrowly instrumental; art has its uses, but is not in the ordinary sense useful.

All the same, the point of an experimental or instrumental philosophy was to focus on what we can do with our resources in the here and now. To throw away tradition would be foolish, but it would be more foolish not to try to extend whatever traditions we inherit. Dewey's *Art as Experience* celebrates modern art, the art of Cézanne and Matisse and

the Barnes Collection, not old-fashioned connoisseurship or the pleasures of detailed art history. Dewey was not a *post*modernist, but he was
adamantly a modernist in intellectual and aesthetic matters.

The war Dewey fought against Hutchins was not of his seeking or
making. Still, it was hardly an accident that he got into a fight with
Hutchins. Hutchins's *The Higher Learning in America* was inspired by
Mortimer Adler's hostility to pragmatism and enthusiasm for Aquinas;
Dewey was reflexively anti-Catholic and implacably hostile to the
moral and epistemological absolutism of Hutchins's insistence that
teachers must teach the Truth, and that the Truth was one and the same
in all times and places. Dewey had little *positive* to say about the alternative, however; he had no great interest in higher education, nor even
in the higher reaches of secondary education. His most useful contribution to the defense of liberal education was his insistence during the
pre-1914 debates over vocational education that education for work
must be a liberal education rather than narrow technical training.

In general, Dewey was not much interested in the content of liberal
education. Like Bertrand Russell, he appears to have thought that most
of the good or harm that was done to children occurred by the time they
were 11 or so; properly started, the human mind reaches out enthusias-
tically into the world in a self-propelled fashion. The process in which
Dewey was interested was that of getting the child's mind to work as a
self-propelled, problem-formulating, and problem-solving entity. In that
area he was a genius; *How We Think* is a small masterpiece in the analysis of the "informal logic" of everyday thought.

Problem solving, however, is not the essence of liberal education. The
disinterested exploration of cultural traditions is. James in person exemplified the exuberant reaching out to the variety of human experience
that I would celebrate as the essence of this exploration. Neither in theory nor in person did Dewey emulate James. I am inclined to say that
Dewey wrote persuasively about all aspects of education *other* than
those that feature most prominently in accounts of liberal education.
Conversely, contemporary writers who wish to defend the educational
verities against postmodernism, feminist epistemology, deconstruction, and whatever other forces of the night they fear, cannot make
friends with anyone of a Deweyan persuasion. They want, as David
Bromwich has eloquently complained, to use tradition for exactly those
purposes to which Dewey objected—to set unquestionable standards, to
fix the intellectual world, to make each generation assess itself by reference to an unchallengeable best that has been thought and written.[4] As I

---

[4] David Bromwich, *Politics by Other Means* (New Haven, Conn.: Yale University Press, 1992.)

have sufficiently said, I find this too coercive a view, but I do not deny its virtues. The narrow point I want to make in this context is only that the competition for the soul of the liberal educator is still on. There is vastly more that Kimball's essay makes me want to say, but this is not the place to do more than thank him for stirring up such an interesting argument.

ALAN RYAN *is professor of Politics at Princeton University.*

Because I Like the Questions

ARTURO MADRID

Reading Bruce Kimball's learned and provocative essay on pragmatic liberal education, and in particular his discussion of the tensions between the model of liberal education found in the research university and what he describes as liberal education informed by pragmatism, I could not help but revisit my own experiences over the past four decades.

When my eldest son entered college in 1979, I asked him—despite myself—what field he thought he would major in. To my surprise he said physics. No one in my immediate or extended family had any interest or talent, much less a praxis, in science or math. I asked him why he had chosen physics. I was even more struck by his response. "Because I like the questions," he answered simply.

I don't believe I realized that there was such a thing as "questions" until I was already on the faculty of an institution of higher education. And yet I was an outstanding student, I had an excellent undergraduate education in the liberal arts, and my graduate training has served me very well over the years. Somehow the research institution model of liberal education, with its undergraduate major and its graduate school emphasis on inquiry as the means to knowledge, either was not explicit at the institutions I attended or just escaped me.

Two years later, in the spring of 1981, I asked my son if he was still planning to major in physics. He said he was not. I asked why and was once again surprised by his response. "Because," he said, "they are not going to let me ask the questions." He went on to explain that his educational preparation was deemed to be deficient and that as a consequence, if he stayed in physics, he would be consigned to life as a technician.

My son—if I may say so—was no intellectual slouch. Quite apart from an excellent record in high school, he had almost perfect SAT and ACT scores. Most important, he had an inquiring mind and he was certainly enrolled in an institution in which the research university model of liberal education was firmly implanted. But the message was very clear. The major, at least in physics, was not about a liberal education. It was about separating the sheep from the goats.

For the past three decades, I have been involved in efforts to change the demographic profile of higher education, and particularly the faculty profile. During the mid- to late 1970s, I directed a major national fellow-ship program toward that end. It was not a felicitous moment to do so. The number of available academic positions declined during the decade, but there was no corresponding drop in the number of persons pursuing an academic career. I was thus faced, at the beginning of the 1980s, with the task of providing job counseling to persons I had earlier encouraged to pursue a Ph.D. and who had not been able to obtain academic appointments.

When dealing with these people, I usually started off with a question, "What do you know?" Irrespective of how long and in how many ways I pursued the question, the answer(s) I got inevitably focused on a base of knowledge in a specific discipline and, in the case of the better students, on methodological considerations. No one ever said, "I am a good researcher; I can give form, coherence, and context to complicated mate-rials; I can draw conclusions from those materials; and I can make them accessible to others." Or to put it another way, no one ever said, "I know how to get information, how to make sense of it, how to evaluate it, and how to make it useful." Certainly no one ever said, "And I furthermore do it on command."

If a liberal education conforming to the research institution model was supposed to prepare students to deal with change and complexity through inquiry, something had gone awry. Mainly, I would say, many if not most of us who sought a liberal education received instead prep-aration for graduate study—whether we subsequently pursued it or not. And of course, those of us who did by and large gave our best efforts to separating out the next generation of sheep from the goats.

I would like to believe that this essentially elitist and flawed model of liberal education is being seriously challenged by a model the pragmatic dimensions of which counter that elitism and correct its flaws. And I would further like to believe that changes in the demographic makeup of the student body are driving fundamental change in the curriculum. But I am not totally convinced. From my perspective, that change is occurring at the margins and not at the core. It is more accommodation than change.

I am more convinced by the argument that a pragmatic approach to liberal education is emerging because students and their parents are anxious about costs, returns, and competition and that these anxieties are propelling students into vocational and professional programs of study. In some of the traditional disciplines, the prospect of becoming superfluous may result in significant and long-term curricular change. A case in point is departments of modern languages in which, except for Spanish, enroll-ment has dropped precipitously, thus forcing a reconsideration of the

curriculum. Whether the change will be cosmetic and simply accommodating or substantive and truly pragmatic remains to be seen.

I am not as convinced that "intellectual dissatisfaction with the
essentialist, fact/value, theory/practice distinctions" (88) is as pervasive
as Kimball believes. That may well be the case among public intellectuals, academic philosophers, and higher education professionals, but I
do not believe that it holds true in the ranks of academia. Most current
faculty are products of an academic tradition that promoted those
distinctions. Many have negative memories of the New Left's challenge
to that academic orthodoxy. Others fear or are leery of the values advocated by the Christian right. By and large, the majority are reluctant to
engage each other or students in discussions of values.

Notwithstanding, the developments Kimball identifies are compelling.
Multiculturalism, although under severe attack, has been affirmed on
most U.S. campuses. Values and service, community and citizenship are
part of the reigning higher education discourse and may well become
widespread academic concerns. General education seems to be experiencing a resurgence. Policymakers understand that education is "all one
system," and multiple projects are successfully connecting schools and
universities. Assessment, despite faculty resistance, is taking hold.

For me, the true test is found in one development in particular—the
reconception of teaching in terms of learning and inquiry. Fund for the
Improvement of Post-Secondary Education staffers, in the 1970s, were
fond of saying that teachers kept teaching long after students had
stopped learning and that the only cure for that condition was to make
learning "learner-centered." Teaching can drive learning and inquiry
and does in many institutions, but it is not a pervasive or deeply rooted
phenomenon. We need to make it so.

I asked my son that spring day what he planned to study instead. He
answered, "Either philosophy or political science." I said, "Because you
are going to be able to ask the questions, right?" I don't know that his
philosophy or political science professors fostered learning and inquiry,
but at least he knew that there were questions to be asked and that
asking them was at the heart of learning. We need to assure that all our
students have that opportunity.

ARTURO MADRID *is the Norine R. and T. Frank Murchison distinguished
professor of the Humanities at Trinity University, San Antonio, Texas.*

Prognostication and Doubt

Predictions stretch toward extremes. The stock market has bulls and bears; economists talk recession and inflation. Around the beginning of every new year, people of many stripes try their hands at predicting important political and social events. In all of these cases, dire predictions get the most attention. Even weather forecasters seem more excited by bad weather; and in idiomatic parlance "weather" actually means bad weather, as if good weather was the absence of climatic or atmospheric conditions. Certainly disasters garner publicity. A stock market crash, a serious recession with many unemployed, an earthquake in California, a hurricane in Florida—as with an Aristotelian tragedy, these events instill pity and fear, and not just when they happen but also when they are foretold. Thus, while negative forecasts frequently precipitate action, positive or neutral predictions are often met with apathy. When told, for example, that the economy was improving, most Americans took a "wait and see" attitude; told it was declining, many immediately changed their living styles. Similarly, when bad weather is predicted, people will take off from work, postpone trips; good weather predictions rarely lead to modifications in schedules.

That dire predictions sell, that they lead to action, is, of course, well known to publishers and the media. The rash of books detailing or predicting the collapse of education in this country rides on this knowledge. And the outcome has itself been predictable. There have been outbreaks of outrage and anger, but also salutary corrections, and much activity has been generated toward the improvement of education. Still, as was the case with the reported death of Mark Twain, the predictions of gloom were greatly exaggerated, and similar to the cable sent by Twain from London, Bruce Kimball sends us this message in his essay on pragmatic liberal education. Kimball sees the recent, "seemingly intractable confrontations" within higher education converging toward the "resurgent intellectual tradition of pragmatism" (iii). There is no call to action. Thus, as with positive forecasts generally, the question is whether we need to pay any attention. If Kimball is correct, if American colleges and universities at the end of the twentieth century are approaching a new consensus, we can only be glad, but if he is wrong, we are no worse off than before. Simply to ignore this prognostication, however, would be to dismiss Kimball as a foolish Pollyanna. A more prudent course would be to consider him a Rumpelstiltskin whose ability to turn straw into gold is something we must harness to save our own lives. Therefore, we must ask whether pragmatism accurately reflects current trends in education, whether it provides a map for achieving education goals, and whether it answers the criticisms that have been raised. In this short response, I will try my hand at each of these three questions in turn, in light of a single but dichotomous educational issue.

First, Kimball asserts that one reason John Dewey's pragmatism has not been better acknowledged in higher education debates is that its reputation is largely limited to education in grades K to 12. The problem, as Kimball admits, began with Dewey himself: "For a philosopher who wrote some 40 books and 800 articles, championed education reform, virtually identified philosophy and education, and posited a continuity between the thinking of schoolchildren and that of scientists, it is surprising to find so little written on liberal education or, for that matter, postsecondary education" (62). This lack helped to fuel a growing sense of disjunction between Dewey's pragmatic philosophy and debates about higher education, and Kimball cites Van Doren, Childs, and Blanshard, among others who dismissed the relevance of pragmatism to college education.[1] Kimball must be credited, therefore, with successfully detailing the relationship of Dewey's philosophy of education to higher education. Unfortunately, however, making this connection does not prove a consensus, especially as the relationship of pragmatism to our current K to 12 system is simply assumed.

Among the seven developments Kimball offers to demonstrate the growing influence of pragmatism on higher education is the commonality and cooperation between college and other levels of the education system. The reasoning seems to be that if pragmatism has always been associated with K to 12 and can now be associated also with higher education, then a continuity of educational philosophy from kindergarten to grade 16 exists, which continuity can be offered as further evidence for the increased influence of pragmatism in higher education. In addition to its circularity, this statement begs the question of K to 12 education, for even if we were to concede a growing consensus arising from the confrontations in higher education, we could hardly say the same for K to 12, where there has also been loud and rancorous debate.

If higher education in this country is hardly monolithic (Francis Oakley described it as "a vast, sprawling, markedly variegated, and

---

[1] Mark Van Doren, *Liberal Education* (New York: Henry Holt, 1943), 100; John Childs, *Education and Morals* (New York: Century, 1950), 101; Brand Blanshard, "Values: The Polestar of Education," in *The Goals of Higher Education*, ed. Willis D. Weatherford, Jr. (Cambridge, Mass.: Harvard University Press, 1960), 102.

extremely decentralized system, embracing secular and religious, public and private institutions, with an independently supported private segment of a strength and size unparalleled anywhere else in the world"[2]), then at least the same can be said for the U.S. K to 12 education "system." With public and private, secular and religious, college preparatory and vocational, magnet schools, charter schools, for-profit schools, not to mention cooperative schools, Montessori schools, single-sex schools, bilingual schools, and so on, there is clearly no single vision of K to 12 education, a multiplicity that is also unfortunately and often disproportionately affected by wealth, class, and race.[3] Responding to criticisms of this system based on much-publicized falling test scores, sweeping comparisons with students in other nations, and an increasing perception of a lack of preparedness for college (with little discussion of what these factors mean), reform efforts, far from the Deweyan principles of interdisciplinary work and emphasis on method, have focused heavily on knowledge-based instruction. The clarion cry seems to be "back-to-basics." *America 2000: An Education Strategy* posited specific fields and specific knowledge that all American children should possess. After much debate and a change in administration, the reformulated *Goals 2000: Educate America Act* added references to such fields as the arts and foreign languages, not previously included.[4] Standards are being set separately by discipline with task-specific or knowledge-driven goals to be met in grades 4, 8, and 12.[5] And college preparatory curricula continue to be governed by fact-based, multiple-choice achievement tests that leave little or no room for fallibilism, contextualization, or methodological solutions. Current trends in K to 12 education, therefore, run largely counter to Deweyan principles. Kimball's reliance on a commonality between college and current K to 12 education and his failure to address the latter in any depth weakens his argument.

---

[2] Francis Oakley, "Against Nostalgia: Reflections on Our Present Discontents in American Higher Education," in *The Politics of Liberal Education*, ed. Darryl J. Gless and Barbara Herrnstein Smith (Durham, N.C.: Duke University Press, 1992), 282.

[3] Andrew Hacker depicted the impact of racism on American education and society in *Two Nations: Black, White, Separate, Hostile, Unequal* (New York: Charles Scribner's Sons, 1992). The recent publication and reception of Richard J. Herrnstein and Charles Murray, *The Bell Curve: Intelligence and Class Structure in American Life* (New York: Free Press, 1994) illustrates racism still at work.

[4] *See also* Ellen T. Harris, "Why Study the Arts—Along with Science and Math," *Aspen Institute Quarterly* 4 (1992).

[5] The National Council on Education Standards and Testing, under the auspices of the U.S. Department of Education, is overseeing the establishment of voluntary national standards in the following fields: mathematics, science, history, the arts, civics, geography, and English. The National Assessment of Educational Progress (NAEP) is developing assessment outcomes.

The relative weighting of science, art, and humanities subjects in the curriculum leads directly into the second question of how and whether education goals are achieved. Although sometimes taken metaphorically to mean the entire range of college education, as in "the faculty of arts and sciences," the literal arts and sciences have played a small role in liberal education, which focuses instead on the humanities and social sciences. Kimball writes at length about this historical disjunction, quoting many writers and paraphrasing a 1943 statement by the American Council of Learned Societies, to the effect that "the understanding of human values, culture, and, indeed, experience, was the special province of...the humanities" (70). This connection between values and humanities on the one hand and between science or the arts and professionalism on the other has frequently led to a lessening emphasis on science and arts education for all students, based on an assumption that one only studies these areas of inquiry vocationally and not because they offer insight into human values.

Although Kimball quotes John Smith as stating that one of "the reasons for reappraising Pragmatism at the present time [is that] the question of the relation between natural science and human values has been given a sharp and urgent focus" (91), Kimball does not address the issue of incorporating science (or art) into the humanities and social science hegemony of college education, and, like most of the debate on higher education, his proposal as written might simply refer to changes in the focus of the humanities and social sciences. This is particularly odd in that scientific inquiry lies at the heart of the Deweyan philosophy (20–23). Kimball, however, offers no pragmatic advice on how to manage separations between disciplines, how to teach the whole spectrum of knowledge without dividing it up into more and more minute fragments, or how to leap traditional boundaries. A turn to pragmatism without a turn to broader exposure to knowledge and creativity might be a contradiction, but it is one that Kimball advances by default. Strangely, he will not even place a value on the "pragmatic" recovery he witnesses, saying "Whether this convergence of pragmatism and liberal education is a good thing is for others to decide" (v). By not discussing the role of the disciplines in the pragmatic recovery he documents, Kimball limits the impact of his proposal; by not valuing this recovery, he sidesteps the pragmatic approach.

Finally, let us address curiosity and application in terms of stated criticisms of pragmatism. Although the relative value of theory and practice is often discussed (separating the critical, historical, and theoretical on the one hand from practical and hands-on work on the other), less is said today about the importance of curiosity-based versus application-based learning. There are actually two dichotomies here: one that divides avocation from vocation and another that distinguishes between types of inquiry within a professional field. Today's education leans toward application in both senses; it encourages vocationalism, as Kimball describes, and it supports proposals that project specific results. Nowhere is this more obvious than in science and the arts. Students are not generally encouraged to take science or art courses unless they plan to pursue such a course of study professionally. And science as well as art funding, and thus inquiry, are more and more tied to practical outcomes with little value placed on wonder and imagination.[6]

Although Deweyan philosophy calls for curiosity-led inquiry in both vocational and avocational studies (22), Kimball implies throughout his essay that science is a professional study only, that it is application-based and therefore highly specialized. He links science with "advanced and specialized research" as opposed to liberal education (7), and he proposes a growing professionalism, quoting Daniel Wilson's comment that "[the shift of philosophy] to becoming as esoteric and as unfathomable to the educated public as nuclear physics or molecular biology [went hand in hand with] the shift to a professional, specialized, academic discipline" as a reason for the decline in the influence of pragmatism (45). He never mentions the arts.

If the "antiprofessional implications" (80) of pragmatism have led to criticism, then the inclusion of science and the arts as part of a curiosity-based, pragmatic education will be essential for its success. A number of years ago, J. Robert Oppenheimer spoke of the joy of avocational learning in the arts, athletics, *and* science: "Though surely we will not all burst into song, or take to skis, or pick up a chisel or a brush, some of us have done some of these things, and some of us will; and it seems a proper hope that in our education both for the young, and for those, in growing number, who like us have kept a lifelong taste for it, we do what we can to open the life of science at least as wide as that of song and the arts."[7] Kimball never explains the relationship of vocation and avocation in the resurgence of pragmatism; he also does not distinguish between the teaching of a practice (which need not have a functional use) and direct application.

[6] The elimination of funding for both the SSC (Superconducting Supercollider) and the SETI (Search for Extraterrestrial Intelligence project) is but one major indication of this trend away from curiosity or wonder-based research that is pursued without known practical advantages, but hardly without enormous potential.

[7] J. Robert Oppenheimer, "Communication and Comprehension of Scientific Knowledge," in *The Scientific Endeavor: Centennial Celebration of the National Academy of Sciences* (New York: Rockefeller University Press, 1965), 278.

In sum, can we say that Kimball offers us, like Rumpelstiltskin, a way of spinning the dissonant confrontations on higher education into a golden convergence based on pragmatism? I do not think so. Happily though, Kimball has given me a reason to believe that doubt is good. He quotes Charles S. Peirce on "What Pragmatism Is": "The irritation of doubt causes a struggle to attain a state of belief. I shall term this struggle *Inquiry*.... With the doubt, therefore, the struggle begins, with the cessation of doubt it ends. Hence, the sole object of inquiry is the settlement of opinion" (25). With the arousal of doubt, Kimball has thus initiated Inquiry, which is both a desired and pragmatic action. And maybe he has also given us, just as the Maiden in the story of Rumpelstiltskin is given, a way to gain dominion over the problems we face simply by giving us the name of a possible solution.

ELLEN T. HARRIS *is associate provost for the Arts and professor of Music at Massachusetts Institute of Technology, Cambridge.*

Reckoning versus Reasoning: A Struggle for the Soul of Mathematics

SUSAN L. FORMAN
LYNN ARTHUR STEEN

> Those who take part in the highest functions of the state must practice calculation, not like merchants or shopkeepers for purposes of buying or selling, but to help in the conversion of the soul from the world of becoming to truth and reality.
> —Plato, *The Republic*, VII

> Master: Wherefore in all great works are Clerks so much desired? Wherefore are Auditors so well fed?...Because by numbers such things they finde which else wold farre excell man's minde.
> Scholar: Verily, sir, these men by numbering their cunning do attain.
> —Robert Recorde, *The Declaration of the Profit of Arithmeticke*, 1540

Since ancient times, reckoning—the practice of calculation—has been valued both as a window on truth and as an instrument of profit. The scholastic tradition led the earliest universities to stress the theory of arithmetic (e.g., Diophantus, *Arithmetica* [c. 275]) and to diminish the practical. Indeed, Philip Melancthon argued at Wittenberg in 1517 that "the art of computation" is "so clear and evident that even children can understand it." Yet the need for instruction in practical calculation was so great that guilds and schools of "reckoning masters" proliferated in the late Middle Ages, parallel to but separate from the emerging universities.[1] *Triveso Arithmetic* (1478), the first Western textbook on practical arithmetic, promised "gratifying usefulness" to diligent students who wanted to learn the mercantile trades of fifteenth-century Venice.

The roots of mathematics penetrate deeply in all the world's great civilizations.[2] In each, we find disconnections between the philosophical and the practical, between the mind and the hand. These differences persist to this day, but now we recognize with increasing clarity that culture greatly influences students' context for learning, even in a supposedly

---

[1] *See* Frank J. Swetz, *Capitalism and Arithmetic: The New Math of the 15th Century* (La Salle, Ill.: Open Court, 1987).

[2] *See* George Gheverghese Joseph, *The Crest of the Peacock: Non-European Roots of Mathematics* (London: Penguin, 1991).

neutral discipline such as mathematics. The multiple roots of mathematics in the world's civilizations, too often oversimplified in Western-oriented histories of mathematics, preclude broad generalizations about intrinsic relationships between these two great strands in mathematics education.

Nonetheless, because of our history, liberal education in the United States does have distinctly European roots. From colonial times onward, colleges in America reflected the British emphasis on natural theology (to demonstrate the glory of God by discovering laws of nature) and Baconian philosophy (to explore and record data, to eschew grand theories, and to use science for the improvement of life). Neither emphasis favored mathematics as a discipline, nor did the circumstances in England at the time, where continued devotion to Newtonian methods had caused English mathematics to fall behind the rapidly advancing frontiers in the rest of Europe.

As a consequence, colleges in early America showed little interest in advanced mathematics. College education was a gentleman's education based on a curriculum designed to develop mental discipline and transmit a fixed body of knowledge. With the exception of West Point, where useful mathematics applied to engineering thrived by adoption of curricula from *École polytechnique* in Paris, mathematics in other colleges focused on rote methods to promote mental discipline. "Few colleges before the Civil War taught even calculus, and almost none required it."[3]

Mathematics in this environment was neither liberal nor pragmatic. Rote learning of arithmetic and geometry neither liberated the spirit nor enabled students to put knowledge to productive ends. Three events in the late nineteenth century changed all that: J. J. Sylvester's acceptance of a post at the new Johns Hopkins University, Charles Eliot's introduction of electives at Harvard, and the growth of land-grant institutions as the academic centers of the western migration.

The renowned Sylvester accepted the position at Johns Hopkins because, as a Jew, he was not eligible for appointment to either Oxford or Cambridge. Between 1873 and 1883, he built a research department whose graduates spread the best of European mathematics to other institutions across the United States. Sylvester founded the first U. S. research journal in mathematics, which became the nucleus of the fledgling American mathematical community. His influence can still be felt today in the dominance of the research universities and in the mathematics community's sense of expectations, identity, and purpose.

---

[3] Judith V. Grabiner, "Mathematics in America: The First Hundred Years," in *The Bicentennial Tribute to American Mathematics, 1776-1976*, ed. Dalton Tarwater (Washington, D.C.: Mathematical Association of America, 1977).

The shift in undergraduate studies from a largely prescribed curriculum (originally designed primarily to prepare ministers and teachers) to a system of electives enabled Sylvester's mathematical program to thrive and spread. Because mathematicians were thus freed to teach only those who elected their subject, courses could be taught at a much more demanding level. And by freeing students to study as deeply as they wished, the elective-dominated curriculum enabled students who loved mathematics to progress rapidly to advanced levels. The ideal of liberal education as the cultivation of enlightenment and civility thrived in those departments that followed in Sylvester's footsteps.

Simultaneously, higher education in the United States underwent a major expansion with the growth of land-grant universities, whose primary mission was to support the building of a nation—in engineering, in agriculture, in business, and in education. In these institutions, as at West Point, applied, practical mathematics provided a foundation for the many skills needed to support the growing population of the United States—surveying, bridge building, telegraphy, statistics, management, etc. These institutions reflected the democratic ideals of the nation—serving all the people, not just the gentleman's class—and paved the way for pragmatism as a distinctive American contribution to higher education.

Thus the evolution of mathematics in U. S. colleges and universities provides an apt example of the historical conflicts between the ideals of liberal and pragmatic education documented by Bruce Kimball. His wide-ranging essay provides numerous points of contact with issues in mathematics education, including, to name but a few, the tradition of privilege accorded to reason (*ratio*); the social context of "warranted belief"; the relation of meaning to application; and John Dewey's "faith in intelligence." In this brief response we will focus on only one of these many possible connections, but one that is of considerable importance in today's effort to reform school mathematics education: the evocation of meaning from application.

In the twentieth century, mathematics as a discipline has advanced simultaneously on two seemingly opposite fronts, historically called "pure" and "applied." Pure mathematics appears to be the natural extension of the Platonic ideal of the rational—the *ratio* in contrast to the *oratio*, the philosophical rather than the rhetorical. Applied mathematics appears to be a natural companion of pragmatism, although its modern roots derive more from the military campaigns of Napoleon than from the philosophical writings of Dewey.

Yet appearances can be deceiving. The epitome—indeed the caricature—of pure mathematics flowered in the postwar years due to the influence of the French mathematicians writing under the *nom de plume* of Bourbaki. This ultra-abstract perspective, which greatly (and many believe negatively) influenced the "new math" movement in U. S. education, derived directly from the applied military-engineering tradition of French mathematics. In the United States, advocates of pure mathematics echoed England's G. H. Hardy in boasting that pure mathematics such as number theory was safe from moral contamination since it could never be applied to anything useful. So it is that today we find at Harvard and Brown and many other universities separate departments of pure and applied mathematics, as well as separate programs in statistics, operations research, and computer science—all applied mathematical sciences. Formalism flourishes in pure mathematics departments while meaning thrives in applied departments.

Ironically, some of today's most powerful tools of applied mathematics, particularly those that form the foundation of computer science and biology, are outgrowths of number theory and abstract algebra, previously thought of as among the purest and least useful areas of mathematics. In mathematics, therefore, we can easily affirm a blending of the liberal and pragmatic traditions—not as a feature of education, but as an essential characteristic of the discipline itself. Indeed, the reunification of mathematics, pure and applied, is one of the most prominent characteristics of research in the last two or three decades.

But in education the large gap between the two traditions remains. The culture of mathematics in the United States continues to be dominated by the tone set at the major research universities, which now, a century after Sylvester, are the envy of the world. The canonical curriculum in mathematics from high school through college is based on a philosophy that each course is intended primarily to prepare students for the next. The teleology of the system is the culture of graduate programs in mathematics that, for the most part, have been purged of the more practical and applied of the mathematical sciences.

Yet more than half the students who study college mathematics today do so in two-year or community colleges, primarily in programs in which mathematics serves a strictly utilitarian purpose. Indeed, the vast majority of credits in postsecondary mathematics are earned in courses that are also part of the traditional high school curriculum, notably intermediate and college algebra, introductory statistics, and variations on finite or business mathematics—all courses that students believe serve very pragmatic purposes.

Mathematics education in U. S. colleges and universities is unique in the world, and unique in history. For one thing, most mathematics taught and learned in higher education is the same mathematics that is taught and learned in high school. (Fewer than 20 percent of all student enrollments in college and university mathematics are in courses at the level of calculus or beyond.) A greater fraction of high school graduates is in college than ever before, as is a growing proportion of adults who return to college to renew or extend their skills. Particularly for the latter group, mathematics is always high in priority because it is so often required for job placement or advancement.

U. S. education also differs from that in other countries in its emphasis on general education at the college level. Students from all disciplines, not just those who plan to major in a mathematics-intensive field, study mathematics in college. These circumstances pose a challenge for college mathematics education that is distinctly American: to educate all students as citizens while at the same time providing the foundation for those whose interests are primarily in mathematics as a tool for another subject. In every mathematics department, these dual goals encapsulate the distinct aims of liberal and pragmatic education.

Fortunately for our students, mathematics education from school to college is currently immersed in reform. Reunification of the pure and applied is one feature of this reform, driven not so much by ideology as by the overwhelming realities of student interests and computer technology. Student motivations to study mathematics are, for the most part, primarily pragmatic. Mathematics is a fundamental tool of literacy in a technological age, a prerequisite for virtually all professional and managerial jobs. The power of computers is now so great that they have become essential tools not only in applied (number-crunching) mathematics, but also in theoretical (symbol-manipulating) mathematics.

The current reform movement in mathematics education, although led by faculty, was driven by students who voted with their feet against the historic, Sylvester-invested tradition of pure, rational, "liberal" mathematics education. So mathematics is moving, as Kimball argues for all of higher education, toward a "pragmatic liberal education." Although the direction in which mathematics education is headed may be consistent with the philosophical tradition of pragmatism (or neo-pragmatism), it is clearly not motivated by the tenets of pragmatism itself. Mathematics education is moving under different stimuli, but achieving the same results.

Much of the emphasis of reform is not on the nature of mathematics—pure or applied—but on its pedagogy. The experience of those who seek to reform mathematics education is that content and pedagogy are inseparable—you cannot improve one without the other. This recognition has led in unexpected directions:

- A new emphasis on communication as an essential goal of mathematics education restores *oratio* to a position comparable to *ratio* in the philosophy of mathematics. This emphasis comes not especially from the humanists in academe, who might be expected to be naturally inclined to stress expression as an essential component of learning, but from business leaders who insist that technical knowledge is worthless absent the ability to express this knowledge clearly both orally and in writing.

- The findings of research on learning emphasize the essential connection of thought and action, the necessity of engaging students in the active construction of knowledge. This Dewey-like notion that understanding follows from activity is a crucial component of the reform movement in mathematics education—not as a goal of education but as a means to educate.
- The metaphor of calculus reform, which has been taken up now by the entire standards movement in mathematics, is to make mathematics education "a pump, not a filter." This emphasis on "mathematics for all" accords with Dewey's progressive views of education, to move away from class-based education for the elite to education for the masses.

We see, therefore, two countervailing tendencies in mathematics education. The new emphasis on pedagogy shifts from the traditional vocation-oriented pragmatism ("just the facts") to a more liberal view that stresses understanding ("explain your reasons"). Yet the broad goals of the reform movement, in emphasizing education for all rather than education for an elite, appear to reflect a shift away from the classical "gentleman's" liberal education to a Dewey-like pragmatic education.

Mathematics traditionally is a discipline that idolizes the individual. Students' sense of self-confidence is enhanced (or destroyed) through competitive examinations and solitary struggles with mind-expanding problems. Dewey's pragmatism, on the other hand, is rooted more in social goals than in individual attainment, in education to serve society (and democracy). The "filter" tradition of mathematics remains acceptable so long as education is viewed as an individual good. But as the "pump" metaphor gains ascendancy, mathematics education is gaining a "social conscience," and will necessarily come to reflect increasingly the ideals of pragmatism.

The challenge of our time, both in high school and in the first years of college, is to unite the pragmatic with the liberal, the vocational with the academic, the hand with the mind. Artificial separation that limits opportunities to learn has no place in American society.

SUSAN L. FORMAN *is professor of Mathematics, Bronx Community College, New York City.*
LYNN ARTHUR STEEN *is professor of Mathematics at St. Olaf College, Northfield, Minnesota.*

The Educated Person, Curriculum Content Standards, and Pragmatic Liberal Education

MILES MYERS

The nationwide effort to describe curriculum content standards is an attempt to fashion a new definition of basic literacy and, thus, a new public-professional compact on what students should know and be able to do as a result of the common curriculum of K to 12 schools.[1] Without some agreement on the "common curriculum," the K to 12 public school system may cease to be a viable public institution, and, in fact, powerful voices are already calling for the abandonment of the K to 12 common schools on the grounds that such schools not only have failed to provide an adequate curriculum for all students but also have failed to construct a public-professional agreement on a core curriculum.

At present, the national discussion of standards has become one of the ways that a public-professional agreement on a core curriculum can be constructed, although agreement on what students should know and be able to do is not coming easily. Two of the recurrent questions in the standards movement is (1) how should standards be described and (2) how do different standards document content to each other. I want to argue in this commentary that Bruce Kimball's description of the recurrent themes in a pragmatic approach to liberal education offers us a valuable guide for how content standards should be described and for what is the core curriculum underlying all standards documents.

The first question focuses on how content standards should be described. Most of the recent history of the current federal standards movement in English content is testimony to the fact that "public policy is a crude instrument for securing social ideals,"[2] especially when federal agencies attempt to define subject-area content standards as a list of specific federal regulations. I think Kimball's paper illustrates the force of an exemplar approach rather than a regulatory approach to curriculum content standards.

---

[1] Miles Myers, *Changing Our Minds: Negotiating English and Literacy* (Urbana, Ill.: National Council of Teachers of English, 1995).

[2] Thomas Green, "Excellence, Equity, and Equality," in *Handbook of Teaching and Policy*, ed. L. S. Schulman and G. Sykes (New York: Longman, 1983), 322.

In the English content standards, the regulatory approach often takes the form of pressure for a finite list of books describing such things as the canon of children's literature and even for the specifications of particular approaches to teaching spelling.[3] The issue for English is not whether literature and spelling would be taught but whether the content standards would mandate a limited list of specific books and spelling words for each grade level. The National Council of Teachers of English (NCTE), the International Reading Association (IRA), and the University of Illinois (Urbana Campus) argued that content standards should be shaped not by a regulatory feature-list but by exemplars of the primary areas of English content, by statements of language principle, by historical reviews of the origins of these principles, by exemplars of grade level variations, and exemplars of student work. Other sections of the NCTE/IRA standards document includes exemplars of classroom instruction (vignettes) and opportunity-to-learn standards (O.T.L.: what resources teachers need to teach the standards). Federal spokespersons charged that the O.T.L. standards were illegal, that the content descriptions and exemplars were too vague, and that the language principles were too focused on process.[4]

[3] National Council of Teachers of English, "NCTE/IRA Say Standards Effort Will Continue," *Council Chronicle*, Urbana, IL (April 1994): vol. 3, no. 5, 1; Karen Diegmueller, "English Group Loses Funding for Standards," *Education Week* (30 March 1994a): 1, 9; Karen Diegmueller, "Flap Over English Standards Sparks Strong Words," *Education Week* (7 September 1994b): vol. XIV, no. 1, 9; "Ed Halts Funding for Project to Set English Standards," *Education Daily*, Washington, D.C. (24 March 1994): vol. 27, no. 57. There was also a management issue in the debate between the Standards Project and the federal agents from FIRST. FIRST thought the development was too cumbersome and needed streamlining. NCTE and IRA believed that FIRST wanted to eliminate the hundreds of task forces and meetings across the country, all of which were reading and responding to drafts of English standards. NCTE and IRA argued that if teachers did not have broad ownership, the standards documents would simply sit on the shelf. In March 1994, after 18 months, the Secretary of Education terminated the contract of the English standards project and announced he was going to issue a new contract to get English standards written. In December 1994, after asking for public comment and hearing from the public that the work should only be done by the National Council of Teachers of English and the International Reading Association, the Secretary of Education announced no new contract would be issued and that NCTE and IRA would do the work (see Diegmueller, 1994(b) for story on public response).

[4] This debate has obvious parallels to the health care debate in its tension over centralized and localized decision making. The Department of Education announced it was abandoning the goal of stamping a *single* federal version of curriculum content in each subject area in December 1994. Many versions were now possible. If the National Education Standards and Improvement Council is eliminated—and it might be—many versions are possible.

Some of the federal pressure to describe content standards as a list of regulatory features resulted from the desire of certain leaders in Congress and in the Department of Education to have the National Educational Standards and Improvement Council (NESIC) regulate the curriculum content of the country. NCTE and IRA argued that there should be several versions based on common exemplars and principles, not a single version, and that the ultimate decision on versions should belong to the states and local districts, not NESIC. NCTE and IRA argued that the purpose of a standards document is to provide a map of a content area and suggested goals, not a road-by-road list of directions. Federal agents in the Fund for the Improvement and Reform of Teaching (FIRST) and various other federal spokespersons charged that several versions will confuse states, that exemplars and principles are too loose to be useful as mandates, and that the NCTE/IRA approach is "too vague."[5]

By March 1994, the Department of Education had announced that it would not continue funding the NCTE/IRA project and that it would fund a new group to produce the English standards the federal government wanted. However, after asking for public comment on the new request for proposals to do English standards, the Department of Education in November 1994 announced it was going to follow the public recommendations and not fund any work on English standards, leaving the national development of English content standards to NCTE and IRA. In addition, in December 1994, the Department of Education announced that it was abandoning its demand for a single version of standards in each subject area, and by March of 1995 there were several bills either to eliminate NESIC or to prohibit NESIC from turning curriculum content into a list of mandated regulations. In the meantime, Congress withdrew all funding from FIRST.

How does one answer the charge that exemplars are a vague and unworkable approach to standards and our common vision of education? Organizational research clearly shows that exemplar images and descriptions are effective ways to guide organizational decisions in schools and in many corporate environments.[6] It is true that images and descriptions do not demand the tightness of fit with local action that we typically find between federal regulations and local behaviors. But Karl Weick argued that because schools are loosely coupled systems that

---

[5] "Standards and Gobbledygook," *Washington Post* (3 April 1994): Editorial.
[6] Karl E. Weick, "Educational Organizations as Loosely Coupled Systems," *Administrative Science Quarterly* 21 (1976): 1-19; T. J. Peters and R. H. Waterman, *In Search of Excellence* (New York: Harper and Row, 1982); T. E. Deal and A. A. Kennedy, *Corporate Cultures* (Reading, Mass.: Addison Wesley, 1982).

must be able to adapt to local needs, schools should be managed by exemplars or enactments of particular values, not by regulatory features.[7] In fact, there is substantial research showing that typical lists of government regulations "not only hinder teachers' responsiveness to students, but over time discourage teachers...from broadening their repertoire of approaches."[8] In loosely coupled systems such as schools, a description of exemplars and principles can provide what Gareth Morgan calls a culture metaphor suggesting directions in "language, norms, folklore, ceremonies, and other social practices that communicate the key ideologies, values, and beliefs guiding action."[9]

The exemplar approach depends for its coherence primarily on its descriptions of content, statements of principle, and exemplars of student work. But in the debate over history standards, the focus of critical attacks was primarily on classroom activities or vignettes, not the descriptions or principles themselves. In fact, Diane Ravitch generally approved the history standards: "Its 31 content standards, with few exceptions, are intellectually challenging. Its description of standards for teaching and learning are excellent. Many of the illustrative activities are well-conceived." But Ravitch was critical of many of the classroom activities proposed for history, generally finding in them "present mindedness," an absence of attention to "shared civic values," and "one-dimensional" portraits of issues.[10] Lynn V. Cheney also focused on classroom activities in her attacks, noting that classroom vignettes did not mention Thomas Edison and other historical figures she thought should be mentioned.[11]

But it is the principles, not the snapshots of classroom activities, which should be the primary focus of the standards debate. We should not be having a national public debate about the absence of Charles Dickens or *Wuthering Heights* from snapshots of selected classroom activities described in the standards documents. Two or three lessons or vignettes cannot be expected to satisfy a principle or a content description. Vignettes are only one element of the classroom experiences carrying out a particular standard, and out of context almost any classroom activity can be made to appear somehow off-kilter. This does not mean that exemplar novels, poems, and short stories should not be named. They should be. This does not mean that the principles should not specify some of our recommended

[7] Weick, "Educational Organizations as Loosely Coupled Systems."

[8] Gary Sykes, "Public Policy and the Problem of Teacher Quality," in *Handbook of Teaching and Policy*, ed. L. S. Schulman and G. Sykes (New York: Longman, 1983), 120.

[9] Gareth Morgan, *Images of Organizations* (Newbury Park, Calif.: Sage Publications, 1986), 135.

[10] Diane Ravitch, "Standards in U.S. History," *Education Week* (7 December 1994): 48.

[11] Lynn V. Cheney, quoted in *Education Week* (2 November 1994).

literary selections. They should. As Kimball makes clear in his description of liberal education, principles, and exemplars can provide a powerful message about the foundations of curriculum content.

The second question addresses how the various standards documents should be integrated into a coherent vision. Kimball's seven trends in a pragmatic approach to a liberal education provide a coherent, overall focus for the core curriculum underlying various standards documents. These seven trends are also a useful portrait of the educated person. The seven themes Kimball identifies in a pragmatic approach to liberal education—each reflecting changes in the physical objects, the cognitive structures, and the ideas of the world—are (1) multiculturalism, (2) general education, (3) community and citizenship, (4) commonality among all levels of the education system, (5) teaching as a form of learning and inquiry, (6) values and service, and (7) assessment (97).

First, multiculturalism. Radical changes in the workplace *and* in the citizenship roles of women and racial minorities, radical shifts of economic power from Western Europe to other parts of the world, dramatic growth in worldwide transportation and in worldwide communication systems, and major population changes resulting from immigration have all increased society's need for citizens and workers with a personal sense of the world's diversity and a capacity to manage gender, ethnic, and racial differences within a democratic society. In other words, the educated person should have an intercultural, situated intelligence. Both Kimball's pragmatic approach to liberal education and NCTE's content standards aim for an educated person who is able to situate an understanding of texts within different perspectives (gender, race, class, ethnicity) and within a range of Western and "non-Western classics... when they address questions relevant to the subject matter."[12]

The roles of diversity and multiculturalism in the teaching of reading and writing have been debated in U.S. schools since 1775: should students read Greek and Latin texts *only* in Greek and Latin or in translation (English); should students read only Biblical materials and paraphrases or should they read secular works from England; and should students read only English "greats" from England or should they read something called American literature? English teachers today, recognizing the need to understand new and old themes in the lives of women and men in "new" roles and in the lives of Latino, Asian, and African Americans in any roles, are asking what new perspectives should be added to the booklist of English classes.

---

[12] Dinesh D'Souza, *Illiberal Education: The Politics of Race and Sex on Campus* (New York: Free Press, 1991), 254.

"Multiculturalism" does not mean that traditional texts are eliminated or that new, contemporary works are added simply to introduce diversity. New works place enduring themes of the humanities in modern settings, and the pairing of old and new texts helps students build bridges between the present and the past. Remember, new texts are not the sole source of diversity in the classroom. Diversity is already present through the influence of immigration, global news, business networks, and labor patterns not present in the societies and classrooms of older literacies. Students who have watched their mothers and fathers assume new roles in the workplace and who have witnessed the diversity in the U.S. Congress—"20 percent of the members of the U.S. Senate have immigrant grandparents"[13]—tend to introduce these themes into their readings of old and new texts, identifying both diversity and commonality in Shakespeare, in Morrison, in Dickens, in Baldwin, in Twain, in Tan, in Hawthorne.

Multiculturalism as a theme in school curricula does not mean that all cultures are "equally good." There is always in English classes a privileged core curriculum based on democratic traditions and on such enduring values as brotherhood, sisterhood, and a belief in the possibilities of justice. As Cornel West and others have indicated, the literature class is one of the places where a larger prophetic framework "of moral reasoning" based on democratic values encompasses discussions of difference, and eschews "putting any group of people or culture on a pedestal or in the gutter."[14] In summary, then, one common theme we should find in our standards is a multicultural understanding of the world, and this is one of the trends Kimball finds in a pragmatic approach to a liberal education.

Second, general education. In Kimball's view of contemporary liberal education, one theme cutting across all subjects is "general education," and a key element of "general education" today is an understanding of how to harness a range of tools, networks, cognitive strategies, and internalized voices to solve problems. A dramatic growth in the United States of information processing machines, self-management systems, information networks, and centers of expertise has contributed to the need for an understanding of modern information tools and the skills of distributed intelligence.

Curriculum content standards in English introduce students to distributed intelligence—to ways of distributing questions and problems to

---

[13] Harold L. Hodgkinson, "A True Nation of the World," *Education Week* (18 January 1995): 32.

[14] Cornel West, *Race Matters* (New York: Vintage Books/Random House Inc., 1994), 43.

various machines, experts, data banks, computer networks, metacogni-
tivestrategies, and collaborative groups. In the curriculum content of
earlier forms of literacy, the use of calculators, computer spell-checks,
and group work was often considered a form of cheating, a way of avoiding internalizing all necessary information in the individual mind. But
the rapid growth of information has made the individual memory bank
approach to information impractical. An understanding of distributed
intelligence, which in most school curricula appears as part of general
education, is now essential in all subject areas, and seems certain to
appear in the various standards documents.

Third, community and citizenship. The combination of an information explosion and the increased rate of information turnover, reflected
in higher levels of gross national product in information production, has
resulted in higher levels of uncertainty about the stability of information and in the increased blurring of disciplinary boundaries. For example, psychology and linguistics have blurred into psycholinguistics;
sociology and linguistics have blurred into sociolinguistics. These
changes have challenged the unified, stable world of information that
was the foundation of earlier forms of literacy and knowledge and have
changed earlier forms of teaching which emphasized only delivering
information, observation, and analysis.

In earlier forms of literacy, a publication like the ninth edition of the
Encyclopaedia Britannica could claim to present a unified world-view
which "was widely, if not universally, shared by his contributors." By
the fifteen edition in 1974, that unified view of the world was gone:

> "but with the Fifteenth Edition it is quite otherwise. Heterogeneous and
> divergent contributions, which recognize the diversity and fragmentation
> of standpoints in central areas, are deeply at odds with the overall scheme,
> in so far as the scheme presupposes any real unity to the work...the ency-
> clopedic mode of inquiry has become one more fideism and a fideism
> which flies in the face of contemporary realities."[15]

One recent example of this uncertainty of information is the debate
over the Smithsonian Museum's exhibit of the Enola Gay, the airplane
that dropped the atomic bomb on Japan. The Smithsonian hoped to use
the Enola to tell two different stories illustrating two principles of citizenship, first our debt to heroes, the U.S. soldiers who fought in World
War II and who ended the war and saved lives by dropping the bomb, and

[15] Alasdair MacIntyre, *Three Rival Versions of* Moral Inquiry (South Bend, Ind.:
    University of Notre Dame, 1990), 56.

second our debt to history and humanity, the beginning of the atomic age and the horrible death of Japanese civilians. The first story had photographs of American heroes; the second had photographs of dead Japanese. On one side of the debate was the Veterans of Foreign Wars (VFW) and on the other were those who wished to "deglamourize" atomic energy and war. The challenge to the Smithsonian was to negotiate a coherent exhibit of the Enola Gay. But by the end of January 1995, the exhibit had been terminated and the community attempt at coherent story telling abandoned.

The objects at the Smithsonian are like the objects listed in the Encyclopaedia Britannica or like books and objects in English classes. Without the stable world unifying *all* information, a stability characteristic of decoding/analytic literacy, the meaning of cultural objects themselves must be continually negotiated and renegotiated. Without the ability to participate and yet to stand back and analyze the principles that bind us, without the principles of citizenship, and without, at the same time, involvement and participation in community, the educated person, in the midst of life's uncertainties, will lose the ability to live with ambiguity—to continue to try to tell a story the premises of which are constantly changing.

Furthermore, without the ability to fluctuate between parts and wholes, between experience and explicit study, the educated person will lose the familiar in the midst of uncertainty: "A large part of the art of instruction lies in making the difficulty of new problems large enough to challenge thought and small enough so that, in addition to the confusion naturally attending world elements, there will be luminous familiar spots."[16] Finally, without the ability to alternate between participation and observation, the educated person will lose the capacity to build bridges between the traditional and the contemporary: "ultimately the teacher must help the student become part of a community of interpreters—which not only carries on the tradition but constantly amends and expands it in active participation."[17] In Kimball's view of liberal education, this ability to shift gears enables us to focus on both community and citizenship, on both involvement and norms of democratic action. In this kind of world, we need to be able to be involved in the contingencies of participation and, at the same time, to stand back and analyze the patterns underlying our behavior.

Fourth, commonality among all levels of the education system. A dramatic growth in the range of sign systems used for entertainment and intellectual inquiry—from the increased use of simulated virtual reality in computer programs to the increased use of film, television, and various

---

[16] John Dewey, "Thinking in Education," *Democracy and Education: An Introduction to the Philosophy of Education* (New York: Free Press, 1966), 157.

[17] Robert N. Bellah et al., *The Good Society* (New York: Alfred A. Knopf, 1991), 174.

electronic devices for displaying data—has heightened the need for an educated person with experience in shifting signs and in different ways of sign-system knowing. Various drafts of the English content standards call for learning to read and compose using a variety of sign systems. There is an underlying assumption in the English content standards that an educated person will have reading and composition experiences in a selected variety of media—film, charts, photographs, graphs, drama, pantomime, poems, essays. This means that teachers will encourage what some call the talents of multiple forms of intelligence.[18]

Not too many years ago, English departments rejected film studies as not serious intellectual work. Today film studies is a legitimate part of English content in both major universities and K to 12 schools. Previously, visual and action signs were associated with the lower grades and with the lower branches on the tree of knowledge. These lower forms were assumed to be stepping stones to the higher grades and higher verbal forms. That radical division between lower and higher knowledge is no longer practical. There is now a general understanding that a commonality underlies intellectual work across the grades.

Kimball argues that liberal education today must recognize that "the different levels of the U.S. educational `system' are equally important and engaged in a common enterprise" (94). Today, the difference between lower and higher grades is not the sign system itself—all levels engage in sign shifting as ways of knowing. The distinctions from one grade to another are matters of differentiation and themes—sign systems become more differentiated and themes change with the age of the student. These distinctions appear to be a common trend in various standards documents and are, at the same time, part of Kimball's portrait of the contemporary educated person.

Fifth, teaching as inquiry. Transportation, teleconferencing, telephones and various other audio visual devices have introduced to everyone an increasing range of rhetorical settings in which the social construction of knowledge can take place. The earlier literacies tended to emphasize academic events—for example, reading an academic paper at a conference— and to ignore conversational and teaching events. The earlier forms of literacy assumed that printed versions of academic speech captured all the knowledge found in all other events and more. Today, we recognize that a way of talking is, in part, a way of knowing and that teaching is one important way of learning ways of talking in different rhetorical settings.[19]

---

[18] Howard Gardner, *Frames of Mind* (New York: Basic Books, 1983).

[19] Del Hymes, *Foundations in Sociolinguistics* (Philadelphia: University of Pennsylvania Press, 1974), 52. The term "speech event" comes from Del Hymes who calls the speech event the largest rule-governed unit of speech patterns.

In each rhetorical setting or speech event (notational events, conversations or most K to 12 teaching, lecturing or public presentations, reading aloud of academic papers), the negotiation of meaning is both a social process, requiring that an educated person know the event's social "rules" for speaker-audience relationships and for interpreting and criticizing the views of others, and a logical process, requiring that an educated person be able to use the logic necessary to warrant the "assertability" of facts. A "warrant" for "asserting" something is simply the social agreement about measurement that underlies statements of facts in various rhetorical settings. It is a fact, for example, that Kansas City is 257 miles from Eastville because we all agree on how to measure miles and how to locate Eastville and Kansas City on our agreed-upon maps. Conversations, which allow much more approximation in their specifications of facts than do presentations and academic events, can estimate distance as "somewhere over 200 miles," but academic events, which insist on exactness, must specify "257." In summary, conversations usually focus on the exploration of ideas, but academic events focus on precise communication.

To understand the social practice of constructing and understanding knowledge, the educated person needs experience in alternating among different speech events. Teaching is one of the central ways to learn the "rules" of those different speech events, and, for this reason, students themselves need to be given the opportunity to teach in various settings (in classroom dialogues, small and large group discussions, tutorials and lecture presentations). Kimball points to Ernest Boyer's conception of the "scholarship of teaching"[20] and Gerald Graff's conception of teaching the conflicts[21] as two examples of the growing importance of teaching as a method of learning in liberal education (95).

Sixth, values and service. In Kimball's view of a pragmatic approach to liberal education (90), the knowledge of the educated person is not always divorced from service to the larger community, facts are not always divorced from values, thought is not always divorced from action. In decoding/analytic literacy, the social sciences were attempting to adopt the paradigmatic methods of inquiry typical of mathematics and physics in which "facts" were almost always made to appear "valueless" or "objective." Recently, the social sciences have adopted narrative or case-based research, where values and action are joined, turning "away from a laws and instances ideal of explanation

[20] Ernest L. Boyer, *College: The Undergraduate Experience in America* (New York: Harper & Row, ;1987), 15-64.
[21] Gerald Graff, *Beyond the Culture Wars: How Teaching the Conflicts Can Revitalize American Education* (New York: W. W. Norton, 1992), 12.

toward a case and interpretation one, looking less for the sort of thing that connects planets and pendulums and more for the sort that connects chrysanthemums and swords."[22]

In the paradigmatic logic of the traditional analytic essay, syllogism, set theory, and on-off methods, an object or idea is defined by a hierarchical system of categorical features, which are the objective facts. Paradigmatic approaches, which are still the method of choice in some schools of philosophy and in most areas of the "hard" sciences, are based, among other things, on the on-off design of the law of contradiction (A cannot be B and not-B), the law of the excluded middle (A must be either B or not-B), and the separability of values and facts.

In case-based methods of inquiry, the test of truth for an event is its lifelikeness or fit with the case or protypical exemplar. For example, we can test the logic of whether a "living thing" is a "bird" by testing the living thing's goodness of fit to a robin or sparrow, both protypical exemplars of a bird according to the research conducted by Eleanor Rosch.[23] Daniel McNeil and Paul Freiberger[24] argued that a case-based approach to logic—what has been called "fuzzy logic"—has become a fundamental operating principle in air conditioners, televisions, and our elevators, as well as in intellectual disciplines. In case-based approaches, the T.V. screen automatically adjusts itself to approximate a prototype screen. In this way, the television user does not have to adjust the T.V. set one feature at a time.

In the old decoding/analytic literacy of traditional English classes, the syllogism, set theory, and true-false and either-or categories of paradigmatic logic were the privileged forms of logic used in writing analysis, inquiry, and reports in secondary English. In these traditional classes, narrative composition was assigned almost exclusively to creative writing in which values and facts would mix while the mainstream English classes taught almost exclusively the paradigmatic, analytical essay in which students were asked to be objective, separating values and facts. That separation is no longer the situation. In the current draft of English content standards, equal status is given to the case-based logic found in narrative and descriptive forms and to the paradigmatic-based logic found in exposition, comparison-contrast, and argument or persuasion. The key intellectual challenge for the educated person in this new world is some skill in shifting modes, enabling the educated person to use a range of organizational structures, some of which join together values and facts, thought and action, knowledge and service. When we change

---

[22] Clifford Gertz, *Local Knowledge* (New York: Basic Books, 1983), 21, 19.

[23] Eleanor Rosch, "Human Categorization," in *Studies in Cross-Cultural Psychology*, ed. Neil Warren (London: Academic Press, 1977), vol. 1.

[24] Daniel McNeil and Paul Freiberger, *Fuzzy Logic* (New York: Simon & Schuster, 1993).

our narratives in which values and facts are mixed into analytic essays in which values and facts are separated, we are engaging in a test of our values and in a study of our ethics. In the new literacy, the educated person, must be able to join together fact and values, knowledge and service.

Seven, assessment. Kimball identifies assessment as a current theme in a pragmatic approach to a liberal education (96), and current drafts of English content standards provide a substantial emphasis on the skills of evaluation, assessment, and judgment. The emphasis on assessment skills grows out of a shift away from traditional distinctions between art and non-art, literature and non-literature, and a shift away from the traditional authorities who defined what books are valued, what books get taught.

First, we will turn to the traditional distinctions between texts. In the traditional decoding/analytic literacy of twentieth century English, literature and non-literature (or transactional texts) were distinctly different categories of books and materials, and in fact, the separation of these two types of objects was the foundation of English as a subject, setting it off from Science, for example, in which the texts or objects of study were declared to be entirely non-aesthetic. The current drafts of the English content standards reflect a shift from an exclusive interest in categorizing texts to some interest in using different ways of reading on the same text. Louise Rosenblatt[25] proposed that literature and non-literature be viewed as the two ends of a continuum of ways of reading, most works inviting a mixture of literary and non-literary readings.

Nelson Goodman[26] has made a similar proposal to shift the question about art from "What is art?" to "When is art?" Thus, Norman Mailer's *Armies of the Night* is packaged for us as inviting a reading as history or novel, and T.V. programs like *Hard Copy* are marketed to us as news or gossip. (I use "gossip" here to mean a casual form of fiction, a kind of pop culture literature.) And Desmond McCarthy sees postmodern art as challenging our assumptions about what is a "real":

> "It may even appear ridiculous to recall the fact that a good rocking horse has often more of the true horse about it than an instantaneous photograph of a derby winner."[27]

[25] Louise Rosenblatt, *Literature as Exploration* [1938] (New York: Noble and Noble, 1968).
[26] Nelson Goodman, *Languages of Art: An Approach to a Theory of Symbols* (Indianapolis, Ind.: Bobbs-Merrill, 1968).
[27] Desmond McCarthy, quoted in Charles Newman, *The Post-Modern Aura* (Evanston, Ill.: Northwestern University Press, 1985), 18.

The result is that "the present jumbling of varieties of discourse has grown to the point where it is becoming difficult either to label authors...or to classify works."[28]

Robert Scholes argued that texts function within a primary code that specifies the non-negotiable rules of the game for the reading of different texts, rules that students learn in the common curriculum of the public schools. Texts, in other words, have inherent properties, and these properties resist some of the interpretations made by readers and various interpretive communities.[29] Because texts have inherent properties, readers have interpretations accepted by the text and interpretations resisted by the text. Thus, readers and writers need substantial practice assessing the differences between resisted and accepted readings.

Why are these labels and classifications important? First, as noted earlier, they tell us how to read texts. Second, they tell us how to behave. Literary codes invite "legitimate" voyeurism into private lives, giving us a "firsthand" view of experience.[30] Nonliterary codes, however, do not invite voyeurism. In fact, in nonliterary situations, we are like PeepingToms if we peer into private lives. Thus, when grocery-counter magazines and television documentaries blur the distinctions between nonpoetic and poetic codes by fictionalizing actual events and people, by pretending to be poetic when they are not, they are inviting "illegitimate voyeurism." The challenge to the educated person is to learn to assess the presence of poetic and nonpoetic codes and the kind of voyeurism thus invited.

Judgments about the differences between the literary and non-literary codes is only one of the assessment issues. The other assessment issue is the judgment of quality. The purpose of English classes is not to institutionalize a nineteenth century booklist and "not to make judgment disappear but to reform the conditions of its practice"[31]—to invite, in fact, all students to engage in judgments of quality in aesthetic and non-aesthetic texts. In the current drafts of English content standards, students are invited into the cultural game of judging "quality"—"what is my best piece of writing?" and "what book is my favorite?" If English classes do not invite students to select their best pieces, to rank the

[28] Gertz, *Local Knowledge*, 20.

[29] Robert Scholes, *Textual Power* (New Haven, Conn.: Yale University Press, 1985), 161.

[30] Chaim Potok, Rebellion and Authority: The Writer and the Community, talk given at the Annual Convention of the National Council of Teachers of English (Orlando, Fla., 20 November, 1994).

[31] John Guillory, *Cultural Capitol: The Problem of Literary Canon Formation* (Chicago: University of Chicago Press, 1993), 340.

books they like, and to rank the writing of other students, then these classes are denying students access to the cultural game of aesthetic judgment. And not only students. Faculty also should post listings of two or three favorite books and favored selections of their own writing.

There are those who will oppose any assessment because they fear that assessment will lead to mandates and enforcement of a single culture, forcing everyone to be the same and marginalizing those left off the list. Peter Elbow discusses this dilemma of "the list" in his description of the English Coalition, which essentially left this issue unresolved.[32] Mandates are legitimate concerns. But the resistance to assessment is often a resistance to making public what is already happening privately in K to 12 schools—behind the closed doors of college admission offices, behind the processes of textbook selections. The fact is that every K to 12 faculty now engages in purchasing some books and not others; a list exists and it is rarely made public. The resistance to assessment—to listing some books or student essays we like also leads to an inability to salvage community—"to get us, with all our differences, nevertheless to work together now and then on the same thing and thereby have some community and shared experience."[33] By including practice in assessment, the English content standards attempt to establish the foundation for this common community.

Both the English content standards and Kimball's description of a pragmatic approach to liberal education attempt to establish in our profile of the educated person a negotiated interaction between community and citizenship, thought and action, belief and understanding, values and service, participation and observation, general and situated knowledge. These negotiations are an essential habit of mind in the educated person because they appear to be productive approaches to contemporary problems. Kimball's portrait of the educated person could be a valuable cultural metaphor for helping the various subject-matter groups think about their common purposes, kindergarten through graduate school, English through math. The portrait helps us to think productively about curriculum content without being pulled into a senseless list of governmental regulations or behavioral objectives outlining a finite list of children's literature and a list of the dangers of invented spelling. In other words, Kimball's discussion of contemporary liberal education helps elevate the discussion of English content standards to a

[32] Peter Elbow, *Growth in English* (New York: Modern Language Association, 1990), 228.
[33] Ibid., 242.

level beyond federal regulations, to a level inviting all citizens to a conversation about the essential themes underlying the liberal education of a citizen at this time and place.

MILES MYERS *is executive director of the National Council of Teachers of English.*

REFERENCES

PART 2 PRAGMATIC LIBERAL EDUCATION: A DIALOGUE

America 2000: An Education Strategy. 1991. Washington D.C.: U.S. Department of Education.

Anderson, Charles. 1993. *Prescribing the Life of the Mind: An Essay on the Purpose of the University, the Aims of Liberal Education, the Competence of Citizens, and the Cultivation of Practical Reason*. Madison, Wis.: University of Wisconsin Press.

Anderson, Charles. 1990. *Pragmatic Liberalism*. Chicago: University of Chicago Press.

Anderson, Martin. 1992. *Imposters in the Temple: American Intellectuals Are Destroying Our Universities and Cheating Our Students of Their Future*. New York: Simon and Schuster.

Arnold, Thurmon. 1937. *The Folklore of Capitalism*. New Haven, Conn.: Yale University Press.

Athens (Ga.) Banner-Herald. 26 December 1994; 29 December 1994.

Atlanta Constitution. 23 November 1994; 11 December 1994; 13 December 1994; 10 January 1995.

Banks, James A. 1993. "Multicultural Education: Historical Development, Dimensions, and Practice." In *Review of Research in Education*, edited by Linda Darling-Hammond, vol. 19, 3-49. Washington, D.C.: American Educational Research Association.

Bardo, John W., ed. 1990. *Defining the Missions of AASCU Institutions*. Washington, D.C.: American Association of State Colleges and Universities.

Barnett, Brian. 1992. "Teaching and Research Are Inescapably Incompatible." *Chronicle of Higher Education* (June 3): A 40.

Belenky, Mary Field et al. 1986. *Women's Ways of Knowing: The Development of Self, Voice, and Mind*. New York: Basic Books.

Bellah, Robert N. et al. 1991. *The Good Society*. New York: Alfred A. Knopf.

Bernstein, Basil. 1990. *The Structuring of Pedagogic Discourse. Volume IV. Class, Codes, and Control*. London: Routledge.

Blanshard, Brand. 1960. "Values: The Polestar of Education," in *The Goals of Higher Education*, edited by Willis D. Weatherford, Jr. Cambridge, Mass.: Harvard University Press.

Bloom, Allan. 1987. *The Closing of the American Mind: How Higher Education Has Failed Democracy and Impoverished the Souls of Today's Students*. New York: Simon and Schuster.

Brantlinger, Patrick. 1990. *Crusoe's Footprints: Cultural Studies in Britain and America*. New York: Routledge.

Bromwich, David. 1992. *Politics by Other Means*. New Haven, Conn.: Yale University Press.

Carnochan, W. B. 1993. *The Battleground of the Curriculum: Liberal Education and American Experience*. Stanford, Calif.: Stanford University Press.

Carter, Deborah J., and Eileen M. O'Brien. 1993. "Employment and Hiring Patterns for Faculty of Color." Washington, D.C.: American Council on Education. *Research Briefs* 4.

Casey, Beth A. 1994. "The Administration and Governance of Interdisciplinary Programs." In *Interdisciplinary Studies Today*, edited by Julie Thompson Klein and William Doty, 53-67. Vol. 58 in the New Directions in Teaching and Learning Series. San Francisco: Jossey-Bass.

Chan, Kenyon S., and Shirley Hune. forthcoming. "Racialization and Panethnicity: From Asians in America to Asian Americans." In *Toward a Common Destiny: Improving Race and Ethnic Relations in America*, edited by Willis D. Hawley and Anthony Jackson. San Francisco: Jossey-Bass.

Cheney, Lynn V. 1994. Quoted in *Education Week*. November 2.

Childs, John. 1950. *Education and Morals*. New York: Century.

Childs, John. 1950. "John Dewey and Education." In *John Dewey: Philosopher of Science and Freedom: A Symposium*, edited by Sidney Hook, 153-63. New York: Dial.

Chronicle of Higher Education. 12 December 1994.

Chronicle of Higher Education Almanac. 1 September 1994: 5, 9.

Coleman, Samuel. 1968. "Is There Reason in Tradition?" In *Politics and Experience: Essays Presented to Professor Michael Oakeshott on the Occasion of His Retirement*, edited by Preston King and B. C. Parekh, 239-82. Cambridge: Cambridge University Press.

Conant, James Bryant. 1945. *General Education in a Free Society*. Cambridge, Mass.: Harvard University Press.

Council Chronicle. 1994. "NCTE/IRA Say Standards Effort Will Continue." Vol. 3, No. 5, April.

Crane, Diana, and Henry Small. 1992. "American Sociology since the Seventies: The Emerging Crisis in the Discipline." In *Sociology and its Publics: The Forms and Fates of Disciplinary Organization*, edited by Terence Halliday and Morris Janowitz, 197-234. Chicago: University of Chicago Press.

Current, Richard. 1989. *Phi Beta Kappa in American Life*. New York: Oxford University Press.

Dahlberg, Ingetraut. 1994. "Domain Interaction: Theory and Practice." *Advances in Knowledge Organization* 4: 60-71.

Davis, Gregson. 1994. "Between Cultures: Toward a Redefinition of Liberal Education." In *African Studies and the Undergraduate Curriculum*, edited by P. Alden, D. Lloyd, and A. Samatar, 19-33. Boulder, Colo. and London: Lynne Reicher.

Deal, T. E., and A. A. Kennedy. 1982. *Corporate Cultures*. Reading, Mass.: Addison Wesley.

Denzen, Norma K. 1992. *Symbolic Interaction and Culture Studies: The Politics of Interpretation*. Cambridge, England: Basil Blackwell.

Dewey, John. 1969–. *John Dewey: The Middle Works*, edited by Jo Ann Boydston. Carbondale, Ill.: Southern Illinois University Press.

Dewey, John. [1910] 1933. *How We Think*. 2d ed. New York: Henry Holt.

Dewey, John. [1916] 1966. *Democracy and Education: An Introduction to the Philosophy of Education*. New York: Free Press.

Dewey, John. 1922. *Human Nature and Conduct*. New York: Henry Holt.

Dewey, John. [1925] 1929. *Experience and Nature*. 2d. ed. La Salle, Ill.: Open Court.

Dewey, John. [1931] 1963. *Philosophy and Civilization*. New York: Capricorn.

Dewey, John. 1934. *Art as Experience*. New York: G. P. Putnam's.

Dewey, John. 1966. "Thinking in Education." In John Dewey, *Democracy and Education: An Introduction to the Philosophy of Education*. New York: Free Press.

Diegmueller, Karen. 1994a. "English Group Loses Funding for Standards." *Education Week*. March 30: 1, 9.

Diegmueller, Karen. 1994b. "Flap Over English Standards Sparks Strong Words." *Education Week*. September 7: 9.

D'Souza, Dinesh. 1991. *Illiberal Education: The Politics of Race and Sex on Campus*. New York: Free Press.

Education Daily. 1994. "Ed Halts Funding for Project to Set English Standards." Vol. 27, No. 57, March 24. Washington, D.C.

Elbow, Peter. 1990. *Growth in English*. New York: Modern Language Association.

Featherstone, Joseph. 1986. "Foreword." In Bruce A. Kimball, *Orators and Philosophers: A History of the Idea of Liberal Education*. New York: Teachers College Press.

Fink, Karl. 1985. Quoted in Charles Newman, *The Post-Modern Aura*, Evanston, Ill.: Northwestern University Press.

Flexner, Abraham. 1930. *Universities, American, English, German*. New York: Oxford University Press.

Flexner, Hans. 1979. "The Curriculum, the Disciplines, and Interdisciplinarity in Higher Education." In *Interdisciplinarity and Higher Education*, edited by Joseph Kockelmans, 93-122. University Park, Pa.: University of Pennsylvania Press.

Fox-Genovese, Elizabeth. 1986. "The Claims of a Common Culture: Gender, Race, Class and the Canon." *Salmagundi* 72 (Fall).

Freire, Paulo. 1990. *Pedagogy of the Oppressed*. New York: Continuum.

Fuller, Timothy. [1950] 1989. "Introduction: A Philosophical Understanding of Education." In Michael Oakeshott, *The Voice of Liberal Learning: Michael Oakeshott on Education*, edited by Timothy Fuller, 1-6. New Haven, Conn.: Yale University Press.

Gardner, Howard. 1983. *Frames of Mind*. New York: Basic Books.

Gertz, Clifford. 1983. *Local Knowledge*. New York: Basic Books.

Gibbons, Michael et al. 1994. *The New Production of Knowledge: The Dynamics of Science and Research in Contemporary Societies*. Thousand Oaks, Calif.: Sage.

Giroux, Henry A. 1992. "Liberal Arts Education and the Struggle for Public Life: Dreaming About Democracy." In *The Politics of Liberal Education*, edited by Darryl J. Gless and Barbara Herrnstein Smith, 119-44. Durham, N.C.: Duke University Press.

Goals 2000: Educate America Act. 1993. Washington, D.C.: U.S. Department of Education.

Goodman, Nelson. 1968. *Language of Art: An Approach to a Theory of Symbols.* Indianapolis, Ind.: Bobbs-Merrrill.

Grabiner, Judith V. 1977. "Mathematics in America: The First Hundred Years." In *The Bicentennial Tribute to American Mathematics, 1776-1976*, edited by Dalton Tarwater. Washington, D.C.: Mathematical Association of America.

Graff, Gerald. 1992. *Beyond the Culture Wars: How Teaching the Conflicts Can Revitalize American Education.* New York: W. W. Norton.

Green, Thomas F. 1983. "Excellence, Equity, and Equality." In *Handbook of Teaching and Policy*, edited by L. S. Shulman and G. Sykes, 318-41. New York: Longman.

Greene, Theodore M., Charles C. Fries, and Henry M. Wriston. 1943. *Liberal Education Re-examined: Its Role in a Democracy.* Report for a Committee Appointed by the American Council of Learned Societies. New York: Harper.

Guillory, John. 1993. *Cultural Capital: The Problem of Literary Canon Formation.* Chicago: University of Chicago Press.

Hacker, Andrew. 1992. *Two Nations: Black, White, Separate, Hostile, Unequal.* New York: Charles Scribner's Sons.

Harding, Sandra. 1991. *Whose Science? Whose Knowledge?* Ithaca, N.Y.: Cornell University Press.

Harris, Ellen T. 1992. "Why Study the Arts—Along with Science and Math." *Aspen Institute Quarterly* 4: 84-105.

Henry, William A. III. 1994. *In Defense of Elitism.* New York: Doubleday.

Herrnstein, Richard J., and Charles Murray. 1994. *The Bell Curve: Intelligence and Class Structure in American Life.* New York: Free Press.

Hodgkinson, Harold. 1995. "A True Nation of the World." *Education Week*, January 18: 32.

Hooks, Bell. 1990. *Yearning.* Boston: South End.

Huber, Ludwig. 1992. "Editorial." *European Journal of Education* 27: 193-99. Special issue on "Interdisciplinary Studies."

Hutchins, Robert M. 1936. *The Higher Learning in America.* New Haven, Conn.: Yale University Press.

Hymes, Del. 1974. *Foundations in Sociolinguistics.* Philadelphia: University of Pennsylvania Press.

Jaeger, Werner. 1939-45. *Paideia: The Ideals of Greek Culture*, translated by Gilbert Highet, 2d ed. Oxford, England: Basil Blackwell.

Jarausch, Konrad H. 1982. *Students, Society, and Politics in Imperial Germany. The Rise of Academic Illiberalism.* Princeton, N.J.: Princeton University Press.

Joseph, George Gheverghese. 1991. *The Crest of the Peacock: Non-European Roots of Mathematics*. London: Penguin.

Kerr, Clark. 1991. *The Great Transformation in Higher Education 1960-1980*. Albany, N.Y.: State University of New York Press.

Kimball, Bruce. 1995. *Orators and Philosophers: A History of the Idea of Liberal Education*. 2d ed. New York: College Entrance Examination Board.

Kimball, Bruce. 1988. "The Historical and Cultural Dimensions of the Recent Reports on Undergraduate Education." *American Journal of Education* 96: 293-322.

Kristeller, Paul Oskar. 1960. *Renaissance Thought: The Classic, Scholastic, and Humanist Strains*, rev. ed. New York: Harper and Row.

Levine, Arthur. 1994. "The Great Debate Revisited." *Atlantic Monthly*, December: 38-44.

Lindenberger, Herbert. 1989. "The Western Culture Debate at Stanford University." *Comparative Criticism* 11: 225-34.

Lorde, Audre. 1984. *Sister Outsider: Essays and Speeches*. Trumansburg, N.Y.: Crossing.

MacIntyre, Alasdair. 1990. *Three Rival Versions of Moral Inquiry*. South Bend, Ind.: University of Notre Dame Press.

Mailer, Norman. 1968. *Armies of the Night*. New York: New American Library.

Marrou, H. I. 1956. *A History of Education in Antiquity*, translated by George Lamb. New York: Sheed and Ward.

Marsden, George. 1994. *The Soul of the American University*. New York: Oxford University Press.

McCarthy, Desmond. 1985. Quoted in Charles Newman, *The Post-Modern Aura*, Evanston, Ill.: Northwestern University Press.

McNeil, Daniel, and Paul Freiberger. 1993. *Fuzzy Logic*. New York: Simon and Schuster.

Mead, Margaret. *And Keep Your Powder Dry*. 1942. New York: William Morrow.

Minnich, Elizabeth Kamarck. 1990. *Transforming Knowledge*. Philadelphia: Temple University Press.

Morgan, Gareth. 1986. *Images of Organizations*. Newbury Park, Calif.: Sage.

Murphy, Arthur E. 1993. "Pragmatism and the Context of Rationality," edited by Marcus G. Singer. *Transactions of the Charles S. Peirce Society* 29 (Spring 1993): 123-78; 29 (Summer 1993): 329-68; 29 (Fall 1993): 687-721.

Myers, Miles. 1995. *Changing Our Minds: Negotiating English and Literacy*. Urbana, Ill.: National Council of Teachers of English.

Newman, Charles. 1985. *The Post-Modern Aura*. Evanston, Ill.: Northwestern University Press.

Oakeshott, Michael. 1983. "Historical Change: Identity and Continuity." In Michael Oakeshott, *On History and Other Essays*, 97-118. Oxford, England: Basil Blackwell.

Oakeshott, Michael. [1950] 1989. "The Idea of a University." In *The Voice of Liberal Learning: Michael Oakeshott on Education*, edited by Timothy Fuller, 95-104. New Haven, Conn.: Yale University Press.

Oakley, Francis. 1992. *Community of Learning: The American College and the Liberal Arts Tradition*. New York: Oxford University Press.

Oakley, Francis. 1992. "Discontents in American Higher Education." In *The Politics of Liberal Education*, edited by Darryl J. Gless and Barbara Herrnstein Smith. Durham, N.C.: Duke University Press.

Oakley, Francis. 1992. "Against Nostalgia: Reflections on Our Present Discontents in American Higher Education." In *The Politics of Liberal Education*, edited by Darryl J. Gless and Barbara Herrnstein Smith, 267-89. Durham, N.C.: Duke University Press.

Oppenheimer, J. Robert. 1965. "Communication and Comprehension of Scientific Knowledge." In *The Scientific Endeavor: Centennial Celebration of the National Academy of Sciences*. New York: Rockefeller University Press.

Osajima, Keith. 1993. "The Hidden Injuries of Race." In *Bearing Dreams, Shaping Visions*, edited by Linda A. Revilla et al., 81-92. Pullman, Wash.: Washington State University Press.

Peirce, Charles S. [1877] 1931-58. "The Fixation of Belief." *Popular Science Monthly* 12: 1-15. In *Collected Papers of Charles Sanders Peirce*, edited by Charles Hartshorne and Paul Weiss (vols. 1-6), with A. Burks (vols. 7-8). Cambridge, Mass.: Harvard University Press.

Peirce, Charles S. [1940] 1955. *Philosophical Writings of Peirce*, edited by Justus Buchler. New York: Dover.

Peters, T. J., and R. H. Waterman. 1982. *In Search of Excellence*. New York: Harper and Row.

Potok, Chaim. 1994. Talk given at the annual convention of the National Council of Teachers of English, Orlando, Fla. 20 November.

Ravitch, Diane. 1994. "Standards in U.S. History." *Education Week*, December 7: 48.

Reports from the Fields. 1991. Vol. 2 of *Liberal Learning and the Arts and Science Major*. Washington, D.C.: Association of American Colleges and Universities.

Revilla, Linda A. et al., eds. 1993. *Bearing Dreams, Shaping Visions*. Pullman, Wash.: Washington State University Press.

Rorty, Richard. 1989. *Contingency, Irony, and Solidarity*. Cambridge: Cambridge University Press.

Rosaldo, Renato. 1989. *Culture and Truth*. Boston: Beacon.

Rosch, Eleanor. 1977. "Human Categorization." In *Studies in Cross-Cultural Psychology*, edited by Neil Warren, vol. 1. London: Academic Press.

Rosenblatt, Louise. [1938] 1968. *Literature as Exploration*. New York: Noble and Noble.

Rosenthal, Sandra B. 1986. *Speculative Pragmatism*. Amherst, Mass.: University of Massachusetts Press. Paperback edition, 1990. Peru, Ill.: Open Court.

Rothblatt, Sheldon. 1976. *Tradition and Change in English Liberal Education: An Essay in History and Culture*. London: Faber & Faber.

Sandler, Bernice R. 1986. *The Campus Climate Revisited: Chilly for Women Faculty, Administrators, and Graduate Students*. Washington, D.C.: Project on the Status and Education of Women, Association of American Colleges.

Scholes, Robert. 1985. *Textual Power*. New Haven, Conn.: Yale University Press.

Seidman, Steven. 1994. *Contested Knowledge*. Oxford: Basil Blackwell.

Sloan, Douglas. 1991. "John Dewey's Project for 'Saving the Appearances': Exploring Some of Its Implications for Education and Ethics." *Revision* 13 (Spring): 23-41.

Smith, Dorothy E. 1987. *The Everyday World as Problematic*. Boston: Northeastern University Press.

Smith, John. 1978. *Purpose and Thought: The Meaning of Pragmatism*. Chicago: University of Chicago Press.

Smith, Page. 1990. *Killing the Spirit: Higher Education in America*. New York: Viking.

Steiner, George. 1984. *A Reader*. Oxford: Oxford University Press.

Stember, Marilyn. 1991. "Advancing the Social Sciences through the Interdisciplinary Enterprise." *Social Science Journal* 28: 1-14.

Stern, Fritz. 1971. *The Failure of Illiberalism: Essays on the Political Culture of Modern Germany*. Chicago: University of Chicago Press.

Swetz, Frank J. 1987. *Capitalism and Arithmetic: The New Math of the 15th Century*. La Salle, Ill.: Open Court.

Swoboda, Marian J., ed. 1990. *Retaining and Promoting Women and Minority Faculty Members: Problems and Possibilities*. Madison, Wis.: University of Wisconsin System.

Sykes, Charles T. 1988. *Profscam: Professors and the Demise of Higher Education*. New York: Kampmann.

Sykes, Gary. 1983. "Public Policy and the Problem of Teacher Quality." In *Handbook of Teaching and Policy*, edited by L. S. Shulman and G. Sykes, 91-125. New York: Longman.

Van Doren, Mark. 1943. *Liberal Education*. New York: Henry Holt.

Veblen, Thorstein. 1918. *The Higher Learning in America: A Memorandum on the Conduct of Universities by Business Men*. New York: B. W. Huebsch.

Washington Post. 3 April 1994: Editorial.

Weick, Karl E. 1976. "Educational Organizations as Loosely Coupled Systems." *Administrative Science Quarterly* 21: 1-19.

Weingartner, Rudolph H. 1993. *Undergraduate Education: Goals and Means*. Phoenix, Ariz.: American Council on Education and Oryx.

West, Cornel. 1994. *Race Matters*. New York: Vintage Books/ Random House.

White, Morton G. 1957. *Social Thought in America: The Revolt Against Formalism*. Boston: Beacon.

Wilson, Daniel J. 1990. *Science, Community, and the Transformation of American Philosophy, 1860-1930*. Chicago: University of Chicago Press.